W9-CJX-141

THE REVOLUTION, THE CONSTITUTION, AND AMERICA'S THIRD CENTURY

We the People

The American Academy of Political and Social Science

THE REVOLUTION, THE CONSTITUTION, AND AMERICA'S THIRD CENTURY

The Bicentennial Conference
on the United States Constitution

Volume I· Conference Papers

A social and philosophical examination of the Constitution, its two centuries of influence on American life, and its implications for future generations

Published for the American Academy of Political and Social Science by the University of Pennsylvania Press

Philadelphia

Library of Congress Cataloging in Publication Data

Bicentennial Conference on the Constitution, Philadelphia, 1976
    The Revolution, the Constitution, and America's Third Century;
The Bicentennial Conference on the United States Constitution.

    At head of title: American Academy of Political and
Social Science.
    Includes indexes.
    CONTENTS: v. 1. Conference papers.—v. 2. Con-
ference discussions.
    1. United States—Constitutional law—Congresses.
2. United States—Politics and government—Congresses.
I. American Academy of Political and Social Science,
Philadelphia. II. Title.
KF4550.A2B47 1976   342'.73'029   78-65110
ISBN 0-8122-7763-5

The Bicentennial Conference on the United States Constitution and
this report on its proceedings were supported by a generous grant
from the Sun Company as a public service

Copyright © 1980 by the American Academy of Political and
Social Science

All rights reserved

Printed in the United States of America

CONTENTS
Volume I

FOREWORD

In Philadelphia, in the summer of 1776, Jefferson, Franklin and John Adams and their colleagues voted to sever the political ties connecting the thirteen English colonies with the Mother Country. In justification, both to their fellow citizens and to the community of nations, they declared their reasons as well as their independence; they recited the many causes of American dissatisfaction with English dominion, and asserted political "truths" Americans held to be "self-evident." Those truths were to be the blueprint of a new nation: "that all men are created equal . . . endowed by their Creator with certain unalienable Rights . . . Life, Liberty and the pursuit of Happiness."

These truths have been the lode star of American political values ever since—not always perfectly realized but ever the guide. Sharing these values is essential to the ordered liberty of a democratic society. But more was needed: a system of political organization allocating authority among levels and branches of government and between public and private sectors. Designing that political system was the work of the second group of extraordinary patriots—Madison, Washington, Ellsworth, James Wilson, and again Benjamin Franklin— meeting in Philadelphia throughout the hot summer of 1787, where they wrought a Constitution. We must not underestimate the difficulties surmounted by those delegates in drafting a document that they could agree on. When the Convention reassembled for the very last time, that great elderly figure, Franklin, attempted to offer some perspective on what had been accomplished as he urged the delegates to sign the document:

> I agree to this Constitution with all its faults, if they are such; because I think a general Government necessary for us, and there is no form of Government but what may be a blessing to the people if well administered, and believe farther that this is likely to be well administered for a course of years. . . . I doubt too whether any other convention we can obtain may be able to make a better Constitution. For when you assemble a number of men to have the advantage of their joint wisdom, you inevitably assemble with those men, all their prejudices, their passions, their errors of opinion, their local interests, and their selfish views. From such an assembly can a perfect production be expected? It therefore astonishes me, Sir, to find this system approaching so near to perfection as it does; and I think it will astonish our enemies. . . . Thus I consent, Sir, to this Constitution because I expect no better, and because I am not sure, that it is not the best. The opinions I have had of its errors, I sacrifice to the public good.

In 1976, to celebrate the bicentennial of the Declaration of Independence, a group of judges, scholars, political leaders, lawyers and representatives of groups in the private sector was convened in Philadelphia by the American Academy of Political and Social Science. Their charge was to reexamine the Constitution—to ask how well our system with its unique federalism has worked, how effectively the United States plays its critical role in the world community, how secure are our liberties, and whether we are satisfied with our mechanisms for separation of governmental powers.

These volumes are the record of that Bicentennial Conference. It is a record which includes numerous formal papers and much vigorous debate. Such serious meditation upon American practices and values was not present often enough during the 1976 commemoration of our independence. It is imperative that in these next years preceding the bicentennial of the Constitutional Convention of 1787, we turn to the fundamental question as to how the aspirations of the framers of that great charter of government have been realized.

As 1976 was an effort to reflect on the aspirations of the Declaration, the interval between that commemoration and that of 1987 calls for a searching inquiry into how well our Constitution has succeeded. It is not enough that we have functioned longer under the ideals of 1776 and the Constitution of 1787 than any other nation.

Is the system of divided, separate powers and functions workable in the complex social, economic and political environment of today and for the future?

Is that document and are our practices under it now such that we can weather new storms and stresses and preserve popular government in the face of conflicts arising from our divided and concentrated sovereignty, the strains and contests between the several branches— and ultimately can the system withstand the external pressures of a changing and troubled world?

The varied insights of the participants to the 1976 conference of the American Academy of Social and Political Science deserve to be widely canvassed. Many lessons—some of them conflicting—can and will be drawn from these materials. But there is one theme which pervades the entire document. It is a theme stated by Mr. Justice Holmes half a century ago, and it captures the essence of our constitutional history:

> (W)hen we are dealing with words that also are a constitutent act, like the Constitution of the United States, we must realize that they have called into life a being the development of which could not have been foreseen completely by the most gifted of its begetters. It was enough for them to realize or to hope that they had created an organism; it has taken a century and has cost their successors much sweat and blood to prove that they created a nation.

Washington
August 1978

Warren E. Burger
Chief Justice of the
Supreme Court of the
United States

PREFACE

Since the American Academy of Political and Social Science was organized on 14 December 1889, its purpose has traditionally been "to promote the progress of political and social science, especially through publications and meetings." Without taking sides on controversial issues, the Academy "seeks to gather and present reliable information to assist the public in forming an intelligent and accurate judgment."

For the celebration of the 200th anniversary of independence in 1776, the Academy Board of Directors suggested a very special tribute that would at once promote reflection on our Revolutionary values, how they were confirmed later in the United States Constitution, and what lies ahead during our third century. Both intellectual history and future public policy were anticipated as major themes of a conference on the Constitution.

That conference took place at historical sites in Philadelphia from 5 April to 8 April in 1976 and may be viewed as one of the most important and ambitious undertakings in the history of the Academy. Since that time, work has continued to edit the original, solicited papers for each of the four committees, to embellish and document more substantially the summaries written by our rapporteurs, and to edit the transcripts of the four working committees so as to maintain the wisdom, information and prescriptions of the participants while reducing redundancy. We hope—and believe—our staff has succeeded in presenting these materials in such a way as to retain the dynamic liveliness so evident during the proceedings.

Discussion about the Constitution almost invariably invites controversy. The stalwart stability of its original language, the flexibility of interpretation, and the capacity of the Constitution to be changed invoke defenders of strict constructionism as well as proponents of significant alteration to levels of intellectual, literary, and sometimes heated advocacy. The Academy, through this conference, is proud to have fulfilled its function of providing a forum for some of these debates. Perhaps more consensus than dissension is expressed in these two volumes; a careful content analysis would be required to determine the validity of that assertion. Either way, the bold strength of our country's most important document, and the world's oldest single-document organic law in existence, is reassured through the essays and dialogues that are found here.

As President of the Academy, I wish to pay tribute to the essayists, rapporteurs, participants, editors, the Board, the organizing committee and the staff of the Academy. All of these persons are identified elsewhere in these two volumes and do not require repetition here. But it must be said that they collectively are the framers of these documents, that it is their erudition, experience and thoughtful insights about the future to which we are indebted. It is also a special tribute to these contributors that this publication enjoys the esteem and respect offered by Chief Justice Warren Burger in writing the Foreword, for which I and the Board are most grateful.

The Academy trusts that the publication of these volumes helps to launch the next decade of intensive and wide public interest in the 200th anniversary of the birth of the Constitution in 1789 and will reinforce the well-traveled course our country has taken to uphold political freedom, liberty for the individual, and the state's concern with the welfare of all its people.

Philadelphia, Pennsylvania   Marvin E. Wolfgang
September 1978   President

As with any collective project, many persons have been responsible for the imagination and production of these volumes. The Board of Directors, the Bicentennial Committee, the Chairman of the Conference, and all of the participants have been, of course, the major

ACKNOWLEDGMENTS

contributors. But special acknowledgment should be made to those who worked directly on the post-conference preparation of these materials.

The Sun Company deserves our special appreciation for its continued and sustained support, both financially and through encouragement to our staff. Dean Chaapel, especially, has never failed to offer advice and support for the project from its inception to its completion.

Varney Truscott, who was our gracious Conference Coordinator, was responsible for the general supervision of these volumes. As principal editor, she oversaw all aspects of their preparation with an intelligent coordination of people, ideas, grammar, and style.

The editor of *The Annals*, Richard Lambert, was not only instrumental as an architect of the conference, but was deeply involved in the second round of the editing of these volumes as well. His expert experience is reflected especially in the volume that reports the several committee discussions.

Without the help of Robert W. Kotzbauer, who initially edited the committee transcripts, this work would be less lively, less coherent. His contribution has been invaluable to the success of the final production.

The firm of Lewis and Gilman and its staff were involved from the inception to the design of the printed production. To all who helped we extend our appreciation.

The staff of the Academy, Ingeborg Hessler, Doris Mackler and Dorothy Lerner, functioned in most efficient administrative ways to provide support for the conference and the final publication.

The Academy reaches back to 1889. With the help of many persons who contributed to these volumes, the Academy will reach forward, we hope, to many more generations of students, scholars and all others interested in the dissemination of important political and social ideas.

Marvin E. Wolfgang
President

ACADEMY BICENTENNIAL COMMITTEE

CO-CHAIRMEN

Marvin E. Wolfgang, President, AAPSS
Professor of Sociology and Law, University of Pennsylvania

Richard D. Lambert, Editor, *The Annals*
Professor of Sociology, University of Pennsylvania*

Lee Benson, Professor of Historical Social Sciences
University of Pennsylvania

Joseph S. Clark, Former U.S. Senator
Philadelphia, Pennsylvania

A. Leon Higginbotham, Jr., Circuit Judge, U.S. Court of Appeals
Third Circuit, Philadelphia*

Covey T. Oliver, Ferdinand Wakeman Hubbell Professor of Law,
   Emeritus
University of Pennsylvania*

Louis H. Pollak, District Judge, U.S. District Court, Eastern District of
   Pennsylvania
Philadelphia*

Henry W. Sawyer, III, Partner, Drinker Biddle & Reath
Philadelphia

Varney Truscott, Conference Coordinator, American Academy of
   Political and Social Science, Philadelphia

*At the time of the conference, Dr. Lambert was Dean of Instruction and
Academic Planning, Faculty of Arts and Sciences; Prof. Benson was Professor of
History of the American Peoples; Judge Higginbotham was District Judge, U.S.
District Court; Prof. Oliver was Hubbell Professor of Law; and Judge Pollak
was Dean and Albert M. Greenfield University Professor of Human Relations
and Law, University of Pennsylvania Law School.

CONFERENCE PARTICIPANTS

Henry J. Abraham
James Hart Professor of
  Government and Foreign
  Affairs
University of Virginia
Charlottesville, Virginia

John B. Anderson
U.S. House of Representatives
Washington, D.C.

Paul Bender
Professor of Law
University of Pennsylvania
Philadelphia, Pennsylvania

Lee Benson
Professor of Historical Social
  Sciences
University of Pennsylvania
Philadelphia, Pennsylvania

Sam Brown[1]
Director, ACTION
Washington, D.C.

Fletcher L. Byrom
Chairman
Koppers Company, Inc.
Pittsburgh, Pennsylvania

José A. Cabranes
Legal Adviser and Director,
  Government Relations
Yale University
New Haven, Connecticut

Joseph S. Clark
Former U.S. Senator
Philadelphia, Pennsylvania

Tom C. Clark
Associate Justice (retired)
Supreme Court of the U.S.
Washington, D.C.

Ruth C. Clusen[2]
Assistant Secretary
U.S. Department of Energy
Washington, D.C.

David Cohen
President, Common Cause
Washington, D.C.

John Sloan Dickey
President Emeritus
Dartmouth College
Hanover, New Hampshire

John Diebold
Chairman
Diebold Group, Inc.
New York, New York

Hedley Donovan[3]
Senior White House Adviser
Washington, D.C.

David P. Eastburn
President
Federal Reserve Bank of
  Philadelphia
Philadelphia, Pennsylvania

Christopher F. Edley
Executive Director
United Negro College Fund
New York, New York

George C. Edwards, Jr.
Circuit Judge
U.S. Court of Appeals
  6th Circuit
Cincinnati, Ohio

Thomas Ehrlich
President
Legal Services Corporation
Washington, D.C.

Daniel J. Elazar
Director
Center for the Study of
  Federalism
Temple University
Philadelphia, Pennsylvania

Heinz Eulau
William Bennett Munro
  Professor of Political Science
Stanford University
Stanford, California

Richard A. Falk
Albert G. Milbank Professor of
  International Law and
  Practice
Center of International Studies
Princeton University
Princeton, New Jersey

John D. Feerick
(American Bar Association)
Partner
Skadden, Arps, Slate,
  Meager and Flom
New York, New York

Martha A. Field
Professor of Law
University of Pennsylvania
Philadelphia, Pennsylvania

Adrian S. Fisher[4]
U.S. Ambassador to the
  Conference of the Committee
  on Disarmament
Geneva, Switzerland

James O. Freedman[5]
Dean
University of Pennsylvania
  Law School
Philadelphia, Pennsylvania

Henry J. Friendly
Circuit Judge
U.S. Court of Appeals,
  2nd Circuit
New York, New York

Gerald Frug
Associate Professor of Law
University of Pennsylvania
Philadelphia, Pennsylvania

Buell G. Gallagher
Vice Chairman, National Board
  of Directors (Emeritus)
NAACP
New York, New York

Richard N. Gardner[6]
U.S. Ambassador to Italy
Rome, Italy

Charles E. Gilbert
Richter Professor of
  Political Science
Swarthmore College
Swarthmore, Pennsylvania

Edwin L. Goldwasser[7]
Vice Chancellor for Research
  and Dean of the Graduate
  School
University of Illinois
Urbana, Illinois

Frank Goodman
Professor of Law
University of Pennsylvania
Philadelphia, Pennsylvania

Jack Greenberg
Director-Counsel
Legal Defense and Educational
Fund, Inc.
NAACP
New York, New York

Jack P. Greene[8]
Andrew Mellon Professor in
the Humanities
Johns Hopkins University
Baltimore, Maryland

Erwin N. Griswold
Partner
Jones, Day, Reavis & Pogue
Washington, D.C.

Charles V. Hamilton
Wallace S. Sayre Professor of
Government
Columbia University
New York, New York

Patricia Roberts Harris[9]
Secretary
U.S. Department of Health,
Education and Welfare
Washington, D.C.

William H. Hastie
Senior Judge
U.S. Court of Appeals,
3rd Circuit
Philadelphia, Pennsylvania

Louis Henkin[10]
Harlan Fiske Stone Professor
of Constitutional Law
Columbia University
New York, New York

Kenneth Holland
President Emeritus
Institute of International
Education
New York, New York

John Honnold
William A. Schnader Professor
of Commercial Law
University of Pennsylvania
Philadelphia, Pennsylvania

R. Gordon Hoxie
President
Center for the Study of the
Presidency
New York, New York

Charles S. Hyneman
Distinguished Professor of
Political Science, Emeritus
Indiana University
Bloomington, Indiana

Albert E. Jenner, Jr.
Senior Partner
Jenner & Block
Chicago, Illinois

Philip C. Jessup
Judge
Norfolk, Connecticut

Sir Otto Kahn-Freund[11]
Cambridge University
Cambridge, England

Evron M. Kirkpatrick
Executive Director
American Political Science
Association
Washington, D.C.

George B. Kistiakowsky
Abbott and James Lawrence
Professor of Chemistry,
Emeritus
Harvard University
Cambridge, Massachusetts

Richard D. Lambert
Professor of Sociology
University of Pennsylvania
Philadelphia, Pennsylvania

Noyes Leech
Professor of Law
University of Pennsylvania
Philadelphia, Pennsylvania

Susan Paris Lewis[12]
Vice Chairman
Common Cause
Washington, D.C.

Sol M. Linowitz
Senior Partner
Coudert Brothers
New York, New York

Leon Lipson
Henry R. Luce Professor of
Jurisprudence
Yale University
New Haven, Connecticut

James R. Mann
Former Member
U.S. House of Representatives
Greenville, South Carolina

Bayless Manning[13]
Partner
Paul, Weiss, Rifkind, Wharton
& Garrison
New York, New York

Myres S. McDougal
Sterling Professor of Law,
Emeritus
Yale University
New Haven, Connecticut

Carl McGowan
Circuit Judge
U.S. Court of Appeals,
D.C. Circuit
Washington, D.C.

Robert B. McKay
Director, Program on Justice,
Society and the Individual
Aspen Institute for Humanistic
Studies
New York, New York

Martin Meyerson
President
University of Pennsylvania
Philadelphia, Pennsylvania

Constance Baker Motley
District Judge,
U.S. District Court
Southern District, New York
New York, New York

James L. Oakes
Circuit Judge
U.S. Court of Appeals,
2nd Circuit
Brattleboro, Vermont

Covey T. Oliver
Ferdinand Wakeman Hubbell
Professor of Law, Emeritus
University of Pennsylvania
Philadelphia, Pennsylvania

Richard L. Park
Professor of Political Science
University of Michigan
Ann Arbor, Michigan

J. R. Pole[14]
Rhodes Professor of American
    History and Institutions
Oxford University
Oxford, England

Louis H. Pollak[15]
District Judge,
    U.S. District Court
Eastern District of Pennsylvania
Philadelphia, Pennsylvania

Nelson W. Polsby
Professor of Political Science
University of California
Berkeley, California

Robert J. Pranger
Director of Foreign and Defense
    Policy Studies
American Enterprise Institute
    for Public Policy Research
Washington, D.C.

Sir Leon Radzinowicz
Fellow, Trinity College
Cambridge University
Cambridge, England

J. Austin Ranney[16]
Co-Director of the Program for
    Political and Social Processes
American Enterprise Institute
    for Public Policy Research
Washington, D.C.

Marcus G. Raskin
Distinguished Fellow
Institute of Policy Studies/
    Transnational
Washington, D.C.

George E. Reedy
Nieman Professor of Journalism
Marquette University
Milwaukee, Wisconsin

Seymour J. Rubin
Professor of Law
American University
Washington, D.C.

Henry S. Ruth, Jr.[17]
Partner
Shea & Gardner
Washington, D.C.

Stephen I. Schlossberg
Director of Governmental and
    Public Affairs
United Auto Workers
Washington, D.C.

Stephen J. Schulhofer
Associate Professor of Law
University of Pennsylvania
Philadelphia, Pennsylvania

Whitney North Seymour, Sr.
Senior Partner
Simpson, Thacher & Bartlett
New York, New York

Chesterfield Smith
Partner
Holland & Knight
Lakeland, Florida

Elmer B. Staats
Comptroller General of the U.S.
Washington, D.C.

John R. Stark
Executive Director
Joint Economic Committee
U.S. Congress
Washington, D.C.

Clyde W. Summers
Fordham Professor of Law
University of Pennsylvania
Philadelphia, Pennsylvania

James L. Sundquist
Director of Governmental
    Studies
Brookings Institution
Washington, D.C.

Henry Teune
Chairman, Department of
    Political Science
University of Pennsylvania
Philadelphia, Pennsylvania

Alpha Trivette
Past National President
Future Farmers of America
Ladysmith, Virginia

Joan S. Wallace[18]
Director
School of Social Work
Western Michigan University
Kalamazoo, Michigan

Herbert Wechsler
Director, The American Law
    Institute
Harlan Fiske Stone Professor of
    Constitutional Law, Emeritus
Columbia University
New York, New York

Charles E. Wiggins
Former Member
U.S. House of Representatives
Fullerton, California

John Minor Wisdom
Circuit Judge
U.S. Court of Appeals,
    5th Circuit
New Orleans, Louisiana

Marvin E. Wolfgang
Professor of Sociology and Law
University of Pennsylvania
Philadelphia, Pennsylvania

Esmond Wright
Director
Institute of United States
    Studies
University of London
London, England

J. Skelly Wright
Chief Judge
U.S. Court of Appeals,
    D.C. Circuit
Washington, D.C.

NOTES

At the time of the conference—

[1]Mr. Brown was Treasurer of the State of Colorado.

[2]Ass't. Sec'y. Clusen was President of the League of Women Voters of the U.S.

[3]Mr. Donovan was Editor–in–Chief, Time Inc., New York.

[4]Amb. Fisher was Francis Cabell Brown Professor of International Law, Georgetown University, Washington, D.C.

[5]Dean Freedman was Professor of Law.

[6]Amb. Gardner was Henry L. Moses Professor of Law and International Organization, Columbia University, New York.

[7]Dean Goldwasser was Deputy Director, Fermi National Accelerator Laboratory, Batavia, Ill.

[8]Prof. Greene was Harold Vyvyan Harmsworth Professor of American History, Queen's College, Oxford University, England.

[9]Sec'y. Harris was a partner in Fried, Frank, Harris, Shriver & Kampelman, Washington, D.C.

[10]Prof. Henkin was Hamilton Fish Professor of International Law and Diplomacy.

[11]Sir Otto was Arthur Goodhart Visiting Professor of Law at Cambridge University, England.

[12]Mrs. Lewis was a member of the Administrative Committee of the National Women's Political Caucus, New York.

[13]Mr. Manning was President of the Council on Foreign Relations, Inc., New York.

[14]Prof. Pole was Reader in American History and Government, Churchill College, Cambridge University, England.

[15]Judge Pollak was Dean and Albert M. Greenfield University Professor of Human Relations and Law, University of Pennsylvania Law School.

[16]Prof. Ranney was Visiting Professor of Political Science, University of California, Berkeley.

[17]Mr. Ruth was Director of Criminal Justice Research of the Urban Institute, Washington, D.C.

[18]Dr. Wallace was Deputy Executive Director of Program Operations, National Urban League, Inc., New York.

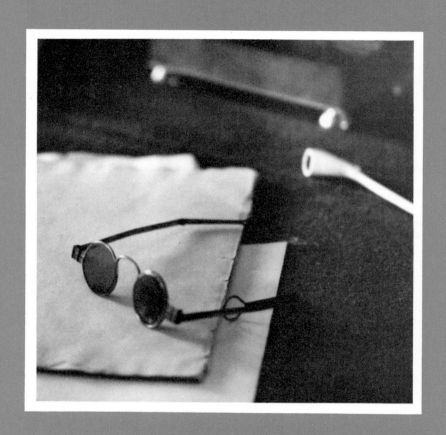

DEDICATION AND OPENING

I hereby open our constitutional conference, which we have entitled "The Revolution, the Constitution, and America's Third Century."

We are mindful that in this Bicentennial year we celebrate 1776 and the Declaration of Independence. We are also mindful that Revolutionary values of that year extended to 1787 and the later adoption of the United States Constitution.

The American Academy of Political and Social Science was founded in 1889 to promote scholarly discussion of political and social issues. It is most fitting that the Academy hold a conference on the Revolutionary values that were codified in the principles of the Constitution,

OPENING REMARKS at Dedication Ceremony

by Marvin E. Wolfgang

and we are gratified that we have been able to bring together a distinguished group whose professional lives, in one way or another, have been concerned with major constitutional issues.

For four days, followed by our annual meeting, we shall meet here and discuss the major issues of the Constitution during our history. Representatives from law, academia, government, business, industry, labor, and consumer interests will meet here to have a scholarly dialogue to discuss the development of the Constitution historically and its viability for America's next century.

It is indeed my privilege and honor on behalf of the Board of Directors of the American Academy and its organizing committee to welcome the conferees to this momentous meeting.

It is fitting that we are here in the hallowed hall of Independence, where men of much merit made the documents that have been so important to our history. Not since that Constitutional Convention has there been a gathering such as we will be having here this week.

There are differences from that first Constitutional Convention. We represent not political states, but intellectual disciplines and various voices of the public. We are men and, unlike our predecessors, women. We are white and black; our society is composed of free citizens all, not free and slave.

Our function is to discuss and disseminate, not to create an entirely new document. We shall question and remold, and our final voices will be guides for thought and decision, not binding rubrics. But neither the White House nor Congress nor the Supreme Court can ignore what is said here.

I am indeed proud to present to you, for the purpose of dedicating this constitutional conference, the distinguished Senior United States Judge of the United States Court of Appeals from the Third Circuit here in Philadelphia, Judge William Hastie, who will now formally open this meeting on "The Revolution, the Constitution, and America's Third Century."

DEDICATORY REMARKS at Independence Hall

by William H. Hastie

This Bicentennial year is a time for sober reflection upon our national beginnings that centered on the place in which we are assembled this morning. But a nation's beginning is a proper source of reflective pride only to the extent that the subsequent and continuing process of its becoming deserves celebration.

The lore of our national beginnings contains many anecdotes. A brief one seems apropos here and now. As the draftsmen of our Constitution, their work almost completed, were leaving this building at the end of a long day, a concerned Philadelphia lady stood outside. Addressing a fellow townsman, she asked: "Mr. Morris, is it a good Constitution you gentlemen have drafted?" Mr. Morris answered: "That must depend, madam, upon how it shall be interpreted and applied." Today, informed by the experience of two centuries, our appraisal can and should be less Delphic.

As political and social scientists and as citizens largely experienced in the functioning of government, the members of this Bicentennial Conference on the Constitution of the United States bring extraordinary expertise to an examination of the merits and demerits of our 200 years of national becoming and the delineation of paths of constructive change as we enter the third century of our national existence. The elegant brochure prepared for this conference by our host Academy quotes this statement of George Washington to his contemporaries who devised our Constitution: "I do not think that we are more inspired, have more wisdom, or possess more virtue than those who will come after us." We must prove deserving of that expression of confidence.

That will not be easy. Forty years ago, observing the great Depression of the 1930s, an eminent British scholar wrote that, under the American constitutional scheme, the powers delegated to the national government were hopelessly inadequate to cope with the economic realities and exigencies of modern industrialized society. Today, although some still question whether Professor Laski has been proved wrong, more voices—certainly the most vociferous ones—are heard decrying the present extent, not to mention abuses, of national power. I cite these polar views merely to suggest the inherent nature and difficulty of many of the matters that will confront this conference. That which has been characterized as "government of the people, by the people and for the people" is as eternally difficult a business as it is an exciting and inciting idea.

I suppose it is human nature on the one hand and the uses of government on the other that make this so. For men will always yearn, and properly so, for both freedom and provision. And in the yearner's mind the relative importance of each will be a variable of time, place, and circumstance. To the extent that there is want in the midst of plenty or the potential of plenty, men will demand that government be more effectively organized and act more aggressively for greater provision. On the other hand, to the extent that governmental impositions prove burdensome or oppressive, there will be outcry for greater freedom. Thus, from generation to generation, it becomes more difficult to satisfy, or even to reconcile, the resulting diversity of deserving, but often contradictory, claims.

Yes, our political legacy includes intractable problems. Yet we continue to believe that the genius of the founders of our nation lay in the devising of political institutions that would both command respect and loyalty because of their decency and exhibit flexibility enough for effective adaptation to the needs of other and different times. For that, we cannot give them too much credit. Yet our belief in the excellence of their work is also the measure of our responsibility to make those institutions serve the people well in our times.

May enthusiasm for participation in that task be the impelling force of this Bicentennial Conference.

INTRODUCTORY REMARKS
at the American Philosophical Society
by Herbert Wechsler, Chairman

President Wolfgang, fellow conferees, distinguished guests, ladies and gentlemen: I approach this conference with the high hope that it may make a useful contribution and deem it a great honor to be asked to take the chair. Before committing myself to the silence and abstention that a chairman must observe, may I venture a brief comment on the task we are assembled to discharge.

THE AMERICAN CONSTITUTION

Two centuries of national existence surely call for the expressions of devotion they will be evoking throughout this year. Our meeting may well be unique in choosing to commemorate the Declaration and the patriots who gave us independence by focusing attention on the sequel to that indispensable achievement, the framing of the polity and government that have endured. Our concern is, therefore, with the Constitution, whose anniversaries it is less customary to observe, though of all the happenings in Philadelphia its formulation has exerted and exerts the largest influence upon the welfare and the destiny of our nation.

In considering the Constitution, we have before us the rich record of the past with its enormous glories and its large frustrations, not the least of which occurred in the election of a century ago. We must learn from that rich record what we can, ambiguous as its instruction often is. That is, however, just the prelude of our task, which is to concentrate upon the present and the future. The Academy, in calling us together, speaks as Antonio, though to a better purpose: "What's past is prologue; what to come/Is your and my discharge."

It is, of course, much easier to call for an assessment of our basic charter in relation to the present and the future than to frame a meaningful response to an assignment of that kind. Such is the human situation that we see the present only through a glass and darkly; our appraisals of the future rarely involve more than the projection of our hopes or our fears. Added to this, the papers that we have before us cover such a range of problems and of speculations than we all would be hard put to do them justice in a period of months instead of days.

In this predicament we must count heavily upon the conferees in each of our committees, guided by their chairmen and keynoters, to focus upon issues that are truly of a constitutional dimension, in the sense that their solution calls for the approval or rejection of specific changes in our fundamental law. This is no doubt to give voice to a lawyer's bias, but as Woodrow Wilson put it long ago, referring to the Constitution: "a written document makes lawyers of us all." I say no more, however, in support of this suggestion than that it will assist us to achieve the most significant conclusions we can reach in the brief time at our command. Think how it helped the Constitutional Convention to agree upon a text that its deliberations started with the fifteen resolutions moved by Randolph, constituting the Virginia Plan.

Needless to say, I do not argue that this conference will not fulfill its purpose unless it achieves agreement on a program of amendment. A consensus in this group against the need for change, assuming that defects have been judiciously identified and gains and losses in removing them judiciously appraised, would be a product as important, in my view, as an agenda for reform. In constitutional affairs as in the rest of life, there is wise counsel in the aperçu of Justice Holmes that "imitation of the past, unless we have a clear reason for change, no more needs justification than appetite."

THE CONSTITUTION AND CHANGE

However our task may be defined, and our committees are autonomous as they define it, its performance will require us to feel as free to criticize as to extol the constitutional positions we examine. I should consider this too obvious to say had not my mailbox told me, as yours may have told you, that there is still a sentiment abroad that it is impious or worse to challenge the perfection of our charter.

That sentiment, however patriotic in its provenance and motivation, is hostile to the spirit of the Constitution and refuted by its text. It is well that we repudiate it now.

The thirty-nine delegates who signed the Constitution did not think the product perfect, not to speak of the sixteen who departed or declined to sign or the eighteen who stayed away. No more was claimed for the convention's draft than that it would surmount the weakness of the Articles and lead to the "more perfect Union" that was sought. That "a constitutional door was open to amendment," as Washington put it in his letters to Virginia, so that deficiencies could be eliminated in the future, was the telling argument against the doubters, crucial to securing the approval here and even more so in the state conventions. The Bill of Rights could thus be promised as demand for that security became insistent and provided promptly as

Herbert Wechsler

the government was formed. So, too, the system chosen for electing Presidents could be prevented from collapsing by the 12th Amendment, though, as we know today, not all the perils were removed.

To be sure, a great consensus is required for amendment, two-thirds of the Senate and the House and approval in three-quarters of the states by legislatures or conventions as the Congress may elect when resolutions are proposed. A less onerous procedure would, of course, have paid more deference to Jefferson's insistence that the "earth belongs always to the living generation," the premise of the Declaration's proclamation that governments derive "their just Powers from the consent of the governed." The revolutionaries in the Constitutional Convention could not have been insensitive to that conception, but neither could they yield to it entirely and create a government that would achieve acceptance by the states and gain sufficient strength to last. They had no choice, therefore, but to impose their present in such large degree upon the future, hoping to obtain its acquiescence by the benefits conferred. We may consider that the hope was not misplaced, for we have had our peaceful revolutions, starting, as Jefferson maintained, with his election as the President but more persuasively, I should suppose, in later years. It is important, though, that we remember that the most transforming changes in the cosmos of the Constitution were produced by civil war.

That cataclysm notwithstanding, we should recognize that the amending clause, which gives this conference its meaning, represented a significant advance in thought about the nature of organic law. In New Jersey, New York, and Virginia, the first constitutions after independence made no provision for amendment, as there was none in Cromwell's Instrument of Government of 1653. Delaware, Georgia, Maryland, Massachusetts, and Pennsylvania did formulate procedures for revision, but only that of Maryland seems viable upon its face. The Articles, as is well known, conditioned change on the consent of all the states. The framers' plan was, thus, an innovation in support of adaptation, stringent as its requirements may be.

That stringency is not without its compensations, for it has contributed to our acceptance of the most distinctive feature of our public law, the scope afforded to revision by interpretation: primarily, of course, interpretation by the courts, with final judgment in the Supreme Court, but also in some part by the Executive and Congress. Bagehot's famous dictum that "the men of Massachusetts could work any constitution," which Wilson properly regarded as a tribute to Americans in general, is supported mainly by the adaptations nurtured in this way. That record is, of course, before us as we move to our deliberations.

There are problem areas in which we may consider that the right solution inheres in interpretative changes as distinguished from revision of the text. Such submissions are, of course, in order, and they have the virtue of reducing or eliminating drafting difficulties that might otherwise be fatal. At the risk of being labeled a misogynist, I refer to the pending Equal Rights Amendment as very possibly a case in point.

INTRODUCTION OF COMMITTEES

I have spoken of the task we have assumed and of the spirit in which I believe we should approach it. That is all an introduction should attempt to say, and I shall say no more. Dean Pollak, who will shortly give the keynote speech, will speak to the substance of the problems that we have before us. Before I call upon Dean Pollak, I would like to introduce the presiding officers of each of our four committees and the authors of the papers that they have before them as a basis for discussion. They are the people who have planned the working sessions of our meeting and will take the lead in their deliberations.

Committee I, with its suggested focus on the "Maintenance of Revolutionary Values," has for its presiding officer Patricia Roberts Harris, and I must confess that I am not quite sure if I should introduce her as professor, dean, ambassador, commissioner, or something else. All of those titles have been hers in a career of great distinction in legal education, government service, philanthropy, business and community service, as well as in the practice of the law.

The keynote paper for Committee I was originally assigned to Professor Alfred H. Kelly of Wayne State, whose sudden and untimely death deprived us of a valued friend and depleted our scholarly resources. Much of his paper had fortunately been completed by the time of his attack, and, thanks to his wife and his associate, Professor Richard D. Miles, the submission is before us. It is buttressed by a second paper by another distinguished historian, Professor Jack P. Greene of John Hopkins, presently visiting at Oxford as the Harmsworth Professor of American History. Professor Greene has come to us from England and will make the keynote presentation in Committee I.

Committee II will center its attention on "Effectiveness of Governmental Operations." Its chairman is Professor Nelson W. Polsby, a distinguished political scientist, now at the University of California in Berkeley. The author or editor of many works related to our subject and managing editor of the *Political Science Review*, he has thought long and hard about our governmental institutions, with special emphasis perhaps upon a subject that arouses a slight interest in our time, the relationship of President and Congress.

The keynote paper for Committee II was prepared by Professor Henry J. Abraham, the Henry L. and Grace Doherty Professor of Government and Foreign Affairs at the University of Virginia. A perceptive student of governmental processes, with special interest perhaps in the judicial, Professor Abraham established his academic reputation at the University of Pennsylvania before succumbing to the gentle graces of Charlottesville.

The emphasis suggested for Committee III, "Shaping of Public Policy," may overlap somewhat that assigned to Committee II, but that is no disaster. Our chairman is the distinguished Comptroller General of the United States, the Honorable Elmer B. Staats. After important service in the executive office of the President, including many years as Deputy Director of the Bureau of the Budget, he was entrusted in 1966 with the immense responsibility of directing the General Accounting Office, established by Congress as an organ of the legislative branch. If there is such a thing in the United States as a senior career public administrator, surely it is he and we are grateful for his presence.

The basic paper for Committee III was prepared by Professor Charles E. Gilbert of Swarthmore, a political scientist with broad, eclectic interest in the problems of self-government, who has written with great insight on many aspects of the subject. He has attempted to provide in his exhaustive paper a guide to the enormous academic literature bearing on this subject during recent years.

Finally, Committee IV has for its subject "The United States and the World." Its chairman, Adrian S. Fisher, was until recently Dean of the Georgetown University Law Center, where he is now Francis Cabell Brown Professor of International Law. Before he took the academic veil, he had had a distinguished career in law and government, including periods of service as general counsel of the Atomic Energy Commission, legal adviser of the Department of State, Deputy Director of the U.S. Arms Control and Disarmament Agency, general counsel to the *Washington Post* and, last but by no means least, chief reporter for the *Restatement of the Foreign Relations Law of the United States* of the American Law Institute.

The issues paper for Committee IV was prepared by Covey T. Oliver, Hubbell Professor of International Law at the University of Pennsylvania. Professor Oliver's career also combines distinguished academic contributions and important public service, including two years as ambassador to Colombia and two more as Assistant Secretary of State for Inter-American Affairs and U.S. Coordinator of the Alliance for Progress. Among his publications, I note with special pleasure that he collaborated with Professor Fisher on the *Restatement of the Foreign Relations Law*.

I wish that time permitted introduction of our conferees, on whom the ultimate success of our venture most depends, but that would plainly be impossible. It is appropriate, however, that I should present the ranking member of the conference, Mr. Justice Tom C. Clark, whose eighteen years of service as an Associate Justice of the Supreme Court of the United States, not to speak of the manifold good works to which he devotes his retirement, merit the thanks of the Republic.

We come now to the main event of our morning, the keynote of the conference, which will be sounded by Dean Louis H. Pollak of the University of Pennsylvania Law School. Dean Pollak is a native of New York, the son of a distinguished lawyer who was much concerned with civil liberty and justice when such concern was not the fashion of our bar. His own career has carried forward that tradition both in practice and in teaching, including almost twenty years at the Yale Law School, five of them as Dean. Two years ago he moved from Yale to Pennsylvania as the Albert M. Greenfield Professor of Human Relations and Law. Then, as if to illustrate the legend of Samarra, the fate that he believed he had escaped in New Haven befell him in Philadelphia, where he again has become Dean.

Louis Pollak is a profound scholar, an able and compassionate lawyer, an ardent citizen and public servant, and withal an unpretentious and delightful man.

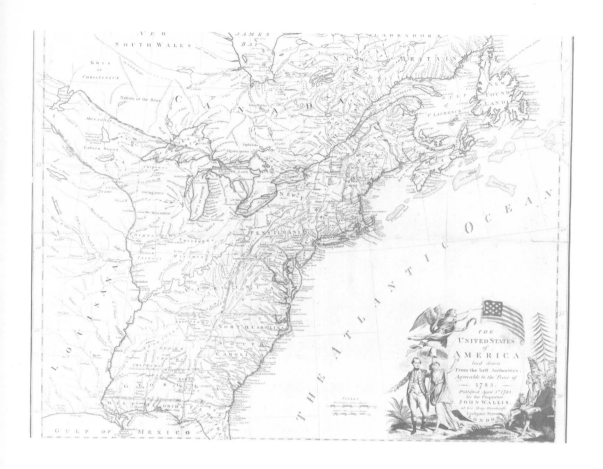

KEYNOTE ADDRESS

by Louis H. Pollak

It was proper—it was necessary—that the first session of this conference took place at Independence Hall. That spare and tranquil house across the green is a home place not alone for Americans but for all those who "hold these truths to be self-evident, that all men are created equal, that they are endowed by their Creator with certain unalienable Rights, that among these are Life, Liberty, and the pursuit of Happiness."

Jefferson, Franklin, John Adams, and the others who signed the Declaration were not preachers or publicists. They were leaders and doers, persons trained to accountability and action. They knew that it was not enough to assert self-evident truths and unalienable rights, and thereby to proclaim liberty throughout the land. They knew that "to secure these rights, Governments are instituted among Men, deriving their just Powers from the consent of the governed." So on behalf of the confederation of free states they constructed a Congress which had the appearance of a national government—but on which no effective power to govern was conferred. Congress, assembled in Independence Hall, strove ineffectively, and within a decade the "Articles of Perpetual Union" wasted into inanition. Whereupon, Madison, Franklin, Wilson, Washington, and the rest repaired again to Independence Hall. And there, "in Order to form a more perfect Union," they drafted and called upon their fellow citizens to "ordain and establish this Constitution." It is this Constitution—amended, and thereby enlarged, and yet in its central elements intact—which we are assembled to discuss for these four days.

How do we address ourselves to our agenda? We gathered first in reverence at Independence Hall, drawing inspiration from that place and from the moving words of the very great lawyer and judge who dedicated our humble labors to the monumental labors which went before. Listening to Judge Hastie, one remembered that the second purpose of the Constitution, following on the formation of "a more perfect Union," was "to . . . establish Justice." And one felt again the force of Holmes's dictum that "continuity with the past is not a duty, it is only a necessity."

I think our first undertaking here in the Philosophical Society should be to come to terms with that past, to see if we can reach agreement on what the enduring values and structures are that still connect us with the business taken in hand by the American people two centuries ago. But I doubt that we could have pursued that inquiry in an expeditious and effective way if we had begun our working sessions at Independence Hall. It is not simply that for us to deliberate where they deliberated would have been presumptuous. It is that, had we lingered in the house across the green, our search for the past would have been trammeled by the overwhelming symbols. We would have engaged in unequal dialogue with that past. We are better met on ground less hallowed—but venerable enough: in this house where Franklin still presides.

I propose that we take active steps to put ourselves in appropriate relation to our beginnings and our growing years before attempting to assess our present condition. The catalytic Declaration and the lasting Constitution establish the legitimacy of the work we are to undertake. But, unexamined, they shed little light on the paths we can most usefully pursue. The Constitution is with us still, not simply because it has no term of years and no later plebiscite has replaced it with another document. The Constitution is with us still because the Declaration summoned it forth to accomplish the Declaration's unfinished purposes. The Constitution, Marshall wrote, was "intended to endure for ages to come. . . ." But, unlike the "perpetual" Articles of Confederation, it has no claim on perpetuity except as it continues to fulfill the "truths" accepted in 1776 by three million white colonists of Western European ancestry. And that continuity of fulfillment, 200 years later and in the century to come, depends on the continuing will to freedom in 1976, and afterwards, of 200 million Americans of all colors and cultures, and four billion others with whom we share the Earth.

I press the point that as a first order of business we should consider the Constitution-in-process—that is, how our constitutional arrangements have carried us to where we now are—before we can fairly measure the effective congruence of the present Constitution with the vision of those who declared independence. In urging this, I have in mind an admonition voiced by Holmes, speaking for the Court, in 1920—an admonition which, if some greet it as platitude today, merely bears witness that we as a nation are slowly acquiring a better understanding of our dominant legal processes than prevailed before Holmes began to cut away the undergrowth which obscured the path of the law. Herewith, Holmes, in *Missouri* v. *Holland*, laying the foundation for a construction of the treaty power broad enough to achieve the needs of a great nation:

Louis H. Pollak

[W]hen we are dealing with words that also are a constituent act, like the Constitution of the United States, we must realize that they have called into life a being the development of which could not have been foreseen completely by the most gifted of its begetters. It was enough for them to realize or to hope that they had created an organism; it has taken a century and has cost their successors much sweat and blood to prove that they created a nation.

Holmes, born in 1841, was in his eightieth year when he wrote those haunting sentences. They move us still because they are instinct with his own experience. His sweat and blood were spent at Ball's Bluff, at Antietam, and at Fredericksburg. Those battlefields were part of the Constitution which he wrought from 1903, when he came to the Court, to 1932, when he gave place to Cardozo.

Holmes and his contemporaries lived the middle of our history. One of that sturdy company—Jeremiah Smith, born when Van Buren was President—came singularly close to linking our century with our nation's beginning. Judge Smith was the erstwhile New Hampshire Supreme Court justice whom President Eliot transformed into a professor in 1890, and who then taught for twenty years. I still recall my father's fond recital of how, one spring morning in the first decade of this century, Judge Smith walked into his classroom in Austin Hall rather more slowly than was his wont, put his books on the lectern, and said gravely: "Gentlemen"—the honorific apostrophe which is today happily obsolete in every American law school— "Gentlemen, I must apologize if I seem somewhat subdued this morning. This is a sad day in my family's history. This is the one-hundredth anniversary of my brother's death." Judge Smith apparently refrained from burdening the embarrassed young gentlemen with the further information that his father, the *first* Judge Jeremiah Smith, had been wounded at the Battle of Bennington in 1777.

No one at this conference, I think, has memories that antedate this century. We, and the people of this nation generally, know America's prior history only at second hand. In this Bicentennial year, we are nearing what Charles Black has called "the beginning of our third life . . . the day when no one is left who was alive when someone still lived who was born before our Constitution came into being."

It is against this fact that I ask us to try collectively to repossess some fragments of our past before we contemplate our present and our future. How is this to be done? I wonder if we may take counsel now with Franklin, who so benignly watches over us. I venture the guess that Franklin would be with us in person, if he could, this morning. To be sure, Franklin did not burden posterity, as Bentham did, with the requirement that he be kept in a glass case and produced on ceremonial occasions. But Franklin was equally mindful of the future and equally curious about it. Witness a letter to his friend, Barbeu Dubourg, written in 1773, in which Franklin was responding with interest to Dubourg's speculations about the possibility that people struck dead by lightning could be restored to life. First, Franklin referred to accounts of toads, trapped in sand, revived years and even ages later; next, he wondered whether delicate plants, uprooted for shipment overseas, might be immersed in mercury and thereby kept alive during a long ocean voyage. Then Franklin said:

> I have seen an instance of common flies preserved in a manner somewhat similar. They had been drowned in Madeira wine, apparently about the time when it was bottled in Virginia, to be sent hither [to London]. At the opening of one of the bottles, at the house of a friend where I then was, three drowned flies fell into the first glass that was filled. . . . In less than three hours, two of them began by degrees to recover life. They commenced by some convulsive motions of the thighs, and at length they raised themselves upon their legs, wiped their eyes with their fore feet, beat and brushed their wings with their hind feet, and soon after began to fly, finding themselves in Old England, without knowing how they came thither. . . .
>
> I wish it were possible, from this instance, to invent a method of embalming drowned persons, in such a manner that they may be recalled to life at any period, however distant; for having a very ardent desire to see and observe the state of America a hundred years hence, I should prefer to any ordinary death, the being immersed in a cask of Madeira wine, with a few friends, till that time to be then recalled to life by the solar warmth of my dear country!

Even as a dreamer Franklin was a pragmatist. "A hundred years hence"—except when computing compound interest—was as far a horizon as Franklin cared to look to. But at least this suggests that he would have been willing to meet us halfway. The 100 years he proposed were the very 100 years which, in Holmes's retrospective view, were required to "create a nation." And I put it to you that before we commence the discussion of America in 1976, we ourselves might derive advantage from a perspective taken in middle course. I propose, therefore, that, as predicate for our own bicentennial perspective, we make a brief survey of the American political enterprise, as Franklin might have surveyed it 100 years after his death.

Franklin died in 1790, one year after Washington was inaugurated and the First Congress set to work. It was almost as if the good doctor had willed himself to stay alive until the Constitution had taken hold. Let us then suppose that Franklin's 1790 casket was a cask of Madeira from which he was to be decanted a century later. Franklin in 1890 might have raised himself on his legs, wiped his eyes, and announced his readiness to finish out the last years of the 19th century in the "solar warmth of [his] dear country." And if, to begin his reacquaintance with his countrymen, he had looked back—through a glass, darkly, as it were—on the ten decades since his initial death, what chiefly would have engaged his scientific scrutiny?

The events of the first decade would have interested Franklin, but not greatly surprised him: the establishment of the government departments, and of the federal courts; the adoption of the Bill of Rights; the debate over the First Bank; the Whiskey Rebellion, and the campaigns against the frontier Indians; Washington's ambivalence about furnishing Congress all requested information; the schism between the Hamilton and Jefferson factions, paralleling the war between Britain and France; the reluctance of the judges to advise the government on legal matters, or to become entangled in other nonjudicial responsibilities; the election of John Adams; the Alien and Sedition Acts; and Madison's Kentucky and Virginia Resolutions.

At the commencement of the 19th century, Franklin would have seen the emergence of two instruments of governance which have proved of decisive importance—the party system and judicial review. Neither of these instruments is described in the Constitution, but each serves to carry out its implicit purposes. The party system—or, to be more precise, the *two*-party system—is the instrument for transmuting parochial interest groups (the factions whose dominance Madison, in his *Federalist* days, had been apprehensive of in a small republic) into coherent, broadly based and enduring majoritarian alliances capable of governing a large and expanding confederation of states. Judicial review is the instrument for curbing legislative and executive acts—at the local or national level—which tend to subvert the allocations of function or the protections of individual rights prescribed by the Constitution.

In 1801 Jefferson took office as President of the United States: he eschewed partisanship—"we are all Republicans, we are all Federalists"—and was the leader of his party. In the same year, Marshall took office as Chief Justice of the United States: he was the principal leader of the scattered remnants of the other party. Two years after taking office, he announced the Court's decision in *Marbury* v. *Madison* and eschewed politics: "Questions, in their nature political . . . can never be made in this Court." It is perhaps not surprising that Jefferson and Madison and their fellow Republicans saw Marshall's assertion of judicial authority to review and invalidate acts of Congress, and in a proper case to issue orders to cabinet members, in partisan terms: the Federalists, defeated at the polls, would continue to conduct guerrilla warfare from the bench.

In conversation with Senator John Quincy Adams, Senator William Giles of Virginia put it this way:

> If the Judges of the Supreme Court should dare, *as they had done*, to declare acts of Congress unconstitutional, or to send a mandamus to the Secretary of State, *as they had done*, it was the undoubted right of the House to impeach them, and of the Senate to remove them for giving such opinions, however honest or

sincere they may have been in entertaining them. . . . Removal
by impeachment was nothing more than a declaration by Congress to this effect: You hold dangerous opinions, and if you
are suffered to carry them into effect you will work the destruction of the Nation.

So persuaded, the Republicans impeached that member of the Court
who was least restrained about voicing his Federalist opinions from
the bench—Justice Chase. But the Senate declined to convict. No
justice has been impeached since that day. And Marshall, though he
never again struck down a law of Congress, went on to establish
federal supremacy over the states, and also the Court's arbitrament of
that supremacy: in *McCulloch* v. *Maryland*, which sustained congressional power to charter the Bank of the United States and barred states
from taxing the bank out of business; in *Gibbons* v. *Ogden*, over-
throwing New York's attempt to close the Hudson and the harbor to
steamboats other than those of a single private monopoly; and in the
other judicial hammer-blows that built a nation.

Franklin, leader of so many causes, was an early abolitionist. For
him the half century which followed the Louisiana Purchase would
have been decades of mounting dismay, as the institution which he
hated was claiming a vast new dominion and, in the process, threatening to destroy the union of states which he had helped to establish.
Taney's opinion in *Dred Scott*, announcing that no descendant of a
slave could be a citizen of the United States, and holding Congress
powerless to end slavery in the territories, would have been hard
reading for the Philadelphian who in 1789, when he was eighty-three,
presented a plan "to qualify those who had been restored to Freedom,
for the Exercise and Enjoyment of Civil Liberties. . . ," and who in
1790, two months before his death, had called on the First Congress
to take the lead in ending slavery in America.

We can suppose that Franklin would have stood with the new Republican, Lincoln, in the great debates with Douglas and the other
political campaigns which followed *Dred Scott*, and also in the military campaigns which followed the political ones. But is it not, also,
fair to guess that with the onset of the Civil War, Franklin would
have urged Lincoln to hold a tighter rein on those of his subordinates,
military and civilian alike, who relied on delegations of presidential
authority to imprison thousands of suspected Southern sympathizers,
to suspend habeas corpus, and on occasion to muzzle particularly
virulent elements of the press? Would not Franklin—would not, perhaps, Lincoln himself—have welcomed the Court's ruling in *Ex parte
Milligan*, decided after Lincoln's death, that military commissions
could not try civilians even in time of war if the civil courts were
functioning: "The Constitution of the United States is a law for
rulers and people, equally in war and in peace, and covers with the
shield of its protection all classes of men, at all times, and under all
circumstances." And again:

Louis H. Pollak

This nation . . . has no right to expect that it will always have wise and humane rulers, sincerely attached to the principles of the Constitution. Wicked men, ambitious of power, with hatred of liberty and contempt of law, may fill the place once occupied by Washington and Lincoln.

For Franklin, 1865 should have been a halcyon year—the end of rebellion and the end of slavery. But the stillness at Appomattox was broken by the firing of a revolver at Ford's Theatre. With Lincoln dead, Congress and the President were soon at loggerheads about how to rebuild the shattered nation. On paper, the nation's purposes seemed clear enough: the 13th Amendment ended slavery; the 14th Amendment exorcised Taney's dread dictum that blacks could never be citizens; the 15th Amendment granted blacks—*male* blacks, that is—the vote. Taken together, the three post-Civil War amendments pointed to the horizon described by Justice Miller, for the Court, in the *Slaughter-House Cases*: "the freedom of the slave race, the security and firm establishment of that freedom, and the protection of the newly-made freeman and citizen from the oppressions of those who had formerly exercised unlimited dominion over him." But how were these objectives to be achieved, and how and on what timetable were they to be squared with plans for readmission of the rebellious states? With these gravest questions of public policy (and sundry others) unanswered and unanswerable, paralysis of government set in. The dominant Republicans tried to use their power base in Congress as a platform for wielding the executive power; but Andrew Johnson, although unable to effectuate his own policies, refused to surrender his authority to Congress. Then the Republicans, turning back the pages to the Republicanism of Jefferson, tried impeachment. But the Senate of 1868 acquitted Johnson, just as the Senate of 1804 had acquitted Chase. Impeachment as an instrument of party conflict disappeared from the constitutional arsenal.

The Court in the late 1860s could do nothing to ameliorate the perilous confrontation between Congress and President. And, in the same era, the Court's expositions of the relationship between the states and the United States showed little understanding of Marshall's great nationalizing judgments, let alone a candid recognition that the Civil War had changed the equilibrium beyond recall. "The general government and the states," said Justice Nelson in 1871, in ordering the federal tax collector to return $61.51 of taxes paid under protest by a Massachusetts probate judge,

although both exist within the same territorial limits, are separate and distinct sovereignties, acting separately and independently of each other, within their respective spheres. The former, in its appropriate sphere, is supreme; but the states within the limits of their powers not granted, or, in the language of the 10th Amendment, "reserved," are as independent of the general government as that government within its sphere is independent of the states.

Little wonder that Henry Adams was later to say, writing of the last year of Andrew Johnson's administration:

> The whole government, from top to bottom, was rotten with the senility of what was antiquated and the instability of what was improvised. . . . [T]he whole fabric required reconstruction as much as in 1789, for the Constitution had become as antiquated as the Confederation. Sooner or later a shock must come, the more dangerous the longer postponed. The Civil War had made a new system in fact: The country would have to reorganize the machinery in practice and in theory.

The election of a new President—the soldier-hero who had suppressed the rebellion—promised much: but it only resulted in debacles of a new kind. For the eight years of Grant's presidency, the nation wallowed in multiple malfeasances of a magnitude not even dreamed of by Franklin's most enterprising contemporaries. As Henry Adams wrote of the earliest of the many tawdry episodes: ". . . the worst scandals of the 18th century were relatively harmless by the side of this, which smirched executive, judiciary, banks, corporate systems, professions, and people, all the great active forces of society, in one dirty cesspool of corruption."

The election of Grant's successor took place in 1876. Had Franklin observed the American electoral process in the centennial year, he would have had little ground for confidence in the party system. Save only for Watergate, 1876–77 may fairly be viewed as the nadir of American politics. The candidate with the lesser number of popular votes—and, it seems likely, the lesser number of electoral votes—was declared the winner by the 8–7 partisanly divided verdict of a jerry-built electoral commission (five Senators; five Representatives; five Supreme Court Justices). Moreover, in exchange for Southern Democratic acquiescence in the installation of Governor Rutherford B. Hayes as President, the Republican leaders agreed to withdraw federal troops from Louisiana and South Carolina, which, in effect, marked the end of popular concern for the great national purpose charted in *Slaughter-House*: "the protection of the newly-made freeman and citizen from the oppressions of those who had formerly exercised unlimited dominion over him."

But did not *Slaughter-House* suggest that at least the judges would keep faith with the commitment made at Bull Run and Gettysburg and then written into the Constitution? In *Slaughter-House*, appellant's counsel—John Campbell of Alabama, the erstwhile justice who resigned from the Court at the outset of the rebellion—had unabashedly relied on the 14th Amendment for the proposition that the Louisiana legislature lacked power to confer on a single butchering

Louis H. Pollak

syndicate the exclusive right to operate an abattoir outside of New Orleans. Four justices agreed with Campbell. But the five justices of the majority did not: they found that the 14th Amendment provided no footing for a claim to constitutional protection from state interference with pursuit of a common calling, since the 14th Amendment and the other post-Civil War amendments were so clearly oriented toward what the Court called "the one pervading purpose" of bringing slaves into full freedom.

But in the decade following the centennial, the 14th Amendment underwent a sea-change. In 1883 the Court held that the amendment gave Congress no power to require railroads, theatres, and hotels to desist from segregating or excluding blacks. However, the decision in the *Civil Rights Cases* was not to mean that the amendment was to become a dead letter. Rather, the amendment was to be put at the service of a different constituency. Thus, three years after the *Civil Rights Cases*, the Court ruled that a corporation was a "person" within the meaning of the 14th (and, correspondingly, the Fifth) Amendment, and thereby ushered in the era of constitutional protection of free enterprise from government regulation adumbrated by the *Slaughter-House* dissenters. Blacks seemed to be falling out of constitutional favor, to be replaced by businessmen.

Surveying America in 1890, and in the ensuing decade which closed out the century, Franklin might have noted certain other data and pondered their significance for the future:

1. In 1887 Congress passed the Interstate Commerce Act, establishing a federal commission to govern interstate railroad rates. In 1890 Congress passed the Sherman Anti-Trust Act. Congress was taking the first steps toward national regulation of a national economy and was beginning to improvise new forms of administrative governance. But the Constitution had lagged far behind Congress. The Court's first case under the Sherman Act affirmed dismissal of the suit brought by the United States to set aside corporate acquisitions, which gave one company control over 98 percent of the sugar refining capacity of the United States:

> Slight reflection will show that if the national power extends to all contracts and combinations in manufacture, agriculture, mining and other productive industries, whose ultimate result may affect interstate commerce, comparatively little of business operations and affairs would be left for state controls.

2. The census taken in 1890 disclosed that the American frontier was a thing of the past. The continent was beginning to fill up. And America was beginning to look outward: Hawaii was soon to become American territory, to be followed in a few years by Puerto Rico and the Philippines. Shortly, the Court would consider whether, and in what respects, the Constitution followed the flag.

3. In 1890 the Louisiana legislature passed a law requiring railroads

to provide "equal but separate accommodations" for the two races. The Jim Crow statute was sustained six years later in *Plessy* v. *Ferguson*.

4. In 1894, Congress adopted an income tax. In 1895, the Court held the tax unconstitutional.

America, Franklin might have concluded in 1900, had lost her innocence and was coming of age.

The America which came of age in 1900 was an anomolous polity. The Constitution which Henry Adams thought antiquated in 1868 was at last obsolete. It was a Constitution sedulously protective of the racist instincts of the many and the acquisitive instincts of the few. It was a Constitution with little feeling for the "truths" proclaimed in 1776 or the structure blueprinted in 1787. And it was a Constitution unfitted to help a modern state govern its own increasingly dynamic economy or its ever-more complex relationships with other nation-states.

With the beginning of the new century, we no longer require Franklin to serve as guide. We enter the years of first-hand recollection of some members of this conference. They can recall for all of us the highlights of the long struggle in this century to restore the Constitution to sensible connection with the needs and purposes of the United States: the 16th Amendment; Holmes and Brandeis dissenting; depression and FDR's fight with the old Court; World War II and the subsequent deployment of the treaty power; and, last and foremost, the new constitutional era shaped by the Warren Court—ushered in by the rejection of *Plessy* v. *Ferguson* and the acceptance of the oneness of the American people.

We come finally to Vietnam and Watergate—events which (to use Justice Miller's phrase in *Slaughter-House*, as he sketched the background of the post-Civil War amendments) are "almost too recent to be called history, but which are familiar to us all." They are the brooding omnipresences overhanging this and every conference on America's future. They are the two Banquos at every Bicentennial celebration.

One could reasonably have expected Lyndon Johnson and Richard Nixon to be more adept than all other elected Presidents at understanding and working with Congress; for of all the elected Presidents only they had served in the House, the Senate, and the vice presidency.

In domestic matters, Johnson indeed knew how to induce Congress, miniaturized since Roosevelt's time, to grow again to life-size—to be the equal partner of the President in the shaping of major national policy. Of this partnership, the Civil Rights Act of 1964 is a triumphant example, and there are others. But when it came to Vietnam, Johnson, from Tonkin Gulf on, induced Congress to grow small again and abdicate the adult exercise of its awesome responsibilities. With respect to the Johnson policies which took us into, and kept us in, that longest of American wars, I am persuaded that they were wrongly

Louis H. Pollak

conceived, badly executed, and profoundly damaging to America's inner fiber and her effective leadership of the free world. Some whom I respect regard this assessment as largely or wholly in error. Whatever verdict history renders on the merits of Johnson's Vietnam policies, I am bound to acknowledge that the President had the courage of his convictions. By contrast, at least at the outset of the war, Congress, taken as a whole (of course there were illustrious exceptions: such as Wayne Morse, a double maverick; and Ernest Gruening, the aging New Dealer who kept forgetting that loyalty to party and President and concern for reelection normally take precedence over unswerving fidelity to the nation's welfare), had at the outset of the Vietnam War no courage and no convictions. Johnson is to be faulted for fostering congressional inattention to duty. But the duty and the inattention belonged to Congress. At its doorstep lies the decisive institutional failure.

Nor is that failure to be explained away on the basis of some constitutional meta-principle that disagreement with presidential leadership in matters of foreign and military policy is unwise and perhaps even unpatriotic. As a matter of law, the President is of course the negotiator-in-chief and the commander-in-chief, but in both roles the President is subject to legislative constraints even more powerful than those which a sovereign Parliament can readily impose on the Queen's ministers. Nor did the proposition—of which the late Senator Vandenberg was the embodiment—that politics stops at the water's edge amend the Constitution. Indeed, to look at the American experience through the prism of that proposition is not merely to misperceive the Constitution's deliberate separation of functions and authorities, it is to misunderstand our history: America's politics *began* at the water's edge, when Hamilton and Jefferson divided the Cabinet and the nation on the proper American response to the outbreak of war between Britain and France.

Nixon came to the White House seeking peace with honor. Two months later, he determined that the way to peace in Vietnam lay through neighboring Cambodia, where North Vietnamese reserves were massed, and he sent in bombers to blaze the trail. But the new war needed to be unacknowledged: public disclosure that Prince Sihanouk's realm was being bombed, and that he was not objecting, might have tended to embarrass the prince's studious neutrality. Nixon's potential embarrassment—waging a new war without asking leave of Congress—was taken care of by his field commanders in a very graceful way. As later described by the House Judiciary Committee, in laying the factual predicate of a draft article of impeachment which the committee did not approve:

> On March 18, 1969, the bombing of Cambodia commenced with B-52 strikes under the code name *MENU OPERATION*. These strikes continued until May 26, 1970. . . . The operational reports prepared after each mission stated that these strikes had taken place in South Vietnam rather than in Cambodia.

Save for a few senior members in whom the Pentagon confided, Congress was not advised that the targets listed in the operational reports were a little wide of the mark. But the official dissemination of these somewhat uninformative reports was not unlawful. We have been reassured on this point of law by the general who was then Air Force chief of staff:

> For falsification to constitute an offense, there must be proof of "intent to deceive." This is a legally prescribed element of the offense and is negated when the report is submitted in conformity with orders from a higher authority in possession of the true facts.

With this aspect of the matter clarified, the only remaining legal question was a technical one: by what constitutional warrant had the President unilaterally initiated and pursued a year-long air war in a neutral country? After the fact, one might even have called it an academic question. But it was a question which continued to worry Congress—the more so, perhaps, because it was the sort of question the federal courts were disposed to term "political," and hence non-justiciable. And the possibility that the question might arise again, in other guises, led at last to the enactment of the War Powers Resolution of 1973—the first major step in the reestablishment of Congress as one of the three co-equal branches of government. The resolution directs the President, absent a declared war, to report to Congress any significant commitment of armed forces in foreign territory, and to withdraw such forces by a date certain. Nixon vetoed the resolution, but Congress passed it over his veto. In rejecting Nixon's veto, Congress must be taken to have rejected a chief argument contained in Nixon's veto message—namely, that the War Powers Resolution is unconstitutional. Congress must have been very sure of its own constitutional ground, because it well knew that Nixon was a lawyer (at that time), and indeed a very accomplished one. Moreover, Congress also knew that Nixon was a "strict constructionist," which presumably meant that it was not his wont to conclude that an act of Congress was unconstitutional. On the other hand, Congress may have felt that Nixon was apt to be a more flexible constructionist in judging federal laws imposing constraints on the President. Nixon has always set great store on maintaining unfettered the plenary authority of the President—for example, Watergate.

The framers contemplated the dread possibility that some day a President sworn to preserve, protect, and defend the Constitution might find it irksome and might seek to reign under a legal code of his own composition. "This nation," as the Court said over a century ago in *Milligan*,

> has no right to expect that it will always have wise and humane rulers, sincerely attached to the principles of the Constitution. Wicked men, ambitious of power, with hatred of liberty and con-

tempt of law, may fill the place once occupied by Washington and Lincoln.

And so in the end, Nixon, corrupt and sick, quit "the place once occupied by Washington and Lincoln." He yielded to the convergence of two inexorable constitutional mechanisms: impeachment, the great engine intended, not for the exorcism of political foes, but for the trial of those charged with betrayal of the public trust; and the subpoena power of a court of the United States.

It will be recalled that Nixon, in *United States* v. *Nixon*, had contended that no court had power to determine the President's obligation to comply with a subpoena requiring the production of presidential records—in that instance, tapes of conversations between the President and his advisers—deemed by the President to be confidential. The President's assertion of executive privilege posed a question, so it was argued, committed by the Constitution to the President alone—in lawyer's parlance, a "political question." And the argument was not without some force. After all, in *Marbury* v. *Madison*, Marshall, in giving assurance that "questions in their nature political . . . can never be made in this Court," had been at pains to abjure any claims to judicial authority "to intrude into the cabinet, and to intermeddle with the prerogatives of the executive." But Chief Justice Burger and his brethren were unpersuaded. They saw the claim of executive privilege as posing a legal question, not a political one. And, therefore, a different sentence in *Marbury* v. *Madison*—"It is, emphatically, the province and duty of the judicial department, to say what the law is"—controlled the result in Nixon's case.

As the last chapter of Nixon's downfall shows, the most extraordinary fact about the American governmental process is the range and magnitude of the public issues which lawyers transpose into litigation and which judges then resolve by saying "what the law is." But the fact is not a new one; it is firmly rooted in Marshall's era, and it was clearly perceived by thoughtful observers dating as far back as Tocqueville. Moreover, criticism of spacious judicial intervention in the formation of fundamental public policy is no new thing. Billboards urging "Impeach Earl Warren" seem almost deferential in contrast to the attacks leveled at Marshall and his brethren: "If, Mr. Speaker, the arch-fiend had in . . . his hatred to mankind resolved the destruction of republican government on earth, he would have issued a decree like that of the judges."

Marshall survived his critics. So did Warren. We continue to look to judges to declare the fundamental values of our nation. In our own time, we have not been disappointed. Jim Crow and its monstrous derivatives—such as the incarceration of Japanese-Americans in World War II—were overthrown by what Richard Kluger has called the "simple justice" of *Brown* v. *Board of Education*. That single judgment connects our America with Lincoln, and with what Lincoln saw at Gettysburg to be the necessary and proper intendment of the

Declaration. The nine justices who achieved the decision in *Brown* v. *Board of Education* have given us the opportunity and obligation at last to fulfill our nation's covenants. We are honored today by the presence in our midst of one of the members of that Court, Justice Clark.

The cases which matter most are those, like *Brown*, which define the fair purposes and processes of a free society and trace the contours of human dignity. The issues build upon one another, and so the Consitution builds. When, last week, the justices heard Anthony Amsterdam and Robert Bork argue the death penalty, they were working within a framework reared, in part, by an intrepid Louisiana lawyer—our distinguished fellow conferee, Judge J. Skelly Wright—who thirty years ago failed by the margin of one vote to persuade the Court that it was unconstitutional to electrocute a man twice. And perhaps the justices, now closeted with these fateful issues, will see relationships to the issues addressed last Wednesday by the New Jersey Supreme Court, when it held that the parents of Karen Ann Quinlan were entitled to help liberate their daughter from an existence which is no longer life.

In similar fashion, but in another part of the constitutional forest, the justices will have the opportunity next year to consider *Brown* v. *Board of Education* in a different context. Does *Brown* apply—or does *Plessy's* "separate but equal" doctrine have continuing dominion—with respect to a school board policy of assigning students who seek a curriculum of academic excellence to high schools segregated on grounds of sex. The Court of Appeals in this circuit, finding the two schools to be of equal academic quality, a fortnight ago sustained Philadelphia's quaint atavism. The Court of Appeals' view that "if there are benefits or detriments inherent in the system, they fall on both sexes in equal measure," seems less than compelling: the Supreme Court observed as long ago as 1948 that "equal protection of the laws is not achieved through indiscriminate imposition of inequalities." Perhaps, notwithstanding the Court of Appeals' finding that the separate schools are equal, the Supreme Court will detect a fundamental disparagement of women in a policy which sends females to a school named "Girls" and males to a school named "Central." If the Court shows itself capable of sorting out issues of this kind, case by case, within the rubric of the equal protection clause, the case for ratification of the stalled Equal Rights Amendment would be less compelling.

Some may think it unmannerly of me to use this public occasion to suggest that our Court of Appeals here in Philadelphia may have fallen into constitutional error and that its judgment should be reviewed, with a view to possible reversal, but the justices in Washington. Perhaps I can make amends by being unmannerly in the other direction—through the indiscriminate imposition of impoliteness on all courts within range. I now put it to you that the Supreme Court took a long backward step three months ago when it reversed our

Louis H. Pollak

Court of Appeals in *Rizzo* v. *Goode*. In that case, it will be recalled, the Court of Appeals, on a record showing numerous instances of police mistreatment of local residents, had sustained Judge Fullam's carefully drawn decree requiring the Mayor and high officials of the Philadelphia police department to develop procedures which would facilitate orderly inquiry into citizen complaints of police misconduct. On certiorari, five of the justices disagreed. Unpersuaded "that the behavior of the Philadelphia police was different in kind or degree from that which exists elsewhere"—which, if the justices are right, suggests a general malaise in the legal order which should give all of us pause—they held that the remedy devised by Judge Fullam and approved by the Court of Appeals was an unwarranted federal judicial intrusion into the governance of local affairs. With all respect, I think the greater wisdom lies with Justice Blackmun and those who joined him in dissent:

> It is a matter of regret that the Court sees fit to nullify what so meticulously and thoughtfully has been evolved to satisfy an existing need relating to constitutional rights that we cherish and hold dear.

In voicing these concerns, I am acting on what I conceive to be a citizen duty to monitor the content of decisions affecting important constitutional claims. I believe there is a parallel duty to be concerned about the forms of constitutional adjudication. I think you will agree that careless judging is apt to produce careless judgments. Accordingly, I submit that if, following Marshall's lead, the judicial department is to continue to "say what the law is," and thus to articulate the central values of our society, justices and judges must take the time to hear reasoned argument, and also to render reasoned opinions based on what Professor Wechsler has tellingly called "neutral principles of constitutional law." If I am right in this, I think it follows that serious problems are posed by what appears to be an increasing incidence of summary dispositions in our appellate courts. Last week witnessed a particularly troublesome example of this practice: the Supreme Court had before it an appeal from a three-judge district court which had sustained a Virginia statute criminalizing the homosexual acts of consenting adults. Although a case can certainly be made for the result reached by the district court, one would be hard put to say, in light of *Griswold* v. *Connecticut* and subsequent decisions, that the appeal was frivolous. There is certainly no recent Supreme Court decision which flatly concluded the issue in Virginia's favor. And indeed one member of the district court had found that the state lacked constitutional authority to intrude on the private conduct of its citizens in so coercive a way. With matters in this posture, three of the justices voted to set the appeal down for argument. But the majority of the Court overrode their brethren: they voted to affirm, without argument *and* without rendering an opinion.

Given the seriousness and sensitivity of the issues presented on that appeal, I think the course of adjudication followed by the Court disserved the judicial process. I suppose it may be said in support of the decision not to hear argument that it would have been a waste of precious judicial time to explore issues a majority of the justices were prepared to resolve without benefit of opinion. And I suppose that dispensing with an opinion may be supported on the ground that explaining a decison in writing is hard and time-consuming and unrewarding labor when one is unsure of the grounds for one's decision. But neither line of defense seems very compelling. The short of it is that summary affirmance in a case of this consequence disposes of the particular controversy but gives no guidance to the bench, the bar, or the nation. Dispositions of this kind command obedience to a judicial mandate, but they do not generate respect for it. But respect for a court's mandate is not a resource to be squandered. It is the entire basis of the authority Marshall asserted and we have confidently acquiesced in. Judges must act as judges.

As the members of the judicial department must—and I trust will —continue to perform their tasks in ways calculated to command respect, so, too, they must be treated with respect. Not the respect of robes and honorifics and "May it please the Court," but the respect contemplated by the Constitution—tenure during good behavior; and, most insistently, a compensation which is suitable to the burdens and responsibilities of judging and which is not to be diminished. The responsibility of seeing to these matters lies with Congress. It is a responsibility Congress has shirked, just as, until enactment of the War Powers Resolution, it shirked responsibility on questions of peace and war. The responsibilities are of comparable dimension. Momentous as they are, the constitutional imperatives to "provide for the common defence" and to "insure domestic Tranquility" are of no higher dignity than the constitutional imperative to "establish Justice." I thought it a mistake to try to litigate the "legality" of the Vietnam War, for it was a tactic calculated to withdraw accountability from Congress. With all respect, I feel the same way about the pending litigation asserting the unconstitutionality of current judicial salaries, eroding under inflation. They are not unconstitutional, they are inadequate, grossly inadequate, and Congress is to blame. The proper venue is in the Capitol, not in the Court of Claims.

An extraordinary thing is happening in our Bicentennial year. A few leading English lawyers are beginning to wonder whether English law would not be well served if England were in some manner to adopt a judicially enforceable bill of rights. One of the foremost champions of the idea is Sir Leslie Scarman, an eminent member of the Court of Appeal. In his Hamlyn Lectures two years ago, the learned judge even argued that the idea is not quite the constitutional heresy it would appear to be to English lawyers trained on conventional notions of parliamentary supremacy. He pointed out that neither Holt nor Coke was fully persuaded that Parliament's authority was without limit. And most insistently he quoted Cromwell:

Louis H. Pollak

In every Government there must be Somewhat Fundamental, Somewhat like a Magna Charta, which should be standing, be unalterable. . . . That Parliaments should not make themselves perpetual is a Fundamental. Of what assurance is a law to prevent so great an evil, if it lie in the same legislature to un-law it again?

In this spirit, and to conclude this prologue to our agenda, I recall us once again to our constitutional beginnings—to Franklin's words on the last of the Constitutional Convention. I hope they may also serve as epiloque:

Sir, I agree to this Constitution with all its faults, if they are such; because I think a general Government necessary for us, and there is no form of Government but what may be a blessing to the people if well administered, and believe farther that this is likely to be well administered for a course of years, and can only end in Despotism, as other forms have done before it, when the people shall become so corrupt as to need despotic Government, being incapable of any other. . . . Thus I consent, Sir, to this Constitution because I expect no better, and because I am not sure, that it is not the best.

COMMITTEE I

VALUES and SOCIETY in REVOLUTIONARY AMERICA
by Jack P. Greene

> In Order that a . . . State should long survive it is essential that it should be Restored to its original principles.[1]

Even if the Bicentennial of the United States did not suggest, the mood and circumstances of post-Vietnam and post-Watergate America would strongly demand a reconsideration of the relevance of the principles and values on which the country was originally founded. The dispiriting and divisive war in Southeast Asia followed by a humiliating "peace with honor" and the rapid "loss" of Vietnam, Cambodia, Laos, and Angola to the free world; the marginal successes of the federal government in coping with the bewildering difficulties of stagflation; the seeming inability of government—at all levels—to deal effectively with the apparently intractable problems posed by the proliferation of crime and violence, the decay of the cities, the continuation of racial and sexual discrimination, and the pollution of the environment; the corruption of the political system itself to a point that required the resignation of the two highest elected officials in the land and permitted agencies of the federal government to violate at will many of the country's most cherished values and to operate essentially beyond the control of all of the elected delegates of the people—this nearly endless litany of abuses, defects, failures, and, at best, marginal successes over the past two decades seems, from a variety of indications, to have led to a manifest loss of confidence—outside as well as inside the United States—in the capacity of the American political system to solve the nation's problems.[2] This loss of confidence has led, within the United States, to a retreat or alienation from public life and, abroad, to widespread predictions of the death of the liberal state as exemplified for the past 200 years by the United States.

In such an apparently desperate situation, the principal question for a gathering such as this becomes, not whether the principles of

1776 can sustain us for a third or even a fourth century, but whether they still have any relevance at all at this moment, whether social and political conditions have not changed so drastically between 1776 and 1976 as to render the political system hammered out between 1776 and 1789 entirely obsolete or at least in need of fundamental revision. To put the question another way, is the alleged incapacity of the United States to deal with the massive problems now confronting it traceable not merely to the sudden agglomeration of a series of unrelated or only tenuously connected short-term problems that are susceptible to manipulation by changes in policy and/or leadership but also to the long-term disintegration and ossification of the political system itself, to some deeper systemic failure rooted in the very foundations of the American nation?

Yet, the very survival of the American political system for the past 200 years is, at the very least, a powerful testimony to its capacity to respond to the most profound kinds of changes in social and political conditions, while the outcome of Watergate and its associated scandals and abuses of power provides vivid—and heartening—evidence that the old system may still have some life in it. Even if that system and the principles, values, and institutions on which it rests and through which it finds embodiment and expression should not turn out to be the causes of our present discontents, however, it is certainly desirable, in the spirit of both Machiavelli and the founding fathers, to seize the occasion of the Bicentennial to take a careful look at the viability of "the original principles" on which the Republic was founded. What the original principles and values of the American Republic as they were formulated during the era of the American Revolution actually were and how they were rooted in and were a reflection of the particular social conditions that obtained in early America are the subjects of this paper. Hopefully, a discussion of these subjects will provide a basis for the consideration of the more pressing questions of which Revolutionary values ought to be reaffirmed, strengthened, and maintained and which eliminated as inappropriate and dysfunctional to a vastly different late 20th century world.

THE REVOLUTIONARY INHERITANCE

[During the Revolution], every thing in America seemed to operate, to promote political knowledge. The principles of civil liberty, which were but imperfectly considered in the writings of Locke, Sydney, and Montesquieu, occurred every moment to the views and feelings of the whole body of the people: Instead of being any longer barely the discoveries of a few enlightened philosophers, they became the prevailing sentiments of the whole body of the American citizens: And from that period until now, they have been constantly operating to produce a more natural form of government, a more perfect system of freedom, and a more flourishing state of society in America, than ever had been known before, among all the associations of men.[3]

Jack P. Greene

American understanding of precisely what the principles and values of the American Revolution actually were has fluctuated widely according to changing social circumstances, political exigencies, and cultural orientations. Part of a sweeping new movement toward greater sophistication in historical studies,[4] the analysis of the Revolution over the past quarter century has produced what seems to be a far more accurate and detailed and a far less anachronistic comprehension of most aspects of the era of the Revolution than we have ever had before. In no area is this more true than in the analysis of the principles and characteristics of what Gordon S. Wood has called the emerging "American science of politics," knowledge of which has been enormously enriched by the careful studies of Douglass G. Adair, Bernard Bailyn, Richard Buel, Jr., Martin Diamond, Cecelia M. Kenyon, Perry Miller, Edmund S. Morgan, J. G. A. Pocock, J. R. Pole, Gerald Stourzh, and Gordon S. Wood, to name only the principal contributors.[5]

The foundation of the "American science of politics," these new studies have revealed, was a hardheaded and, we would now say, realistic view of human nature. Rejecting the belief of a few of the more radical thinkers of the European Enlightenment in the perfectibility of man, the founding fathers were virtually unanimous in their distrust of the human animal. Man was an imperfect creature whose actions and beliefs were often shaped by passion, prejudice, vanity, and interest and whose boundless ambition, though sometimes diverted into socially desirable channels by his craving for public approval and fame, made it difficult for him to resist the temptations of power and vice. Man's feeble capacities for resistance thus turned power and vice into corrupting and aggressive forces, the natural victims of which (in the public arena) were liberty and virtue, those central pillars of a well-ordered state.[6] Yet, this unflattering view of man was counteracted by a belief that, through reason, man could use his own imperfections as a basis for constructing a stable and effective political system that would provide him with all the benefits that could be expected from political society. That politics, to quote David Hume, could "be reduced to a science," that the application of intellect to the problem of human governance could yield, in the phrase of the Society for Political Inquiries, a body established by Benjamin Franklin, Thomas Paine, and others in Philadelphia, in 1787, "mutual improvement in the knowledge of government, and . . . the advancement of political science," was the confident expectation of most of the men who assumed responsibility for working out the new political systems for the United States during the Revolution.[7]

This belief in the efficacy of reason underlay an animated, engaging, and, for the participants, exhilarating search for what the Vermont divine and historian Samuel Williams referred to in the previously quoted passage as "a more perfect system of freedom . . . than ever had been known before, among all the associations of men." There had been no comparable opportunity presented to mankind, said Thomas Paine, "since the days of Noah." Americans had it in their "power to begin the world over again" by discovering what Douglass Adair has called those " 'constant and universal principles' of . . . government in regard to liberty, justice and stability." Yet, Americans did not, as Paine supposed, have an entirely "blank sheet to write upon."[8] "In the establishment of our forms of government," said George Washington in his circular letter to the governors of the states at the conclusion of the War for Independence, Americans were able to draw upon "the treasures of knowledge, acquired by the labours of philosophers, sages, and legislators, through a long succession of years." The classical tradition, the English common law, the writings of 17th century New England Puritans, the political thought of John Locke and other natural rights theorists of the 17th and 18th centuries, the social and political thought of British opposition writers, and the ideas of both the Scottish and the continental European Enlightenment provided Americans with a plentiful stock of political wisdom to which they could, and did, turn for guidance. But practical experience derived from a century and a half of internal self-government, the lessons of which had been vivified by a decade of intense political interchange with Britain just prior to the Revolution, may have been even more helpful in the quest for an American science of politics. For the men who worked out the major components of the new American system were—almost to a man—experienced politicians. In marked contrast to virtually all later political revolutions, the American Revolution occurred in a society that had already undergone extensive political development and had at its command impressive political resources in the form of experienced and acknowledged leaders, tested institutions, and a politically conscious and socialized electorate.[9]

If Americans had a large body of theory and tradition and a broad range and deep level of experience to draw upon, however, little of it could be applied to the conditions of an independent America without considerable modification. What emerged from this process of adaptation was a political system that was in its working principles, characteristics, and underlying goals distinctively American.

The departures from traditional theory and practice, in relation to most of what may be referred to as the main working principles of government, were in many respects substantial. In the best British tradition, Americans would retain a strong belief in the principle of limited government: they, like Britain, would have a government of laws, not men. But they quickly rejected the contemporary British orthodoxy that the supreme legislative power was omnipotent and could alter the fundamentals of the Constitution as well as ordinary statute law—"the power and jurisdiction of parliament," said Sir William Blackstone in his enormously influential *Commentaries on the Laws of England*, "is so transcendent and absolute, that it cannot be confined . . . within any bounds." To defend themselves against Parliament's efforts to tax them after 1764, Americans had fallen back on the higher law doctrine of Sir Edward Coke and other 17th century interpreters of the common law who had suggested that the fundamental rights of Englishmen were beyond the reach of a mere legislative body. Over the next quarter century, they incorporated into the American system of government the basic principles that the natural rights of men were not conferred by but existed independently of a limited government and that neither those natural rights nor any other component of the fundamental law, as laid down by the Constitution, were susceptible to change by government. Indeed, Americans developed the "important distinction," a distinction, said *The Federalist* papers, that seemed "to have been little understood and less observed in any other country," between fundamental law and statute law, between "a Constitution established by the people and unalterable by the government, and a law established by the government and alterable by the government." Unlike the British constitution, that amorphous result of a series of discrete actions by the ordinary organs of government, the American constitutions were written documents, ideal designs of government constituted by the people in specially elected conventions and designed to confirm the fundamental rights of the citizenry at the same time that they specified a form of government that would secure those rights.[10]

Governments were, moreover, to be limited not only by constitutions established by the sovereign power of the people but also by the very character of government itself. For American government was *representative* government and representative throughout, not just in one of its parts. Americans rejected the European idea that society was divided into separate orders or estates and that each order needed its own organ of government to protect its special interests. In America, there would be no "distinction of rights in point of fortune," "no distinctions of titles, families, or nobility," no legally privileged "family interests, connexions, or estates," no "hereditary powers." "*Representative government*," said Paine, "is freedom," and the "floor of freedom" had to be "as level as water." Among *citizens*, at least, there had to be an absolute equality of rights. Thus, in the American conception of politics, government was divided into separate branches, not because each part represented a different social constituency, but simply because it would act as a check upon the others. Because each branch derived its "whole power from the people," moreover, it was directly "accountable to them for the use and exercise" it made of that power, and the chief "security of the people," Samuel Williams pointed out, derived less "from the nice ideal application of checks, balances, and mechanical powers, among the different parts of the government" than "from the responsibility, and dependence of each part of the government, upon the people." Representative government was to be responsive and responsible government.[11]

The notion that all power derived from the people was the foundation for still another and, in many ways, the most crucial innovation in the American science of government: the idea that sovereignty resided in the people themselves rather than in any institution of government. Earlier British and European thinkers had been unanimous in their belief that sovereignty was indivisible, and during the 1760s and 1770s British political writers found the American argument that there might be two or more taxing powers in the same political society, a multiplicity of parliaments each with a separate jurisdiction over a specific area, incomprehensible. Such an argument seemed to imply the existence of more than one sovereign power within a single state, but to most Britons the very idea of an *imperium in imperio*—a sovereign authority within a sovereign authority—was nothing but a solecism, a total contradiction in terms. The colonies were either part of the British Empire and therefore under the authority of the King-in-Parliament assembled, the repository of sovereign power in the empire, or they were separate states each operating under its own sovereign authority. There was—there could be—nothing in between.

Faced with the same problem of how the essential powers of sovereignty might be divided between the state governments and the national, American political writers solved the problem of the indivisibility of sovereignty and thereby made possible the creation of a workable federal system, perhaps the most important political innovation of the Revolutionary era, by relocating sovereignty not in governments but in the people themselves. If the people were sovereign, as the federal Constitution of 1787 assumed, the "state governments could never lose their sovereignty because they had never possessed it," and the people could delegate the essential powers of sovereignty to any government or governments they wished, giving some powers to one government and other powers to another. According to this theory, all governments at all levels were the agents of the sovereign people. Thus, as James Madison wrote in *The Federalist*, both the state governments and the national government were "but different agents and trustees of the people, constituted with different powers, and designed for different purposes." Such a distribution of power between state governments and the national government, and the countervailing pressures arising from that distribution, would, in fact, be still another device for protecting the people against too great an assumption of power by either.[12]

In many ways, the most considerable departure from traditional political wisdom was the idea that, contrary to the dictum of Montesquieu, public virtue might not be requisite for a popular republican government—especially if such a government extended over a large area. The establishment of republican governments in the states in the mid-1770s had been accompanied by widespread expressions of the conviction that no popular government could long survive without a virtuous citizenry which would eschew vice and luxury and put aside all individual concerns in pursuit of the common good. By the mid-1780s, however, some writers were beginning to sense, somewhat in the spirit of Bernard Mandeville, that private vice might render public virtue unnecessary in a free government, that the clashing of self-interest might in fact provide "the energy of true freedom." How precisely this situation might be achieved was, as Douglass Adair has shown, the special insight of James Madison as derived from David Hume and revealed in *The Federalist* no. 10. Whereas earlier republics had invariably fallen prey to the tyranny of a majority faction, the United States, Madison predicted, would be saved from that unhappy fate by its enormous size and the multiplicity of interests that would necessarily result from that size. With so many separate and diverse interests, there could be no possibility of enough of them submerging their differences and getting together to form a majority faction. In a large republic, Madison thus suggested, the struggle of manifold interests would operate, to quote Martin Diamond, as a "safe, even energizing" force that would operate to safeguard the liberty and stability of political society. Not a single unitary interest, then, but a plurality of conflicting interests was the proper foundation for a free government. Traditional hostility to faction and party as the instruments of partial and self-interested men would no longer be functional in the new American regime: within a generation after the ratification of the federal Constitution, in fact, political parties would come to be seen as essential to mobilize the diverse and multiple interests of the country for the purpose of providing effective government.[13]

The new science of politics that emerged in the United States during the Revolutionary era was not, of course, in all ways a departure from the past. Traditional skepticism about the political capacities of the broad body of the citizenry, though sharply mitigated by the already highly inclusive character (in relative terms) of American political society, continued to be manifest in a variety of constitutional checks on the power of the electorate: by bicameral legislatures and such institutions as the council of censors in Pennsylvania and Vermont and the council of revision in New York, at the state level, and by the indirect selection of the President, Senate, and Judiciary at the federal level. Similarly, there was no real revision in traditional criteria of who might be admitted to citizenship: all categories of people thought either not to be free from external control (such as slaves, servants, and propertyless adult males) or lacking in sufficient discretion (such as women and free people of color) were routinely denied the franchise, despite a few proposals for universal manhood and even universal adult suffrage.[14] Finally, political leadership continued to be considered as the preserve of the "aristocracy of talent," those people of unusual wealth, education, merit, or talent who were sufficiently expert to provide effective government. American political leadership would, like that in much more traditional societies, designedly continue to be elitist in character and the broad body of electors deferential to their political superiors. The power of the people was still intended not primarily "to facilitate their will in politics but to defend them from oppression."[15]

What Americans wanted their governments to be like, the specific characteristics they expected them to exhibit, was implicit in these many working principles of their political system. Governments were to be representative (popular and responsive), responsible (competent and attentive to the general interests of political society), equal (without any distinctions of rights among citizens), open (subject to review by the citizenry), and concerned with the single end of the "public business" and "not the power, the emolument, or the dignity, of the persons employed" in government. A proper concern with the public interest, moreover, necessarily demanded that government also be mild (in the construction and application of the law), simple (with no more officials in either civil or military capacities than were absolutely necessary), and inexpensive.[16]

But a government exhibiting these characteristics and built upon the principles described above might have been turned to any number of purposes, and the primary question must surely be what goals the American political system as fashioned in the era of the Revolution was supposed to achieve, what values, or larger ends of government, the Revolutionary generation had in mind when it was constructing that system.[17] Most of these values were explicit in the major American state papers.

The primary purpose for which governments were instituted, said the Declaration of Independence, was to secure the inalienable rights of men, of which the Declaration listed three: life, liberty, and the pursuit of happiness. Security of each of these three rights was certainly among the most fundamental values of the Revolutionary generation. Security of life, the first in the trilogy, and liberty, the second, were ancient goals of British government and require little examination here. But the reader should be reminded that in the American Revolutionary context, liberty was beginning to mean something more than a bundle of inherited liberties and rights that were the prescriptive possessions of citizens. During the Revolution, liberty had in fact come to carry a double meaning: it referred to both the right of the citizen to participate in the political process and, as the American conception of natural rights discussed above suggests, those inherent rights that pertained to all citizens *qua* citizens which could not in any way or to any extent legitimately be violated by government.

Implicit in these first two objects of political society were two further ones that were made explicit in the Preamble to the federal Constitution—order, variously referred to in Revolutionary state papers as safety or domestic tranquility, and justice. If Americans believed in liberty as an end of political society, it was an ordered liberty justly distributed among all citizens by an impartial government. Liberty was not to be confused with licentiousness, which was liberty carried to such an excess as to produce its direct opposite. The "blessings of liberty," said the Virginia Declaration of Rights, could only "be preserved to any people . . . by a firm adherence to justice . . . [and] moderation." Justice had to be the guiding principle behind all government actions. The list of grievances in the Declaration of Independence bristles with indignation at the many alleged injustices of the British government toward the Americans during the previous thirteen years.[18]

Jack P. Greene

"Pursuit of happiness" was certainly the most novel and the most ambiguous of the inalienable rights or fundamental values of political society asserted by the Declaration of Independence. The happiness of individual citizens had not previously been considered a concern of government in traditional European thought and practice: unlike property, the third component of the traditional trilogy of rights as laid down by John Locke in his *Second Treatise of Government*, happiness, as Cecelia M. Kenyon has pointed out, was not susceptible to objective definition and varied enormously from one individual to another. What Jefferson and his colleagues meant to imply by substituting it for property has been a perennial subject of scholarly debate. Almost certainly, however, they did not mean to assert, as an earlier generation of historians assumed, the supremacy of human rights over property rights. Most of the leaders of the Revolution would probably have agreed with Thomas Paine that liberty should always take precedence over "the defence of property." But in the Anglophone world of the late 18th century, few people ever suggested that there might be any conflict between the two. Like most contemporary British political writers, Americans regarded security of property as one of the most important components of liberty, and in the years after 1776 they also assumed a similar link between property and happiness: security of property was, in all quarters, said to be a basic ingredient of happiness.

Upon a close inspection, in fact, happiness, as it was conceived by the Revolutionary and later generations, turns out to have been composed of several such ingredients. Not just security of property, but peace and a situation in which citizens might become prosperous and achieve a state of what was referred to as "competency and independence" were said to be important components of happiness and legitimate goals of political society. Whereas systems of government, in the old world, supported themselves "by keeping up a system of war," Thomas Paine told Europeans in *The Rights of Man* in 1792, the system of government in the new world promoted "a system of peace, as the true means of enriching a nation" by enriching the inhabitants that composed it. Peace was thus a means of achieving a still more fundamental objective. True happiness, Paine told his European readers, had been discovered in America to be the product of a situation in which every citizen might "pursue his occupation, and enjoy the fruits of his labors, and the product of his property, in peace and safety, and with the least possible expense." Every citizen should have the opportunity to pursue his happiness in peace and safety, and the pursuit of happiness was the quest for property, prosperity, and independence from control by any other man. Government was thus expected both to facilitate the pursuit of happiness by the citizens who lived under it and to protect them in the enjoyment of whatever fruits their efforts had borne.[19]

If, as Charles Pinckney declared in the Federal Convention in 1787, the "great end of Republican Establishment" was the creation of a government "capable of making" its "citizens . . . happy" by fostering an environment in which they could, in peace and safety, pursue and enjoy prosperity and independence, the Declaration of Independence suggested through the assertion of the "self-evident" truth that "all men are created equal" that equality, in some form, might be a goal of American political society. Whether by this assertion Jefferson and his colleagues were talking about equality in the state of nature, a conventional proposition found in the political theory of Hobbes, Harrington, Locke, and most other natural rights philosophers, or equality in civil society, a potentially radical idea, is still an open question. Given the American tendency, noted by Cecelia M. Kenyon, "to blur the differences which Locke [and others] had either stated or implied between the state of nature and the state of civil society," it cannot safely be assumed, however, that they meant to confine their concern with equality to the state of nature. Certainly, as much of the rest of the Declaration makes explicit, the form of civil equality they had chiefly in mind was equality between Americans and Britons—formerly as subjects of the same empire and thenceforth as members of "separate and equal" political societies.[20]

But the concept of equality was widely recognized to have far broader implications, and during the Revolution a rough consensus emerged as to precisely what equality in civil society did—and did not—imply. It emphatically did not mean that all men were equal by nature, or that all men should have "an *equality of wealth and possessions.*" What it does seem to have meant was equality both of opportunity and of rights—for citizens. Equality of opportunity connoted the equal right of every individual citizen to pursue his happiness, to achieve the best life possible within the limits of his ability, means, and circumstances; equality of rights meant that all citizens—and certainly not all men who were not all citizens—would, as Samuel Williams put it, have "an equal right to liberty, to property, and to safety; to justice, government, laws, religion and freedom." The American belief in equality of opportunity can be witnessed in the widespread insistence that there should "be no monopolies of any kind, that all trades shall be free, and every man free to follow any occupation by which he can procure an honest livelihood, and in any place, town, or city, throughout the nation," while the commitment to an equality of rights is best illustrated by their rejection of all suggestions for the recreation in America of the European system of privileged "orders and degrees." In America, said Thomas Paine, there would be "no other race of men . . . but the people."

How far the Revolutionary commitment to equality extended can be surmised from the treatment of the two issues of established religion and chattel slavery. The commitment extended far enough to permit most states to disestablish formerly legally established churches and to enunciate principles of religious toleration and equality of all denominations. Thenceforth, each American would be left at "full and perfect liberty, to follow the dictates of his own conscience, in all his transactions with his maker" and "all denominations" would "enjoy equal liberty, without any legal distinction or preeminence whatever." But the commitment was not strong enough to force them to abolish chattel slavery wherever it was economically viable or even to extend citizenship to those people who had successfully escaped slavery. Free people of African and Amerindian descent, like women and children, were not thought to have the discretion requisite for the responsible exercise of citizenship. For the time being, the American commitment to equality would be limited to citizens, that is, to white adult independent males.[21]

Another value that was widely manifest during the Revolution was the insistence that American political society encourage public-spiritedness or public virtue. Somehow, George Washington told Americans upon his leaving his command at the end of the war, they had to acquire

> that pacific and friendly disposition . . . which will induce them
> to forget their local prejudices and policies; to make those mutual
> concessions, which are requisite to the general prosperity; and,
> in some instances, to sacrifice their individual advantages to the
> interest of the [whole] community.

Despite the insights of James Madison and others concerning the possibility of building a stable state on the clash of self-interest, most members of the Revolutionary generation still believed that public virtue—as principally defined by a concern for and willingness to subordinate individual and local interests in behalf of the common welfare—was necessary to the successful functioning of any republican political society.[22]

One final value that received strong emphasis during the Revolution was unity. Prior to the 1760s, the disunion of the colonies was notorious. For 150 years they had been, in most cases, more directly connected with Britain than with each other, and they had often quarreled over boundaries and even refused aid to one another against enemy attacks. During the long altercation with Britain prior to the Revolution, however, they learned the importance of maintaining a united front, and, from 1774 through the end of the war, American political leaders, acutely aware of the extreme fragility of the extensive union they were trying to establish because of the multiplicity of conflicting interests and traditions it contained, stressed the importance of a firm and steady union, lest division contribute to the failure of the Revolution by permitting the British to divide and rule. Following the war, these same leaders emphasized the necessity for a strong and perpetual union as the only device through which the new American states could achieve either their full potential as republican polities or their rightful place among the rest of the nations of the world. On "the *Union of the States*," said Paine at the conclusion of the war, "our great national character depends. It is this which must give us importance abroad and security at home. It is through this only that we are, or can be known in the world." In the late

Values and Society in Revolutionary America

1780s, *The Federalist* declared hopefully, "the utility of the *Union*" was "deeply engraved on the hearts of the people in every State." But it would take another century and a civil war before such a declaration could be applied with full confidence to the United States as a whole.[23]

The Revolutionary generation did not, of course, give each of these values equal emphasis, and a rough system of priorities can be established among them. They may be broken down into four categories according to their importance to the people of the Revolution. Life and liberty were given the highest priority and belong in the first and most important category. Only very slightly behind them, the pursuit of happiness falls into a second category. Of only somewhat less importance, public virtue, justice, order, and peace comprise a third category, while, as least valued by the Revolutionary generation, unity and equality can be assigned to a fourth and last category.

SOCIAL FOUNDATIONS OF REVOLUTIONARY VALUES

> In the state of society which had taken place in America, the foundations of her freedom were laid.[24]

Unity; public virtue; equality of opportunity and rights for citizens; public happiness as represented by peace and tranquility and the ability of all citizens to strive for prosperity and independence, secure in the knowledge that the property acquired as a result of their strivings would be secure; order; justice; liberty as both the sanctity of individual liberties and the right to participate in the political process; security of life—these were the principal values of the Revolutionary generation, the fundamental goals political society was expected to promote. They were values that were expressive of and appropriate to a special combination of social conditions that obtained in early America. "Writers upon American politics" during the Revolution, Samuel Williams accurately observed, learned their political "principles from the state of society in America," and the salient characteristics of that society, at least as it existed for those segments of the population who were of European extraction, were simplicity, openness, relative plenty, relative equality, and activity.[25]

Despite the efforts of the colonists to transplant to the new world as much of the world they had left behind as possible, circumstances of life in the colonies had never been congenial to their success. The easy availability of land and a high demand for labor to exploit it and the resources it contained produced a wide diffusion of property and a society that was more equal and less differentiated than any in the Western world at that time. Every one of the fundamental supports of the traditional society of the old world—the legally sanctioned distinctions of rank and degree, the scarcity of land and other resources, the psychology of passive dependence among the vast majority of the population, and the feelings "of subordination that property, ancestry or dignity of station . . . naturally excited" in Britain and Europe—all of these were either missing altogether or

Jack P. Greene

extraordinarily weak in the new world. The result was that the traditional patterns of family and corporate authority that lay at the heart of the patronage societies of the old world never managed to achieve much vigor in the new. Thus, as Crèvecoeur remarked in his famous *Letters from an American Farmer*, the European coming to America was confronted with a society totally

> different from what he had hitherto seen. It is not composed, as in Europe, of great lords who possess every thing, and a herd of people who have nothing. Here are no aristocratical families, no courts, no kings, no bishops, no ecclesiastical dominion, no invisible power giving to a few a very visible one.

Instead, he found "a people of cultivators" with but few towns scattered among them, "a pleasing uniformity of decent . . . habitations," and a lexicon "short in words of dignity, and names of honour." As Tocqueville later remarked, free men in America were "seen on a greater equality . . . than in any other country of the world, or in any age of which history has preserved the remembrance."[26]

Along with an extraordinary laxity of political control on the part of Britain, the vast opportunities and profuse abundance of the American environment exercised a profound effect upon the development of values and personality. Whereas in the old world, many, probably most, of the colonists had been, in the words of Crèvecoeur, "as so many useless plants, wanting vegetative mould, and refreshing showers" and had been "mowed down by want, hunger, and war," in America as a result of transplantation they had, "like all other plants, . . . taken root and flourished." "From involuntary idleness, servile dependence, and useless labour," they "passed to toils of a very different nature, rewarded by ample subsistence." As Crèvecoeur penetratingly observed, this "great metamorphosis" had "a double effect": first, it extinguished "all . . . European prejudices," encouraged men to forget "that mechanism of subordination, that servility of disposition which poverty had taught" them in the old world, and nourished a jealous sense of personal independence, marked impatience with restraint, and a profound antagonism to any barriers to the pursuit of individual happiness; second, it greatly enlarged their expectations for themselves and their children and prompted them to form "schemes of future prosperity," to marry earlier and produce more children to fill up the vast open spaces, to endeavor to educate their children in preparation for the bright new world they had before them, and to develop "an ardour for labour" unknown in the old world. The ease "of acquiring subsistence, and estate," said Samuel Williams, both produced "a spirit of universal activity, and enterprise" and encouraged men to preoccupy themselves with the pursuit of their own individual interests to the exclusion of all other concerns. Men were "careful and anxious to get as much as they can," said Crèvecoeur, "because what they get is their own." In America, then, "nature and society . . . combined" to raise free men from a state of passive dependence to one of active independence, to produce a "natural, easy, independent situation, and spirit," and to nourish a "spirit of freedom," industry, and economy, a thirst for property, knowledge, and improvement, and—because most free men were free from want and too preoccupied with their own pursuits to have time for dissipation and vice—habits of virtue. "Industry, good living, selfishness, litigiousness, country politics [that is, the politics of skepticism and dissent], the pride of freemen, religious indifference"—these were the personal characteristics that were "produced, preserved, and kept alive, by the state of society" in America.[27]

The political system established in the United States during the Revolution was thoroughly compatible with this "state of society" and the character and values of the men who composed it. Government in America was to be the servant of the individual citizens who created and lived under it; they were not to be the servants of the government. Independence from Britain and the establishment of a more perfect union through the federal Constitution were not ends in themselves but means through which the citizenry could help to make sure that neither external interference nor internal divisions would prevent political society from achieving its most fundamental purpose: the promotion of the liberty, prosperity, and happiness of individual citizens. The main object of concern to most Americans, Charles Thomson complained in 1786, was their own "individual happiness," and this strong predisposition among individuals to preoccupy themselves with their own private concerns at the expense of public obligations was productive of a powerful tension between the pursuit of happiness and public virtue, between the insistence upon personal independence and the need for public-spiritedness. This tension, strongly manifest during the War for Independence, was temporarily resolved in the early 19th century by giving precedence to the pursuit of happiness over public virtue, by defining the public good as the sum of private happinesses. Except in times of war and public distress, this resolution was workable so long as resources were plentiful and private interests did not interfere excessively with the welfare of the whole society.[28]

Government, Thomas Paine wrote with the American model firmly in mind, was thus *"nothing more than a national association acting on the principles of society."* That those principles were not universal, that the "form of government which was best suited to . . . one stage of society" might cease "to be so, in another," was widely recognized by the men of the Revolution. They also understood that unless a government could adapt to changes in the nature and circumstances of society it would "lose much of its respectability, and power; become unsuited to the state, and injurious to the people." Not just the dangers of corruption, but also the changing character of society itself made a "frequent recurrence to fundamental principles" desirable. What was "written upon paper respecting govern-

Jack P. Greene

ment," said Samuel Williams, was not sacred and not "otherwise good or bad, than as it is applicable to mankind, and may be beneficial, or disadvantageous to them."[29]

CONCLUSION

> No policy would appear more puerile or contemptible to the people of America, than an attempt to bind posterity to our forms, or to confine them to our degrees of knowledge, and improvement: The aim is altogether the reverse, to make provision for the perpetual improvement and progression of the government itself.[30]

That the values of the Revolution and the system of government through which they were expressed would eventually have to be modified to meet changing social conditions was clear to most men of the Revolution. For the first century of the Republic, however, there were no *social* changes sufficiently profound to demand fundamental changes in either the political or the value systems that had been articulated during the Revolution. Such changes as occurred tended simply to remove or modify existing anomalies discovered to have been incompatible with the original values of the Republic. Thus, it is hardly surprising that the principle of equality should have been given ever greater emphasis in the most egalitarian society in the Western world. The substitution of faith for skepticism in the political capacities of the broad body of citizens, the expansion of the suffrage to include all adult white males, and the growing insistence upon equal access to public office for all citizens both undermined the last vestiges of traditional political mentality in the American political system and testified to the increasing importance of equality as a political value within American society. Similarly, the abolition of slavery and the adoption of the 13th, 14th, and 15th Amendments to the Constitution committed that society to the eventual destruction of the racial limits within which liberty had hitherto been confined.

If American society underwent few basic alterations during the first century of the American Republic, it has changed profoundly during the second. It has moved from simplicity and (relative) homogeneity to complexity and (relative) heterogeneity: from a country of mostly independent rural proprietors of British and/or North European stock, it has become a nation largely composed of urban dwellers of extraordinary ethnic diversity who, to a very great extent, depend for their livelihood, either directly or indirectly, upon large-scale business, industrial, and political organizations. As concentrations of wealth have become greater, so has poverty and social inequality. Relative plenty, vast open spaces, and an optimistic sense of boundlessness and activity have been replaced by impending scarcity and anxious fears of constriction and passivity. The new state of dependence in which most Americans have come to live over the past century has produced a widespread and a totally new value:

economic security or freedom from want. Government has long since ceased to be inexpensive and—for some segments of society—even mild. The isolation and reliance upon a pacific disposition in foreign affairs has been replaced by involvement and reliance upon the threat of force.

Given the fundamental character of these and other changes, it is perhaps surprising that Revolutionary values have proved as viable as they have. Many restraints have had to be imposed upon the pursuit of happiness as Americans discovered early in the 20th century that in a society with resource limitations private vices were not always public benefits, but there has been an enormous expansion of the ideals of liberty, justice, equality (racial and sexual), and privacy—a value that had received little emphasis in the Revolutionary era—to the point, some commentators have argued, that they threaten their companion values of order and stability. The adaptability of these values strongly argues, in fact, that they are still laudable and appropriate goals for American society. But changing social and political (especially international) conditions may make it necessary to revivify and to reorder priorities among them, perhaps even to reconstruct the American science of politics so that it may be better able to secure them in a more complex world. Such an effort would be entirely commensurate with the expectations of the founders of the American Republic.

Jack P. Greene

NOTES

1. Niccolò Machiavelli, *The Discourses*, ed. Bernard Crick (London: Peter Smith Publishers, 1970), p. 385.

2. The latest Harris Poll in March 1976 revealed the lowest confidence in American institutions among the American public ever recorded during the ten years during which such polls have been taken.

3. Samuel Williams, *The Natural and Civil History of Vermont* (Walpole, N.H., 1794), p. 310.

4. See Jack P. Greene, "The New History: From Top to Bottom," *New York Times*, 8 January 1975, p. 37, for a brief description of this movement.

5. The works of most of these scholars are discussed at length in Jack P. Greene, "Revolution, Confederation, and Constitution, 1763–1787," in William H. Cartwright and Richard L. Watson, Jr., eds., *The Reinterpretation of American History and Culture* (Washington: National Council for the Social Studies Social Education, 1973), pp. 259–96. But see, also, J. G. A. Pocock, *The Machiavellian Moment: Florentine Political Thought and the Atlantic Republican Tradition* (Princeton: Princeton University Press, 1975), pp. 462–552, and Gerald Stourzh, *Alexander Hamilton and the Idea of Republican Government* (Stanford: Stanford University Press, 1970).

6. See, especially, Arthur O. Lovejoy, *Reflections on Human Nature* (Baltimore: Johns Hopkins University Press, 1961), pp. 37–65, and Bernard Bailyn, *The Ideological Origins of the American Revolution* (Cambridge: Harvard University Press, 1967), pp. 55–93.

7. Douglass G. Adair, "That Politics May Be Reduced to a Science: David Hume, James Madison, and the Tenth *Federalist*," *Huntington Library Quarterly* 20 (1957), pp. 343–60; Thomas Paine, "The Society for Political Inquiries" (1787) in Philip S. Foner, ed., *The Complete Writings of Thomas Paine*, 2 vols. (New York: Citadel Press, 1945), vol. 2, p. 42.

8. See Adair, "That Politics May Be Reduced to a Science"; Paine, *Common Sense*, and "The Forester's Letters" (1776) in Foner, ed. *Complete Writings*, vol. 1, p. 45, vol. 2, pp. 82–83.

9. Washington's Circular Letter, 8 June 1783, in ed. Jack P. Greene, *Colonies to Nation 1763–1789: A Documentary History of the American Revolution* (New York: W. W. Norton & Co., Inc., 1975), p. 438; Bailyn, *Ideological Origins*, pp. 22–53; Jack P. Greene, "The Growth of Political Stability: An Interpretation of Political Development in the Anglo-American Colonies, 1660–1760," in John Parker and Carol Urness, eds., *The American Revolution: A Heritage of Change* (Minneapolis: Associates of the James Bell Library, University of Minnesota, 1975), pp. 26–52.

10. Sir William Blackstone, *Commentaries on the Laws of England*, 4 vols. (Philadelphia, 1771–72), vol. 1, pp. 160–62; Bailyn, *Ideological Origins*, pp. 175–98; Robert R. Palmer, *The Age of Democratic Revolution: A Political History of Europe and America, 1760–1800*, vol I: *The Challenge* (Princeton: Princeton University Press, 1959), pp. 213–35; ed.

Edward Mead Earle, *The Federalist* (Washington, D.C.: National Home Library Foundation, 1937), no 53, p. 348.

11. Williams, *History of Vermont*, pp. 342–44; Paine, *A Serious Address to the People of Pennsylvania.* . . . (Philadelphia, 1778) and *Rights of Man, Part Second* (London, 1792) in Foner, ed., *Complete Writings*, vol. 1, p. 390, vol. 2, pp. 282–83, 287; and Gordon S. Wood, *The Creation of the American Republic, 1776–1787* (Chapel Hill: University of North Carolina Press, 1969), esp. pp. 519–618.

12. Bailyn, *Ideological Origins*, pp. 198–229; Wood, *Creation of the Republic*, pp. 524–47.

13. Wood, *Creation of the Republic*, pp. 65–70, 610–11; Adair, "That Politics May Be Reduced to a Science"; Martin Diamond, "Democracy and *The Federalist*: A Reconsideration of the Framers' Intents," *American Political Science Review* 53 (1959), pp. 52–68.

14. On this point, see Jack P. Greene, *All Men Are Created Equal: Some Reflections on the Character of the American Revolution* (Oxford: Oxford University Press, 1976).

15. J. R. Pole, "Historians and the Problem of Early American Democracy," *American Historical Review* 67 (1962), pp. 626–46; Richard Buel, Jr., "Democracy and the American Revolution: A Frame of Reference," *William and Mary Quarterly*, 3d ser., 21 (1964), pp. 165–90.

16. See Williams, *History of Vermont*, pp. 342, 347–59, for a discussion of the attributes of American government.

17. The term "values" is used here and throughout this paper in its general vernacular sense of the larger goals, purposes, or objects which constitutions, institutions, laws, and other political instruments are designed to achieve. See Judith Blake and Kingsley Davis, "Norms, Values, and Sanctions," in Robert E. L. Faris, ed., *Handbook of Modern Sociology* (Chicago: Rand McNally & Co., 1964), pp. 456–57.

18. Most of the major state papers of the Revolution are conveniently reprinted in Greene, ed., *Colonies to Nation*.

19. See Cecelia M. Kenyon, "Republicanism and Radicalism in the American Revolution: An Old-Fashioned Interpretation," *William and Mary Quarterly*, 3d ser., 19 (1962), pp. 153–82; Paine, "Thoughts on Defensive War" (1775) and *Rights of Man, Part Second*, in Foner, ed., *Complete Writings*, vol. 1, pp. 363, 388, vol. 2, p. 54; Williams, *History of Vermont*, pp. 337, 359.

20. Charles Pinckney, Speech, 25 June 1787, in Greene, ed., *Colonies to Nation*, pp. 532–33; Kenyon, "Republicanism and Radicalism"; David S. Lovejoy, " 'Rights Imply Equality': The Case Against Admiralty Jurisdiction in America, 1764–1776," *William and Mary Quarterly*, 3d ser., 16 (1959), pp. 459ff.; J. R. Pole, "Loyalists, Whigs and the Idea of Equality," in Esmond Wright, ed., *A Tug of Loyalties:*

Anglo-American Relations, 1765–85 (London: Institute of United States Studies, 1975), pp. 66–92; Robert Ginsberg, "Equality and Justice in the Declaration of Independence," *Journal of Social Philosophy* 6 (1975), pp. 6–9.

21. Williams, *History of Vermont*, pp. 330, 336–37; Paine, "Six Letters to Rhode Island" (1782) and *Rights of Man, Part Second*, in Foner, ed., *Complete Writings*, vol. 1, p. 281, vol. 2, p. 337; Greene, *All Men Are Created Equal*. Discussions of American considerations of the meaning of equality may be found in Wood, *Creation of the Republic*, pp. 70–75, and Willie Paul Adams, *Republikanische Verfassung und bürgerliche Freiheit: Die Verfassungen und politischen Ideen der amerikanischen Revolution* (Darmstadt und Newwied, 1973), pp. 162–90.

22. Pocock, *Machiavellian Moment*, pp. 527–45.

23. Paine, "The American Crisis" (1783) in Foner, ed., *Complete Writings*, vol. 1, p. 232; Earle, ed., *The Federalist*, no. 1, p. 7.

24. Williams, *History of Vermont*, p. 369.

25. Ibid., p. 372.

26. Jack P. Greene, ed., "William Knox's Explanation for the American Revolution," *William and Mary Quarterly*, 3d ser., 30 (1973), p. 300; Michel-Guillaumme Jean de Crèvecoeur, *Letters from an American Farmer* (1782), as reprinted in Willard Thorp, Merle Curti, and Carlos Baker, eds., *American Issues*, vol. 1: *The Social Record* (Philadelphia: J. B. Lippincott Co., 1941), pp. 104–6; Alexis de Tocqueville, *Democracy in America* (New York: Vintage Books, 1954), vol. 1, p. 55.

27. Crèvecoeur, *Letters*, pp. 104–6; Williams, *History of Vermont*, pp. 324–33, 372–76.

28. Wood, *Creation of the Republic*, p. 610.

29. Paine, *Rights of Man, Part Second*, in Foner, ed., *Complete Writings*, vol. 1, pp. 360–61; Williams, *History of Vermont*, pp. 345–46, 358.

30. Williams, *History of Vermont*, p. 346.

MAINTENANCE OF REVOLUTIONARY VALUES

by Alfred H. Kelly and Richard D. Miles

The American system of constitutional liberty, which first flowered in the era of the American Revolution, has roots buried deep within the colonial, English, and Western cultural heritage. Its values and institutional structure have to some extent exhibited an extraordinary continuity; nonetheless, the system has evolved and developed with the growth of the American social and political order and with the successive political crises through which the United States has passed. Paradoxically, as American constitutional liberty enters its third century of national identity, it has not only flowered magnificently once more, it also has entered a new era of crisis which again threatens its existence and which almost certainly will result in profound changes both in the system's values and in its institutional structure.

The Revolutionary era of two centuries ago saw the emergence for the first time of two or three closely related ideas about man and his relation to the state which were to serve as the foundations of the American system of constitutional democracy. Put too briefly, these were the idea of limited government or constitutional supremacy, the idea of natural rights, and the concept of an open society. All were closely associated both in theory and practice; all had venerable origins, some of which in fact went back to the ancient world.

If the modern reader will turn to the first book of Plato's *Republic*, he will find a dialogue between Socrates and Thrasymachus the Sophist upon the nature of law and the state. Thrasymachus, in a direct anticipation of an argument that Marx would invoke more than 2,000 years later, adopts a totally cynical view of the nature of law. The dominant classes in any society, he says, get control both of the priesthood and the instruments for lawmaking; thereupon they fashion both the law and religious belief to suit their own interest, persuading the populace that what they wish to be secular and profane law is, in fact, the command of the gods. But Socrates, whom Plato sets up as Thrasymachus's antagonist, will have none of this. Admittedly, he says, men in power may seek to corrupt law to their interests. But true law is something much more than that; it reflects certain eternal truths which flow from the nature of the gods themselves. Thus, for the first time the idea of natural law was explicitly stated: that there is a certain natural harmony in the universe which reflects the nature of God himself and which certainly God cannot and would not change. Further, the fundamental principles of natural law can be discovered by the application of human reason, to serve as the foundation of a rational and more legal system. A few centuries later, Cicero, the great Roman lawyer-philosopher, would give expression to the same idea in his *De Legibus*, proclaiming that man-made law must so far reflect the natural harmony of the universe that if the Senate and the Roman people themselves (the highest source of sovereignty he could conceive of) should make robbery, adultery, or the falsification of wills law, such pronouncements still would not be such, for they would defy the natural harmony of the gods.

This notion of a natural harmony in the universe which men could discover by reason and incorporate in a system of rational positive law passed down into the medieval era, where it reappeared in the writings of Aquinas and the other great churchmen. And in the late 16th, 17th, and 18th centuries, it came to maturity in an extraordinary flowering of political theorists, virtually all of whom seized upon the idea of natural law as the theoretical foundation upon which to erect a theory of sovereignty and the parameters of the power of the state. There were a great many such, from Richard Hooker and John Milton to John Locke, Algernon Sidney, John Harrington, Emmerich de Vattel, Samuel Pufendorf, Jean Jacques Burlamaqui, and a host of others. By far the most important of these writers for subsequent American history was John Locke, the theorist of the Glorious Revolution of 1688–89, whose *Second Treatise of Government* by the eve of the American Revolution was so well known as to serve as a kind of bible of political theory for the American colonists.

Like several other natural law writers, Locke began by formulating the idea of a state of nature—a hypothetical time in the remote past, antecedent to the creation of the state, when men had existed in "a state of nature." The state of nature, Locke held, was not one of chaos and anarchy; on the contrary, it was one in which natural law prevailed and under which men recognized certain fundamental principles of right and justice, which determined the relations of men with one another.[1]

Locke thereupon argued that because some men would not obey the dictates of natural law, it had become necessary for good men to covenant together to erect the state, into whose hands they surrendered the protection of natural law and the concomitant body of natural rights that now were recognized as derived ultimately from natural law.[2] Thus Locke adopted for himself the compact theory of the state, which, in fact, certain radical Calvinist writers had formulated a century earlier. The concept solved at one stroke both the problem of the legitimate origins of the state itself (a difficult one for

Alfred H. Kelly and Richard D. Miles

political theorists after the disintegration of the idea of divine right) and the problem of the theoretical limits upon state power.

The state, in other words, legitimized by its origins in natural law and by a political compact that brought it into being, in the final analysis existed solely to protect the rights derived from natural law. Thus, the state was obliged to guarantee all men certain fundamental rights, both against one another and paradoxically against government itself. It was this concept of natural law, natural rights, and limited state power to which virtually all the great political theorists of the age subscribed.

Locke was very certain what the fundamentals of natural rights amounted to. They were the basic guarantees of life, liberty, and property which were to be found incorporated in successive great charters of English liberty from the time of King John: Magna Charta, the various confirmations of the charter, and so on. By the time Locke's *Second Treatise* was published, certain of the most fundamental guarantees of liberty and natural rights had been reduced to positive law in the so-called Bill of Rights of 1689.

In reality, the English common law courts had for some centuries been engaged in formulating certain fundamental rights of Englishmen which the law guaranteed against the state. Over a long period, these courts had developed a series of procedural guarantees for defendants in criminal prosecutions and for the parties in civil cases, which one day would be described under the rubric of procedural due process. Originally, such guarantees had been developed with little or no reference to natural law or natural right; they were, instead, merely the "rights of Englishmen." But in the early 17th century, Sir Edward Coke of King's Bench had on at least two occasions invoked common law guarantees with language which at least implied a certain link between the rights of Englishmen and natural rights. It was an association which would become very familiar to the pamphleteers and political spokesmen of the American Revolution more than a century and a half later.

It is necessary to add here only that the idea of the rights of Englishmen as embodied both in common law decisions and in the great charters, along with both natural law and natural rights theory and the compact theory of the state, made their way to the American colonies in the course of the 17th and 18th centuries, where in intimate association with one another they provided the foundation for the political ideas of the American Revolution. The basic American Revolutionary argument as first stated was that the British government, in the Sugar Act, Stamp Act, and Townshend Acts, was violating the fundamental rights of the colonists, who, as Englishmen, were entitled to all those rights commonly extended to Englishmen in Britain. After about 1769 or 1770, the colonists tended to broaden their argument to include the notion that the rights of Englishmen were derived ultimately from natural law and natural right, so that the charters, the critical parliamentary statutes such as the Habeas Corpus Act of 1679, and the great guarantees developed in the common law courts were no more than expressions of positive law of the great fundamental guarantees inherent in natural law and natural right.

JEFFERSON'S REVOLUTIONARY IDEAS

It was this theory of natural law, natural right, the compact theory of the state, and limited government that Jefferson incorporated in the Declaration of Independence, with its affirmation of the "self-evident" truth that "all men are created equal," and that "they are endowed by their Creator with certain unalienable Rights," and that "among these are Life, Liberty, and the pursuit of Happiness." There were, however, two rather revolutionary ideas in the concept of natural rights as Jefferson set forth the theory in the Declaration: first, that natural rights somehow were associated with a principle of human equality, and second, that there was a more fundamental human right than that of property—"the pursuit of Happiness."[3]

To grasp how revolutionary Jefferson's ideas were in their immediate meaning as well as in ultimate impact, one needs only to reflect that all governments everywhere up until that time, even in Britain, had been based upon what the historian Edward Channing (speaking of London's attitude toward her colonies) called "the great plum pudding" principle: the government and the social order at large existed for the benefit of the privileged classes, whose superior wisdom, virtue, and social position entitled them to exploit the state for their own ends. It was this principle which Jefferson now was repudiating. His repudiation was inherent, also, in his rejection of property as the most fundamental human right after life and liberty and in his insistence that there was a greater right: the right of every individual to pursue his self-interest free of the restrictions of class privilege or unreasonable restrictions upon liberty imposed by the state.

To put it differently, the Declaration gave expression to a nascent American idea of equality of opportunity in an open society. It was an idea which Tocqueville would hail some sixty years later as a fundamental operative principle of the American social order. Jefferson did not invent the idea; on the contrary, the growth of fluid class systems and of a measure of political democracy had been distinctive phenomena in several of the American colonies for decades. The Revolution strengthened the democratic thrust of these forces and others already at work along the Atlantic seaboard. It destroyed established churches (only three, all in New England, survived beyond 1785, and they died out in the next forty years), liberalized criminal codes, opened the West to mass acquisition of land by the middle class, and liberalized somewhat the franchise requirements. And while the Revolution did not destroy aristocracy anywhere, it shifted its base, ruining many old Tory families and weakening others, thrusting former petty bourgeoisie into new positions of influence, prestige, and power, and generally weakening the hold of the old aristocracy, in particular in the North, upon the social and political order.

Alfred H. Kelly and Richard D. Miles

THE MAGISTERIAL TRADITION IN AMERICAN SOCIETY

But it must not be assumed from any of the foregoing that the Declaration and the Revolution completed the putative union between the doctrine of natural rights and the idea of human equality. The courtship had begun, but the marriage had by no means yet been celebrated. In a great many critical respects the socio-political structure out of which the Declaration and the Constitutional Convention of 1787 came was not democratic at all; indeed, from our point of view, even the impulse to a society in which all men and women were to be conceded real equality of opportunity was only a modest one. Most important, that was a society which still tolerated slavery. It is true that the Revolution itself released a substantial antislavery impulse in the United States, which in New England and the middle states resulted either in the outright abolition of slavery by court decision (Massachusetts) or in the passage of gradual emancipation laws, as in Pennsylvania, New York, and New Jersey. And in response to the same antislavery impulse, the Confederation Congress in 1787 incorporated in the Northwest Ordinance of that year a provision forever banning slavery and involuntary servitude from the region north of the Ohio and west of Pennsylvania. But most of the Revolutionary leaders were only mildly disturbed, it would appear, at the continued existence of black slavery among them. Either they were blinded by self-interest to the incongruity of their position, or—as some Southerners would presently declare—they simply did not believe that natural rights applied to black people.

As further testament to the very limited role which the idea of equality and universal human rights played in the early American Republic, it is necessary only to recall that the aristocratic tradition in politics was still extremely powerful. Most white males now had the vote, but landed and mercantile aristocrats, together with the more prosperous smaller merchants and small landed gentry along with their lawyer-spokesmen, were expected as a matter of course to take the lead in the political process. Since the early colonial era, there had been a powerful magisterial tradition in colonial politics, in which the magistrates were conceived of as holding power in a kind of trust bestowed upon them through the social compact but which nonetheless left the magistrates free to rule as they thought best. For at least a generation or so after the Revolution, the magisterial tradition continued almost uninterrupted in the state and federal politics of the new Republic.

Thus, the convention which met at Philadelphia in 1787 and which drafted the Constitution of the United States was very much in the magisterial tradition. The convention has on occasion been viewed by certain historians as something of a counterrevolution, which reversed the egalitarian thrust of the Declaration of Independence and restored the idea of magisterial authority. We believe that is almost certainly an incorrect view of the matter. The men who assembled at

Philadelphia were, by and large, drawn from the same class as those who had sat in the Second Continental Congress and put their names to the Declaration. (The names of six of the signers of the Declaration, in fact, are to be found among those of the thirty-nine men who signed the Constitution in 1787.) It was not that a counterrevolution was in progress; rather the convention's objective was, of necessity, a radically different one from that of the Continental Congress eleven years earlier. The task of the Continental Congress had been to formulate a rationale for revolution, that is, for the destruction of an outworn and unacceptable system of sovereignty. The convention's task was an almost precisely opposite one: to establish a new system of sovereignty, to describe, validate, and confine its mechanisms, and to describe, validate, and confine its sweep of power. This task the convention performed with extraordinary wisdom, insight, and success.[4]

But the fact that the Constitution in no sense was a counterrevolution should not obscure the generally magisterial character of the gathering. The aristocratic tradition in the convention was very strong, as the names of George Washington, Edmund Randolph, Alexander Hamilton, Gouverneur Morris, Robert Morris, George Mason, Charles Cotesworth Pinckney, Rufus King, John Rutledge, John Dickinson, and John Langdon attest. Most of these men had been born to the purple; a few, like Dickinson, Hamilton, and Franklin, had risen to the top of the social order through fortunate marriages, successful business enterprise, or sheer brilliance. But with one or two possible exceptions, they thought and acted within the magisterial tradition; the word "levellism" (the 17th century Puritan Revolution equivalent of advocacy of egalitarian democracy) was a hateful term to them.

Moreover, the document which they drafted, while it was an extraordinarily liberal and enlightened document for its day, reflecting as it did the best Enlightenment and Republican thought of the time, was nonetheless essentially a magisterial document. Very cleverly, the framers recognized and fitted the new constitutional system into the prevailing state distributions of political power, as indeed they were obliged to do if the document they were drafting were to have any chance of acceptance by the prospective state conventions. Thus, they equated the electoral franchise for the House of Representatives with that of the most numerous house of the various state legislatures, while in effect they allowed the legislatures of the various states to establish any system they wished for the choice of presidential electors. But in the resultant system, only the House was drawn directly from the electorate, however limited, of the several states. The Senate, chosen by the several state legislatures, was two steps removed from the people. The President, chosen by electors who conceivably might themselves be elected by the state legislatures, was at least two steps removed from the people; if the electoral college failed to cast a majority for a presidential candidate so that the final election was thrown into the House of Representatives, the chief executive was

Alfred H. Kelly and Richard D. Miles

three steps removed from the people. And the members of the prospective new federal judiciary, nominated by the President and confirmed by the Senate, would in turn be three or four steps from the people.

The result was most emphatically a magisterial Constitution, highly intelligent and enlightened, but in no immediate sense democratic. The saving grace in all this, it would eventually turn out, was that virtually all the critical provisions involved were sufficiently flexible to be adaptable to the rise of political democracy. Without that flexibility and adaptability, the Constitution hardly could have survived.

THE BILL OF RIGHTS

The amendments submitted to the states in 1789 by the First Congress under the new Constitution, ten of which were to be ratified and to become known collectively as the Bill of Rights, represented a return once more to the problem attacked in the first portion of the Declaration: a statement of natural and historic rights, which now were to be translated into positive law. The authors of the Constitution had not believed a Bill of Rights to be necessary. As James Wilson put it, the new government, unlike that of the states, was to be one of limited and derived powers rather than residual sovereignty; therefore, under a familiar common law principle, it would be unnecessary to enumerate the limitations upon that government or to state the things it could not do. Such an enumeration, Wilson argued, might even be dangerous; enumeration of specific prohibitions and guarantees imposed on the national government might imply that it possessed other powers not specifically denied it. But this argument had yielded to the exigencies of the ratifying process: the proponents of the Constitution had used the promise of a Bill of Rights to win waverers over to ratification, and the First Congress considered itself to be morally bound to carry out the promises of the Constitution's advocates.

The guarantees the new Bill of Rights imposed upon the national government fell generally into four categories. Most important for the great growth of constitutional liberty in the 20th century were those laid down in the First Amendment, setting forth what were to be considered the great fundamental guarantees of an open society: the prohibition upon any "establishment of religion"; the "free exercise" clause; and a prohibition upon any abridgment by law upon freedom of speech, press, assembly, and peaceable petition. Every one of these guarantees had a century or more of history behind it; and their original meaning has been the subject of very considerable controversy among historians in the late 20th century. Thus E. S. Corwin thought the establishment clause prohibited only a state church in the formal European sense but not at all other accommodations between state and church, while Leonard Levy has argued that the Jeffersonian "wall of separation" theory was historically correct. And Zechariah Chaffee was to argue that the guarantees of freedom of speech and press radically altered the English common law meaning of these guarantees, literally prohibiting all or very nearly all restraints upon speech, a stance adopted also by Alexander Meiklejohn; while Leonard Levy was to argue with equal conviction that the speech and press provisions of the amendment did no more than incorporate the prevailing English common law guarantee of no prior restraint, leaving the English law of seditious libel still in force. What is certain is that the amendment, except for the little flurry at the time of the Alien and Sedition Acts, was to sleep almost undisturbed into the 20th century, in part because of the obvious fact that the amendment's restrictions applied only to a government already limited by enumeration in its specific powers, in part because of the restricted and cautious role played by federal sovereignty in state-federal relations until nearly the end of the 19th century. Until 1925 there was almost no hint of the constitutional "explosion" which has surrounded the amendment since that time, either in church-state relations, sedition law, or censorship.

The second great set of guarantees, those of the Fifth, Sixth, Seventh, and Eighth Amendments, set down in positive law the ancient common law guarantees of the rights of Englishmen in criminal and civil procedure in the courts. Taken all together, they added up to the great fundamental guarantees of the fair trial which had been growing and developing since Magna Charta: due process, a prohibition upon double jeopardy and compulsory self-incriminating testimony, jury trial, venue in the vicinage, confrontation of witnesses, compulsory process for defense witnesses, the right to be informed of the nature of a criminal charge, and a prohibition upon excessive bail, excessive fines, and cruel and unusual punishment. Lurking behind all these guarantees, also, was a further one scarcely hinted at in the Fifth Amendment but fundamental to constitutional liberty: the subordination of military to civil power and a severe restriction upon the former's legitimate sphere of authority. Significantly, several of the procedural guarantees involved had only lately been the subject of controversy during the Revolutionary quarrel with Britain; thus the Administration of Justice Act of 1774 had grossly violated the guarantee of vicinage trial found in the Sixth Amendment.

The Second, Third, and Fourth Amendments stated certain traditional guarantees of the rights of Englishmen running back to the quarrel between Crown and Parliament in the 17th century. Significantly, several of these had also been involved in some fashion in the Revolutionary quarrel. The Second Amendment's guarantee of the right of the people to keep and bear arms had arisen out of demands of the Puritan militia trainbands before the civil war of the 1640s, while the Third Amendment's prohibition upon the quartering of troops in private houses in time of peace not only antedated the Puritan Revolution but also had been the subject of recent disputes between America and Britain involving the Quartering Acts of 1765 and 1774. And the Fourth Amendment, with its prohibition against unreasonable search and seizure and its stipulation of warrants based upon probable cause, not only stated an ancient English

Alfred H. Kelly and Richard D. Miles

common law right but called up for most Americans memories of James Otis's celebrated attack upon writs of assistance on the eve of the Revolution, in 1761. Again, also, the Second, Third, and Fourth Amendments carried the flavor of the supremacy of civil over military authority.

Finally, the Ninth and Tenth Amendments fell into a special category: they represented two generalized attempts to guard against the possibility of federal tyranny. The Ninth Amendment sought specifically to counter the Federalist argument that a national bill of rights might, by enumeration, imply a denial of rights which the new amendments did not succeed in listing; it provided that the enumeration of certain rights shall not be construed to deny or disparage others retained by the people. The amendment actually changed nothing and was essentially declaratory, in that it stipulated that which James Wilson and other nationalist lawyers had argued was the case anyway. Not until far down into the 20th century would the amendment acquire any substantial constitutional importance. The Tenth Amendment also was essentially declaratory: it reserved to the states or to the people powers not delegated by the Constitution to the United States or prohibited by it to the states. Significantly, the Congress, at Madison's instance, specifically refused to incorporate the word "specifically" in the amendment. Thus, the proposal left the enumerated powers of Congress potentially open to Hamiltonian and Marshallian construction and thus paved the way for the vast expansion of federal powers, notably through the commerce and taxing powers, which was to take place in the 20th century. Long afterward, states' rights conservatives, arguing that broad construction was a threat to liberty, would attempt to interpolate the word "specifically" into the amendment, but they were destined to ultimate failure.

The new Bill of Rights, taken in the large, was entirely consistent with the Constitution ratified two years earlier. Its statement of the doctrines of limited government and an open society, and its enumeration of certain traditional common law guarantees, were like the Constitution itself, entirely within the value system of the Revolutionary era. And just as the Constitution in no sense had added up to a counterrevolution against the values laid down in the Declaration, so the guarantees of the new Bill of Rights were not in any fashion a repudiation of the charter drafted at Philadelphia. The amendments, for the most part, expressed familiar ideas which scarcely altered the limited federal Republic the authors of the Constitution had established.

REVOLUTIONARY VALUES AND CONSTITUTIONAL LIBERTY TODAY

If we now engage in a great leap forward in time and subject this system of constitutional liberty and natural rights as formulated in the Declaration, the Constitution, and the Bill of Rights to a very broad and generalized scrutiny, it is possible at once to see certain very great evolutionary changes in the ideas of individual rights (they are not often called natural rights anymore), in the character of such rights themselves, and in the means whereby they are defined, implemented, and guaranteed.

Crucial to any consideration of modern constitutional liberty is the fact that the very concept of self-evident natural rights derived from natural law has nearly died out of contemporary constitutional theory. In reality, the demise of the idea of natural rights began in philosophic theory in the late 18th century. At the very time that the Declaration gave the concept its noblest expression, David Hume had already launched a devastating attack upon the conception that man could, by a process of reasoning from a priori premises, discover certain fundamental principles of right and justice inherent in the universe, which could in turn be translated into coherent propositions about human right and human liberty.

The higher law idea lived on throughout the 19th century, although with diminishing vitality, occasionally winning overt expression, as it did from William H. Seward at the time of the slavery extension crisis of 1850. Occasionally, also, the Supreme Court gave it some recognition of sorts. In the 20th century, however, the idea lives on in the writings of only a few Catholic philosophers, such as Leo Strauss. Such thinkers as Roscoe Pound, John Dewey, and Morris Cohen turned away from it completely, recognizing that it was a part of what Oliver Wendell Holmes, Jr., called "the illusion of certainty."

In short, the great "self-evident" truths of the Declaration and the natural rights philosophers are no longer self-evident. In their place are the truths of various ideologies, grounded in many instances in the great propositions about man and society derived originally from the Enlightenment, but which are no longer capable of demonstration except through an overt stipulation of unprovable premises. To put the matter differently, the underlying values of our contemporary explosion in civil rights and civil liberties may appear self-evident upon superficial perusal, but upon close inspection they appear to be compounded of our Enlightenment faith in reason and progress, a latter-day utilitarianism (the greatest good for the greatest number), which is in reality a logical extension of the Jeffersonian-Benthamite approach to social theory, and a latter-day concept of egalitarianism—one which in origin goes back to the Declaration and has been nurtured for two centuries by economic dynamism and class fluidity, but which in our own time has taken on a populistic flavor unknown to earlier generations. To all this, one must add that expressions of so-called rights very often contain a power-relationship component (those associated with the Black Revolution are a good example of this fact) and that they may, on occasion, reflect the half-disguised competition for power of competing pressure and self-interest groups.

There is potential for tragedy in all this, for it means that at the very time when the concept of individual rights in everything from due

Alfred H. Kelly and Richard D. Miles

process to racial equality is receiving unprecedented homage, both from the Supreme Court of the United States and from the society at large, the theoretical underpinning which gave such rights their vitality is gone. Rights have become pragmatic, not natural. What this means ultimately is that the rights so confidently proclaimed in the last generation are in reality the product of the shifting realities of the dynamics of the social process. A "right" which the Warren Court thought to be fundamental may be broken in upon, modified, or become inconsequential at the hands of the Burger Court tomorrow, simply because the ideological and power relationships reflected in the Court's membership have changed.

This does not mean that the justices themselves do not suffer from "the illusion of certainty" in the formulation of the propositions about the nature of right and justice which they proclaim. They do not often refer to natural law in cultivating truth; rather they discover either historical truths or self-evident sociological truths which are formulated out of certain half-hidden ideological assumptions about contemporary society and the nature of the social process. There is nothing very new in this process; indeed the ideological and rational procedures by which the Warren Court arrived at some of its landmark decisions about private right resemble strikingly the fashion in which the Court at the turn of the century translated the economic and social myths of laissez-faire capitalism into conceptions of rights in private property against the state.

The self-evident truths of *Lochner* v. *New York* (1905) with its translation, as Holmes put it, of Herbert Spencer's *Social Statics* into constitutional law have vanished now. But the judicial approach to social reality, while it is a different apparent reality which is approached, and a reality seen through very different judicial glasses, remains unchanged. The most spectacular example of this enduring fact is perhaps to be found in *Griswold* v. *Connecticut* (1965), the celebrated decision holding unconstitutional state legislation regarding the dissemination of birth control information. As Justice Black observed correctly, the Court had resorted in its opinion to essentially the same discovery of a self-evident ultimate reality—in this instance a right of marital privacy—as Peckham had indulged himself in in his *Lochner* opinion sixty years earlier.

All this gives rise to a somewhat disturbing thought: the libertarian-oriented rights which we proclaim so confidently with respect to racial minorities, women, accused persons, "far-out" dissidents, and the like, must be seen ultimately as nothing more than the product of the institutions, social pressures, and values of a certain sector of American society. It is not even certain, in many instances, whether they represent majority-held values. In turn, this may well mean that they will prove just as frail and as vulnerable to the terrible erosive process of time as the link between due process and vested interest once proved to be. The only alternative to such a conclusion is the acceptance of some kind of theory of progressive revelation of social truth as a manifestation of cultural progress. In reality, however, such a notion amounts to nothing more than a disguised version of natural law theory.

The fact remains that, from the standpoint of a latter-day Enlightenment-oriented observer, the Supreme Court since the 1930s and in particular in the Warren era brought about through the decision-making process an extraordinary flowering of the idea of constitutional right and of constitutional liberty. In certain fundamental respects, also, the Court has worked directly within the value system generated by Locke, Coke, Milton, Harrington, Sidney, and the other natural rights philosophers of the 17th and 18th centuries. Other portions of the Court's decisions, those having to do with search and seizure, for example, are directly within the tradition of liberty formulated by the leaders of the American Revolution.

Moreover, the Court's vast concern with procedural due process and the rights of accused persons which the *Miranda, Escobedo, Powell, Wainwright,* and *Coolidge* cases embody hearkens back to the centuries-long English concern with the rights of accused persons, the formulation of which already had been evolving for centuries at the time of the American Revolution. The colonists before 1770, with their reverence for Coke, had considered them to be integral to the rights of Englishmen, and Jefferson alluded to them in the third portion of the Declaration in the course of his charge against George III.

Finally, the present Court is directly within the Revolutionary tradition in its concern for the great guarantees of an open society. Issues having to do with separation of church and state, for example, spring directly out of the Revolutionary movement for the disestablishment of state churches, the Virginia Statute of Religious Liberty of 1785, and the incorporation of the establishment and free exercise clauses within the First Amendment. And the Court's concern for free speech and in particular for the rights of dissident political minorities lies directly within the libertarian tradition of freedom of speech which took its departure from the very limited guarantees of "no prior restraint," but which by the time of the crisis over the Sedition Act of 1798 had progressed to the point where Albert Gallatin and his colleagues in Congress had formulated the first broad American-style guarantees of freedom of expression.

A NEW IDEA: ENFORCEABLE EQUALITY

Nonetheless, the modern Court's decisions on occasion carry within them implicit value systems which the Revolutionary era doubtless would have found foreign or at least strangely distorted. Thus the concept of equality within which the Warren and Burger Courts have operated has altered vastly since Jefferson first gave overt expression to the idea in the Declaration; indeed the idea of enforceable guarantees of equality as the Court has conceived them has altered substantially within the last thirty years.

Since the time of the Declaration, in fact, the American idea of equality, which the modern Court translates into legal right, has gone

Alfred H. Kelly and Richard D. Miles

through four or five distinct stages of evolution. The first stage, which Jefferson undoubtedly had in mind in part when he penned the Declaration, had to do with the centuries-old English idea of procedural justice for accused persons (habeas corpus, jury trial, evidentiary safeguards, and the like). The English caste system had interfered with the perfection of this system, but in America by the time of the Revolution formal caste as recognized at law had so far disappeared with respect to white persons that procedural equality was everywhere recognized. The second stage in the evolution of American egalitarianism, the extension of equal political rights to all white males, was well under way at the time of the Revolution and was to be consummated almost completely by the time of the Jacksonian era. Significantly, several states between 1820 and 1840 adopted new constitutions which embodied the guarantees of white male political equality.

Meanwhile, a novel idea, which Jefferson may well have had in mind in 1776, was working its way into American society: the idea of equality of opportunity, a notion closely associated with the concept of an open society and a fluid class system. Already in the 1830s Tocqueville, Dickens, Harriet Martineau, and Mrs. Trollope remarked upon the American sense of social egalitarianism, which did not at all carry any guarantee of equality of condition, but rather merely that all white men were entitled, without regard to prior rank, family, or social status, to participate equally in the economic scramble incident to a highly fluid society. Associated with this was another nascent Jeffersonian idea: that of the utilitarian approach to public policy. The concept of the greatest good for the greatest number assumed that no one social group would be favored overtly by the state without reference to the general public welfare. It is this concept of equality of opportunity along with those of equal justice and equal political rights which dominated the American scene far down into the 20th century.

With the adoption of the 13th, 14th, and 15th Amendments, the evolution of the American idea of equality entered still another stage: the extension of the guarantees of procedural justice, political rights, and equality of opportunity to a succession of minorities formerly excluded from the American social process. The amendments were, of course, intended principally to liberate the black man and to incorporate him in the body politic. For the first time, the interpretation of the egalitarian ideal became a judicial function. But the Court at first entered this field with extreme caution and even reluctance, refusing to endow the 14th Amendment's "privileges or immunities" clause with any content of consequence, rejecting an interpretation of the equal protection clause which would have allowed Congress to legislate against private discrimination, and reconciling, through the "separate but equal" myth, the idea of a racial caste system with a concept of a constitutional democracy.

Within the last forty years, however, as everyone is aware, the Court has become a powerful champion of racial equality, first insisting upon a rigorous interpretation of the "equal" standard in the separate but equal formula, then, beginning with *Brown* I and *Brown* II, destroying first in education and then everywhere else in public facilities the very concept of separate but equal and legalized caste. The Court, moreover, within the last few years has reached out to extend the benefits of an all-inclusive egalitarian idealism to other minorities hitherto partially or completely shut out from the benefits of an open constitutional democracy and fair system of procedural justice: to women, to illegitimate children, to recipients of public welfare, to impoverished prisoners, and so on. All these are logical and rational extensions of the idea born in the Civil War and Reconstruction era: that it is not logically feasible in a constitutional democracy to exclude any minority from the benefits of an open constitutional society.

Even as this process unfolded, however, a novel conception of the egalitarian ideal entered the marketplace of constitutional ideas and found its way both into legislation and into judicial decision: that it was not merely the duty of the government to remove the caste or other legal restrictions upon an open constitutional society but, in addition, the duty of both the federal government and the states to guarantee equality of position within the educational, social, and economic order through positive intervention by government. This is a novel and extraordinary development in the American egalitarian ideal, which to some extent may fairly be said to stand the old notion of equality of opportunity on its head and to replace it—as far as the concept goes—with an enforced equality of position. Insofar as this has received judicial sanction, it appears to be one major way in which the concept of constitutional liberty is being very significantly altered.

There are numerous manifestations of this tendency, but undoubtedly the introduction of affirmative action by the Court into school desegregation cases beginning with *Green* v. *County Board of New Kent County* (1968) and continuing through the *Swann, Wright, Keyes,* and *Bradley* decisions is undoubtedly the most dramatic. It now becomes the duty of the state, once a finding of de jure segregation occurs, not merely to prohibit such segregation, but also to pass beyond that to a positive remedial program to correct the consequences of past racial injustice by altering the distribution of the races in the public schools. On occasion this has meant resort to racial quota systems of a kind which Justice Frankfurter, within another context, only a few years ago pronounced contrary to the spirit of American constitutional liberty. Through Title VI of the Civil Rights Act of 1964, moreover, the federal government, through Health, Education and Welfare, has taken it upon itself to assure the existence of appropriate quotas and salaried equality by race, sex, and cultural origin for university faculties and for student bodies, as well as in the great mass of industries that have any kind of contract status with government. The consequence of all this in many instances has been a curious kind of government-guaranteed equal status altogether at

Alfred H. Kelly and Richard D. Miles

odds with the traditional American conception of an open market equality of opportunity.

Very often, however, affirmative action has gone beyond a mere guarantee of equality for the minority or minorities involved and has embraced attempts at inverse discrimination in an effort to remedy long-standing social wrongs, both public and private. Whether one views such attempts with dismay, in the light of their obvious conflict with the traditional open-opportunity concept of American equality, or considers them to be merely the latest and grandest manifestation of the egalitarian dream released by the Declaration is in considerable part a matter of one's individual value system. The Supreme Court thus far has refused to plunge into the maze of constitutional, legal, social, and political issues involved, preferring instead to dispose of the one major reverse discrimination case it confronted, *DeFunis* v. *Odegaard* (1974), on a technicality.

Sooner or later, however, the Court, and ultimately American society, will have to deal with the inverse discrimination issue. The critical questions are obvious: does state imposed discrimination as a means of remedying past social injustice or inequalities in the class system purify such policies of the taint of violating the equal protection clause, as Justice Douglas's tortured and contradictory dissent in the *DeFunis* case at least implied? Or are such programs, at last, hopelessly unconstitutional? The answer, obviously, is tied intimately to the question of whether the Court stays with a traditional Tocqueville concept of American equality or adopts the guarantee of position concept of the last few years.

Of even greater lasting significance: what are the implications for the long-run structure of American society of a government program of enforced equality of opportunity? Does inverse discrimination penalize superior ability, enforcing a lockstep of position, achievement, and eventually of class position which may ultimately reduce the creativity of American society? Will it alter class relationships significantly, by lifting hitherto suppressed minorities into adequately competitive positions in the American social order? Or will it prove unable to make any real impression upon the distribution of wealth, income, membership in the professions, and lucrative occupations that have traditionally characterized American society? Will it operate to reduce social tensions, or will it, in the long run, prove to have generated so many hatreds and tensions of its own as to have frustrated more or less completely the noble aspirations such policies have embodied? The answers to all of these questions will ultimately have to work their way into the law of liberty. One tentative and highly controversial proposition may be advanced here: in the long run, a populistic conception of rights—one that involves state-enforced equality of position as distinct from the guarantee of equality of opportunity— may break in very gravely upon a system of liberty which traditionally has been highly individualistic in its legal and theoretical foundations.

One notable aspect of the new egalitarianism which calls for particular comment is the proposed Equal Rights Amendment (ERA) for women, which at present writing is at least within striking distance of ratification. No enlightened person can quarrel with the amendment's general objective: presumably the elimination of whatever remains of social and economic discrimination against women in American society. A substantial portion of the criticism directed against the amendment has come from highly conservative traditionalists, who in spite of the major social currents of the 20th century to the contrary still believe that "woman's place is in the home." It constitutes a line of argument not likely to win many friends among those who have watched and studied with sympathy the long struggle, now more than a century old and going back to Lucretia Mott, the Grimke sisters, Carrie Chapman Catt, Susan B. Anthony, and so on, to eliminate discrimination against women in American society.

However, analysis of the matter hardly ends there. To paraphrase Justice Holmes slightly, the amendment rests upon the proposition that there are no biological or psychological differences between men and women which either the law or private social institutions properly can take account of. But, in fact, the statute books of the several states are full of protective legislation for women based upon a contrary premise: that both biology and social structure on occasion impose special burdens upon women which in some circumstances demand special intervention and special classification by the state on their behalf.

Nor has it been merely benighted males who have defended legislation and court decisions of this kind. The Progressive era—between the turn of the century and World War I—was one in which a great many highly intelligent women, among them Grace Abbott, Sophonisba Breckinridge, Jane Addams, and Florence Kelley, fought strenuous battles on the floor of one state legislature after another to get special protective legislation for females: hours of labor laws, factory sanitary facility laws, pregnancy leave laws, statutes creating special civil rights for women in marriage, special protection for female prisoners, and so on. Much of this legislation is still on the books. But as Professor Paul Freund has shown conclusively, ERA if adopted would cast doubt upon the special position of women at law in a great variety of respects, many of them damaging to women's rights. It is an argument that can hardly be disregarded lightly.

There is quite evidently a class element in the debate over ERA. The women who sponsor the amendment most strongly are generally drawn from a professional and business background, for whom the special protective legislation of the Progressive era has little meaning. Thus, Martha Griffiths, lately a Representative from Michigan and a principal sponsor of ERA in the House, has directed her fire in considerable part at the discrimination which women encounter in law, medicine, college teaching, and so on. By the same token, some of the opposition to ERA has come from female labor leaders, among them Myra Wolfgang of the waitresses union, who sees ERA as

Alfred H. Kelly and Richard D. Miles

menacing the kind of special protection she still deems to be valuable for working women. It is conceivable, of course, that if the amendment actually wins ratification, it will undergo a process of judicial interpretation which eventually will allow women to have the best of two worlds.

THE FURTHER EXPANSION OF THE OPEN SOCIETY

A second major respect in which constitutional rights and the law of liberty have undergone substantial change within the last generation or so is through the vast expansion of the dimensions of an open society. At the time of the Revolution, the concept of an open society already was winning general recognition, but the channels of expression involved were as yet rather limited. So far as the Constitution and the Bill of Rights were concerned, it meant little more than a guarantee of religious liberty and the disestablishment of religion; certain very elementary guarantees of freedom of speech, press, assembly, and petition; and the implicit subordination of military to civil authority. In actual practice, the dimensions of freedom of expression were extremely limited, as Leonard Levy has shown. Moreover, the unwritten philosophic assumptions of an open society were almost certainly stronger and more important than those involving formal legal guarantees: the notion of maximum freedom of movement, maximum economic discretion in a free market, and so on. These were primarily matters of institutional process and the silent operation of mores rather than of constitutional law.

For a surprisingly long time, the constitutional dimensions of the American open society changed relatively little. In the area of freedom of expression, for example, the Supreme Court, as late as 1919, in defining the permissible constitutional limits of governmental suppression of seditious activity, could endorse formally the bad tendency doctrine as an offset to the "clear and present danger" which it had accepted the year before. And while the technical constitutional rationale and limits of the bad tendency concept were very different from the rationale the high Federalists had resorted to in 1798 in defending the constitutionality of the ill-starred Sedition Act, the practical limits which the doctrine set upon freedom of political dissent were not very different from those of a century and a quarter earlier. Much the same thing might be said of the Court's decision in the *Dennis* case in 1951, in which, by means of the so-called sliding scale doctrine, it managed to rationalize "bad tendency" prosecution of eleven Communist party members convicted, in effect, of a charge of having propagated a series of ideas about government and society alleged to be dangerous to national survival. The practical dimensions of the Smith Act, it appeared, were not very different from those of the Sedition Act of 1798 or the Sedition Act of 1918. It is worth observing, also, that the Court during World War II almost completely abdicated its task of protecting the civil liberties of the loyal Japanese-American population, abjectly surrendering to the argument of military necessity to which the Army, the Executive, and Congress in effect all subscribed. The result was an infamous 'concentration camp" stain on the record of American constitutional liberty.

This was a by-product of the gravest of national emergencies, war, as were the suppressions of allegedly seditious activities before and since. But the Cold War era, reminiscent in so many ways of the circumstances of the 1790s which produced the first American Sedition Act, produced even more restrictions on civil liberties. Along with the Smith Act and the wave of prosecutions inspired by the *Dennis* decision, the McCarran Act (1950) and the Communist Control Act of 1954 provided further effective checks on freedom of speech and political activity. To these legislative enactments was added the action of the executive branch with the establishment of loyalty programs by Presidents Truman (1946–47) and Eisenhower (1953). All of this raised serious constitutional questions, but for the most part, no important judicial assessments of constitutional liberties were forthcoming for some time. This may have been in part due to the reluctance of the judiciary to move against coordinate branches of government, though it may equally be surmised that among the members of the U.S. Supreme Court there was no sure majority of strong devotees of personal liberty. Furthermore, there is ample evidence that determined efforts to strengthen national security, however crude, however abusive of the delicate fabric of constitutional liberty, were popular. Popular will, it seemed, actually supported governmental power to make the open society somewhat less open.

And yet, in a sequel familiar in the unfolding story of American constitutional liberty, it became clear that the idea of the open society survived the exigencies of war, both hot and cold, and, indeed, received a reaffirmation which carried it to such lengths as to form a major change in our idea of freedom. The role of popular attitudes was important in this, too—quite possibly the decisive factor in the long run, thus testifying to the profound significance of a newly aggressive populistic democracy in the determination of the dimensions of constitutional liberty. But clearly the resolution of the problem of freedom during dangerous times was achieved by the advent of a new Supreme Court, "the Warren Court," as common usage now has it. That presumably conservative decade, the 1950s, saw a remarkable change in the personnel of the Court, as President Eisenhower, in an exercise of appointive power rare in American history, was able to appoint five new justices to that tribunal. And President Kennedy, in his abbreviated tenure, appointed two more. So by the middle or late 1960s, when the new dimensions of the open society became abundantly apparent, it was indeed a decidedly different Court which had accommodated the new thrusts of popular feeling to the law of constitutional liberty.[5]

The central matter of constitutional concern during the Cold War, the civil liberties of alleged subversives, began to receive constructive judicial attention toward the end of the 1950s. The Warren Court, without actually striking down the *Dennis* opinion, in *Yates* v. *U.S.* (1957) modified its interpretation of the Smith Act so radically as

Alfred H. Kelly and Richard D. Miles

virtually to end prosecutions under that statute, while its opinions on the McCarran Act rendered the registration provisions of that law to all intents and purposes unenforceable. And a whole series of state loyalty program laws and loyalty oath statutes failed to pass the Court's scrutiny, most of them condemned because they suffered from the "vice of vagueness" or, by implication, infringed upon First Amendment rights. Even congressional and state legislative investigations, for a moment in 1957 (*Watkins* v. *U.S.*; *Sweezy* v. *New Hampshire*), were given a sharp check.

Meanwhile, a good many forces were at work in American life to produce an unparalleled growth of egalitarianism: a larger and larger percentage of people were achieving a middle-class standard of living; organized labor became a part of the political and economic establishment; various minority groups (Jews, Poles, and others) were now well beyond the desperate struggles of the urban slums and became significant elements of the mainstream of American culture; there was a comparative decline of the old "White Anglo-Saxon Protestant" ascendancy; and there was an extraordinary expansion of higher education, which poured into business and the professions a flood of educated men and women, most of whom were libertarian in outlook and aggressively egalitarian in their attitudes toward politics and society. The resulting surge of an importunate spirit, kindled to new heights by the pervasive immediacy of television, wrested striking concessions to the claims of personal liberty from the body of established constitutional ideas. The moderately open society of American Revolutionary tradition was rendered impressively more open.

The accommodations to this movement made by the Warren Court, and in many ways continued by the Burger Court, pertained to a wide range of matters; so wide, indeed, as to raise a serious question in the minds of many, including thoughtful libertarians, as to whether the extremes of openness might threaten to replace the fundamental notion of "ordered liberty" with a liberty so disorderly as at last to shake apart the very system long relied on for freedom's guarantee.

Such a turn of thought was for some time pretty much restricted to extremely conservative opinion, or to those with a palpable self-interest in the status quo. Thus the great movement to open American society to black people seemed to have majority support, at least until the appearance of the more advanced development of the idea of equality of position and affirmative action noted above. The next major expansion of the open society became important in the 1960s when the Court saw fit to interfere in state legislative and congressional apportionment. The new activism of the Court in this matter, launched in 1960 in the *Gomillion* case, was wholly apparent in *Baker* v. *Carr* (1962) and further developed within another two years in the *Gray*, *Reynolds*, and *Lucas* cases, among others. As a result, all voters throughout the United States had something like equal access to representative government, whereas before many had been virtually excluded by the happenstance of residence.

When it came to extending the fullest possible measure of constitutional liberty to persons accused of crime, however, it began to appear that there might be some incompatibility between the spirit of populistic democracy and important American traditions. The rights of the accused, particularly the very explicit ones of the Fourth, Fifth, and Sixth Amendments, have often been misunderstood and misinterpreted in popular thought. The notion that invoking the Fifth Amendment protection against self-incrimination is a confession of guilt has been a painfully obvious example in recent decades. When the Warren Court undertook, in effect, an extensive reform of criminal procedure as evidenced in the *Mapp, Gideon, Escobedo*, and *Miranda* decisions, faithful adherence to constitutional guarantees seemed to produce results which were plainly contrary to justice: the "criminal," it was widely assumed, went free because of some esoteric technicality.

This happened at a time when Americans were newly conscious of crime in their lives, for it was dramatized daily, and often quite explicitly, on television; it was prominent on many a page of the newspaper; it was constantly discussed in home, office, and shop; it was summarized in regular announcements of statistical summaries expressing a crime rate; and it invariably summoned up the picture of some repugnant person who was brutal, violent, and probably drunk or drugged. For a great many people, to talk of such a person having constitutional rights strained to the utmost the credibility of the very concept itself.

None of this was lost on those running for political office, including the highest in the land. "Crime in the streets" became a theme of the Goldwater campaign in 1964, and contenders for high office have been obliged to discuss the matter ever since. This has provided an interesting case study of the durability of the judicially-promulgated reform of criminal procedure, for Richard Nixon made the matter, through denunciations of the Warren Court and talk of "law and order," a prominent theme of his 1968 campaign. He was the winner that year, and an impressive winner in 1972; he actually did have the opportunity to make four appointments to the Court, including that of a new Chief Justice; and the new Court has had ample opportunity to change the tenor of decisions regarding the procedural rights of the accused in criminal trials. By early 1976, it seemed clear that the Burger Court would at least stop the process of strengthening the constitutional protections of such rights and when at all possible would render decisions sympathetic to those engaged in prosecutions. This was especially evident in *Harris* v. *New York* (1971), which limited seriously the *Miranda* decision, and the reaffirmation of the credibility rule in *Oregon* v. *Hass* (1975). Another strong indication is found in *Kastigar* v. *U.S.* (1972) where the protection against self-incrimination provided by the Fifth Amendment was further weakened.

It would seem, then, that the political process has been successfully employed to check the expansion of constitutional liberty in this area —ominous to some people, heartening to others. It is hard to believe that there are immediate practical consequences in this—that is, that

Alfred H. Kelly and Richard D. Miles

the crime rate has been changed by the new pronouncements of the Court. But there is a reenactment of an ancient problem of constitutional government based on the idea of people as the constituent power: how can we prevent the system which the people have created from diminishing the liberties it was intended to serve, when a current majority wishes to do so? In the matter of criminal procedure, we might say that the Constitution, in the Fourth, Fifth, and Sixth Amendments, seeks to embrace all people in the enjoyment of certain precious rights; but recently it seems that many Americans wish to exclude some from the full access to the protections therein set forth. The eagerness of so many to restrict these rights is distressing to anyone who believes in the enduring value of limited government. No doubt it arises from a sense of crisis about crime in American society, a motive similar to alarm about national security in time of war. The extremity of the danger, then, becomes the justification for the limiting of freedom, or at least for a lack of interest in making it secure to all. In the case of war, Americans have generally been confident that the war would some day end, and then the freedoms, which have been suspended rather than canceled, might be resumed. With regard to crime, a somewhat less confident expectation is probably in order, unless we can recover the Enlightenment assumption of the benevolence and perfectibility of our fellow citizens. Meanwhile, we might capitalize on the strong tradition we have from the Revolutionary era to create a truly open society, including therein even the poor and underprivileged, even when they are so unfortunate as to be accused of crime.

Anyone who lived as an adult through the 1960s must be impressed with the startling expansion of the dimensions of permissible speech and publication, including movies. When the results are surveyed as of 1976, it seems fair to suggest that American society has accommodated a range of expression in writing, speaking, and pictures which would in some respects astound the Revolutionary generation—though, of course, the content would not really be novel to many of them. More and more people, it seemed, were convinced that there should be virtually no bounds to their utterances and that the First Amendment could be invoked as an absolute bar to legal restraint. The most spectacular controversy was the one over obscenity, still not satisfactorily resolved. It may well continue for some time to be what it was called years ago: "a constitutional disaster area."

There had long been something of a tradition that material which was "lewd and obscene" lay outside the protection of the First Amendment. To a large extent, this had been a widely accepted philosophical premise, a matter of common understanding so well respected as to be generally observed. Review by the U.S. Supreme Court of state laws on the matter had been rather inconclusive when the Warren Court in the late 1950s undertook a decisive effort to reconcile the conflict between the new First Amendment claims of free speech with the imprecisions of tradition. The principal result was the finding in the *Roth* case (1957) which set forth "appeal to prurient interest" as a test of obscenity; yet this elusive quality, which the Court meant to separate from a mere literary concern with the mysteries of sex, was nowhere defined. To that was added a reliance on "contemporary community standards," which introduced the supple element of fad and fashion in public opinion. Subsequent to *Roth*, where censorship was upheld, a number of additional decisions seemed to support the First Amendment claim of free expression. Then came the curious *Ginzburg* decision with its assertion that marketing methods (pandering) had tainted the materials themselves, and a criminal conviction was thus sustained. Yet in the same year, 1966, the Court found that *Fanny Hill*, an 18th century book which some of our founding fathers may have known, was not *"utterly* without redeeming social value," hence protected by the First Amendment.

The Burger Court in the 1970s has tried to grapple with this matter, and has even undertaken once again a definition of obscenity. In the *Miller* case (1973) there appeared a reliance on some familiar ideas (contemporary community standards), new verbal puzzles (depicts or describes in a patently offensive way), and a revised reference to value (lacks serious artistic, political, or scientific value). Punishment for the sale of obscene matter and for exhibiting obscene movies was sustained in the 1973 decisions (*Miller* and *Davis* cases), yet the larger consequences somehow were not consistent with those results. The ensuing proliferation of x-rated films and adult bookstores is familiar enough to anyone who looks around in any city. It may well be that there is a substantial acceptance among the American people that obscenity is more a sin than a crime, hence personal, philosophical, and impossible of legal definition. In some indirect fashion, it may be that private opinion, informally supporting a tradition of an open society will settle this matter more surely than formal constitutional pronouncements can.

Religious freedom is one of the most firmly established features of the American tradition. The very founding of many of the colonies from which the United States grew was related closely to this matter. Well before the Revolution, a generous measure of religious freedom flourished in several places, religious toleration in many others, and religious pluralism was a distinctive feature of American society. Among the most revolutionary things which happened within America after 1776 was the change in public policy regarding religion. To organize a body politic without a preferred state church, which is what happened in all but three states, was a most unusual arrangement, scarcely known throughout Western Christendom, then or now. Following disestablishment in the states, came the Jeffersonian idea of thorough separation of church and state, and then the incorporation of these ideas into the new national Constitution through the First Amendment.

Exactly what was meant by the First Amendment, however, became a matter of continuing controversy after World War II, much of it centering around the relationship between religion and education. The critical question, then and since, has been: how complete must sepa-

Alfred H. Kelly and Richard D. Miles

ration of church and state be? The Jeffersonian idea, which is the principal 18th century source of American practice, included a strong emphasis on the privacy of religious thought and practice, the neutrality of the state, and the immunity of the citizen from governmental compulsion, including involuntary participation in any particular religion indirectly through an activity of his government which either supported or suppressed this absolutely private enterprise. It is hard to avoid the conclusion that this mode of thought, coupled as it was with a strong aspiration for an open society, calls for the wall of separation to be pretty nearly absolute.

Nonetheless, during the last two or three decades, the Court has held otherwise a number of times. The arrangements at issue in the *McCollum* case (1948), it seems, could hardly have been approved, since public school facilities were plainly being used for religious purposes—a rather common practice at the time. But, this case apart, when the support of religious purposes has been more indirect, the Court for a while acted on Justice Douglas's assertion in the *Zorach* case (1952) that the wall of separation is not absolute and that to assert that it is would be to demonstrate hostility to religion.

To be sure, Justice Black, who had dissented in *Zorach*, was able ten years later to incorporate a reply to that idea in his opinion for the majority who held in *Engel* v. *Vitale* (1962) that a "Regents' Prayer" in New York violated the First Amendment. The "establishment clause," he said, is not irreligious in spirit; instead it "relied on the belief that a union of government and religion tends to destroy government and degrade religion." And compulsory Bible reading in Pennsylvania met a similar fate when the Court declared the practice unconstitutional the following year.

These decisions, though, prompted a renewal of the bitter controversy over the role of religion in the public schools which had lain uneasily quiescent for some years. There was a formidable drive for a "pro-prayer" amendment, an idea still in the air in the 1970s. As the crisis in school financing became grave, particularly so for parochial schools, in the 1960s, there were renewed demands for federal financial assistance to schools, public, private, and parochial. In 1963, Congress enacted a higher education facilities act which provided construction grants for institutions of higher education, including church-related colleges; and in 1971, in *Tilton* v. *Richardson*, the Court sustained the law. By 1968 the Court had sustained, in the *Allen* decision, a New York law which provided for public financing of textbooks in private schools in grades seven through twelve. State laws providing direct subsidies of one kind or another to parochial schools—"parochiaid"—were stricken down by the Court in 1971 and 1973, but the matter is far from settled, for the techniques of indirect aid suggested by the *Everson* and *Allen* decisions encourage continuing efforts to find further avenues of support for church schools from public funds.

Of all the areas where efforts have been made to expand American society by an even treatment of all, the tradition of state neutrality

Maintenance of Revolutionary Values

where religion is concerned is as clear a heritage of the Revolutionary era as any. Yet, of those discussed above—freedom of speech, apportionment, criminal justice procedures, obscenity (extreme freedom of speech), and religion—it is the last which portends the gravest danger, as the potential for divisiveness and antagonism is so great. The development of constitutional meaning here reflects the ambivalence of the latter 20th century on the matter. On the one hand, we have the end of required religious exercises in public schools, including prayers and Bible reading; on the other, we have public funds providing support, if often indirectly, for the operation of schools whose purpose is to a considerable extent a religious one. Historically, Americans have been for the most part an unchurched people, for until about the middle of the 20th century most of them did not profess membership in any church at all.[6] The statistics, of course, have their own peculiar infirmities, but they seem to tell us that in recent decades the small majority of church members has increased somewhat. The relationship, if any, of this trend to an apparently rising crime rate and the widely held belief that there is a decline in personal morality is not quite the kind of puzzle with which we are concerned. But a constitution must serve an actual people with actual beliefs. One must assume that the populistic democracy prevalent at the dawn of the third century of national life has on its immediate agenda the reconciling of traditional constitutional values respecting religious freedom and the new, energetic impulse to modify them in important ways.

THE NATIONALIZING OF CONSTITUTIONAL LIBERTY

Finally, a third major change in the nature of constitutional rights is one which has been an integral part of the advent of enforceable equality and the expansion of the open society: it is the virtual triumph of the recent, powerful tendency to nationalize constitutional liberty. The libertarian values of the Revolutionary era have a far greater reach and play a far more conspicuous part in American lives today than ever before. This is in some measure a product of the apparently relentless expansion of the national government so evident throughout American history; but, more important, it is the result of a kind of judicial activism which must have seemed most improbable only twenty years ago.

During the first years of the Constitution, there had been some inclination to assume that constitutional liberty in certain fundamental respects flourished throughout the land, simply as a matter of the inherent purpose and meaning of constitutional government. And lying directly behind that thought was the philosophy of natural rights so recently and repeatedly proclaimed in the Revolutionary era. Certain federal judges in the 1790s, furthermore, assumed that such an abstract principle of justice implied that, under the U.S. Constitution, final authority to articulate such fundamental rights was vested in the federal judiciary rather than in the state legislatures. Thus, Justice William Paterson found an act of the Pennsylvania legislature

Alfred H. Kelly and Richard D. Miles

invalid in 1795 because it was "inconsistent with the principles of reason, justice, and moral rectitude" and "contrary to the principles of social alliance in every free government." And Justice Samuel Chase criticized an act of a state legislature because it was "contrary to the great first principles of the social compact."

Such rhetoric, and the awesome magnitude of national judicial power it implied, receded in a few years as new issues diverted constitutional development into new channels. Most of the practical concerns for personal liberty were determined by state and local law, presumably limited by the bills of rights and other restraints on government found in state constitutions. While the 14th Amendment provided another kind of restraint on state government, it became clear in the closing decades of the 19th century that it had not, in fact, brought about the expansion of liberty which its framers had expected.

It was not until well into the 20th century that the real potential of the 14th Amendment for constitutional liberty became active. Between 1925 and 1932 the Court found in a number of cases that the federal Bill of Rights was a limitation on state police power by virtue of the due process clause of the 14th Amendment; for the most part, it was First Amendment freedoms which were protected in this manner. A most significant resumption of this idea came in 1937 when Justice Cardozo, while denying that the 14th Amendment automatically protected all the rights found in the first eight amendments, nonetheless said the rights "implicit in the concept of ordered liberty" were so protected. He also spoke of principles of justice "so rooted in the traditions and conscience of our people as to be ranked as fundamental." This was distinctly reminiscent of the language of Paterson and Chase in another era; the 18th century was speaking to the 20th.

By mid-century the Court had incorporated fully the guarantees of the First Amendment within the due process clause of the 14th Amendment, and modernized the meaning of First Amendment freedoms in many ways so that constitutional protection was given to picketing by labor unions, meetings in public parks, parades, pamphlet peddling, and other matters which state and local governments had so often forbidden. And one member of the Court, Justice Black, in *Adamson* v. *California* (1948) plainly asserted that the Court ought at once to declare the entire content of the federal Bill of Rights formally incorporated in the 14th Amendment. This was rejected by his colleagues at the time, and has not yet quite been embraced by the Court. But the Warren Court (of which Black was a member) ultimately performed most of what Black had urged. This was most conspicuous in the field of criminal trial procedures. In the 1960s, in one case after another, the process was evident, making it clear that the states were restrained by the Fourth, Fifth, Sixth, and Eighth Amendments—and they had long been restrained by the First. As Leonard Levy has said, "The Warren Court's criminal-law revolution, then, consisted in nationalizing the Bill of Rights."

In addition, the Warren Court formulated a new constitutional law protecting an extraordinary range of private activities against interference by a state. Notable here were a controversial 1965 decision striking down long-standing state birth control legislation as a violation of a new-found right of marital privacy, a judicial nationalization of the law of libel that made public political criticism virtually immune from either private or criminal libel suits, the development of a new law of obscenity which was quite broadly permissive, and the new reach of separation of church and state which banned prayers and Bible reading from public schools.

The momentum of change has not been sustained by the Burger Court; yet it had its moment of dramatic humanitarian-liberal activism in 1973 when it found state antiabortion statutes to be an unconstitutional violation of a right of privacy guaranteed by the 14th Amendment. And in a series of cases involving scurrilous, vulgar, and perhaps obscene language provocatively uttered in public, the Burger Court denied state and local authorities the right to prosecute the offenders, very nearly overruling the 1942 decision in *Chaplinsky* v. *New Hampshire* where the punishment of somewhat milder language had been sustained.

The traditional weight of governmental restrictions on civil liberty in the United States had long been heaviest at the state and local level; this was now substantially lightened. However, it had been achieved by the exercise of a newly expanded power in the federal judiciary. Such activism in the national government would have been shocking and even repugnant to most people in an earlier day, but it now seemed more or less plausible because Americans had for some time witnessed a considerable expansion in government as a whole. Here, then, was a price which had to be paid for the nationalizing of constitutional liberty: the amazing growth in only a generation or two of the national government. If one branch, the judicial, had done much to enhance liberty, what was the record of the other two?

As to the legislature, the record is extremely complex. Many of the nation's new laws during the last half-century or so have been attempts to enhance the status and prospects of large numbers of people. On the other hand, some of those very laws have had mixed and limited results. The Social Security system, for example, virtually confiscates money from both an employee and his employer (who usually have no choice in the matter) for the sake of an extremely modest, if distinct, improvement in the employee's later life after he stops working. And it is remarkable that we have had three major laws which deal with sedition and subversion (1940, 1950, 1954) in this period and only two important ones (1798, 1918) in the preceding century and a half. Presumably Congress is within reach of the people, though, since most of its members must stand for reelection every two years, and one must assume that over a generation's time any laws which are strikingly unpopular will be changed. Yet there is an important check on that process, for there is one person whose vote is worth that of nearly two-thirds of the members of Congress, namely the President.

Alfred H. Kelly and Richard D. Miles

Here, it seems, in the growth of executive power is a major potential menace to constitutional liberty. It may well be that the sheer growth of government in general is a great departure from the thinking of the Revolutionary generation; the one part of it which is most striking is surely that of modern presidential power. The central theme of the Declaration of Independence was the assigning of the loss of American liberty to the acts of the King; the first organization of a common government was one which had no executive power at all in any direct sense; even the newly devised state governments often provided only a limited executive authority; and the opponents of the U.S. Constitution in the ratification controversy made much of the potential for tyranny in the office of President, expressed by Patrick Henry when he denounced it by saying, "It squints toward monarchy."

Most of modern presidential power has developed in response to the great national crises of recent generations: depression, war, and quasi-war. There had been intermittent experiences with this along the way, of course: one thinks particularly of Lincoln and Wilson as assuming a virtual war-time dictatorship in the interest of national survival. But it was understood at such times that the extraordinary conditions would one day end, and things would return to a less regimented order. Recently, however, there has arisen an unarticulated assumption that we are always going to be menaced with the threat of war or depression, and therefore we must accept great reaches of presidential power in order to preserve the country.

The spectacular events of recent presidential history are too well known at this moment to require repeating here; they are still being kept before us in books and movies. The most disturbing dimension of this is the persistence of the idea that we must expect Presidents to exercise great power; that it has been the abuse of power rather than power itself which is the evil; and the faith that this Bicentennial year is, happily, also an election year in which we can find a good person to whom this power may be entrusted. A careful reading of the U.S. Supreme Court's opinion in *U.S. v. Nixon* (1974) reveals a good deal of judicial self-restraint; most of the awesome power of the President remains intact. Little has been proposed for the reduction of presidential power. The election, it would appear, is expected to solve the problem by selecting an honorable person to whom such power may be entrusted. Few people seem impressed with the old notion that power corrupts.

In striking contrast, the new reach of judicial power has generated a good number of proposals for its limitation. Those who have been disappointed in recent rulings have felt a bitter resentment that men in distant Washington have allowed offensive conduct to go unpunished. As one controversial decision has followed another, the ranks of the disappointment have grown. Some are angry about crime, others about pornography, many others about abortion, and perhaps the greatest number of Court-haters are those who are upset by court-ordered busing of school children. All this puts a considerable strain on the American political and constitutional system, just at a time when populistic democracy seems ascendant. The dominant thought in many people's minds is that the Supreme Court has frustrated popular will in many states and communities, where strong majorities have wished to close adult bookstores and x-rated theaters, get tough with suspected criminals, outlaw abortion, establish parochiaid, and send their children to the neighborhood schools which prompted them to take up their current residence in the first place.

Inescapably, this will spill over into the political process even more conspicuously than it has in the recent past. What elected officers of government can do in response to these pressures is not entirely clear. The most serious proposal is for new amendments to the Constitution which have the effect of overruling the Court. There is something of a precedent for this, of course, in the 11th Amendment, which restored a dignity to the states which the Court had destroyed, and perhaps in the 16th Amendment as an example of achieving that which the Court had forbidden. Yet we have been doing a good deal of amending lately. More to the point, no doubt, is the question of whether Constitution-amending is a sound way of formulating social policy. The experience with the 18th Amendment is not reassuring. A constitution should endure, and that of the United States gets much of its veneration because of its durability.

But it is the durability of constitutional liberty which is the more particular concern. The essence of constitutionalism is the limitation of power, the foremost of the principles derived from the Revolutionary era; together with the commitment to natural rights, this made people confident in their expectation of an open society. The growth of constitutional liberty in recent decades is impressive, and it has been in the main guided by the values present at the founding of the nation. While grave problems await Americans in their third century of national life, the ideals of Jefferson, Madison, Adams, and the other libertarian-minded founders may still serve the cause of constitutional liberty.

Alfred H. Kelly and Richard D. Miles

NOTES

1. Thomas Hobbes, who published his *Leviathan* in 1651, disagreed with Locke; to him, the state of nature had been one of endemic war of "every man against every man," in which life was "poor, mean, nasty, brutish, and short." But Hobbes, who thus disagreed with the great majority of natural law writers, had virtually no influence upon the development of early American political theory.

2. Or as Tom Paine would have it in the opening pages of *Common Sense* 100 years later, "Governments are founded upon the ruins of the bowers of paradise."

3. It is true that George Mason had used a similar phrase a month earlier in the Virginia Bill of Rights, but it was left to Jefferson to give the idea its universal appeal.

4. William Gladstone, as every student of the Constitution knows, a century later was to describe the Constitution as "the most wonderful work ever struck off at a given time by the brain and purpose of man." Of course, the Constitution, while a brilli-antly creative work, was not simply "struck off"; it was the end product, rather, of the political philosophy of the Enlightenment in which the framers for the most part were steeped.

5. Two of the members of the Court who were not replaced, Justices Douglas and Black, furthermore, were usually among the most ardent advocates of strong restrictions on government efforts to limit constitutional liberty.

6. According to one set of statistics, church members were less than 35 percent of the total population of the United States in 1890; in all likelihood, the percentage was no larger, and quite possibly was smaller, in earlier years. By 1940, church members were 42.8 percent of the population; by 1950, 56.2 percent. This figure rose to 63.6 percent by 1960. U.S. Bureau of Census, *Historical Statistics of the U.S., Colonial Times to 1957* (Washington, D.C., 1960); and U.S. Bureau of Census, *Statistical Abstract of the U.S.: 1966* (Washington, D.C., 1967).

REPORT on the DELIBERATIONS of COMMITTEE I
by Paul Bender and Martha A. Field

The task of Committee I was to discuss the Maintenance of Revolutionary Values. The committee understood this topic as meaning to refer to Revolutionary values relating to individual rights.

SOURCES OF REVOLUTIONARY VALUES

It was suggested at the outset that the committee ought to determine what the Revolutionary values were. This proposal led directly to a discussion of the sources of Revolutionary values. The committee observed that there were several different possible sources for what might be considered Revolutionary values, and that some of these sources were quite different in content and tone. The sources identified were: (1) The Declaration of Independence (1776); (2) The Constitution of 1787; (3) The Bill of Rights (Amendments I–X to the Constitution) (1791); (4) The Civil War Amendments (Amendments XIII, XIV and XV) (1865, 1868, 1870); subsequent constitutional amendments such as Amendment XIX (1920).

Discussion of the differences between these sources centered at first on differences between the original Constitution and the Declaration of Independence. The Declaration contains ringing phrases concerning rights, including equality, the topic on which the committee spent the major part of its time. The original Constitution, by contrast, contains virtually no guarantees of individual rights. This difference was attributed by the committee to the fact that the Declaration was a revolutionary document, an "indictment," a "series of impieties," not "a document to form a government." The Constitution, on the other hand, was a sober, responsible document designed to work, to create a stable system that could last. As one committee member expressed it, when you write a "manifesto" you use "high-blown" language, but when you "get down to divvying up and deciding who gets what —when you really form an organization" then you write a document concerned with "organization and the distribution of power: who is in charge around here and how do you decide when they have over-stepped their boundaries."

The committee, however, did not take the view that the absence of individual rights guarantees in the original Constitution indicated that the "ringing phrases" of the Declaration—that "all men are created equal," that they are "endowed by their Creator with certain unalienable Rights," and that "among these are Life, Liberty, and the pursuit of Happiness" were words only, rather than reflections of genuine values. As one committee member put it, the Declaration did indeed

> set forth the political philosophy of the leaders of the country at that time. "We the People" were, for the first time in the history of mankind, undertaking to establish a government. Some of the declarations in the early part of the Declaration of Independence were to give substance to this notion and to set forth what the framers believed were the basic political philosophies that they wanted to live by.

As confirming the fact that the Declaration reflected deeply held values, the committee pointed to the adoption of the federal Bill of Rights shortly after the original Constitution, as well as to the presence of similar declarations of rights in the state constitutions.

In comparing the Declaration of Independence with the Bill of Rights, the committee noted the absence of any express reference to equality in the Bill of Rights. The committee observed, however, that the commitment to equality by the signers of the Declaration was not as strong as sometimes supposed. That all "men" were thought to be created equal certainly embodied the contemporary view that women were not equal to men. Nor did all men mean, literally "all" men, for slaves and perhaps descendants of slaves were excluded. The final draft of the Declaration even deleted what one committee member referred to as "Jefferson's noble condemnation of slavery" (actually a condemnation of the King for permitting slavery) in order to "have all the colonies together." This same committee member went on to observe that "[h]aving deleted the phraseology with reference to slavery, they then proceeded to add a number of references to Providence. This is not, in my judgment, the first nor the last time that piety has been used to cover perfidy." Another committee member thought that the deletion of the criticism of the slave trade "constricted the future by establishing the priority of the Union over the question of equality."

The Bill of Rights itself was the product of compromise in the ratification process. In the words of one committee member:

> The people who were in the Philadelphia convention were not representative of the totality of the people who ultimately participated in the decision-making at the ratification conventions in the states. . . . In general, the haves of the society at that time

Paul Bender and Martha A. Field

wrote the Constitution, and in general those who were more or less aligned with the have-nots were the force among the anti-federalists who resisted the Constitution sufficiently to secure the adoption of the Bill of Rights.

The Bill of Rights, in all events, certainly reflected revolutionary values. The committee also believed that the extension of the principle of equality to blacks in the Civil War amendments, the further extension to women in the 19th Amendment, and the fundamental judicial development extending the protection of the Bill of Rights to the states through the 14th Amendment, reflected what, for its purposes, should be considered Revolutionary values. The committee, in the end, found itself discussing basic *constitutional* values relating to individual rights, rather than only those values which it could specifically attribute to the Revolutionary period. In part, the committee appeared to take this view because of its belief that the framers of the Declaration of Independence, the original Constitution, and the Bill of Rights intended a "living" Constitution, an idea discussed in the next section of this report.

THE PROCESS OF CONSTITUTIONAL INTERPRETATION—THE CONSTITUTION AS A LIVING DOCUMENT AND THE ROLE OF THE JUDICIARY

Some members of the committee suggested that a useful way of clarifying the constitutional values would be to ask what kind of men the framers of the Constitution were:

> [W]ho were these people who were responsible for the Declaration of Independence and for the Constitution? What strata of society were represented? Were the people really represented? We know that the blacks, the women, were not represented. The framers represented the upper classes; they accepted the caste system that was part of the English situation at that time, modified to some extent by the privations of the New World. Was it really just a few propertied whites who were responsible for this whole thing? Then after that discussion it would be useful to try to determine which of the English legal principles these men sought to retain.

Other members of the committee said that neither small landholders nor merchants were well represented among the framers. The views and background of the framers, it was said, would give a better perspective as to which of the expressed values were meant to be taken seriously and which were simply "felicitous phrases," thrown in for their ringing quality, but not intended to be effectuated except, perhaps, in the remote future.

The committee appeared to accept a characterization of the framers as upper class and elitist, but less so than other ruling groups in other nations at the time. They came from diverse backgrounds and they represented a relatively broad spectrum. In the committee's words, they saw themselves, not as "free agents," but as "responsible to an electorate" and, although it was a "propertied electorate," "there was a higher proportion of property owners in American society than there was in any other." Nevertheless, there was a reluctance to trust even a propertied electorate with too much power, as is shown by the electoral college system of electing the President and the lack of a provision for direct election of senators. Several committee members observed that property qualifications were probably justified in the framers' minds by the theory that, "in order to be a worthy participant and to possess virtue in the public sense of the word . . . it is necessary for the individual to be free of domination by the will of another man," to have "free will." Ownership of property was thought to provide the necessary independence. (A somewhat different view of property qualifications at the time of the Revolution was suggested by a committee member who said that "if people today had property in the same way that people then had property, they would certainly be in jail, and not be free property holders, because by and large it had been stolen from somebody.")

The committee did not pursue a lengthy inquiry into the views and background of the framers because it concluded, fairly swiftly, that constitutional interpretation today was not—and should not be—governed to a great extent by what the framers specifically intended. One committee member remarked that, while we tend to think of the Constitution today as "a kind of immutable law,"

> there wasn't the kind of expectation among the bulk of American political society [at the time the Constitution was adopted] that the Constitution would achieve the kind of sanctity that it now has. The expectation was that the Constitution, like all other documents of government, would eventually have to be modified, perhaps in very fundamental ways, as society changed, and that social change would inevitably mean constitutional change.

There was general agreement that "a dynamic Constitution is a necessity," that the Constitution is "a living document." From the time of Chief Justice Marshall[1] we have interpreted the Constitution "in line with the political imperatives and the social imperatives of the day." Where the language of the Constitution presents "a blank wall," then amendment is necessary, but otherwise "the language can be informed by the realities of the day and the Constitution is thus preserved." One member of the committee, who is from England, remarked that

> it is an absolutely fundamental point to me as a European that, as I understand it, here in the United States, what Jefferson meant in the Declaration of Independence, what the fathers of the Constitution meant by the words which they used, is, of course, a matter of profound interest, but only a matter of his-

Paul Bender and Martha A. Field

torical interest, . . . a matter for historians and not a matter for lawyers. Words like "people," "men," "liberty," or "equality" all have completely changed their meaning. Here you have a point which distinguishes American legal methods in a very significant way from legal methods on the other side of the Atlantic and especially in England.

One committee member placed great stress on the amendment process, rather than the judicial process of constitutional interpretation, as the vital aspect of a living Constitution:

I think that is the genius of the Constitution and that's why it survived—because it had that built-in device of amendment, and not so much [because of] the interpretation of the meaning in light of contemporary conditions. Every time a major problem has presented itself in the nation, the Constitution has been amended to deal with the problem, as with the right of women to vote and eighteen-year-olds subsequently. [Although it took a long time for the 14th Amendment to be construed] to prohibit segregation in schools . . . the 14th Amendment was [nevertheless] an amendment. . . . But for the amendment provision, the Constitution probably would not have survived.

Most committee members, however, saw the ongoing process of judicial interpretation of the Constitution as the most vital element of constitutional dynamics. In one member's view "the most Revolutionary value of them all is the constant reinterpretation of the Constitution." Another member linked the practice of judicial interpretation to serious shortcomings in the original text, and proposed an extremely broad scope for judicial interpretation:

I would challenge the rubric under which we are gathered: the maintaining of Revolutionary values. I should think we should be concerned with "attaining" rather than "maintaining," on the grounds that the actions that took place 200 years ago were not what they should have been. They disregarded the real concerns of equality and settled down mainly on the question of liberty. . . . [I]f we box ourselves in permanently to the horizons foreseen by the founding fathers, we will wind up continuing their errors. We need, therefore, to have at least a certain amount of irreverence for that document to which we pay supreme reverence. Or it may be that the most reverent attitude is one which seeks to complete the Constitution's unfulfilled intent.

Another member saw the interpretative role of the courts as vital because of the limitations of the other branches of the federal government:

[T]he war, if war it is, between the Congress and the Executive— or inside the Congress itself—is so shortsighted, is so immediately partisan, that it forgets the longer-term Revolutionary values and ideals, and it is in the courts in this country and in the judges that there is being preserved that vision of an 18th century order, however adapted and changed by our interpretation of it, that is relevant in the 20th century.

A number of reasons were given for the belief that, to serve their intended purpose, constitutional provisions regarding individual rights had to have the quality of incorporating new specific meanings. Society, in changing dramatically, has presented us with a whole new set of individual rights problems. In one member's words, the original Constitution

> assumed a kind of society that was simple and open; one in which there was relative plenty and a small amount of poverty; one in which there was a relative equality, at least among those people who could be considered men; one in which there was an extraordinary amount of activity, industry and enterprise unleashed by the openness, space and opportunities that were available throughout American society; and finally [one in which there was] a preoccupation with individual happiness—people were able to be concerned with that because there was so much space.

Another member saw significance in the fact that "growth . . . is visibly running out as a means of giving satisfaction." A third observed that the Constitution was drafted

> at a time when the frontier was open, when there was a large percentage of land ownership, at least among the white male population. . . . [But] now we face a closed frontier. Now there is a much smaller percentage of ownership. And, more importantly, that percentage of the population which owns a controlling interest in the important institutions of society is smaller now . . . and power is more concentrated. Nobody ever conceived this. They conceived . . . that you should be free from a union between the church and the state. They never conceived of a union between corporations and the state. . . . [Yet] all of a sudden today . . . we are faced with corporations as powerful as the church was when unified with the state and as potentially dangerous to our ongoing freedoms as the church was 200 years ago.

A fourth committee member saw enormous significance in the loss of "an assumption of shared values. . . . [A]s we have demonstrated around this table in two days, it's very difficult to identify the values which we may share."

Although there was general agreement within the committee that the judiciary had a vital role to play in the process of interpretation

Paul Bender and Martha A. Field

of constitutional values, restrictions on judicial freedom to make value choices for society were also emphasized. Relatively little attention was paid to formal restrictions, such as concepts of justiciability. Some attention was paid to judge-made rules seeking to avoid the resolution of constitutional issues wherever possible,[2] and to the judiciary's inability to enforce its own judgments, thus requiring ultimate dependence on popular acceptance. One committee member, a legislator, wanted it made clear that if

> this group affirms the right of the Supreme Court to give expanded meaning to the Constitution, that power which the Court asserts has to be asserted most judiciously. The Court can take a leadership role, but if it gets too far ahead of the masses, it's going to undermine confidence in government itself, and the reaction will be restrictive, and perhaps very shortsighted, amendments to the Constitution. The people can be steered but they cannot be led in the long run in some direction in which they don't wish to go.

The committee as a whole seemed to view judicial imposition of constitutional values as a last resort. As one member, a federal judge, put it:

> [T]he Courts act when they are confronted by facts that just are impossible to live with, and I think that we are going to have to continue basically in that fashion. . . . I think we make a mistake, a serious mistake, if we look upon the Supreme Court of the United States as the primary tool for social change. . . . [Power flows to the judiciary] when one or another branch of government fails really to give effect to the aspirations of the peoples of the United States. When the Supreme Court acts on an essentially Revolutionary concept . . . they do it *in extremis.* They do it when there isn't anything else that decent human beings can do—and usually these are essentially decent human beings we have on the Court. Why did they move on the school [segregation] problem?[3] Not because that was a logical way to go about things. They moved because the separate but equal doctrine[4] didn't even begin to work. It was being ignored, flouted in every place in these United States, and they finally moved after [Oklahoma had put a black law student] in a box, a three-sided box, so as to screen her from the white students. This was such an inhumane thing that the Supreme Court couldn't stand it.[5] . . . Or take *Brown* v. *Mississippi.*[6] The Fifth Amendment has been on the books since the beginning, since the passage of the Bill of Rights, in any event. Yet in *Brown* v. *Mississippi* they hung a man, with the deputies who were his legal guardians present. And they raised him up until he was choking, and then they lowered him down and asked him questions. And when he didn't give the answers they wanted, they raised him up and lowered

him down again. This was when the Supreme Court acted to enforce the Fifth Amendment against the states under the due process clause. My point is that so many of these things could be dealt with by the President of the United States, by the Congress. This is the regular route for the validation of the concepts of the Constitution. And when you wait to where the courts are going to act . . . you wait for a period where the court acts in crisis or perhaps even *in terrorem*.

Other committee members also lamented the failure of the executive and legislative branches of the federal government to exercise "the kind of leadership which the founding fathers would have thought legislators and presidents would routinely exercise."

Several other important points regarding the role of the judiciary in the formulation of constitutional values were discussed. A member of the committee who is a legislator stated his view that the courts act most properly in protecting minority rights: "If we were to leave it to a majority [such as a democratically elected legislature] to react to the preservation and protection of minority interests, we would move very, very slowly, simply because the majority is looking out for its majority interests." The entire committee agreed upon the enormous importance of Congress joining with the courts in furthering constitutional development and implementation. For example, even such a vastly important decision as the school segregation case[7] did not win popular acceptance and was not effectively implemented until supported by Congress through legislation. As a federal judge put it,

> it's probably true that the courts were ahead of Congress [on the issue of segregation], but the people in this country were not really convinced of the importance of desegregation until Congress moved, and there was no real accomplishment in the schools toward attainment of desegregation until Congress acted [in the Civil Rights Acts of 1964 and 1965].

Finally, a number of committee members cautioned against relying too heavily on the judiciary to enforce constitutional values. It has only been recently—a development of the 1950s primarily—that the Supreme Court has assumed the role of leader in the area of individual liberties. Another federal judge observed that

> [a]ll these encomia that have been showered on the federal courts and the Supreme Court about being liberal, being interested in human rights and individual rights, should be limited in time. The Warren Court is the only strongly liberal Court in our history that was interested in human rights. . . . The present Court, as everyone agrees, is likewise interested [to some extent], but there is no question that there has been a cutting back. . . . The history of our court system, particularly the federal court system,

Paul Bender and Martha A. Field

has been one of conservatism, not individual or human rights.
. . . So I don't think we should bask in the sunlight of all this
glory that's being heaped on us. I think the federal courts'
record has improved only in the last quarter century, and, as I
say, we have a period of regressive judgments going on right
now.

Still another federal judge linked judicial responsiveness to minority
political power: "The Court began to respond to the demands of
blacks [because], by 1954, blacks represented some kind of political
group in the society (which had not been true previously) and were
beginning to have some political influence."

REVOLUTIONARY VALUES

Equality

The Revolutionary value most extensively discussed by the committee
—indeed, the only value investigated by it in depth—was the value
of equality. The committee paid its respects to the irony of this situation since, as has been noted earlier, the principal aspect of the value
of equality as we think of it today—i.e., the protection of minorities
and politically powerless groups from hostile discriminations—was
apparently not an important value at the time of the Revolution and
original Constitution. The central statement pertinent to equality in
the Declaration of Independence referred to equality only among "all
men" and not even *all* men were included—slaves were clearly excluded, freed blacks may well have been excluded,[8] and non-propertied
men were excluded, for at least some purposes. Nevertheless, the committee concluded that equality was a Revolutionary value in the sense
that there was a principle strongly favoring equality among that
group of persons who were recognized as full citizens. The development of the principle of equality under the Constitution has, in large
part, been a process of adding groups of persons to the category of
full citizens; once they are added, the Revolutionary principle of
equality becomes applicable to them.

There are two respects in which the committee's discussion of the
value of equality differed in approach from the constitutional principle of equality as it has been developed in the Supreme Court, primarily under the 14th Amendment. Little attention was paid by the
committee to the "state action" limitation in the 14th Amendment,
under which only inequalities imposed by the government or its
officials (or by a narrow range of private entities that, for one reason
or another, are treated as the "state" for constitutional purposes) are
subject to constitutional scrutiny.[9] The committee appeared to believe
that private discriminatory action often raised the same problems as
governmental discrimination. In part, this failure to distinguish between state and private action may be accounted for by the fact that
the committee addressed itself to the values that ought to underlie
legislative action, as well as to the values shaping judicial interpretation of the Constitution, although the committee did not explore the

limits that exist upon federal legislative power to enforce the 14th Amendment.[10]

A second way in which the committee's discussion of the value of equality differed from the judicial development of the equal protection clause of the 14th Amendment was in the committee's primary focus on the *effects*—rather than the purposes—of action or inaction challenged as a violation of the constitutional equality guarantee. As will be seen immediately below, the committee was most troubled by the question whether the constitutional value of equality encompassed equality of result, or only equality of opportunity—both questions of effect. The Supreme Court, on the other hand, has often seen equality cases as necessarily involving a challenge to the internal integrity of the governmental process—was it rational, rather than arbitrary; did it betray a hostile or other impermissible purpose?[11]

The committee engaged in extensive, and often unstructured, discussions of the nature of the equality value incorporated in the Constitution. There was general agreement that in the United States, unlike many other countries, "people have a fundamental sense that they are all made of the same common clay." There were attempts to break the equality value down into components, and one committee member suggested six possible categories: equality of law; equality of political power; equality of religion; equality of opportunity; equality of esteem; and equality between the sexes. There was no general agreement that these or similar categories were either meaningful, independent of each other, or sufficiently comprehensive. Why, for example, should it be necessary to specify equality between the sexes— why didn't the other equalities take care of that?

Ultimately, the committee's discussions focused on the difference between equality of opportunity and equality of result—the latter often referred to as equality of status or of position. Equality of opportunity suggests the obligation to give everyone the same *chance* at the good things of life, equality of position, the obligation to see that there is, in fact, an equal distribution of those goods. Affirmative action programs, such as minimum racial quotas for hiring or admission to academic programs, represented instances of enforced equality of position in the committee's view, whereas the equal application of identical standards to all applicants represented apparent equality of opportunity. When approaching these concepts as abstract generalities, the committee seemed to favor equality of opportunity, rather than equality of result, as the constitutional ideal, in large part because, as one member put it, "one of the prime values of our American society is diversity and the right to be different. . . . I do not conceive our object to be to make human beings interchangeable."

The separation between the two kinds of equality, however, soon broke down. It was observed that true equality of opportunity, viewed from the perspective of the people involved, is impossible unless there is substantial equality of position. A child born into a poor, uneducated family does not often have the same opportunity to compete under equal standards with a child born into a rich, well-educated

Paul Bender and Martha A. Field

family. To consider equal standards as affording equal opportunity to people from advantaged and disadvantaged backgrounds was a delusion. Equality of position is a necessary part of equality of opportunity in a society where economic goods are limited. One committee member said that "[W]e sort of suppose in these discussions that everybody starts off at the same starting line with the same blocks under their feet to shove off from. The fact of the matter is, that just is not so in our society."

The committee ultimately resolved the dilemma between the ideal of equal opportunity and the reality of vastly unequal position by favoring a compromise between the two concepts. In the committee's view, the constitutional value of equality should be thought to demand the achievement of certain minimal standards of living for every person. These minimal standards would cover, among other things, food, housing, health care, education, and general opportunities for human self-fulfillment. These minima were necessary to ensure an adequately equal opportunity for every person. Diversity would, of course, exist above the minimum, but the minimum should be provided for all. The constitutional basis for ensuring a minimally decent life to all persons was not agreed upon; the committee was not dissuaded by its inability to draw directly upon the text of a particular constitutional provision.

Another main thread which ran through the committee's discussions of equality was the concern that there might be an irreconcilable tension between equality and liberty—that achieving adequate equality of opportunity for all people would necessarily deprive some people of their freedom to make full use of their advantages. The view eventually emerged that the tension between liberty and equality was less serious than it at first appeared, because limiting the constitutional equality value to equality of opportunity plus the universal attainment of minimal living standards adequately protected both interests. Liberty was essentially freedom from governmental repression. The "liberty" which had to be surrendered to achieve a minimum of equality of position should be seen, not as a loss of liberty, but as a redistribution or sharing of liberty. As one committee member put it,

> [e]very single step in the direction of social progress is a limitation of somebody's liberty to do something. I don't care whether you call this a socialist attitude—I think it is—but I am convinced that all discussions about equality of opportunity or equality of anything else are meaningless unless one faces the fact that a considerable restriction of so-called freedom, especially economic freedom, is a precondition for the achievement of anything that is worth the name of equality of opportunity.

In the words of another committee member, "the liberty of one person to have access to well-paid employment or to go to college may be gained at the expense of the liberty of another person who has previously had rather more choice in the matter, or whose class has. I do not see this as a loss of liberties; I see it as a redistribution of them." In the words of a third,

> I find myself just sitting here really rejecting the concept that we lose liberties by giving liberty to others. . . . If the liberty we were giving up was to somebody to start oppressing me, I would understand that. But, my Lord, what we are really doing is sharing the liberty concept . . . with people who have been excluded from it. . . . I can't seriously debate the statement that an employer feels restricted by the Equal Employment Act. . . . But the affirmative fact is that we are bringing people into the full light of American democracy who have been excluded before, and that's the way I would like to see us think and talk about it. . . . It seems to me that when most people talk about liberty they are talking about individual freedoms. They are talking about the right to speak, the right to think, the right to worship, the right to live, to hold property, not to govern other people either economically or otherwise. . . . [T]he right to exploit . . . is not the typical concept of liberty as we know it in this country.

The committee spent a considerable time discussing minimum affirmative action quotas, and whether they are consistent with or mandated by the constitutional value of equality. Consistently with its preference for the value of equality of opportunity as contrasted with equality of result, the committee expressed a general distaste for quotas. It appeared to accept them, however, as an appropriate and often necessary remedy, for limited periods of time, to redress past discrimination, even past discrimination not specifically addressed to the people who benefit directly from the quotas, but to the class to which they now belong. The committee's apparent theory for requiring result equality here, in the form of minimum quotas, was that only such a remedy would restore conditions to where they would have been had equality of opportunity never been denied. Moreover, quotas in many areas would lead directly to enhanced equality of opportunity. One member cautioned, however, that "the curse of history, whether it is the great tragedy of the black race in the United States or the social history of a class-ridden country like England, cannot be removed by a stroke of the pen out of the legislature or the judge."

There was an interesting discussion of quotas in regard to particular areas of society. Some members of the committee appeared to believe that the legitimacy of affirmative action quotas for minimum hiring depended on the position to be filled. While quotas were generally accepted as proper for hiring police and firepersons, there was skepticism (in a committee made up in large part of lawyers) about their use in bar admissions. Would quotas in the professions establish a group of lower-qualified or unqualified minority practitioners who would primarily serve a minority clientele? A discussion of

Paul Bender and Martha A. Field

quotas for academic hiring produced a distinct division within the committee, with the academic members generally taking the position that they were inappropriate. High minimum qualifications were necessary, in their view, in the interests of future generations, and only members of academic disciplines could judge, on an individual basis, whether applicants had those qualifications. The judges on the committee, however, saw no distinction between academic and other hiring. Finally, some members of the committee expressed dismay at a developing legal situation in which "a court may order affirmative action which might involve quotas, but if the employer, whether a university or a public agency, attempted to do it privately by admitting, in effect, that it was guilty of a past pattern of discrimination, it might be placing itself in great jeopardy."

In the limited situations where the committee endorsed equality of result as an appropriate constitutional value, great concern was expressed over who should pay the price of equalization. A recent decision of the Supreme Court[12] granting retroactive seniority rights to blacks discriminated against in past hiring practices was the subject of much discussion. It was observed that those who paid the price of retroactive seniority were neither those responsible for the discrimination nor those best able to pay. Instead, the burden of equalization was unfairly placed on persons—i.e., non-black employees—who were only one rung higher on the economic ladder than those discriminated against. The burden should be placed on those at "the top of that ladder. . . . [O]therwise what you end up doing is having working class white people feeling that they are having to pay for all the injustices of society . . . and that they're the people least able to pay, and it creates an . . . almost irresolvable class conflict." Some committee members believed that the insulation of persons living in the suburbs from sharing any proportionate economic burden for the problems of the inner cities was an analogous problem. The limitations on the powers and abilities of courts to devise more equitable remedies were stressed, and there was strong sentiment that Congress should turn its attention to these remedial problems.

Other Values

By the time the committee reached the discussion of Revolutionary values other than that of equality, there was little time to discuss those values in any detail. The format followed was for members of the committee to contribute to a list of those values that were considered most important.

The first value discussed was, somewhat surprisingly perhaps, the value of domestic tranquility. The main question raised here was whether this was a true Revolutionary value or whether it was, instead, an expected result of respect for other values, the result of a fair and open society. The question was raised as to how domestic tranquility, if a Revolutionary value in itself, was to be enforced, without violating other constitutional values. With regard to domestic tranquility, one member gave his opinion that

I don't think that domestic tranquility has to give a picture of America as a cow peacefully chewing her cud in a green meadow on a sunny day. I think domestic tranquility can encompass vigorous debate, can encompass marches in Birmingham, can encompass all sorts of things. [But] I would hope that it rejected violence as an acceptable technique for social progress.

Another member suggested that domestic tranquility was not a value at all because "we all know that inherent in the Declaration of Independence is the right to revolt . . . [w]hen you become sufficiently dissatisfied with the government."

Discussion next turned to the possible Revolutionary value of exporting democracy. The committee believed that the framers may have thought of their handiwork as a model for the world, but some members expressed concern that any statement by the committee that our governmental system should be so viewed today was both smug and incorrect. At the same time, deep concern was expressed over the fact that in our foreign policy we have often undermined, rather than promoted, democracy by supporting dictatorships over democratic movements. When the suggestion was made that the committee speak out against this practice as inconsistent with the Revolutionary value of serving as a democratic model, the matter was resolved by deciding that the issue was outside Committee I's jurisdiction, but was within the jurisdiction of Committee IV instead.

A value that was mentioned often, but was little discussed, was the value of free speech and expression. The committee appeared to believe that this was not a controversial value—that it met with universal acceptance within relatively well agreed upon boundaries. Its great importance was assumed. Nor were freedom of religion or the separation of church and state much discussed, again apparently because these values were deemed to be noncontroversial and not under serious attack. One substantive point made regarding free speech was that abstract freedom wasn't enough. More effective platforms needed to be provided for the ordinary citizen:

I would hope that the individual people themselves would have more of an opportunity to exercise First Amendment freedoms; not just the networks, not just the newspapers, not just the licensees of radio and television stations. I would like the people themselves to have access. It's not enough to turn over the streets to the people under the harassment of police in order to make parades and assemble and petition. I think in the third hundred years of the Republic . . . the people, the ordinary people, ought to have a means of expression, if that part of the First Amendment is going to mean anything.

Another value mentioned was the respect for individual autonomy and privacy. The committee believed that this value should lead government to let persons do as they wished so long as they did not

Paul Bender and Martha A. Field

harm others in any tangible way.[13] This would require an end to legislation punishing truly victimless crime.

Finally, fairness of treatment by government—including fairness of procedures and rules against arbitrariness on the part of the government in treating individuals—was stressed as of the utmost importance. Freedom from harsh government oppression is perhaps the most basic value of all. One committee member, a European, volunteered that

> I suspect that I am the only person in this room who has ever lived under a dictatorship. If one has lived under a dictatorship, the question of what are the important values, the really fundamental values, answers itself: the very elementary fact that if there is a knock at the door it is the milkman and not the Gestapo.

One member of the committee sought to sum up all the Revolutionary values as follows:

> I find it difficult, if not impossible, to assign priorities. . . . [T]he [Supreme Court] debates about preferred positions [as between various constitutional rights[14]] have been an astonishing waste of time. I do think, though, that I can find a kind of triad of values which supplement one another and ultimately reduce to a central value. They are freedom of expression—and I include in that the whole range of political, religious, philosophic and aesthetic expressions; the equality value in its total range; and finally the protection of people from being dealt with arbitrarily by the regulating forces of the society. [These three values] reduce to the single central value of the society, which is promotion of individual fulfillment.

CONCLUSION

The committee concluded its discussions on an optimistic note, although it recognized that there was still much to be accomplished. As one committee member put it, "I wouldn't give anybody the impression that I think the fight is over, that vigilance should not be maintained, that injustice is not throughout this land, and that we should put down our oars and coast. I would not want to be a party to that." The committee wished to pay tribute to the enormous accomplishments that have been made, if for no other reason than to encourage attempts at further accomplishments. It is important to note that past efforts have succeeded and that future efforts can succeed as well. On the other hand, the committee believed that most accomplishments have come relatively recently, primarily since 1950. One member said that "a good part of these 200 years that we have known gives us no reason to be proud." Some members of the committee also took encouragement from the fact that questions of equality were not exclusively racial any more, that "sex has been thrown into the pot," so that "sex and race are marching side by side in the right direction." Others took encouragement from the belief that there has recently been increased voluntary compliance with constitutional values, which was seen as a sign of increased societal commitment to those values.

Frequently mentioned shadows across the optimistic outlook were these: a feeling of "growing apartheid in American cities," flowing primarily from the school segregation situation. Meanwhile the Supreme Court refuses to break the line between the inner city and the suburbs for school integration purposes.[15] An increased amount of crime, especially in the cities, was also noted with alarm. Finally, several committee members emphasized the Supreme Court's recent tendency to reduce federal judicial jurisdiction in both the technical and real senses, so as not to get involved, as the federal courts must occasionally if a living constitution is to work, with some of our most serious current problems.[16] In one member's words, "I think this session should say that the access to the Bill of Rights is being endangered by the closing of the courtroom doors in recent days in the Supreme Court of the United States."

Paul Bender and Martha A. Field

NOTES

1. See *McCulloch* v. *Maryland*, 4 Wheat. 316 (1819):

[The] nature [of a Constitution] requires that only its great outlines should be marked, its important objects designated, and the minor ingredients which compose those objects be deduced from the nature of the objects themselves. That this idea was entertained by the framers of the American constitution, is not only to be inferred from the nature of the instrument but from the language. . . . [W]e must never forget that it is a *constitution* we are expounding.

2. See *Ashwander* v. *TVA*, 297 U.S. 288, 346–348 (1936) (Brandeis, J., concurring).

3. *Brown* v. *Board of Education*, 347 U.S. 483 (1954).

4. See *Plessy* v. *Ferguson*, 163 U.S. 537 (1896).

5. *McLaurin* v. *Oklahoma State Regents*, 339 U.S. 637 (1950).

6. 297 U.S. 278 (1936).

7. *Brown* v. *Board of Education*, 347 U.S. 483 (1954).

8. The Dred Scott case, *Dred Scott* v. *Sandford*, 19 How. 393 (1857), subsequently held that freed blacks or their descendants could not be citizens of the United States within the meaning of the Constitution. This decision was reversed by the first sentence of Section 1 of the 14th Amendment.

9. See the *Civil Rights Cases*, 109 U.S. 3 (1883). For a leading case treating a formally private entity as the state, see *Marsh* v. *Alabama*, 326 U.S. 501 (1946) (involving a company town). A recent case refusing to treat a public utility company as the state is *Jackson* v. *Metropolitan Edison Co.*, 419 U.S. 345 (1974).

10. See *Katzenbach* v. *Morgan*, 384 U.S. 641 (1966); *Oregon* v. *Mitchell*, 400 U.S. 112 (1970). Expansive federal legislative power has been recognized under the 13th Amendment, which does not contain a state action limitation, but which is limited to eradicating slavery and the "badges and inci-

dents" of slavery. See *Jones* v. *Alfred H. Mayer Co.*, 392 U.S. 409 (1968). In addition, equality concerns can be vindicated by Congress under other affirmative powers, such as the commerce power, having nothing to do with discrimination as such. See *Heart of Atlanta Motel* v. *United States*, 379 U.S. 241 (1964); *Katzenbach* v. *McClung*, 379 U.S. 294 (1964).

11. See, most prominently, *Washington* v. *Davis*, 426 U.S. 229 (1976), decided two months after the committee's meetings were concluded: "[T]he basic equal protection principle [is] that the invidious quality of a law claimed to be racially discriminatory must ultimately be traced to a racially discriminatory purpose." Effects alone have appeared significant to the Court, however, where inequalities touch upon constitutionally protected or certain "fundamental" rights. See *Shapiro* v. *Thompson*, 394 U.S. 618 (1969) (right to travel); *Kramer* v. *Union Free School District No. 15*, 395 U.S. 621 (1969) (right to vote); *Griffin* v. *Illinois*, 351 U.S. 12 (1956) (poor persons effectively denied initial appeal from non-capital criminal convictions).

12. *Franks* v. *Bowman Transportation Co.*, 424 U.S. 747 (1976).

13. In upholding the constitutionality of prohibitions upon the distribution of so-called "obscene" material to adults wishing to obtain the material, the Supreme Court has recently apparently decided otherwise. See *Miller* v. *California*, 413 U.S. 15 (1973); *Paris Adult Theatre I* v. *Slaton*, 413 U.S. 49 (1973).

14. See, for example, Justice Frankfurter's concurring opinion in *Kovacs* v. *Cooper*, 336 U.S. 77 (1949).

15. See *Milliken* v. *Bradley*, 418 U.S. 717 (1974).

16. See, e.g., *Warth* v. *Seldin*, 422 U.S. 490 (1975); *Simon* v. *Eastern Kentucky Welfare Rights Organization*; 426 U.S. 26 (1976); *Rizzo* v. *Goode*, 423 U.S. 362 (1976); *Laird* v. *Tatum*, 408 U.S. 1 (1972); *Younger* v. *Harris*, 401 U.S. 37 (1971); *Stone* v. *Powell*, 428 U.S. 465 (1976).

COMMITTEE II

EFFECTIVENESS of GOVERNMENTAL OPERATIONS*
by Henry J. Abraham

If it has perhaps not been universally efficient, there is but little doubt that our Article III branch, the judiciary, has been the most effective operationally. In any event, despite the winds of fortune that have buffeted it, and despite its posture as an easy target for public criticism and blame, it has—with but rare exceptions—always received a higher rating of esteem and regard from the body politic than either of the other two branches. Concededly, the percentage of voiced approbation is rarely, if ever, much higher than one-third of those polled among the electorate, yet that figure has been consistently higher than that accorded the legislative or the executive branch. This is hardly an astonishing fact of governmental life, for, in the main, it has been the judges who have kept the American Constitution alive— by, in Anthony Lewis's words,

> giving its 18th century phrases the flexibility to meet new conditions while at the same time applying its broad language of freedom to meet new dangers. They have articulated our ideals.[1]

Whether reliance on that judicial power is wise or even sanctioned is a different, and always alive, source of controversial concern—of which more below. But whatever one's conclusions on that question, our jurists have long demonstrated that they are eminently capable of keeping the constitutional "spirit alive by their judgments and their words."[2] Rare is the visitor to the Supreme Court of the United States, whether he came to praise or scold, who does not stand in awe of its institution and its members—who does not willingly conclude that it is indeed, in Lewis's prose, "entitled, as an institution, to our faith."[3]

---

*Portions of the original issues paper that overlapped with material in the other issues papers are omitted here.

THE JUDICIARY

The judicial branch is not, of course, free from either pragmatic or philosophical operational problems. Two among these most vital to enhanced effectiveness are, first, that eternal question of finding a viable line between "judging" and "legislating" (or, as it might be put more descriptively, "judicial self-restraint" and "judicial activism") and, second, the ever-alive issue of what may be broadly subsumed under the concept of "court reform." Let us examine the latter first.

Any judicial system or structure in democratic society with a constitutional base must essentially meet two basic requirements of public policy: namely, to protect society and to be fair to those accused of infractions of its legal structure. These two are naturally not incompatible, but they do demand the kind of line-drawing and/or balancing of which philosophical as well as pragmatic concepts of government and politics are made.

Whatever one's views of the particular success or failure of specific judicial systems to draw these vital and so often vexatious lines may be, in the eyes of knowledgeable students of courts and judges there is always room for improvement. Suggestions abound. In general, they fall into three broad, interrelated categories: (1) those dealing with the institution and modus operandus of the courts themselves; (2) those concerned with the human beings who staff the courts; and (3) those dealing with the legal framework mandated by a society's lawmakers and its constitutional constellation. All three categories presumably are dedicated to the fundamental goals of any free, democratic, judicial system, which are those of:

1. peaceful resolution of "private" civil conflicts;
2. enforcement of criminal laws;
3. safety valve for the amelioration of "repressive laws";
4. efficient operation;
5. restraint of government intrusions—both in the realm of individual rights and that of the separation of powers.

Couching the following analysis chiefly in the form of questions that are sometimes, but not always, followed by suggested answers, we turn first to the institution of the judiciary and its modus operandus under our particular branch of the common law system.

At the trial and pre-trial level, these questions arise: How effective is the adversary process, the "sporting game," in the quest for truth and justice? The late Judge Jerome Frank, in his still indispensable critique of that process and its substructure, *Courts on Trial*,[4] could think of none less effective for and in that quest! Between the "lawyer game" and the "jury game" in a system "that treats a lawsuit as a battle of wits and wiles,"[5] he could thus visualize none less likely to bring out the truth than our adversary process. Indeed, it is a system geared crucially to the discovery of facts in a hostile, an adversary, setting in a court of law, in which a body of jurors—who are usually, at best, but marginally qualified to judge the issues and

Henry J. Abraham

are increasingly chosen from panels of noncontroversial individuals whose regular activities society apparently does not value, with ample time on their hands and opinions, let alone training, on preferably nothing—pronounces a verdict more often than not on the basis of its views as to which of the two sides had the better (more colorful?, more attractive?, more vocal?, more charismatic?) lawyer. It may well be doubted that juries are in fact capable accurately to answer the general question of guilt or lack thereof; at best, they can probably respond to specific questions.[6] This is not the place to discuss the ethics of lawyers in an adversary system, but as an increasing body of literature[7] has begun to reemphasize, the average attorney's quest is more often than not victory for his client (and thus concurrently for himself) and not for principled justice. The Canons of Ethics, the Code of Professional Responsibility, seem to offer no serious competition, no particular barrier, in the pursuit of that victory, which is commonly attained—if not without hard work and careful planning— as a direct result of what Judge Frank pungently termed the successful invocation of the "Fight" v. "Truth" theory cum game.[8] It is one, as he concluded acidly—in words written twenty-seven years ago and still decidedly apposite—in which

> the lawyer aims at victory, at winning in the fight, not at aiding the court to discover the facts. He does not want the trial court to reach a sound educated guess, if it is likely to be contrary to his client's interests. Our present trial method is thus the equivalent of throwing pepper in the eyes of a surgeon when he is performing an operation.[9]

It may thus well be asked whether the continental inquisitory system (the French enquête, featuring the institution of the *juge d'instruction*) might not be considered as a viable alternative to our accusatory one? How long can our society continue to practice a criminal trial system in which, in the words of attorney Jerry Paul, who successfully defended Joan Little in August 1975 in a widely publicized and dramatized murder case, "the question of innocence or guilt is almost irrelevant."[10] In an interview following the trial, Mr. Paul said he "bought" Miss Little's acquittal and that it cost $325,000. "I can win any case in this country," he cockily-proudly contended, "given enough money. I'm going to tell you the truth. You must destroy the charade, the illusion of justice." Mr. Paul continued that, by admitting that the acquittal was "bought"—the money was there to hire the best counsel, to mount an extensive jury selection process, to hire investigators, to fly in expert witnesses, to spend thousands on "counseling" for Miss Little to prepare her for her testimony—he was pointing up the defects of the system.[11] The presiding jurist in the case, North Carolina Superior Court Judge Hamilton Hobgood, observed that he thought Mr. Paul was quite wrong—that the American legal system, not money, should be credited with the acquittal of the accused.[12] Yet the haunting doubts are not readily stilled. There is a crying need for dramatic change in the adversary system and its protagonists; and as Frank put it, "a considerable diminution of the martial spirit in litigation."[13] Neither minor nor major changes, however, can be effected absent active cooperation, and some genuine largesse, by and of the legal profession—whose members, after all, comprise fully two-thirds of the nation's legislators.

What of the efficacy and adequacy of the sundry tribunals that presently exist at the trial and the appellate levels of the judiciary? Actually, our federal system of constitutional, special, and legislative tribunals is well-organized, relatively simple in design, and would conceivably be quite capable of handling the enormous load of litigation—were it not for the increasingly overly-easy access (especially to the appellate level); excessive jurisdiction (on both trial and appellate levels); excessive jurisdiction (on both trial and appellate levels); chronic understaffing of lower and intermediate courts; and the almost axiomatic resultant delays (notwithstanding some noble statutory efforts to speed trials—noble in theory, irresponsible in design, for, as the Chief Justice of the United States has consistently complained publicly, the laudable statutory demand for speeding up of trials was not accompanied by the obviously vital statutory authorization for the concomitantly essential increases in court staffing). There is no dearth of advocacy[14] for reform to alleviate the fundamental problems alluded to, yet changes in the judicial structure have chronically been even more difficult to sell to the public and its representatives in legislative halls than have other measures and matters.

De minimis, the following changes ought to be effected in the federal realm: (a) Three-judge courts should be abolished forthwith; their work has tripled in the past ten years, their jurisdiction and relative promise of Supreme Court review being tailor-made for stimulated as well as genuine litigation. Their functions should be submerged in the general orbit of the district courts. (b) Congress might be well-advised to consider some tightening of the rather generous appellate as well as trial pathways for habeas corpus and in forma pauperis cases, which presently constitute half of the Supreme Court's work load. Legislative tampering with the former is admittedly fraught with danger, yet it should be possible to continue to provide access for bona fide habeas corpus claims without entertaining "court games" (Justice Douglas's words!) and uncalled for duplicate filings and transfers. The latter have gotten out of hand and need jurisdictional as well as statutory remedial consideration. (c) There is simply no excuse for the continuation of the federal jurisdictional luxury of diversity of citizenship suits. These suits, which, of course, ought to be handled at the level of the states— especially since the federal courts have since 1938 been obliged to apply state law[15]—now constitute the single most numerous category of cases filed as civil suits. Chiefly comprising insurance claims, automobile accident, and personal injury suits, they should preferably be removed totally from judicial tribunals and placed at the bar of ad-

Henry J. Abraham

ministrative, ideally arbitration, panels. Some states, such as Pennsylvania for its first-class cities, have mandated resort to arbitration panels, requiring resort to such panels in all civil cases up to $3,000 in value, and permitting them up to $10,000.[16] Found administratively at the county court level, Pennsylvania's arbitration panels handle an average of 10,000 cases annually—inexpensively, speedily, effectively.[17] (d) Notwithstanding Justice Douglas's often-voiced denial—and indeed his insistence, even during the months immediately prior to his health-dictated retirement from the Court after more than thirty-six and a half years of service thereon, that the highest tribunal was not overworked but underworked!—and, as the Chief Justice once again pleaded in his Year End Report 1975, help is needed.[18] The Supreme Court's case load is staggering. Whether the much-debated, widely suggested and almost equally widely condemned, proposal of the creation of a new appellate tribunal between the courts of appeals and the Supreme Court, to be known as "The National Court of Appeals," is the appropriate answer to the very real problem, is contentious. In any event, the current debate in the legal profession and in Congress is healthy.[19] My own preference would be for a reduction of jurisdiction along the lines of some of the above-suggested remedial steps rather than for the establishment of the new tribunal.[20] (e) To increase judicial effectiveness in terms of time utilization at the level of the Supreme Court, it has been suggested that it abandon oral argument; yet the latter's drama, its visibility, and its undoubted educational facets, both internal and external, are born of the kind of commendable values that underlie the democratic process under law. (f) Periodically, Congress—as it, fortunately unsuccessfully, endeavored in the draconian Jenner-Butler Bill in the mid and late 1950s—toys with the notion of depriving the federal courts of significant areas of jurisdiction in favor of state courts. While there may well be considerable merit in some modest proposals along these lines of what is a periodic love affair with the federal system—some have been suggested immediately above—there must be no tampering with fundamental constitutional appellate prerogatives (as distinguished from trivial and frivolous ones). The presence of a multiple judicial structure of fifty-one separate systems is a fascinating dichotomy of blessing and bane. As long as our federal system endures—and Professor Tugwell makes an intriguing case for what to all intents and purposes is its abandonment—both the problem and promise inherent in such a structure in terms of the judicial process represents a genuine opportunity for the enhancement of governmental efficiency. But the baby must not be thrown out with the bathwater.

Second, what of the status of court personnel, court staffing? There is neither space nor need in this forum to embark upon a detailed examination of the "who," "why," and "how" of court staffing—it has very recently been done in two extensive book-length studies for the federal judiciary[21]—but a few basic observations[22] antecedent to analyzing the profile of that personnel and possible reforms are warranted.

The question of the principles that govern the selection of the men and women who sit on our judicial tribunals is both a moral and a political one of the greatest magnitude. Their tasks and functions are awe-inspiring indeed, but it is as human beings and as participants in the political as well as the legal and governmental process that jurists render their decisions. Their position in the government framework must assure them of independence, dignity, and security of tenure. The two basic methods of selecting jurists under our system are still appointment and election, although today a system combining the two is becoming increasingly prevalent. Yet the process of selection is assuredly more complex than that suggested by W. Curtis Bok's fictional Judge Ulan in *Backbone of the Herring*, who quips: "A judge is a member of the bar who once knew a Governor."[23]

Most of the roughly 12,000 judges on our state and local courts continue to be elected, although the gubernatorial appointive method, often with legislative or bar advice and consent, is being resorted to increasingly—generally a development to be welcomed. On the other hand, the number of states adopting versions of the California and Missouri plans, which combine the elective and appointive methods,[24] is growing rapidly.

The founders of the Constitution struggled at length over the selection of the federal judiciary. Under the Randolph Plan of Union, selection as well as confirmation by the "National legislature" was proposed; an inevitable counter-suggestion would have vested that power in the chief magistrate alone. Representatives from the small states were unhappy with the notion of exclusive executive appointment, fearing favoritism toward the large states, which they suspected might "gratify" the President to a greater extent. Madison recommended appointment by the Senate alone, but after second thoughts disassociated himself from this proposal. Ultimately, Ben Franklin's efforts and a spirit of compromise between large and small interests resulted in the adoption of a system modeled after one then being used in Massachusetts. It is still used today, and on balance it has proved to be workable professionally as well as politically.

It is not universally understood that no legal or constitutional requirements for a federal judgeship exist—an especially surprising fact since each state in the Union has at least some statutory and/or constitutional requirements for at least some judicial posts. There does exist, however, an unwritten prerequisite for a post on the federal bench—a bachelor of laws degree. No one can become a member of the Supreme Court without that degree. Although it is not necessarily mandatory either to have practiced law or to have been a member of the bar, the American Bar Association Standing Committee on Federal Judiciary not only demands trial experience of a candidate for the judiciary, but also requires some fifteen years of legal practice to qualify the candidate for a passing rating. As a matter of historical record, no non-lawyer has ever served on the Supreme Court of the United States. Yet since most of the important questions to come before the Supreme Court, for one, today raise social and

Henry J. Abraham

political issues, one might well ask why does an appellate jurist, especially at the highest level, have to be a lawyer? In one of his last public statements prior to his retirement and death, Justice Black formally urged the appointment of "at least one non-lawyer" to the Court. The chances of affirmative action on that proposal are nil— but it raises intriguing questions about the role of the Court, one so frequently criticized as "legislating" rather than "judging."

In a learned essay calling for selection of Supreme Court justices "wholly on the basis of functional fitness," Justice Frankfurter keenly argued that judicial experience, political affiliation, and geographic, racial, and religious considerations—characteristics that have loomed large, indeed, in presidential selections to date—should *not* play a significant role in the selection of jurists.[25] He contended that, instead, Supreme Court jurists should be at once *philosopher, historian, and prophet*—to which Justice Brennan, in a conversation with this writer, proposed to add "and a person of inordinate patience." Justice Frankfurther viewed their task as requiring "poetic sensibilities" and "the gift of imagination," as exhorting them to

> pierce the curtain of the future . . . give shape and visage to mysteries still in the womb of time. . . . [the job thus demands] antennae registering feeling and judgment beyond logical, let alone quantitative proof. . . . One is entitled to say without qualification that the correlation between prior judicial experience and fitness for the Supreme Court is zero. The significance of the greatest among the Justices who had such experience, Holmes and Cardozo, derived not from that judicial experience but from the fact that they were Holmes and Cardozo. They were thinkers, and more particularly, legal philosophers.[26]

Felix Frankfurter was quite right on the "functional fitness" issue. Objective merit, competence—and, why not, qualities of "philosopher, historian, and prophet"—should be the sole criteria. Their presence need by no means vitiate considerations of political and ideological compatibility—there is nothing whatsoever wrong with so-called court packing, provided the selectee is indeed meritorious and competent—but "personal friendship," unless quite secondary to the basic qualifications, and "equitable" considerations of geography, race, sex, and religion should have no place in choice motivations. Even, indeed infinitely, more so than judicial experience, they are rank nonsequiturs qualitatively and should be shunned resolutely. The judicial branch was neither intended to be, nor should it be, a representative body! For representation, let the body politic turn to the legislative and executive branches. The judiciary's role is a dramatically different one—and ought to remain so.

If the nominating authorities on both the federal and state levels will overridingly base their actions on considerations of merit and competence, there seems little need for any drastic overhaul in present selection methodologies—provided they are either of the appointive/elective (Missouri-California model) variety. The practice of election, however—still so widely present in most of the fifty states—be it partisan or what is often euphemistically called "nonpartisan," should be shunned resolutely. Neither pragmatically nor philosophically is election compatible with judicial service. With regard to the appointive mode, proposals abound for alterations in present practices, above and beyond the adoption of Missouri-California plans. Although, as suggested, there appears to be no pressing need for changes in the typical appointive practice, assuming the presence of the appointees' qualifications, a good many thoughtful observers, troubled by the continuing practices of senatorial courtesy, executive political cronyism, and the political role of the Department of Justice, have advanced the possibility of moving toward some type of judicial selection commissions. Variously conceived, a typical one of the federal level would be composed of individuals designated by the President upon recommendation of the Chief Justice, drawn from both the organized bar and citizens' groups—confirmed by the Senate or not, depending on the plan's authorship. In either instance, however, the commissioner would recommend circa five candidates for each vacancy, with the President required to select one within thirty days (or advance a viable reason to the Senate why none of the five is acceptable to him and thus request a new group of names). Other plans for alteration of the existing method of selection would vest the appointive function in upper level sitting jurists.[27]

A matter of infinitely more pressing concern, and of a far more vexatious and subtle nature, is the already severally alluded-to central question in the judicial process of the basic role of the judge or justice, namely, how to confine him or her to judging rather than legislating. A truly fascinating problem, it has defied line-drawing, and will assuredly continue to defy it—with apologies to Professor Wechsler's "neutral principles." Viewing this matter at the highest judicial level, does the Supreme Court, do its justices, merely judge each case on its intrinsic merit or do they also legislate? In textbook theory—and virtually in the eyes of the average observer—all the members of any judicial tribunal do is to judge the controversies over which they have jurisdiction and arrive at a decision in accordance with the legal aspects of the particular situation at issue. Yet the nine justices of the United States Supreme Court especially are often charged with legislating rather than judging in handing down their decisions. This charge usually admits, and indeed grants, that the Court must, of course, possess the power to interpret legislation, and if "absolutely justified" by the particular issue at hand, even strike down legislation that is unconstitutional beyond "rational question." The charge against the high tribunal insists, however, that a line must be drawn between the imposition of judicial judgment and the exercise of judicial will. The latter is described as legislating, presumably the function of the legislature, and hence reserved to it. But, no matter how desirable one may be in the eyes of a good many observers, is it possible to draw such a line?

Henry J. Abraham

It is, of course, impossible. As with every line, questions arise at once as to how, where, when, and by whom it shall be drawn. But it is obvious that the judges do legislate. They do make law. One of the most consistent advocates of judicial self-restraint, Justice Holmes, recognized without hesitation that judges do and must legislate. But, he added significantly that they "can do so only interstitially; they are confined from molar to molecular motions."[28] Judges are human, as indeed all of us are human—but also they are judges, which most of us are not. Being human, they have human reactions. "Judges are men, not disembodied spirits; as men they respond to human situations," in Justice Frankfurter's words. Justice McReynolds insisted that a judge neither can, nor should, be "an amorphous dummy, unspotted by human emotions." (He certainly sported many such spots!) And Justice Cardozo spoke of the cardiac promptings of the moment, musing in his lively prose that "the great tides and currents which engulf the rest of men do not turn aside in their course and pass the judges by."[29]

But, being human, as indicated, does not stand alone in the judicial decision-making process. A jurist is also presumably a qualified and conscientious member of the tribunal; he or she is in no sense of the term a free agent—free to render a decision willy-nilly. There is a deplorable tendency on the part of many observers to over-simplify the judicial decision-making process. Judges are "rigidly bound within walls that are unseen" by the average layman. These walls are built of the heritage of the law; the spirit of the Anglo-Saxon law; the impact of the cases as these have come down through the years; the regard for stare decisis (although there are, conveniently, often several precedents from which to choose), for a genuine sense of historical continuity with the past, as Holmes put it, "is not a duty, it is only a necessity";[30] the crucial practice of judicial self-restraint[31]—in brief, *the taught tradition of the law.*

Moreover, to reiterate an earlier point, the judges are very well aware of at least two other cardinal facts of judicial life: that they have no power to enforce their decisions, depending, as they do, upon the executive for such enforcement; and that they may be reversed by the legislature, albeit with varying degrees of effectiveness and if not without some toil and trouble—as the Crime Bill of 1968, for one, with its three-pronged attack on the Court, demonstrates. But not only do we often expect too much from the Court, we consciously or subconsciously encourage it to endeavor to settle matters that ought to be, yet for a variety of reasons are not, tackled by the other branches—witness such contentious issues as desegregation, reapportionment, redistricting, criminal justice, and separation of church and state.

How to draw the lines? Anthony Lewis has observed perceptively—but hardly definitively—that "judicial intervention on fundamental issues is most clearly justified when there is no other remedy for a situation that threatens the national fabric—when the path of political change is blocked."[32] This was the case with the areas of endemic racial desegregation and persistent legislative mal-, mis-, and non-apportionment. But it was not the case with such contentious criminal justice decisions as *Miranda v. Arizona*.[33] There, by reading a particular code of police procedure into the general language of the Constitution, the Court may well have overreached itself (although the police were hardly hobbled by the decision). Nor was it the case with the Court's recent involvement with a host of nonjudicial and perhaps nonjudicious aspects of the vexatious realm of abortion[34] (though I happen to agree with the results it reached), where, in effect, it created a federal abortion code. Nor, to point to another realm, is it true of the Court's increasing involvement—some have styled it meddling—with discipline in the public schools.[35] Even its extended forays into the realm of morals are of dubious wisdom, given profound and widespread popular opposition. Our courts should not be viewed as wastebaskets of social problems, which does not mean, of course, that law does not play an efficacious role in social reform. It does, however, point to the inescapable fact that the other branches *must* do their jobs.

Of course, the Supreme Court of the United States is engaged in the political process. But, in Justice Frankfurter's admonitory prose, it is "the Nation's ultimate judicial tribunal, not a super-legal-aid bureau."[36] Neither is the Court, in the second Justice Harlan's words, "a panacea for every blot upon the public welfare, nor should this Court ordained as a judicial body, be thought of as a general haven for reform movements."[37] It may, thus, be questioned on grounds of both wisdom and justifiability—and ultimately governability—whether the Court should be involved, as it has become increasingly, in such realms as economic, as distinct from political and legal, equality, and private as distinct from public morality.

Moreover, the type of judicial activism evinced by the highest tribunal in the land is hardly confined to it. Indeed, whether it be because of cue-taking from above, or because of indigenous oat-feeling, the lower federal courts, particularly the United States district courts, have ventured forth in policy-making of the most obvious kind, policy-making that should be left to the legislative function by the people's representatives. Thus, to question just two or three recent federal trial court actions that veritably smack of legislation—no matter how noble their intent and how desirous their consummation at the bar of public policy—is it really a judicial function to decree-prescribe:

> the F degree of temperature of thermostatically controlled hot water for state mental patients or residential use (110 F at the fixture) and for mechanical dish-washing and laundry use (180 F at the equipment);[38]

or

> that dieticians *and* recreational officers in state penal institutions possess college degrees;[39]

or

that the percentage of women who receive job offers from a certain law firm in the next three years must be at least 20 per cent higher than the percentage of women in the graduating classes of the law schools from which the firm recruits new lawyers?[40]

Decisions such as the above, and a host of others, give pause for thought and raise fundamental role-questions, not only in the mind of professionals[41] and students of government, but also in those of the general public.[42] Caveat Judiciary!

Withal, that public has continued to turn its face toward the judicial branch for the resolution of issues that had better be settled elsewhere. It has done so because courts in general, and the Supreme Court in particular, seem to provide responses to issues where the other branches, especially the legislature, fear to tread.

When all is said and done, the Court, at the head of the United States judiciary, is viewed—and quite properly so—as not only the most fascinating, the most influential, and the most powerful judicial body in the world, it is also the "living voice of [the] Constitution," as Lord Bryce once phrased it. As such, it is both arbiter and educator, and, in essence, represents the sole solution short of anarchy under the American system of government as we know it—witness its seminal role in *United States* v. *Nixon*.[43] It must act, in the words of one commentator, "as the instrument of national moral values that have not been able to find other governmental expression"[44]—assuming, of course, that it functions within its authorized sphere of constitutional adjudication. In that role, it operates as the "collective conscience of a sovereign people."[45] And no other institution "is more deeply decisive in its effect upon our understanding of ourselves and our government."[46] In other words, through its actions the Court defines values and proclaims principles.

Beyond that, moreover, the Supreme Court of the United States is the chief protector of the Constitution, of its great system of checks and balances, and of the people's liberties; it is the greatest institutional safeguard Americans possess. The Court may have retreated, even yielded to pressures now and then, but without its vigilance America's liberties would scarcely have survived. Within the limits of procedure and deference to the presumption of the constitutionality of legislation,[47] the Court—our "sober second thought"[48]—is the natural forum in American society for the individual and for the small group. It must, thus, be prepared to say "no" to the government—a role which Madison, the father of the Bill of Rights, fervently hoped it would always exercise. There are many citizens—indeed most, once they have given the problem the careful thought it merits—who will feel more secure in the knowledge of that guardianship, one generally characterized by common sense, than if it were exercised primarily by the far more easily pressured, more impulsive, and more emotion-charged legislative or executive branches. All too readily do these two yield to the politically expedient and the popular, for they are close, indeed, to what Judge Learned Hand once called "the pressure of public hysteria, public panic, and public greed." The Court, which thus often has had to act as a "moral goad" to the latter two, is neither engaged in, nor interested in, a popularity contest—its function is emphatically not one of counting constituents! Should that time ever arrive, the supreme judicial tribunal, as we now know it, will have lost its meaning.

Even if a transfer of that guardianship to other institutions of government were theoretically desirable, which few thoughtful citizens believe, it would be politically impossible. "Do we desire Constitutional questions," asked Charles Evans Hughes, then not on the bench, in his fine book on the Court, "to be determined by political assemblies and partisan divisions?"[49] The response must be a ringing "No!" In the 1955 Godkin Lectures which he was to deliver at Harvard University when death intervened, Justice Robert H. Jackson had expressed his conviction eloquently and ably:

> The people have seemed to feel that the Supreme Court, whatever its defects, is still the most detached, dispassionate, and trustworthy custodian that our system affords for the translation of abstract into constitutional commands.[50]

And we may well agree with Thomas Reed Powell that the logic of constitutional law is the common sense of the Supreme Court of the United States—which continues valiantly and admirably to strive to maintain that blend of continuity and change which is so vital to the stability of our basic democratic governmental processes.

FEDERAL SYSTEM

Our federal system is the structure that underlies a generous number of both the disappointments and the accomplishments of the American government "of, by, and for the people," as we know it. Federalism is either a failure or a success, depending upon the point of view of the protagonist, both extremes being represented at the Academy's Bicentennial Conference on the United States Constitution in the persons of two leading experts on the subject: Rexford Guy Tugwell and Daniel J. Elazar, respectively. The latter, while duly acknowledging the obvious need for constant reexamination and amelioration, is basically committed to its overall viability;[51] the former, more than twice as old in years and the holder of sundry responsible high government posts in the past, has long been convinced that only radical surgery, perhaps even extinction, will do.[52] A host of views hues to intermediate shadings. Neither the controversy nor the difference in perception is astonishing. For, as a team of contemporary commentators puts it well, the

> genius of the Constitution is also its vulnerability. A document that gives powers to different political institutions is sooner or later going to be caught in a squeeze when the interests of those are in sharp conflict.[53]

Henry J. Abraham

The answer to the questions—at which level, national or state, (1) was power supposed to lie?; (2) where does it lie?; and (3) where should it lie?—are basic to both the argument(s) and to any proposed solution(s).

But there is no argument, whatever, on the patently obvious fact of federal life that, notwithstanding lip-service to the contrary, and notwithstanding such questionably honest decentralizing concepts or measures as revenue sharing, the long apparent trend toward centralization of federal power at the seat and in the hands of the national government is, at once, an axiom of modern American federalism and irreversible—absent drastic and dramatic constitutional changes, which simply will not take place. New York City's 1975 financial Waterloo, its own and its parent state of New York's desperate turn to Washington for the sole practical source of tangible succor, and the New Year's Day 1976 urgent appeal by four leading governors to have the national government take over the entire welfare aid program because "it is out of control . . . a patchwork . . . and not working"[54] are merely the latest and most visible indices of that conclusion's proof positive. This does not, of course, mean that one needs to embrace the off-with-his-head solution of Professor Tugwell; but it does mean listening to his reasoned critique.[55] It may well be that there is really no effective reversal of the trend toward centralization of power—assuming we could agree that reversal were in the system's best interest—and that we ought to adapt the subterfuge so charmingly suggested severally by ex-Senator George Aiken (R.–Vt.) during the agonizing years of the Vietnam War, when he repeatedly, and quite seriously, importuned Presidents to proclaim victory and withdraw all forces forthwith!

As I have had occasion to suggest elsewhere,[56] federalism is a point on a continuum reaching from complete isolation to complete absorption, neither of which is really ever found in the actual life of actual states. As Aristotle might have said, there is no such thing as federalism; there are only federal states—states reflecting the federal principle. Hence, the federal idea, defined by the then Governor Nelson A. Rockefeller in Harvard's Godkin Lectures as a

> concept of government by which a sovereign people, for their greater protection and progress, yield a portion of their sovereignty to a political system that has more than one center of sovereign power, energy and creativity,[57]

features dramatic differences.

These differences point to a salient underlying aspect of federalism: its pragmatism. Thus it was for entirely pragmatic reasons that the Constitutional Convention on Fifth and Chestnut Streets in Philadelphia almost 190 years ago determined upon a federal structure, then as now appropriately known as a dual form of government, calculated to reconcile unity with diversity: the pressing common interests and purposes shared by the uniting colonies, which were desirous of securing themselves against any European imperialism, and the desire of each of the uniting communities to maintain their identity and a large measure of independence—a desire that, in part, springs from the same mysterious sources as national pride and national exclusiveness. In those days, the framers' main concern was whether the fledgling nation, about to be created, would and could endure. Today, as has been true for some time, the question must be stood on its head: will the states, that is, the component parts of the nation, endure? Three major developments have occurred that have prompted that role-reversal. In chronological order, they are: (1) the predisposition of the Supreme Court of the United States, and notably its Chief Justice for thirty-four and a half years (1801–34), John Marshall, to resolve all doubts in favor of the nation via a broad and decisive interpretation of Article VI, the "Supremacy Clause"; (2) the military triumph of nationalism under Abraham Lincoln in the Civil War; and (3) the still accelerating growth of economic and social welfare service demands by the electorate that have inexorably commanded national action for their solution.

The naked facts today, as they have been for several decades, are that it is the federal government that has to deliver the goods. No matter how well-intentioned the component parts may be, they are more often than not incapable of the kind of service performance for which a seemingly steadily increasing popular demand clamors—even while concurrently mouthing platitudes about "returning power to the local levels of government." On the other hand, since the excessive rigidity of centralization is a serious weakness, regional, state, and local governments, with control over matters of unique concern to their own areas, should retain a substantial sphere of independence. And they do—which proves that federalism is not obsolete, although particular aspects may badly need revision. Moreover, as the Canadian as well as the American federal system have proved amply, it is doubtful, indeed, that democratic government could survive except through the device, or at least the trappings, of federalism.

Democracy, which essentially is government by consent, needs mechanisms through which to construct electoral majorities that can agree on what the government should do. The states and localities, by providing such mechanisms under our federal systems, are often able to settle political squabbles in their decentralized realms without forcing them into the national forum where they might cause the sharpest of conflicts. Federalism, at its best, hence enables many regional interests and idiosyncrasies to have their own way in their own areas without ever facing the necessity of reconciliation with other regional interests. Individuals can thus identify themselves with particular regional interests and find in them a satisfying expression of many facets of their personalities. When thus viewed, federalism approaches the textbook ideal: a device for combining unity and diversity in accordance with the requirements of liberal democratic ideals.

The problem with the aforegone analysis of federalism is that,

Henry J. Abraham

while undoubtedly true in democratic theory, and devoutly to be wished as a manifestation of the liberal democratic ideal, it but scarcely has practical application to the pressing issues of the day. The overriding key contemporary issues are simply beyond local, state, and even regional solution. Witness such as the cascading plight of the great cities of the nation; the incessant augmentation of demands for economic and social security; affirmative egalitarianism; and yes, even the once sacred bastion of local control, education. It is visionary to exhort the states to be innovative: their financial plight—with but rare exceptions, such as Texas—renders innovation a luxury; day-to-day survival is the contemporary preoccupation, inexorably bringing with it longing, albeit not necessarily fond, glances toward Washington. No wonder, then, that the Advisory Commission on Governmental Relations wondered officially as long ago as 1968–69 whether contemporary crucial questions, such as those of the urban centers, were still solvable by the American federal system "or if only a centralized and unitary governmental system will be equal to the task."[58] Or can our leadership somehow devise, and sell, reforms that will adapt the venerable federal structure to "the needs of a technological, urban society in an age of onrushing change?"[59] It is excrutiatingly difficult to still the haunting doubts.

And yet, federalism is at least one answer to the vexatious problem of how to conduct effectively the affairs of a nation-state as large, diverse, and complex as ours; provided we do not become the slaves of political theory or terminology; provided that we are not afraid to experiment; provided that we are willing to share/distribute economic bounty (and bane); and further provided that we allow an umpire—that is the federal judiciary, with the Supreme Court at its apex—to decide winners and losers in governmental-societal combat. Many a crime has been, and undoubtedly is being, committed on the altar of federalism, commonly referred to as "states' rights," particularly when the issue at hand deals with the realm of civil rights and liberties. Yet, considerable advantages have also accrued, and will continue to accrue, from the federal system, not the least of which is that it allows more voices to be heard, more governmental experiments to be rendered—in short, more direct and more personalized political participation at a grass-roots level.

Given the inexorable centripetal force of governmental power during the past four decades, however—led by the power of the purse—it may well be asked whether the United States is still properly classifiable as a federal state at all? That the period indicated has witnessed a drastic modification in the role of the constituent states is beyond dispute. Yet they are hardly in total eclipse, and assuredly not in terms of their identity. Their individualized administrative, basic internal governmental structures continue to exist, antiquated as many of them are; they are usually faithfully, probably too faithfully, represented—at least in terms of state and local interests—by their generally parochial congressional delegations; their often provincial and obstructive veto power is omnipresent (and occasionally omnipotent) vis-à-vis general national programs; grants-in-aid continue to abound; revenue sharing programs, while probably visionary and at least partially self-deceptive in their long-range implications, have provided a proverbial shot-in-the-arm; multitudinous social service and welfare programs of a host of stripes are increasingly financed by the national government, underscoring contemporary facets and notions of cooperative federalism, and, on many a delicate matter involving civil rights and liberties, the states have been taken off the hook by one or more of the three branches of the central government in Washington. The national psyche could probably not accept a departure from the federal arrangement: the knowledge of its existence, far more than its fact, represents a veritable security blanket to the average citizen! Perhaps that knowledge, so dear to our heterogenous society, vitiates basically more crucial questions of its effectiveness in the governmental modus operandus—and, indeed, its future role.

Henry J. Abraham

NOTES

1. Anthony Lewis, "A Day in Court," *New York Times*, 16 October 1975, p. 39.

2. Ibid.

3. Ibid.

4. Jerome Frank, *Courts on Trial: Myth and Reality in American Justice* (New York: Atheneum Publishers, 1963).

5. Ibid., p. 85.

6. For a less than complimentary, extensive analysis of juries, see Henry J. Abraham, *The Judicial Process*, 3rd ed. (New York: Oxford University Press, 1975), pp. 110–33.

7. For example, Monroe H. Freedman (Dean of the Hofstra Law School), *Lawyers' Ethics in an Adversary System* (Indianapolis and New York: Bobbs-Merrill Co., Inc., 1975).

8. Frank, *Courts on Trial*, chap. 6—a brilliant, devastating analysis.

9. Ibid., p. 85.

10. "Justice," *New York Times*, 26 October 1975, sec. 4, p. 16E.

11. Ibid.

12. Ibid.

13. Frank, *Courts on Trial*, p. 102.

14. For example, the sixteen-member "Commission on Revision of the Federal Court Appellate System" (known as the "Hruska Commission") and the Report of the Study Group on the Case Load of the Supreme Court (known as the "Freund Report"). See also the Chief Justice's "Annual Report on the State of the Judiciary" (A.B.A. Mid-Winter Meeting, 23 February 1975).

15. *Erie* v. *Tompkins*, 304 U.S. 64 (1938).

16. See the description in Abraham, *The Judicial Process*, p. 142, n. 10.

17. Ibid.

18. See *New York Times*, 4 January 1976, p. 1.

19. See the special issue of *Judicature*, "Bail Out the Supreme Court?," vol. 59, no. 4 (November 1975).

20. Some colleagues have suggested that, conceivably, my position is influenced by the vista of having to revise four books were the proposed court to be established!

21. Harold W. Chase, *Federal Judges: The Appointing Process* (Minneapolis: University of Minnesota Press, 1972), for lower federal judges, and Henry J. Abraham, *Justices and Presidents: A Political History of Appointments to the Supreme Court* (New York: Oxford University Press, 1974) for Supreme Court judges.

22. They are taken largely from chaps. 2 and 3 of Abraham, *Justices and Presidents*.

23. W. Curtis Bok, *Backbone of the Herring* (New York: Alfred A. Knopf, Inc., 1941), p. 3.

24. See Abraham, *Justices and Presidents*, pp. 13–15.

25. His one-time colleague on the Court, Sherman Minton, in a letter to "FF," fully seconded the latter's view: "A copy of your letter should be sent to every member of Congress. Your statement explodes entirely the myth of prior judicial experience. I am a living example that judicial experience doesn't make one prescient." (Frankfurter's Papers, Library of Congress, S. M. to F. F., 18 April 1957. Minton had served eight years on lower courts.)

26. "The Supreme Court in the Mirror of Justices," *University of Pennsylvania Law Review* 105 (1957), p. 781.

27. Ex-Senator Ervin would thus like to see all federal judges selected by a panel of sitting senior jurists, followed by Senate confirmation. Professor Chase, *Federal Judges*, favors the selection of all lower federal judges by the U.S. Supreme Court alone. Professor Peter Graham Fish of Duke University, also disdaining any senatorial role, suggests the vesting of the appointive power of all judges in the Chief Justice of the United States alone, acting under the "Heads of Department" provision of Article II(2)(1) of the Constitution.

28. *Southern Pacific Co.* v. *Jensen*, 224 U.S. 205, 221 (1916).

29. Benjamin N. Cardozo, *The Nature of the Judicial Process* (New Haven: Yale University Press, 1921), p. 169.

30. As quoted by Alpheus T. Mason and William M. Beaney in *American Constitutional Law*, 5th ed. (Englewood Cliffs: Prentice-Hall, Inc., 1972), p. xxvi.

31. For a list of sixteen "maxims" of this self-restraint, see Abraham, *The Judicial Process*, chap. 9.

32. *New York Times*, 15 November 1971, p. 41.

33. 384 U.S. 433 (1966).

34. *Roe* v. *Wade*, 410 U.S. 113 (1973) and *Doe* v. *Bolton*, 410 U.S. 179 (1973).

35. *Goss* v. *Lopez*, 419 U.S. 565 (1975) and *Baker* v. *Owen*, 44 LW 3235 (1975), 423 U.S. 907 (1975).

36. *Uveges* v. *Pennsylvania*, 335 U.S. 437 (1948), at 437.

37. *Reynolds* v. *Sims*, 377 U.S. 533, 624 (1964).

38. *Wyatt* v. *Stickney*, 344 F. Supp. 373, 382 (M.D. Ala. 1972).

39. *New York Times*, 14 January 1976, p. 1.

40. Ibid. 7 February 1976, p. 1.

41. See Louis Lusky's searching new book, *By What Right?*, *A Comment on the Supreme Court's Power to Reverse the Constitution* (Charlottesville: Michie Co., 1975).

42. See the special issue of *U.S. News and World Report*, 19 January 1976, pp. 29–34.

43. 418 U.S. 683 (1974).

44. Anthony Lewis, *New York Times Magazine*, 17 June 1962, p. 38.

45. U.S. Court of Appeals Judge J. Skelly Wright, "The Role of the Courts: Conscience of a Sovereign People," *The Reporter* 29 (26 September 1963), 5.

46. Alexander Meiklejohn, *Free Speech and Its Relation to Self-Government* (New York: Harper & Co., 1948), p. 32.

47. Justice Holmes once stated this (his own) constitutional philosophy to the then sixty-one-year-old Stone: "Young man, about seventy-five years ago I learned that I was not God. And so, when the people . . . want to do something I can't find anything in the Constitution expressly forbidding them to do, I say, whether I like it or not, 'Goddammit, let 'em do it'" (As quoted in Charles P. Curtis, Jr., *Lions under the Throne* (Boston: Houghton Mifflin Co., 1947), p. 281).

48. Charles L. Black, Jr., *The People and The Court* (New York: Macmillan Co., 1969), p. 12.

49. *The Supreme Court of the United States* (New York: Columbia University Press, 1928), p. 236.

50. Robert H. Jackson, *The Supreme Court in the American System of Government* (Cambridge: Harvard University Press, 1955), p. 23.

51. Daniel J. Elazar, *American Federalism: A View from the States*, 2d ed. (New York: Thomas Y. Crowell Co., Inc., 1972).

52. Rexford G. Tugwell, *The Emerging Constitution* (New York: Harper's Magazine Press, 1974).

53. Kenneth Prewitt and Sidney Verba, *An Introduction to American Government* (New York: Harper & Row, Publishers, 1974), p. 303. See their excellent chap. 10, "White House, State House, and City Hall: Federalism in America," pp. 312ff.

54. See *New York Times*, 4 January 1976, p. 1.

55. See chap. 3, "Parts and the Whole," pp. 89ff, of Tugwell, *The Emerging Constitution*.

56. J. A. Corry and Henry J. Abraham, *Elements of Democractic Government*, 4th ed. (New York: Oxford University Press, 1964), chap. 6, "Federalism" *passim* (from which much of this section is adapted).

57. "The Future of Federalism," February 1962.

58. *Urban America and the Federal System: Commission Findings and Proposals* (Washington: U.S. Government Printing Office, 1969), p. 1.

59. Milton C. Cummings, Jr., and David Wise, *Democracy Under Pressure: An Introduction to the American Political System*, 2d ed. (New York: Harcourt Brace Jovanovich, Inc., 1974), p. 89; chap. 3, "The Federal System," pp. 65ff., is a pithy, succinct evaluation and exposition of essentials.

He in a trice struck Lyon thrice
Upon his head, enrag'd, sir.

Who seiz'd the tongs to ease his wrongs,
And Griswold thus engag'd, sir.

Congress Hall,
in Philad⁴ Feb.15.1798.
S.E. Cor. 6ᵗʰ & Chesnut S

REPORT on the DELIBERATIONS of COMMITTEE II
by James O. Freedman and Frank Goodman

THE CONCEPT OF GOVERNMENTAL "EFFECTIVENESS"

In its opening session, the committee attempted to clarify the concept of governmental "effectiveness" and to agree upon yardsticks for its measurement. At the outset of discussion, two criteria were put forward as appropriate measures of the effectiveness of government in general or of any particular institution of government: 1) the degree of public approval it enjoys; and 2) the extent to which it has been able to provide solutions to important societal problems. Judged by either of these standards, it was agreed, all three branches of our national government would be found seriously wanting. Congress and (in lesser degree) the presidency receive consistently low approval ratings in public opinions surveys; and even the judiciary, the least disfavored branch, falls short of majority approval. Similarly, the existence of unremedied social problems—urban blight, the energy crisis, crime in the streets, and others—would be strong evidence of governmental default if government could fairly be held accountable for all in society that is wrong.

Most members of the committee, however, were dissatisfied with both criteria. Public disapproval of government, it was noted, may simply reflect an unrealistic level of expectation and demand, a tendency to look to Washington for solutions to problems that are beyond the capacity of government to solve. Many writers, moreover, have observed the tendency of the public, both in the United States and elsewhere, to demand more and better government services and programs while at the same time strongly resisting the taxes necessary to pay for them. Those who fail to appreciate that there are no free lunches cannot help but be dissatisfied with whatever lunch is served, whatever bill presented, or both.

Furthermore, the increasing unpopularity of the presidency owes much to circumstances that have little to do with how effectively any particular President does his job. In the words of Aaron Wildavsky:

Since the proportion of people identifying with the major parties has shown a precipitous decline, future Presidents are bound to start out with a smaller base comprised of less committed supporters. This tendency will be reinforced by a relative decline of the groups—the less educated and the religious fundamentalist—who have been most disposed to give unwavering support regardless of what a President does or fails to do. Education may not make people wise, but it does make them critical.[1]

Thus, Wildavsky concludes, "future Presidents will have to work harder than have past Presidents to keep the same popularity status," and, in the end, the office is bound to become less popular even as it becomes more active and powerful.[2]

In the case of Congress, too, popularity data must be viewed with some caution. While opinion surveys indicate that most people strongly disapprove of the performance of Congress as a whole, they tend to be satisfied with the performance of their own representatives. To some of the discussants, however, this seeming contradiction did not weaken the significance of the public disesteem for Congress as a whole but merely helped to explain why members who collectively disappoint their constituents nevertheless repeatedly get reelected.

The discussants were equally skeptical of the notion that the persistence of important social evils, such as poverty, urban blight, and crime, bespeaks the ineffectiveness of federal government. For one thing, not all of these conditions are properly the government's responsibility. Government, as one member of the group put it, is no more to be blamed for crime in the streets than to be credited for the gross national product. Moreover, the failure of government to remedy an undesirable social condition may be entirely consistent with the value preferences of a majority of the electorate, its unwillingness to accept the costs of remediation. To the extent that social amelioration requires massive transfer payments from rich to poor, suburb to city, region to region, inaction by government may simply indicate the greater political power of the transferor classes. Finally, even if government were thought to be answerable for major social ills, a balanced assessment would have to take account of its accomplishments as well as its shortcomings. While the federal government has not distinguished itself in certain fields—e.g., energy policy, welfare reform, health-care delivery—it can claim notable achievements in others—civil rights and pollution control, to mention only two. In the last analysis, the discussants agreed, a meaningful evaluation of the effectiveness of government must be built upon a careful balancing of the benefits and costs of each governmental program and agency in relation to the probable benefits and costs of feasible alternatives.

In the course of discussion, there emerged for consideration a third possible criterion of "effectiveness"—the extent to which government succeeds in giving the public what the public wants—that is, adopts special programs and policies demanded or favored by a clear majority of the electorate. This criterion, too, was generally rejected by the

James O. Freedman and Frank Goodman

committee. It was pointed out not only that government has obligations to the minority as well as to the majority but also that, when Congress fails to enact legislative measures (such as gun control) clearly favored by the majority, the reason may be that the minority cares about the issue more intensely, a factor which, in democratic theory as well as in political practice, is entitled to no small weight.

In the end, the committee was unable to agree, at least without substantial reservations, upon any single criterion, or combination of criteria, as the operative test of governmental effectiveness. In the ensuing discussions, that concept remained largely undefined.

ASSESSMENT OF THE THREE BRANCHES OF GOVERNMENT

CONGRESS

From its threshold exercise in definition and clarification, the committee moved to an evaluation, one by one, of the three branches of the federal government. The discussion of the legislative branch took for its point of departure the familiar criticism of Congress as a do-nothing body incapable of effective national planning and policy-making. Nearly all the members of the committee agreed that this criticism largely misapprehends the nature and proper function of the Congress. Above all, it was stressed, Congress is a political institution, a representative body; as such it cannot fairly be judged by the criteria of rationality, foresight, and purposefulness that are rightly applied to the administrative and bureaucratic sectors of government. It is the arena in which conflicts of interest, philosophy, and values within the body politic are thrashed out and compromised, the forum in which political issues are crystallized, clarified, and resolved. Congress enacts, and properly should enact, only those legislative measures which are supported by a broad popular consensus and is moved to action only after sufficient pressures have built up to overcome the inherent inertia of the legislative process. Those who seek favorable action from Congress must therefore do more than make an argument; they must build a constituency.

Developing a measure of consensus sufficient to move Congress is no easy matter. The difficulty is compounded by the absence in this country of a disciplined party system on the British or continental model. Here it is not enough for a group seeking legislation to bring persuasion or pressure to bear on a few party leaders; they must disperse their efforts among nearly 500 individual congressmen, many of whom are more sensitive to currents of opinion in their own local district than to the prevailing views of the national parties. Indeed, some members of the committee expressed the view that the power of the central leadership in both houses to influence the behavior of the rank and file has greatly declined in recent years, and that we are unlikely ever to see again a Speaker Cannon, or even a Speaker Rayburn. The average congressman has little to lose by bucking the leadership, other than the opportunity for favorable committee assignments, and even that threat is far less intimidating than it used to be. To a considerable extent, Speaker Rayburn's legendary leverage stemmed from his close relationship to the President, and from the latter's power to withhold federal projects from the districts of un-cooperative congressmen. Nowadays, however, the mainstream of funds from the federal government to congressional districts flows from ongoing programs rather than isolated projects, and the President is not in a position to turn the faucet on or off. One member of the committee was unconvinced that the era of strong leadership in Congress has passed and cited Senator Lyndon Johnson as recent evidence. Others, however, questioned how much even Senator Johnson, as Democratic majority leader, had really influenced the course of legislation, suggesting that the Civil Rights Act of 1957,[3] often credited to President Johnson, would almost certainly have been enacted within five years anyway, and that even the strongest congressional leadership can do little more than advance the time-table of legislation to a small degree.

Congressional inertia is reinforced by other considerations: The average congressman sees it as more important politically to avoid making enemies than to make new friends, and the risk of making enemies is greater when he supports controversial legislation than when he finds reasons for withholding that support. A vote in favor of the disputed proposal is more likely to be punished at the polls than a vote against that same proposal, assuming supporters and opponents to be equally numerous and caring. The phenomenon was perceptively described by Judge Henry Friendly in a passage quoting and paraphrasing a noted French authority:

> When the legislator is asked to legislate, he knows the benefits he will be conferring on some will be matched by burdens on others; he will have his eye fixed on the relative number of his constituents on one side or the other. Moreover, he realizes that the benefit accorded to some will bring less in gratitude than the loss suffered by others will in resentment; the optimum is thus to do nothing, since failure will be understood by those desiring the legislation whereas success will not be forgiven by those opposing it. If legislation there must be, the very necessity of a text arouses further opposition, hence the tendency to soften it in the sense of compromise or even of unintelligibility.[4]

Because of this strong inertial bias, it is usually far easier, even for powerful interest groups, to block adverse congressional action than to generate favorable action. The oil industry, for example, has been notably more successful over the years in preserving its special tax advantages than in persuading Congress to deregulate natural gas or relax burdensome statutory restrictions against air pollution.

Several committee members noted that racial minority groups seeking protection against discrimination and segregation have found it particularly difficult to move Congress. The other branches of the

James O. Freedman and Frank Goodman

government have been far more responsive. It is no accident that the process of racial desegregation began in the 1940s with presidential action (President Truman's 1948 order banning discrimination in the armed forces[5]), gained momentum in the 1950s with judicial action (most notably, the Supreme Court's 1954 school desegregation decision[6]) and, only after another decade had passed, culminated in congressional action (the enactment of the Civil Rights Acts of 1964[7] and 1968[8] and the Voting Rights Act of 1975[9]).

On the other hand, the point about congressional inertia must not be overstated. Conservative critics often lament the ease, even alacrity, with which Congress grants the demands of special interest groups for subsidies of various kinds at the expense of the general taxpayer. Congressional immobility, they argue, is much more in evidence when legislation is opposed by a cohesive and articulate minority than when it is opposed—if that is not too strong a word—by a quiet and unorganized taxpayer majority, which may not object so much to the particular proposal as to the cumulative effect of many such proposals.

Prospects for Reform

Surprisingly, this perception of Congress as a vessel floating more or less passively on shifting political currents was not seriously challenged. Nor was there any real attempt to evaluate the effectiveness of Congress in terms of this model.

There was, however, some discussion, and a measure of disagreement, as to the possible utility of procedural and structural reform. Some committee members felt that no amount of tinkering with the machinery of Congress would significantly affect its work product. According to this view, the presence or absence of the seniority system, the number of committees, the degree of power exercised by committee chairmen, the existence or nonexistence of a rules committee or a seniority system make little difference; Congress will behave in much the same way regardless. Not all members of the group, however, shared this view. It was noted, for example, that the effectiveness of the individual congressman is unnecessarily impaired by lack of information about fiscal matters, about the internal workings of the executive branch agencies subject to congressional oversight and, less importantly, about conditions in society at large. A suggested remedy was the establishment by Congress of a special legislative branch agency responsible for gathering, digesting, and transmitting in usable form such information as Congress may need for purposes of legislation and effective oversight. Other committee members, however, were doubtful that this service would do much good and noted that agencies charged with informing members of Congress already exist.

Apart from such procedural and organizational matters, the committee also considered structural reforms of a more fundamental nature. The discussion revolved around two areas of possible reform:

first, enlargement of congressional districts and corresponding reduction in the membership of the House of Representatives; second, lengthening of the congressional term of office.

In support of the first, the main argument was that larger districts would strengthen party responsibility in Congress. Candidates would be forced to campaign on issues of national or at least regional scope rather than on purely local and parochial questions. They would find it more difficult to disassociate themselves from the program and performance of their party at the national level, both in Congress and in the White House and at the same time would become more dependent upon national-party funds to finance their costlier campaigns. Larger constituencies, it was said, would enhance the prestige of the congressional office, draw more and abler candidates and by the same token, increase voter interest and participation at the polls. Congressional candidates, responsible to a larger and more diverse constituency, would be forced to seek the support of coalitions more closely approximating those to which presidential candidates must appeal. Most of the discussants, however, appeared unimpressed by these arguments. Larger districts, they replied, would make for less effective representation. Congressmen would be less aware of and responsive to the needs and wishes of their constituents, less able to play the ombudsman's role. Members of minority groups would have greater difficulty winning congressional seats. Reduction in the size of the House would result in increased committee burdens for each member and thus impair the quality of the congressional work product. These significant costs would not be offset by any corresponding benefits in the form of party discipline. And the example of the Senate shows that these significant costs would not purchase any real increase in party discipline: party discipline in the Senate, with its statewide constituency, is not stronger, and may be weaker, than in the House.

The second proposal—to lengthen the term of office for members of the House of Representatives—met with a more favorable reception. Discussants pointed out that the existing two-year term forces congressmen to invest an inordinate part of their time and energies, and those of their staff, in campaigning for reelection. Moreover, facing reelection every two years, congressmen are hesitant to cast controversial votes: the moratorium on serious legislation that observers have noted in every American presidential election year descends upon the House of Representatives every second, rather than every fourth, year. A longer term of office, it was argued, would enable members to devote a large amount of their time to the business of deliberation and legislation rather than to the business of getting elected. It would increase the attractiveness of the office and make elections more competitive and interesting. And with fewer elections, their total cost would be reduced.

One committee member ventured the proposal, often suggested by critics of the present two-year term, that members of both houses be elected concurrently with the President every four years.[10] Under

James O. Freedman and Frank Goodman

that procedure, members of Congress who belong to the President's party would be forced to defend his record and to correlate their own positions with those of the national party; the President, moreover, would stand a better chance of carrying into office a Congress that shares his goals and policies. Other discussants were unpersuaded by these arguments. They argued that an election is the principal mechanism in our democracy for enlisting public participation in the governmental process, for airing and debating issues and crystallizing public opinion into a consensus. Less frequent elections would lead to greater public apathy about politics. In the lengthened intervals between elections, changing public opinion could less easily make itself felt at the legislative level. Nor would synchronization of presidential and congressional elections actually contribute very much to the strengthening of the party system in Congress or to coordination between the presidential and congressional parties. It is notable that President Eisenhower failed to carry Congress in 1956, and that President Kennedy would have been better off with the House elected in the mid-term of 1958 than with the House elected with him in 1960.[11] Lack of coordination between the presidential and congressional parties is due not so much to the existence of biennial elections as to factors—such as the committee system, the seniority system, and the rules of the House—which would not be affected by changing the length of congressional terms.

Congressional Oversight of Regulatory Agencies

The committee devoted relatively little attention to one of the central responsibilities of Congress—the oversight of the executive departments and independent regulatory agencies. Congress performs that function through a variety of mechanisms, maintaining fiscal oversight through the appropriations committees, investigative oversight chiefly through the government operations committees, and legislative oversight through legislative committees with specialized subject-matter jurisdiction. In the view of most observers, these mechanisms have not enabled Congress to maintain effective supervision over the practices and policies of the regulatory agencies, so as to assure that regulation is rational and coherent, in accordance with congressional intent, and effective for its purposes. Neither the appropriations process nor ad hoc investigations provide an opportunity for comprehensive review of agency policies. And, for the most part, the laws creating agencies and defining their missions have been cast in such vague and general terms as to provide them scarcely any policy guidance.[12] Although these regulatory statutes are frequently amended, the amendments seldom revise or refine the original grants of power; more often, they merely confer additional power of an equally vague and unspecific character.

There are strong indications that Congress has become acutely conscious of its shortcomings in the field of oversight and of the urgent need both to reform and reorganize the regulatory agencies and to strengthen its own supervisory role.[13] In the last two sessions of Congress, a host of bills have been introduced with a view to accomplishing these purposes. These proposals contemplate a variety of approaches and techniques, many of them highly innovative.

One such method, increasingly in vogue, is a device known as the "legislative veto," a statutory requirement that executive or administrative action, before becoming effective, be reviewed by Congress and approved—or in the more typical variation, not disapproved—within a specified period.[14] The veto power is sometimes lodged in both houses, more often in one house, occasionally even in a congressional committee. Such provisions are to be found in 196 statutes enacted since 1932, more than half of them (89) since 1970, and nearly one-fourth (46) between 1973 and 1975.[15] They have been employed in such diverse areas as national defense, foreign affairs, interior affairs, public works, immigration, transportation, and executive reorganization.[16] In the 94th Congress, a bill that would have subjected the administrative regulations of all departments and agencies to veto by concurrent resolution of both houses, or by a concurrent resolution of disapproval adopted by one house and not acted upon by the other, was narrowly defeated in the House of Representatives.[17]

The constitutionality of the legislative veto is a matter of sharp dispute.[18] There are those who say that both houses cannot validly delegate to a single house, let alone to a single committee, the power to approve or disapprove administrative regulations; that a congressional veto, whether exercised by one house or both, circumvents the constitutional requirement that every "Order, Resolution, or Vote" be presented to the President for his approval; and that a determination by Congress as to whether a proposed regulation is *ultra vires* invades the province of the judiciary under Article III.[19] The opposing view is that a law which conditions the effectiveness of an administrative regulation on the subsequent approval (or non-disapproval) of Congress is merely a limitation upon the original, admittedly valid, delegation of rulemaking authority to the agency in question.

Constitutionality aside, the legislative veto is also open to objection on practical grounds. Congressional review of the thousands of regulations annually generated by the federal agencies would place a staggering burden on the limited resources of Congress and its staff; would expose each member to greatly intensified pressure from special interest lobbyists of all stripes; would subject the agencies themselves to new political pressures, putting powerful committee chairmen in a position to dictate the detailed content of regulations as the price of their approval; and would add a further element of delay to administrative processes already notoriously slow-grinding. At best, moreover, it is doubtful whether review of individual regulations on a current basis would supply the agencies with that basic policy guidance they have so long needed.

Another much discussed oversight mechanism is the "sunset law,"

James O. Freedman and Frank Goodman

which would establish fixed expiration dates for federal agencies and programs and require affirmative reauthorization by Congress in order to perpetuate them. The device has not been widely used to date; only 14 of the 235 agencies, boards, and commissions created between 1960 and 1973 were given a fixed lifespan.[20] Still, the "sunset" idea is not new. Justice Douglas once suggested to President Roosevelt that the lifespan of all New Deal agencies be limited to ten years.[21] More recently, Professor Theodore Lowi proposed a tenure-of-statutes act that would set a time limit of five to ten years on the life of every organic act.[22] Supporters of this approach argue that the need for continuing renewal of their congressional mandates will not only give Congress an opportunity to reexamine the need for the agency and weed out obsolete and duplicative programs, but will also help to avoid the hardening of arteries that so often seems to afflict aging regulatory agencies that have outlived their mandates. Lloyd Cutler has suggested that the greater vitality and effectiveness that seems characteristic of younger agencies "may result less from their youth than from their role in pursuing goals that our political institutions have just recently proclaimed and continue to support."[23] But a Senate bill introduced in the 94th Congress and reintroduced in the 95th, would comprehensively "sunset" all government activities and programs.[24] For each category of program, it would establish a termination date for existing budgetary authority and require, in connection with any future reauthorization, that the standing committees of both houses conduct, every four years, a zero-based evaluation of all programs within their respective jurisdictions. In this way, all related governmental activities in each area of regulation would be reviewed quadrennially and obsolete and duplicative elements identified and weeded out.

Yet another approach to regulatory reform is the congressionally mandated presidential reform plan, which would require the President to submit to Congress a comprehensive plan of reform for each of the major areas of regulation.[25] Each such plan would contain an evaluation of the existing regulatory framework and recommendations—procedural, structural, and substantive—for its reform. The underlying premise of this proposal is that the President is in a better position to initiate regulatory reform than congressional committees which, over the years, have developed strong vested interests in the existing system. In one proposed variation, the President's reform plans would in each instance become law unless vetoed by either house within a sixty-day period.[26] The one-house veto approach traditionally used in reorganizations of the executive branch would thus be extended to regulatory activities outside the executive branch and to matters of substantive as well as structural reform. This variation recognizes the difficulty of mustering a national, and therefore a legislative, consensus for any particular reform—even when there is universal dissatisfaction with the existing state of affairs—and deals with the problem by shifting the burden of overcoming congres-

sional inertia from those who favor to those who oppose the execu-
tive-initiated reform, so that the inevitable legislative discordance
will result in change rather than perpetuation of the status quo.

One member of the committee noted these developments in passing
but took a dim view of them. Congress, he cautioned, ought not involve itself too deeply in the detailed business of administration. It
lacks the resources to do so and, in the attempt, may weaken its
effectiveness as a representative body. Even without ambitious new
ventures in oversight, congressional committees consume a large proportion of the total staff and informational resources of Congress;
the individual congressman, who lacks these resources except in his
capacity as a committee member, is hard put to make an independent
judgment, on behalf of his constituents, on the great volume of
legislation emanating from committees to which he does not belong.
Very often, perhaps too often, he is forced to defer to the more
informed judgment of the committee.

This last observation significantly qualifies the earlier general picture of Congress as passively subservient to public opinion. That
picture ignores the central role of the congressional committee system.[27] The 200 standing committees and subcommittees of both
houses, each with its own staff and special subject-matter jurisdiction,
is a reservoir of specialized knowledge, competence, even expertise,
in many cases rivaling that of the bureaucracy itself. In their committee work congressmen often display a craftsmanship and creativity
in the art of legislation, an independence of judgment in matters of
policy, that stamps them as far more than mere registrars of their
constituents' opinions. Certain committees, moreover, and their powerful chairmen, serve as pressure points upon which minority and
other interest groups can exert effective influence without having to
buttonhole the entire membership of the Congress. To be sure, assignment to some House committees (e.g., Interior and Insular, Post
Office and Civil Service) is valued chiefly as a means of serving local
constituency interests and thus strengthening the member's reelection
prospects. Seats on other House committees, however, are viewed as
opportunities to promote policy-oriented goals, (e.g., Education and
Labor, International Relations) or to enhance the member's prestige
and influence in the House (e.g., Appropriations, Ways and Means).[28]
In either case, the legislation that emerges from committee is often
quite different, in detail and even in basic concept, from that which
would be produced (if any would) by men and women interested only
in following the orders of those who elected them.

THE PRESIDENCY

The committee's discussion of the presidency focused almost exclusively upon what might be called "the lessons of Watergate." The
pervading theme was that the presidency, and in particular the White
House staff by which the President is increasingly surrounded and
insulated, has grown too great, is insufficiently accountable either to
Congress or to the public, and by one means or another should be

James O. Freedman and Frank Goodman

cut down to size. The White House staff, it was argued—persons appointed without senatorial confirmation and, by virtue of the executive privilege doctrine, largely immune to congressional oversight—cuts the President off from vital sources of information and experience and wields enormous power in his name but often without his knowledge. Two specific correctives were put forward for discussion: that the appointment of principal members of the White House staff be made subject to senatorial confirmation and that the concepts of national security and executive privilege be clearly defined and narrowly circumscribed either by statute, judicial decision, or, if necessary, by constitutional revision.

Neither proposal found much support among the discussants. Senatorial confirmation of chief White House aides was viewed as a futile gesture. Rarely if ever would, or should, the Senate reject the President's choice for a position of such close personal trust. The President is the best judge of who and how many should labor at his right hand. Furthermore, the power to confirm is not necessarily the power to control and, even if it were, the power to confirm those who nominally hold high ranking White House titles is not necessarily the power to confirm those to whom the President actually listens and assigns responsibilities. Congressional scrutiny of top White House appointments would not prevent the President from relying, in whatever way he wished, upon nominally inferior aides of his own sole choosing. The White House is essentially a political institution; its formal structure is unimportant, while its true operating structure cannot be imposed from the outside. "The structure of the White House," observed one of the panelists, "is, inevitably, the structure of a bowl of jello."

The second proposal—that national security and executive privilege be clearly defined—likewise stirred no enthusiasm. Some discussants took the view that, in the long run, these concepts will mean as much or as little as the President can persuade the country to accept; and, in any case, even if executive privilege were defined more narrowly and governmental secrecy considerably relaxed, it is unlikely that Congress or the public would be any better informed. Pressed for information, the President might simply send to Congress a paper haystack without disclosing where the critical needles of information were to be found.

One proposal relating to executive privilege did have some appeal—that the privilege should be available only when invoked by the President himself, on a case-by-case basis, in writing and with accompanying reasons. These procedural requirements, it was hoped, might reduce the number of occasions on which executive privilege is claimed, and even more important, might be the most effective means of scaling down the White House staff: a President might be more reluctant to surround himself with a legion of assistants if he knew that each could be called before congressional committees without the shield of executive privilege.

Some members of the committee questioned whether the White

House staff was really a major long-term problem after all. Helpless though Congress may be to affect the matter, the President himself—any President who has learned the lessons of Watergate—can be expected, on his own, to scale down his staff. Indeed, it was noted, President Ford had already done so. (It might be added that in February of 1977 President Carter announced that White House personnel would be reduced by as much as one-third[29]).

Furthermore, a transfer of functions from the White House to the cabinet departments might not be an unmixed blessing from the standpoint of increasing the political accountability of the federal bureaucracy. The transferred activities might become more amenable to congressional oversight but only by becoming less amenable to presidential direction and control.

Indeed, the diminishing ability of the President to impose his policy preferences upon the vast bureaucracies of the executive branch, let alone the independent regulatory agencies, is one of the central problems of American government. In the words of one authority:

> The President is not strong but weak: He has lost control of the departments, of domestic policy, and, as we see in Watergate, even his own House. He has retreated into foreign policy, but even there he must share his authority with Congress . . . So much attention has been given, in recent years, to the growth of executive power that an essential point has been overlooked. It is true the executive branch has taken upon itself extraordinary powers—war, peace, control of the economy. This does not mean, however, that the man elected by the people to the presidency can actually wield these powers. He does not rule, he reigns—with the deplorable result that no one responsive to the people governs the country.[30]

The political unaccountability of the federal bureaucracy is thus a problem which far transcends the White House staff or the executive office of the President. Indeed, the growth of the "presidency" largely represents an effort by successive Presidents from Roosevelt through Nixon to gain more effective control over, and thus increase the political responsibility of, the departments and agencies of the executive branch. Diminishing the "presidency," as a reaction to Watergate, will not solve the larger problem and could even exacerbate it.

Still in the Watergate vein, the committee addressed itself also to the problem of impeachment. It was proposed that the Constitution should be amended to make easier the removal of the President who has abused his office or can no longer govern effectively. Several specifics were discussed.

One was to institute at the federal level the recall device so widely adopted in the states. Another was that Congress, by a suitably large majority, should be permitted to cast a vote of no-confidence in the President and, thereby, secure his removal. Still another suggestion was to relax the present standard for impeachment—"high crimes and

James O. Freedman and Frank Goodman

misdemeanors"—so as to permit removal for "conduct unbecoming the presidency."

None of these ideas got much support. The prevailing view seemed to be that both the recall and no-confidence devices would seriously destabilize the office and that loosening the constitutional standard for impeachment would introduce too large a measure of subjectivity and discretion. The one suggestion along those lines that met no opposition was that the Congress, by statute, should spell out the concept of high crimes and misdemeanors and set up an ongoing institutional mechanism for impeachment, perhaps in the form of a standing impeachment committee with jurisdiction to investigate charges against executive officers.

On the whole, the committee's discussion of the presidency seems remarkably narrow in scope. In light of the committee's earlier consensus that Congress could not be looked to as an effective instrument of national planning, one might have expected a searching examination of the strengths and weaknesses of the executive branch as a policy-making body. Instead, the executive was regarded exclusively through Watergate lenses as a potential public enemy which ought to be weakened, rather than strengthened. The central question left unanswered, indeed unasked, was whether in our federal government, there is any institution which can effectively perform the vital planning function, a responsibility that becomes ever more important in a world of shrinking resources, environmental fragility, and inflated public expectations.

THE JUDICIARY

In discussing the effectiveness of the judiciary, the committee had before it an issues paper by Professor Henry J. Abraham, one of the nation's leading political scientists, who has written extensively on the work of the Supreme Court. Professor Abraham's paper reviewed a body of evidence suggesting that the American people regard the judiciary as the most effective of the nation's major governmental institutions, as well as the one most conscientious in protecting their civil liberties. Why have the American people reached this conclusion?

Performance of the Supreme Court

Several members of the committee suggested that the Supreme Court, by the character of its performance, has contributed to this high public estimate in at least two important respects. First, the Court has shown decisive capacity, particularly in the last generation, to resolve significant public issues of a kind that the American people believed should be resolved and that the political process had been unable to resolve. When the political process has been paralyzed on the resolution of such issues, the Supreme Court has been the institution that has rescued the nation from the stalemate.

Two of the most important recent examples of such action by the Court are *Brown* v. *Board of Education*,[31] which resolved the historic dilemma of segregation, and *Reynolds* v. *Sims*,[32] which resolved the historic problem of malapportioned legislative representation—issues as to which the political process was peculiarly unable to achieve reform in ways that the American people quite clearly understood reform was needed.

Second, the Supreme Court, over the course of generations, has more satisfactorily met public expectations as to its appropriate role in American life than the other major institutions of government. Its decision in *United States* v. *Nixon*, enforcing the Special Prosecutor's subpoena for certain presidential tapes, is perhaps a pertinent recent example.[33] By deciding that case at all, the Court met public expectations that it would serve as an umpire in a significant contest between two major centers of power within government. By deciding the case expeditiously—within three months of the issuance of the subpoena by the district judge—the Court met public expectations that it would not permit the constitutional confrontation facing the nation to be protracted. And by deciding the case on the merits in the manner that it did, the Court met public expectations as to the proper result; indeed, the American people almost certainly would have been surprised, if not chagrined, had the result been different.

These considerations led many members of the committee to the view that recommendations for changes of a constitutional dimension in the role of the Supreme Court in American government should be considered only with the greatest deliberation.

Selection of the Judiciary

The committee gave considerable attention to the quality of the nation's judiciary and to the criteria by which judges should be selected. That judges should be selected by merit was readily agreed to. But what constitutes merit, and what qualities in addition to merit may properly be given weight?

Few would disagree that professional competence—possession in a very high degree of the technical skills of the lawyer—was an appropriate, indeed essential, factor for a President to take into account in appointing a justice of the United States Supreme Court. One committee member suggested that a lawyer's stature within the profession would provide a President with a reliable index of a prospective nominee's professional competence. Although this will often be the case, the memory of seven former presidents of the American Bar Association asserting that Louis D. Brandeis was not qualified to sit on the United States Supreme Court is not reassuring.[34]

To professional competence, some students of the Supreme Court would add prior judicial experience as a desirable, if not indispensable, qualification for effective service on the Court. Measures that would require that Supreme Court justices have judicial experience of a specified duration, either on a lower federal court or on a state court, have been introduced into Congress regularly during the last three decades.

The argument that a justice of the Supreme Court should have

James O. Freedman and Frank Goodman

some prior judicial experience has a superficial plausibility. But that plausibility dissolves when one examines the history of the Court. Among those justices who had no judicial experience at the time of their appointment to the Supreme Court are some of the most distinguished in that institution's history, including Wilson, Marshall, Story, Taney, Miller, Bradley, Hughes, Brandeis, Stone, Jackson, Black, Frankfurter, and Warren. However, a number of the Court's most distinguished justices did have judicial experience before their appointments, including Brewer, Field, White, Holmes, and Cardozo. The fact that some justices of intellectual distinction had prior judicial experience while others did not suggests the wisdom of Justice Frankfurter's conclusion that "it would be capricious, to attribute acknowledged greatness in the Court's history either to the fact that a justice had had judicial experience or that he had been without it."[35]

Indeed, Justice Frankfurter argued that, beyond the *ad hominem* refutation, prior judicial experience "has no significant relation to the kinds of litigation that come before the Supreme Court, to the types of issues they raise, to qualities that these actualities require for wise decision."[36] For this further reason, too, he concluded that "the correlation between prior judicial experience and fitness for the functions of the Supreme Court is zero."[37]

Even if prior judicial experience is discounted as a qualification for a Supreme Court justice, personal qualities of mind and character beyond professional competence are surely desirable. One member of the committee recalled the prescription, attributed to Justice Brennan, that a Supreme Court justice ideally should be a lawyer, a historian, a philosopher, a prophet, and a person of inordinate patience. Learned Hand, perhaps our wisest judge, refined the prescription:

> I venture to believe that it is as important to a judge called upon to pass on a question of constitutional law, to have at least a bowing acquaintance with Acton and Maitland, with Thucydides, Gibbon and Carlyle, with Homer, Dante, Shakespeare and Milton, with Machiavelli, Montaigne and Rabelais, with Plato, Bacon, Hume and Kant, as with the books which have been specifically written on the subject.[38]

In selecting justices of the Supreme Court, a President is often urged to give weight to considerations of geographical distribution and experiential diversity. For Justice Frankfurter, geographical considerations were an irrelevance that could lead a President to a narrower range of choice than that to which the nation was entitled. Had President Hoover heeded such considerations, he might not have named Benjamin N. Cardozo, a New Yorker, to a Court on which two justices from New York already sat.[39] "The pride of a region in having one of its own on the Court," Justice Frankfurter concluded, "does not outweigh the loss to the Court and the country in so narrowing the search for the most qualified."[40]

Yet for some members of the committee geographical distribution among the members of the Supreme Court was an important factor in enhancing the acceptability, the persuasiveness, and the legitimacy of the decisions that the Court reached. Thus, the suggestion was made that the decision in *Brown* v. *Board of Education* may have gained a greater measure of acceptance in the South because of the fact that Justice Black, an Alabaman, sat upon the Court that pronounced it.

One member of the committee, in explaining his support for considering geographical diversity, invoked a psychological dimension as to how the values of Supreme Court justices are shaped during their service. He argued that public officials who live in Washington, D.C. for long periods of time tend unconsciously to absorb (or be absorbed by) what he described as an eastern United States world view. When decisions of the Supreme Court in a number of significant areas are seen as reflecting a single set of coherent values identified with a particular region of the country, the acceptability of the Court's work among those who regard this view as merely provincial is jeopardized.

The proponent of this argument said that an eastern United States world view could be seen as working itself out in the Court's decisions in areas in which societal standards were changing, such as civil liberties and the regulation of morals. He called particular attention to decisions involving school prayer, abortion, and the rights of criminal suspects and defendants.[41] Whether these decisions are properly attributable to an eastern United States world view, there are surely exceptions to the hypothesis, as the Court's recent decision sustaining the constitutionality of state criminal regulation of adult consensual homosexual conduct done in private suggests.[42]

The arguments supporting experiential diversity as a consideration in the appointment of Supreme Court justices are easily understood. A Court is strengthened in its competence and self-assurance when it includes among its members those whose professional experiences—whether it be as corporate specialists, civil rights litigators, labor negotiators, administrative lawyers, law professors, or political officials—supplement each other.

The committee divided sharply, however, when its discussion moved beyond considerations of professional competence, prior judicial experience, geographical distribution, and personal experience to considerations of race, religion, and national origin. Those who argued that a President might properly take such considerations into account in the selection of Supreme Court justices stressed the strengths by way of insight and experience that members of minority groups in the population can bring to the Court's deliberations. They also maintained that the presence of members of minority groups on a court inspires confidence in its work-product. If the Court's decisions are accorded a greater measure of legitimacy and acceptability in the country at large when they are reached by a group of justices who are geographically diverse, these committee members asked, why would not the same consequence follow from decisions reached by a group of justices which included representatives of significant minorities in the population?

146   *James O. Freedman and Frank Goodman*

But many committee members argued that consideration of racial, religious, or ethnic factors in the appointment of Supreme Court justices was subversive of the basic American principle that individuals be considered solely on their merits as individuals. They argued further that reliance on the premise that, as a matter of fairness or right, there should be a Jewish seat or a black seat or an Italian seat or a female seat on the Supreme Court could too readily result in acceptance of such single seats as quotas or limitations upon the appointment of additional Jews, blacks, Italians, or women to the Court, to the possible detriment both of the group and of the institution.

Role of the President and Senate

A rather different concern with respect to the appointment process was also expressed: that in recent years Presidents of the United States have chosen increasingly to play little more than a perfunctory role in the appointment of judges to the lower federal courts.

The institution of "senatorial courtesy" has traditionally constrained a President's freedom in the nomination of federal judges. Under this custom, the Senate refuses to confirm a judicial nominee if a senator from his state declares him personally obnoxious to him, particularly when the senator making the objection is of the same political party as the President.

One consequence of this custom has been to permit one member of the Senate to dictate that body's rejection of a President's nominee. Another consequence has been to require the President to share his appointment power with particular senators in particular cases—a consequence that has often prompted private negotiations between the White House and the senator involved until agreement on a nominee could be reached.[43]

Several members of the committee reported that Presidents of both political parties have followed a practice in recent years of essentially delegating the task of selecting judges for the lower federal courts to the senators from the state in which the appointment is to be made, so that there is no effective presidential act of judgment in the selection process at all. This means that the quality of individuals nominated to federal judgeships is often no better than the quality of the senators from the state in which the prospective judge will sit. This practice is particularly alarming when seen in light of the fact that the Senate rarely devotes the kind of consideration and scrutiny to the qualifications of those nominated for positions on the lower federal courts that it does to prospective justices of the Supreme Court.

Thus, the formalities of presidential nomination and Senate confirmation do not operate—as the framers undoubtedly intended—as separate stages of independent judgment and of effective restraint upon the appointment of undistinguished individuals to the federal bench. If the quality of the federal judiciary is to be sustained or improved, Presidents must reassert a serious interest in the appointments made in their name, and the Senate must examine the qualifications of judicial nominees with greater care than it has in the recent past.

Utility of the Adversary System

At the suggestion of Professor Abraham, the committee focused, although only briefly, upon whether the adversary system adequately serves the ends of justice.[44] In recent years a number of thoughtful commentators have questioned whether the adversary system is the method best suited to try issues of constitutional significance, to attain justice in mine-run lawsuits, or to provide legal redress to the poor in civil cases.[45]

Professor Abraham's issues paper had suggested that the United States consider adoption of an inquisitorial system of justice, a system used in many European countries, in place of the adversary system we now use. Under an inquisitorial system, the investigation and assembling of the facts is done primarily by an impartial state official rather than by the lawyers engaged to vigorously represent the interests of the respective parties. The role of juries, so central to the functioning of justice in an adversary system, is small or nonexistent.

Some commentators believe that an inquisitorial system places a greater value upon the ascertainment of truth and is more expeditious than the adversary system.[46] In a period when many persons are concerned that the adversary system contributes to the "law's delay" and too often turns results on tactical technicalities, consideration of alternate systems of justice is surely desirable.

But the committee was not persuaded that adoption of the inquisitorial system was desirable. One member argued that the chief virtues of an inquisitorial system were the maintenance of order and the enforcement of discipline, rather than the refined attainment of individualized justice. He added that for this reason inquisitorial systems work best in military contexts, such as courts-martial. Because the adversary system is so deeply embedded in the traditions of our nation, any attempt to replace it, even if only in selected areas, can be expected to be greeted skeptically.

Organization of Judicial Resources

The committee discussed briefly a series of questions relating to what might be called the organization of judicial resources. The questions included the following:

First, should the jurisdiction of the federal district courts to hear cases based upon the diversity of citizenship of the litigants be abolished, in order to relieve the federal courts of a class of litigation that many judges and scholars regard as more properly decided by state courts?[47] Several committee members suggested that the greatest barrier to elimination of diversity jurisdiction was the bar's conviction that the quality of justice was higher in federal courts than in state courts.

Second, should the requirement that certain kinds of federal claims must be heard by three-judge federal district courts, with a direct appeal to the Supreme Court, be modified or eliminated, in order to con-

James O. Freedman and Frank Goodman

serve federal judicial resources at the trial level and reduce the obligatory workload of the Supreme Court?[48]

Third, should the salaries of federal judges be raised in order to insure that the most competent men and women are attracted to, and retained by, the federal bench? This subject had a particular immediacy since a number of federal judges had resigned during the preceding year because they said they could not support their families and educate their children on a judge's salary. Some members of the committee thought it contextually inappropriate to argue that the salaries of federal judges should be raised when, at the same time, it was being argued that the crisis of the nation's cities was attributable in part to the excessive salary demands of other public employees who did not happen to be judges, such as postal workers, firemen, policemen, and sanitation men.

Election or Appointment of State Court Judges

The committee considered the relative wisdom of the election or appointment of state court judges. Although most judges were appointed by state governors during the nation's early years, many states moved to an elective system during the period when the theories of Jacksonian democracy were dominant. The election of judges was regarded then as a device for protecting workers and tenants of land against judges too closely allied with the interests of the landed gentry. In later generations, those who support the election of judges have argued that it is more consistent with democratic theory than the appointment of judges, and that it produces a judiciary more nearly reflective of the diversity of groups in the community and more sensitive to the climate of social change.

In many states, of course, the elective system has become involved with politics in the worse sense. For this reason, many persons believe that a system providing for the appointment of judges, whatever its faults, reduces the influence of political factors and permits the appointment of judges who would refuse to seek the office in a contested election. Because the evaluation of judicial performance is an inexact art, the question of which system produces the more qualified judges is not easily answered.

The Role of the Supreme Court

The committee spent relatively little time, perhaps surprisingly, on questions of the proper role of the Supreme Court in American society. Professor Abraham's paper had described the most significant of these questions—as well as the most vexatious and crucial—as requiring line-drawing for their resolution: the separation of the judicial function from the legislative function, the delineation of the proper bounds of judicial self-restraint and judicial activism, and the separation of the process of adjudicating winners and losers in lawsuits from the process of making large policy determinations in the course of deciding those lawsuits.

There was brief discussion of whether the Supreme Court should undertake to play a larger role in the area of national security than it has in the past. One member of the committee argued vigorously that the Supreme Court should assert jurisdiction over cases seeking· to place judicial controls upon what he called the police bureaucracy, particularly the FBI and the CIA. The argument was that bureaucrats engaged in paramilitary activities should be judged by the same standards and made subject to the same scrutiny in the exercise of power as other civil servants are.

If the Court were to assert jurisdiction in this area, it would in some instances have to change its traditional position, based upon Article III's case-and-controversy requirement, that considerations of national security, properly pleaded, render such cases nonjusticiable.

Other members of the committee suggested that Article III properly restricts many judicial interventions of the kind proposed because the Supreme Court lacks the resources—for example, its own State Department—to permit it to be adequately informed in deciding such cases. This position was forcefully outlined by Mr. Justice Jackson in *Chicago and Southern Air Lines* v. *Waterman Steamship Corp.*,[49] in which the Court held that it could not review presidential orders, issued pursuant to the Civil Aeronautics Act, granting or denying certificates of convenience and necessity to American air carriers for foreign air transport:

> The President, both as Commander-in-Chief and as the Nation's organ for foreign affairs, has available intelligence services whose reports are not and ought not to be published to the world. It would be intolerable that courts, without the relevant information, should review and perhaps nullify actions of the Executive taken on information properly held secret. . . . They are decisions of a kind for which the Judiciary has neither aptitude, facilities nor responsibility and which has long been held to belong in the domain of political power not subject to judicial intrusion or inquiry.[50]

FEDERALISM

In creating the Constitution, the framers made the national government supreme within its compass. But the national government was limited in that compass to the specific powers granted it. All of the powers not granted to the national government were retained by the states or by the sovereign people.

The federal system described by the Constitution thus contemplates that governmental power will be distributed among many political units. One commentator has defined federalism as

> the mode of political organization that unites smaller polities within an overarching political system by distributing power among general and constituent governments in a manner de-

signed to protect the existence and authority of both national and subnational political systems, enabling all to share in the overall system's decision-making and executing processes.[51]

By diffusing governmental power among many constituent units, the structure of federalism seeks to protect the nation against the dangers that might be presented if excessive authority were centralized in the national government. It also permits the constituent units of government, in a theme often sounded by Louis D. Brandeis, to be laboratories for social experimentation, thereby creating the possibility of a greater degree of diversity in governmental styles and political responses than could be achieved if all authority were centralized in the national government. Finally, in a nation of continental scope a federal system permits many policies that affect the daily lives and welfare of the people to be adopted at a nearer rather than a farther reach, thereby creating the opportunity for a greater degree of citizen participation in their formulation.

But federalism is more than merely an arrangement of governmental structures. It is also a mode of political activity calling for the creation of a partnership properly balanced to achieve its goals.

For much of the nation's history, political scientists regarded the achievement of the efficient delivery of governmental services as perhaps the central goal of the federal system. Under this conception, a well-designed federal system would strive to eliminate the duplication of the governmental services by limiting the provision of any particular service to the governmental unit equipped to provide it most efficiently. The possibility that redundancy in the provision of certain services might sometimes be a useful device for accomplishing national goals received little consideration. This conception of federalism was reinforced by many of the attitudes of the Progressive era, which typically sought to find apolitical means of accommodating the nation's governmental structure to the contemporary understanding of political realities.

In recent years, political scientists have formulated a more sophisticated conception of the challenges of federalism. This newer conception suggests that questions distributing governmental power among many political units are primarily questions of politics, rather than of efficiency or structure, that must be judged from a political perspective. The maintenance of the federal system as a balanced partnership among the constituent units of government requires that political choices be made.

In considering the implications of some of the choices that the United States has made, the committee's discussion focused on four major themes: the trend toward centralization of power in the national government; considerations of scale in the design of governmental units; citizen participation in governmental decision-making; and the need for more empirical information on how the federal system actually works in the administration of specific programs.

Deliberations of Committee II   151

The Trend Toward National Centralization of Authority

It is a fact of national life that power in the federal system has increasingly gravitated from the states to the federal government during the past half-century. This trend has been the result of many factors, including the nation's desire for economic regulation and welfare protections that only the federal government could provide.

Perhaps the central question for a contemporary consideration of federalism is whether this trend toward national centralization of authority can be reversed or in principle ought to be reversed. As this trend has developed, the shape of our federalism has undoubtedly changed. Some commentators, such as Rexford G. Tugwell, go so far as to argue that federalism as it has evolved no longer serves a useful purpose and should be formally replaced with a pattern of regional governmental units.[52]

Many committee members expressed the belief that the scale of modern economic activity and the dimensions of contemporary social problems left the nation no effective alternative to centralizing increasing amounts of regulatory power in the national government.

Two examples upon which the committee focused are illustrative. First, control of air pollution is one of the essential goals of the nation's environmental policy. If the achievement of that goal were left entirely to state and local governments, each such government would surely have an incentive to set pollution standards at a level sufficiently low to attract industry to it at the expense of states with more stringent standards. The enactment of low pollution standards by one state would also have a deleterious impact on the environmental quality of neighboring states. In such a situation, the federal government has no alternative to a chaotic competition among states except the setting of national minimal standards.

Second, the growth to public prominence of multinational corporations having a momentous impact upon the American and world economy, as well as upon communities, citizens, investors, and smaller businesses, has inspired concern for more effective public regulation. It seems unlikely that such corporations—many of which are larger than some state governments in resources and influence—can truly be regulated effectively by any authority less powerful than the federal government.

The fiscal crisis of New York City figured prominently in this discussion. Many committee members thought that New York City's experience demonstrated that local governments could no longer be expected to be effective in responding to economic and social problems of the magnitude of those now facing our urban areas. They argued that centralization of power in the federal government is inevitable if these problems, particularly the care of the poor, the unemployed, the ill, and the elderly, are to be addressed effectively.

But what factors caused New York City's fiscal crisis? Two were mentioned most frequently: (1) the federal preemption of control with respect to many programs having a significant local impact, often by

James O. Freedman and Frank Goodman

attractive federal statutes mandating local spending commitments; (2) the city's lack of a prosperous tax base and a thriving productive capacity.

Some committee members believed, to the contrary, that New York City was itself the author of many of its problems, having created its financial crisis by choosing to pay higher salaries to public employees and to provide a wider range of public services to its citizens than almost any other city in the country.

Whatever the underlying factors, many members of the committee seemed persuaded that New York City's financial crisis had demonstrated the inadequacy of classic formulations of federalism and of conventional arguments for decentralization. The events in New York City may prove to be a watershed in the realization that many of the nation's most severe domestic problems can be solved only by the national government.

The committee also discussed one of the more heralded of recent political initiatives bearing on the allocation of power in the federal system—the "new federalism" of the Nixon administration.[53] The stated purpose of that program was to return a measure of authority and responsibility to state and local governments by means of various revenue sharing devices. But the committee's discussion seemed to suggest that the term "new federalism" was more Orwellian than precise.

Several committee members reported that the primary political consequence of the "new federalism" had been an increase, rather than a decrease, in the authority of the federal government with respect to the substantive programs involved. One of the most significant administrative consequences of the "new federalism" was a strengthening of the authority of the Office of Management and Budget over programs not previously within its ken. In addition, the "new federalism" permitted the President to exercise greater authority across bureaucratic and departmental lines with respect to diverse programs that had formerly resisted efforts at a coordinated White House domination.

In short, many committee members believed that the administrative methods chosen to implement the "new federalism" had had the effect, whether coincidental or intended, of increasing the authority of the President and weakening the power of the federal bureaucracy, without enlarging the authority of state and local governments in any important respects. A program described as a "new federalism" thus became, in the view of many committee members, a new centralization.

Some committee members expressed the further view that the revenue sharing programs that comprised the heart of the "new federalism" had been too modest in dimension to be regarded as significant experiments in federalism, since the funds transferred represented only a marginal increase in state and local budgeting over a wide range of domestic functions.

Still, as other committee members contended, these programs had, in small ways, brought a new public focus to federalism and given

Deliberations of Committee II   153 support, even if only moral or largely symbolic, to the belief that state and local governments are important and responsible units in decision-making that affects the people directly. These programs were, in short, at least symbolic gestures toward strengthening the *sense* of federalism.

Many committee members thought that any significant federal attempt to enlarge the dimensions of revenue sharing programs would inevitably be accompanied by the imposition of greater federal control over these programs. Political history suggests that the federal government, in giving substantial amounts of money to the states and to local governments, invariably imposes increasingly restrictive conditions upon how the money may be spent—an action that would reverse the ostensible purpose of delegating power to state and local governments in the first place.

Considerations of Scale in Designing Governmental Units

If the respective units of government in a federal system are to be efficient as well as responsive to political realities, they must be designed to be appropriate in scale to the functions they are expected to perform.

The relationship between scale and function in the performance of tasks generally has been trenchantly discussed in E. F. Schumacher, the British economist, in his book, *Small is Beautiful:*

> For every activity there is a certain appropriate scale, and the more active and intimate the activity, the smaller the number of people that can take part, the greater is the number of such relationship arrangements that need to be established. Take teaching: one listens to all sorts of extraordinary debates about the superiority of the teaching machine over some other forms of teaching. Well, let us discriminate: what are we trying to teach? It then becomes immediately apparent that certain things can only be taught in a very intimate circle, whereas other things can obviously be taught en masse, via the air, via television, via teaching machines, and so on.[54]

What Schumacher writes of the relationship between scale and function in the process of teaching has equal applicability to the process of governing a nation of more than 200 million people.

But how does one decide what is an appropriate scale—an appropriate order of magnitude—for a particular unit of government, whether it be the national government, a state government, or a local government? Put most simplistically, the answer must depend upon the nature of the tasks that the governmental unit is expected to perform.

Many functions that government is expected to perform can be performed effectively only by a unit of government as large as the national government itself. The defense of the nation against foreign enemies is a ready example of one such function. Other governmental

James O. Freedman and Frank Goodman

functions are probably performed most effectively by local units of government. Maintenance of streets and parks are examples of such functions.

The committee began with the premise that the assignment of specific functions to particular units of government must be guided by criteria that seek to optimize such values as the efficient and humane performance of the functions involved, the maintenance of a productive economic and tax base for the unit of government involved, the creation of effective and meaningful opportunities for citizen participation in governmental decision-making, and the provision of cultural activities, recreational resources, and social amenities to all groups of citizens.

If all of the basic units of government were alike, it would be possible to ask what the appropriate scale of government should be in order to optimize the desired values in the performance of particular functions. But the reality is that the basic units of government are not alike. Rather, they are almost kaleidoscopically heterogeneous in many significant respects.

Thus, many of the major cities of the nation have become poorer every year as middle class families have moved to the suburbs in increasing numbers, leaving the cities with reduced productive and financial resources and a higher percentage of poor people having a disproportionate need for social and welfare services. By contrast, most suburban communities have become enclaves for the rich and the moderately affluent, with an increasing capacity to provide an expanded range of governmental services. In short, the social and economic bases of many communities have changed drastically. Similarly, some states and counties are relatively compact and have a homogeneous population, while other states and counties are far-flung geographically and embrace diverse kinds of communities.

In light of these considerations, the committee's members seemed in agreement that abstract efforts to allocate governmental functions to units differentiated only by the word "state" or "city" or "county" would not produce a workable scheme. Efforts to assign governmental tasks had to be made on a more realistic, more empirical basis.

Much of the committee's discussion focused, once again, upon the economic crisis of New York City. Did that crisis demonstrate, as some members of the committee thought, that cities were obsolete in many significant respects and could no longer be regarded as effective units of government in the federal system? Did it also demonstrate, as other members thought, that a city of eight million people was hardly of an appropriate scale to perform the functions expected of a local government? Or did it further demonstrate, as still other members argued, that the problems of urban areas have become so severe that they cannot be met by city governments as presently designed?

Some members of the committee thought that the economic crisis of New York City demonstrated all three propositions and left little alternative to the centralization in the national government of the power to cope with many of the basic problems—such as the provision of welfare and the construction of adequate housing—that states and cities have proven quite unable to confront effectively.

This conclusion suggests that one of the central challenges for a contemporary theory and practice of federalism is to devise means of meeting the problems of the cities—a task made more urgent by the fact that cities, as one committee member poignantly noted, have been enormously influential social organizations in American life as well as the producers and conservers of much that is valuable in our culture.

Citizen Participation in Governmental Decision-making

A third theme in the committee's discussion was the implications of federalism for citizen participation in governmental decision-making. What is the appropriate degree of citizen participation in governmental programs? How should a federal system be structured to achieve the desired degree of citizen participation? Would a federal system that placed more authority at the local level result in greater citizen participation in the decision-making processes of government?

The impulse toward increased citizen participation in governmental decision-making has been particularly strong during the last fifteen years. The slogan of the War on Poverty—that government policies should be framed and administered with the "maximum feasible participation" of those they are intended to serve[55]—anticipated a number of related developments that were to form a discernable pattern. Included among these developments were the enactment of the Freedom of Information Act[56] by the federal government, the adoption by many states of Government in the Sunshine Acts, and the growth of citizen and consumer groups under the guidance of figures like Ralph Nader.

These developments shared some common premises: that the growth of governmental power and bureaucracy had obliterated the voice of the average citizen, and that the government's claim of expertise in the administration of specialized programs was not alone a sufficient guarantor of the formulation of sound public policy or of the consideration of a sufficiently wide variety of views.

It now appears that the demand for greater opportunities for citizen participation in governmental decision-making was part of the nation's response to the larger crisis of accountability now attending many of our governmental institutions.[57] For this reason, it is likely that formal opportunities for greater citizen participation in many governmental processes, particularly those of administrative agencies,[58] will increase in the years just ahead.

Citizen participation may be regarded as an end desirable in itself—as a symbolic demonstration that sovereignty does indeed reside in the people, as a therapeutic act in the drama of citizenship, as a device to insure that decision-making is kept responsive to the needs of widely representative individuals. The committee's discussion was concerned with exploring how, if at all, effective citizen participation can be achieved.

One committee member suggested the need for fundamental con-

James O. Freedman and Frank Goodman

stitutional change. He argued that greater citizen participation and control could be achieved by redefining—in order to reinvigorate—the Ninth Amendment.[59] The argument was that the Ninth Amendment should be redefined from being concerned primarily with protecting individual privacy to being concerned primarily with strengthening local control and local power.

A Ninth Amendment so conceived might, for example, permit local chartering of banks and greater local control over commerce. In any event, so the argument went, the purpose of redefining the Ninth Amendment would be to achieve a fundamental constitutional statement that related issues of the appropriate relationship between scale and function in a federal system to issues of local control and participation.

But many committee members seemed to believe that changes of a constitutional dimension were premature in the present state of our knowledge about how citizen participation works and why it frequently does not work effectively. Indeed, these committee members questioned whether the experience of recent years gives any basis for believing that the creation of opportunities for citizen participation results in any significant degree of local control of governmental decision-making.

Repeated reference was made to the War on Poverty's attempt to enlist citizen efforts in ways that went beyond such conventional forms of participation as voting, becoming active in politics, running for elective office, and lobbying in the legislature.[60] The War on Poverty sought to change the character of citizen participation in the policy-making counsels of government.

Many members of the committee believed that the War on Poverty's efforts in this respect must be regarded as a failure. Few citizens apparently made the effort to participate or succeeded in participating at all, and those who did often found that local government officials were able to successfully resist sharing their decision-making authority with persons whom they regarded as outsiders.

Some members of the committee attributed the apparent failure of the War on Poverty's efforts in this direction to the fact that the attempt to change the character of participation was conceived by a few influential officials at the federal level but never received adequate support from the local governments that would be most affected. Other committee members observed that local bureaucrats and professional staff members can always retain control of small units of government, such as county health commissions and community action groups, more readily than they can of larger units. One committee member even noted, only partly in jest, that ordinary citizens often complain that town meetings, the most inclusive form of democratic governance, are "status ridden." Thus, some committee members concluded that the decision of the War on Poverty to focus upon small local units of government in an attempt to increase the capacity for, and the degree of, citizen participation in decision-making may have been unwise from the start.

These melancholy observations on the fate of the War on Poverty's efforts to increase citizen participation led several committee members to the belief that the task of structuring effective citizen participation in a federal system may be best achieved at levels other than the local. Some committee members suggested that, perhaps paradoxically, most citizens regard the federal government as the most open of the various units of government to which they are subject, as well as the most responsive to expressions of citizen opinion.

If these conclusions are correct, the goal of increasing the scope and enhancing the quality of citizen participation in governmental decision-making may finally be best achieved by structuring the federal system so that opportunities for participation exist especially at the national level, rather than at the state or local levels.

The Need for Empirical Studies

The committee's final theme concerned the implications of the fact that our knowledge of how the federal system actually operates in the administration of governmental programs is, at best, limited.

A number of committee members stated that although there is a considerable body of literature indicating what lawyers believe the public law of federalism ought to be, there are few significant studies that explore the interaction of local, county, state, and federal agencies at the level where services are actually rendered. What we need, they argued, are serious and substantial empirical studies of federalism in operation that approach in quality the studies we have of many of the nation's other governmental institutions.

By way of illustration, reference was made to the limited extent of our understanding of how the thousands of community mental health centers that were established during the Kennedy administration actually work. Creation of these centers was part of a new movement to treat the mentally ill and emotionally disturbed in community settings rather than in institutions. It was also part of a movement to commit the federal government to a share of responsibility in an area formerly left to state and local governments.

And yet, more than a decade later, we know very little about how the program has worked in practice. We know little about the effectiveness of the treatment and other services that these centers provide. We know little about the policies that these centers actually follow, and whether they are established by federal authorities or by local authorities, by bureaucrats, professionals, or citizens. Most important of all, we know little about whether community mental health centers have in any way proven a better method of delivering mental health services because of their relationship to every level of government in the federal system.

Committee members suggested that answers to questions such as these must be explored—with respect, of course, to the hundreds of programs administered cooperatively by the various levels of government—if we are to be in a position to decide wisely on what kinds of services are provided most effectively to whom by what levels of

James O. Freedman and Frank Goodman

government. The empirical challenge, as one member of the committee suggested, is a large one, since there are 3,500 counties that administer federally-originated programs; studies would have to be done of at least 100 of these counties if a serious contribution to our understanding of the federal system in operation were to be achieved.

The committee seemed persuaded that it may be more important at this stage of our political and intellectual development to acquire a more detailed empirical basis for understanding the functioning of "street-level bureaucracy" in administering a governmental program than it is to further refine the political science theories of federalism that the program may implicate. It is surely possible that case studies of the kind envisioned will take a generation to complete.

NOTES

1. Aaron Wildavsky, *"The Past and Future Presidency,"* The Public Interest 41 (Fall, 1975), p. 56 at p. 59.

2. Ibid., p. 59.

3. P.L. 85-315, 71 Stat. 634, 9 September 1957.

4. Henry J. Friendly, *The Federal Administrative Agencies: The Need for Better Definition of Standards* (Cambridge: Harvard University Press, 1962), p. 167.

5. Executive Order 9981 (26 July 1948).

6. *Brown v. Board of Education*, 347 U.S. 483 (1954).

7. P.L. 88-352, 78 Stat. 241, 2 July 1964.

8. P.L. 90-284, 82 Stat. 73, 11 April 1968.

9. P.L. 94-73, 89 Stat. 400, 6 August 1975.

10. A good statement of the pros and cons is found in Nelson W. Polsby, *Political Promises* (New York: Oxford University Press, 1974), pp. 101-7. See also Charles M. Hardin, *Presidential Power and Accountability* (Chicago: University of Chicago Press, 1974).

11. Polsby, *Political Promises*, p. 104.

12. See generally, Friendly, *The Federal Administrative Agencies*; Theodore J. Lowi, *The End of Liberalism* (New York: W. W. Norton & Co., Inc., 1968).

13. See, for example, Senate Committee on Government Operations, *Study on Federal Regulation*, 95th Cong., 1st Sess. (1977); Senate Committee on Government Operations, *Hearings on Improving Congressional Oversight of Federal Regulatory Agencies*, 94th Cong., 1st Sess. (1976).

14. See generally, Senate Committee on Government Operations, *Study on Federal Regulation*, vol. II, *Congressional Oversight of Regulatory Agencies*, pp. 115-22; Geoffrey S. Stewart, "Constitutionality of the Legislative Veto," *Harvard Journal on Legislation* 13 (1976), p. 593; Note, "Congressional Veto of Administrative Action: The Probable Response to a Constitutional Challenge," *Duke Law Journal*, (1976), p. 285; H. Lee Watson, "Congress Steps Out: A Look at Congressional Control of the Executive," *California Law Review* 63 (1975), p. 983.

15. *1976 Congressional Quarterly Almanac*, p. 508.

16. See generally, Senate Committee on Government Operations, *Study on Federal Regulation*, 95th Cong., 1st Sess. (1977).

17. H.R. 12048, 94th Cong., 2nd Sess. (1976); *Congressional Record* 122, (daily ed. 21 September 1976), pp. H-10718-10719.

18. See materials cited *supra* note 12.

19. The last objection is applicable particularly to proposals which require that the legislative veto be based upon a congressional finding that the proposed regulation is contrary to law, inconsistent with the intent of Congress, or goes beyond the mandate of the legislation it is designed to implement. See, e.g., S. 2258, 94th Cong. 1st Sess. (1975).

20. See generally, Senate Committee on Government Operations, *Study on Federal Regulation, supra* note 13 at p. 130.

21. William O. Douglas, *Go East, Young Man* (New York: Random House, Inc., 1974), p. 297.

22. Lowi, *The End of Liberalism*, p. 309.

23. Lloyd N. Cutler and David R. Johnson, "Regulation and the Political Process," *Yale Law Journal* 84 (1975), p. 1395.

24. S. 2925, 94th Cong., 2nd Sess. (1976); S. 2, 95th Cong., 1st Sess. (1977).

25. For example, S. 2258, 94th Cong., 1st Sess. (1975); S. 2812, 94th Cong., 1st Sess. (1975).

26. S. 2812, 94th Cong., 1st Sess. (1975).

27. Richard Fenno, *Congressmen in Committees* (Boston: Little, Brown & Co., 1973).

28. Ibid.

29. *New York Times*, 3 February 1977, p. 22.

30. Hugh G. Gallagher, "Presidents, Congress, and the Legislative Functions," in Rexford G. Tugwell and Thomas E. Cronin, eds., *The Presidency Reappraised* (New York: Praeger Publishers, Inc., 1974), pp. 217, 219.

31. 347 U.S. 483 (1954).

32. 377 U.S. 533 (1964).

33. 418 U.S. 683 (1974). Compare *Senate Select Committee on Presidential Campaign Activities* v. *Nixon*, 498 F.2d 725 (D.C. Cir. 1974).

34. Alden Todd, *Justice on Trial* (New York: McGraw-Hill, Inc., 1964).

35. Felix Frankfurter, "The Supreme Court in the Mirror of Justices," *University of Pennsylvania Law Review* 105 (1957), p. 781 at p. 784.

36. Ibid., at p. 785. Justice Holmes expressed similar views shortly after his appointment to the Court, following twenty years of service on the Supreme Judicial Court of Massachusetts. See Mark deWolfe Howe, ed., *Holmes-Pollock Letters*, vol. 1 (Cambridge: Harvard University Press, 1941), pp. 109-10.

37. Frankfurter, "The Supreme Court in the Mirror of Justices," p. 795.

38. Learned Hand, "Sources of Tolerance," *The Spirit of Liberty* (Alfred A. Knopf, Inc., New York, 1952), p. 81.

39. See Henry J. Abraham, *Justices and Presidents: A Political History of Appointments to the Supreme Court* (New York: Oxford University Press, 1974), pp. 191-94.

40. Frankfurter, "The Supreme Court in the Mirror of Justices," pp. 795-96.

41. See, e.g., *Engel* v. *Vitale*, 370 U.S. 421 (1962) (school prayer); *Roe* v. *Wade*, 410 U.S. 113 (1973) (abortion); *Miranda* v. *Arizona*, 384 U.S. 436 (1966) (criminal suspects).

42. *Doe* v. *Commonwealth's Attorney for City of Richmond*, 403 F. Supp. 1199 (E.D. Va. 1975), affirmed, 425 U.S. 901 (1976).

43. See generally, Joseph P. Harris, *The Advice and Consent of the Senate* (Berkeley: University of

160   *James O. Freedman and Frank Goodman*

California Press, 1953); Harold W. Chase, *Federal Judges: The Appointing Process* (Minneapolis: University of Minnesota Press, 1972).

44. See Jerome Frank, *Courts on Trial: Myth and Reality in American Justice* (New York: Atheneum Publishers, 1963), pp. 80–85.

45. See, e.g., Marvin E. Frankel, "The Search for Truth: An Umpireal View," *University of Pennsylvania Law Review* 123 (1975), p. 1031.

46. Mirjan Damaska, "Evidentiary Barriers to Conviction and Two Models of Criminal Procedure: A Comparative Study," *University of Pennsylvania Law Review* 121 (1973), p. 506; Mirjan Damaska, "Presentation of Evidence and Factfinding Precision, *University of Pennsylvania Law Review* 123 (1975), p. 1083.

47. See generally, H. M. Hart and Herbert Wechsler, eds., *The Federal Courts and the Federal System*, 2nd ed. (Mineola: Foundation Press, Inc., 1973), pp. 1050–1102; Henry J. Friendly, "The Historic Basis of the Diversity Jurisdiction," *Harvard Law Review* 41 (1928), p. 483.

48. See generally, Hart and Wechsler, *The Federal Courts and the Federal System*, pp. 45–47, 967–79; David Currie, "The Three-Judge District Court in Constitutional Litigation," *University of Chicago Law Review* 32 (1964), p. 1.

49. 333 U.S. 103 (1948).

50. Ibid. at 111.

51. Daniel J. Elazar, *American Federalism: A View from the States* (New York: Thomas Y. Crowell Co., Inc., 1966), p. 2.

52. Rexford G. Tugwell, *The Emerging Constitution* (New York: Harper's Magazine Press, 1974).

53. See generally, Michael D. Reagan, *The New Federalism* (New York: Oxford University Press, 1972).

54. E. F. Schumacher, *Small is Beautiful* (New York: Harper & Row Publishers, 1973), p. 66.

55. See Daniel P. Moynihan, *Maximum Feasible Misunderstanding* (Glencoe: Free Press, 1969).

56. 5 U.S.C. sec. 552.

57. See e.g., Alexander M. Bickel, *The Supreme Court and the Idea of Progress* (New York: Harper & Row Publishers, 1970); Robert A. Dahl, *After the Revolution* (New Haven: Yale University Press, 1970); Herman Finer, *The Presidency: Crisis and Regeneration* (Chicago: University of Chicago Press, 1960); Lowi, *The End of Liberalism*; Arthur M. Schlesinger, Jr., *The Imperial Presidency* (Boston: Houghton Mifflin Co., 1973).

58. See *Office of Communication of United Church of Christ* v. *FCC*, 359 F.2d 994 (D.C. Cir. 1966); Roger C. Cramton, "The Why, Where and How of Broadened Public Participation in the Administrative Process," *Georgetown Law Journal* 60 (1972), p. 525.

59. The Ninth Amendment reads: "The enumeration in the Constitution, of certain rights, shall not be construed to deny or disparage others retained by the people."

60. The Economic Opportunity Act of 1964 (42 U.S.C. sec. 2781(4)) required that anti-poverty programs be carried out with the "maximum feasible participation" of the residents of the communities involved.

Deliberations of Committee II

COMMITTEE III

SHAPING OF PUBLIC POLICY*

by Charles E. Gilbert

This is a drastically abbreviated version of the paper written as background for the Bicentennial Conference on the U.S. Constitution. I thought the original paper stringently selective and even summarily obscure, so its distillation presents a problem. In this version I shall omit some topics of the original entirely and truncate discussion of others severely.

The four topics of the Bicentennial Conference overlap constructively. In particular, issues about "the shaping of public policy" and "the effectiveness of governmental operations" seem reciprocal. "The Shaping of Public Policy" might equally be construed as the public shaping of policy—as reflecting concern about the republican or democratic or popular aspects of constitutional government in the United States. That is how I have construed it, with a weather eye on "Revolutionary values," governmental effectiveness, and foreign affairs.

In this interpretation, which relates the constitutional order to liberal democratic values primarily, the topic remains immense. Still, if we can refer without hubris to the proceedings at Philadelphia in 1776 and 1787, we can see that the popular dimension of government was for the participants in those proceedings just that—a dimension of government presumptively critical for most and pervasive for many, but not the entirety of government for anyone. Liberty, equality, justice, and the effectiveness of government in behalf of security and welfare were all concerns potentially limiting the popular dimensions of government as well as dependent on "popular sovereignty" in degree. But these issues of limitation and dependence—of the scope and structure of "popular sovereignty"—are, I suppose, more difficult today institutionally than they were in the founding period; and there is probably no more theoretical agreement about them today.

*Revised 15 November 1976.

In my definition of the topic and appraisal of the issues it presents, formal revision of the Constitution turns out to be of marginal concern. For the most part this paper deals with extraconstitutional institutions; and I conclude that constitutional amendment is unlikely to contribute substantially to their improvement.

This seems to me so despite vast changes in American life since the founding period—changes accompanied, however, by operative changes in the Constitution as well—and despite the changes in our immediate experiencing and in prospect today. But neither my constitutional conclusion nor the changing conditions of American public life should be taken for granted. So this exercise begins with an attempt to identify trends and prospects in American society that seem most likely to be troublesome for the shaping of public policy.

I. TRENDS AND PROSPECTS

Nearly two centuries ago the movement toward the American Constitution was grounded consequentially in analysis of American society and of its relation to the world abroad. Now American society sustains professions for "planning" and "futurism," and our literature of grand analysis and extrapolation is enormous. But there is no avoiding the controversial task of selection from this literature, as well as from one's own observations and speculations; one must ask what tendencies may shape fundamentally the shaping of policy in the nation's third century. I shall identify ten elliptically, prescinding, I hope, from the most obviously topical, attempting to steer between apocalypse and complacency, pursuing no particular order of urgency or priority, and foregoing elaboration.

1. Environmental Constraint

This might be termed the Heilbroner prospect, consisting in resource shortages and growing pressure on the human habitat, posing limits to economic growth and prompting prodigies of public regulation or even allocation.[1] If this is ultimately a controversial prospect, scenarios short of the ultimate—nevertheless entailing slower growth and more collective allocation—are less so; and in almost any version of this prospect public regulation appears more pervasive and the "people of plenty" hypothesis about American democratic politics is qualified.

2. The Modern Mixed Economy

This economy may be more susceptible to inflation than its pre-Keynesian precursor—not just politically, but endemically. If so, it poses hard decisions both technically and politically in pressures for regulation and redistribution, complicating social justice; and the destructive effects of inflation on modern democracies have been considerable. This economy is also more characteristically a service economy whose "new property" and "new income" tend to enlarge dependence on public institutions and collective decisions.[2] The governmental sector bulks larger in its national-income accounts, enlarging the scope

Charles E. Gilbert

of public policy; but it also exhibits a growing "third sector" largely dependent on public policy and raising difficult issues of subsidy and accountability.[3] This economy is further characterized by large organizations in all sectors, raising political issues of elephantine pluralism difficult to compass for individual actors and for democratic theory, allegedly generating a bureaucratic symbiosis of public and private organizations and pressure for "planning" in and from the private sector.[4]

3. The Changing International Order

Certainly international considerations, political and economic, played a large role in the constitutional movement and in the evolution of early American political alignments. Arguably, our international conditions today are more like those of the late 18th century than like those of the late 19th century; but the critical question for the shaping of public policy now is how they may be historically and categorically unique—a question considered more extensively in Professor Oliver's paper. Some aspects of that question stem from topics already mentioned—from, for example, environmental and resource controls and the multinational corporation, along with inchoate issues of global income distribution. In the shaping of American public policy national security bulks conspicuously in the federal budget; and foreign affairs nearly preoccupy the President. The capacities of political organization and of Congress to relate the national interest to the rest of the world are taxed; and they are strained by the close interpenetration of foreign and domestic policy. The issue of political and governmental capacity is perhaps most cogent in foreign affairs, where the case for constitutional reform is perhaps most apparent; but one may also ask whether the reality of "bureaucratic politics" is ineluctable in both foreign and domestic policy, regardless of constitutional framework.

4. Postindustrial Society

This complex, problematical tendency is a nest of implications. As Daniel Bell and others have adumbrated the trend, its educational and professional base poses a prospect of more stringent social stratification, or of meritocratic tensions and the white-collar unionism they tend to engender.[5] The large, labor-intensive service sector of this society may generate implicit tensions between social sectors apparently and independently productive in markets and those dependent on public subsidy of the functions they perform.[6] The technological and educational bases of such a society may produce demands for more explicit policy-making—for "systemic" approaches to policy beyond our political, administrative, or intellectual capacity; for more attention to "quality of life" not only in the environment but also in side effects of social transactions on life styles as well as on life chances and in "social" as well as economic development. Arguably, these emphases tend toward a more importunate, moralistic politics in which interests construed as "values" are difficult to aggregate or integrate. Historically, economic issues are commonly said to have been easier to compromise than social or cultural issues; but these types may be more closely combined in "postindustrial society."[7] In such a society public policies may seem more arbitrary as they are more general; claims for consultation and participation may be more urgent; and sensitivities to "power" may circumscribe public authority. Governmental devolution is apt to seem a logical response to such problems; but it may also exacerbate them while complicating accountability and neglecting general issues of regulation and redistribution.

5. Changing Political Values and Ideologies

"Postindustrial society" may or may not materialize as an aggregate; its emergence may or may not rival that of the industrial revolution in profundity of effects on politics and policy. But some putative post-industrial attributes are already affecting American political organization and alignments; and some scholars think they are altering American "Revolutionary values" toward a more ideological and divisive politics.[8]

Most speculations I have read suggest growing strains on governmental authority and political capacity resulting from something like elite or middle-class populism. Among the values and attitudes expected to contribute to these problems are: an assumption that public "solutions" to "problems" can and should be handled technologically instead of politically; a kindred expectation of continuous technological change or progress and of institutional "lag," thus challenging institutional legitimacy; a heightened emphasis on active participation, especially in the professional classes, as a moral imperative or mode of self-realization instead of a contingent protection of discrete interests and traditional rights; a resulting inflation of "liberty" toward the negation of "power" construed as arbitrary decision or interference with self-development or failure of consultation and opportunity for participation; a growing stress on equality in the Tocqueville sense of envious leveling down as well as the charitable sense of leveling up—not necessarily with centralizing tendencies, but with chronic meritocratic tensions; more particularistic interests in "communities" defined by attributes of culture or "life style"; increasing attention to "quality of life" through public provision of amenities and environmental regulation; and rejection of political bargaining and compromise, as opposed to participation and integration.

Such tendencies may be adduced pejoratively, as threats to political legitimacy and stability, or they may be approved as natural extensions of American Revolutionary values. They might be both; they may not develop anyway. The likeliest trend in "Revolutionary values," I think, is the progressive assimilation of liberty to equality. There is probably also some tension between "Revolutionary values" (including humanistic, altruistic values) and the conditions of large-scale, programmatic, and pluralistic government. Apparent disjunctions between "overt" and "covert" policies—between the rhetoric

166 Charles E. Gilbert

of electoral politics, the terms of interest-group negotiations and the mechanics of political coalition can stimulate the issue of "trust," so much discussed today.[9]

While political tolerance and understanding might as plausibly wax in the technological and educational circumstances of "postindustrial society," this seems likeliest to occur in diffusions of authority and devolutions of function at odds with systemic conceptions of policy. In any case, there are outstanding claims for racial equality and social welfare left over from "agrarian" and "industrial" stages that can hardly be settled equitably in a generation.

6. Modern Mass Communications

Social science seems to be agnostic on the effects of electronic mass communications for individual development and social organization. I think common sense suggests they are pervasive; and I suppose the effects of television for political organization and opinion formation have been profound—taken in tandem with other tendencies mentioned here and together with the role of electronic data processing in election campaigns. The most general effects, I suggest, have been toward more nationalization of political issues and organizational erosion of political parties, especially in presidential politics. Technology, market organization, and professional ethos have arguably tended toward a homogeneity in the mainstream media that has heightened their influence contingently and in agenda setting. The concentration and scale of the major journalistic institutions may entail tendencies of monopolistic competition—marginal product differentiation without risking radical dissimilarity; but common professional conventions and perspectives are also probably no less effective in the working press than in other fields.

More serious than that of homogeneity is the allegation that during the past decade the major media adopted a doctrine of active opposition to governmental policy, especially at the presidential level, and emphasized the shaping, not merely the informing, of public opinion.[10] On this view the fourth estate now plays a more deliberate and partisan role in shaping policy, competing more directly with political and governmental institutions. I don't profess to know whether the allegation is well founded with respect to intentions; but I suspect the problem results from the greater scale and visibility of our principal journalistic enterprises and is perhaps reciprocally enhanced by decline of political organization as well as by serious issues of governmental secrecy and publicity, including opportunistic use of the press by pluralistic public bureaucracies. These factors may intensify the intrinsic journalistic difficulty of steering between cooptation and opposition. The more apparent national scale of the media in television may condition the industry's sense of public responsibility for visible autonomy. It also seems conceivable that concern for audience ratings among more educated viewers could tilt electronic journalism toward personal exposure in national politics after the pattern of local reporting (and there has been ample provocation for this). If television *has* contributed to the decline of party organization in national politics, then its influence has probably gained reciprocally, much as the press is thought to be most influential locally where politics is nonpartisan.

Allegations of journalistic partisanship are not new in American politics with respect to either substantial accuracy or systemic bias: remember Thomas Jefferson! Still, the corporate interest and professional ethos of our principal journalistic enterprises are more strictly important issues of public policy today as journalistic insistence on total disclosure contends implicitly with political leadership for institutional authority. And as public policy becomes more technical and multifarious, so do the problems of informative reporting. The technology and economics of electronic journalism seem to predispose it toward the surface and the instant of the news, toward the personal over the circumstantial in its definition, aside from exceptional documentaries. As television marginally displaces print the danger is that even literate viewers may too easily satisfy conventional standards of cognitive civic obligation and vicarious participation without the kind of information that stimulates deliberation.

7. An Urban Society

Preceding "postindustrialism" logically and chronologically, urbanization changed American political organization and challenged its Jeffersonian doctrines. This has long been an urban nation; but the problem of the "spread city" is more recent in its demands on politics and policy. These include disparities between territorial "community" and large-scale industrial organization or association.[11] They probably also include the public-service diseconomies of large agglomerations—not only economic and environmental, but also in the problems of bureaucratic capacity and responsiveness in dealing with people directly where they live. Such urbanization has raised potentially serious jurisdictional issues in relating the functional logic of public management to political organization and civic participation based on residential patterns within governmental boundaries, while the urban regions and their jurisdictional divisions are the loci of basic cleavages—racial, class, and cultural—in American politics. They long have been. But these tendencies are more apparent in national policy now and prospectively; and, as remarked below, national policies reach more deeply into local governance today.

8. The Growing Density and Changing Balance of Federalism

Probably the majority view among scholars is that American federalism has always been a system more of shared than of compartmentalized functions as well as of close public-private collaboration, though interpretations differ in degree.[12] But in the last fifteen years particularly there has been a quantum increase of density, complexity, and (less certainly) centralization in American federalism. In that period federal grants to state and local governments have risen from 16.4 to about 28 percent of national domestic expenditures and from 11.6

Charles E. Gilbert

to about 21 percent of state and local revenues. Direct federalism (i.e., grants to localities bypassing states), private federalism (i.e., grants to nongovernmental institutions), and regional federalism (i.e., grants to regional planning or functional agencies) are, frequently in combination, responses to problems or importunities in urban and "postindustrial" society. They strengthen new program constituencies and establish new professions; they are sometimes attempts to "target" on national objectives through new jurisdictions or quasi-governments; and their clientele-participation requirements seem an equalizing sequel to earlier civil service requirements.

Scholars disagree about whether the balance of centralization and decentralization has really altered much in recent years (prescinding here from the role of the federal courts).[13] But the national policy role in such fields as education, child and youth development, and health care has probably grown by comparison with state and local roles since 1960, and federal regulatory measures for environmental control and resource conservation have developed the putative national police power through state and local governments and sanctioned state and local policies through grants.[14]

Anent the shaping of public policy the new patterns of federalism exemplify tendencies remarked in the preceding topics. They also pose political complexities of their own through new functional or professional constituencies and some further erosion of general-purpose local government. Thus they raise issues of public accountability at all governmental levels, as well as through devolution to private institutions, even as they create new channels of participation and marginal redistribution.

9. The Modern Administrative State

The problems of this topic are familiar enough, although the basic change in scale of the federal bureaucracy has occurred in less than the last half century.[15] In the shaping of public policy this has been a change of constitutional importance, although the federal bureaucracy hardly holds the implicit constitutional status of administration in Britain or in some European nations: it raises issues of accountability to elected officials, of internal conceptions of responsibility and technical rationality, of appropriate responsiveness to clients, and of "cost-productivity." The inertial properties of bureaucratic pluralism raise obvious problems for popular sovereignty. What effects public-employee organization and collective bargaining may have at the federal level remain to be seen; but this uncertain prospect assumes a constitutional importance similar to that of the decline of the legal doctrine of "privilege." Both tendencies depart potentially from traditional democratic understandings of administrative responsibility, as do modern "developmental" doctrines of organization and management or, in another direction, conceptions of "efficiency" adapted from conglomerate management. Clearly the organization, staffing, public relations, and managerial premises of public administration are central in the shaping of public policy.

10. The Changing Character of Public Policy

The more public policy there is, the more it is shaping—cumulative and reflexive—as well as shaped. Moreover, in a "systems" conception of politics, policies are not only outputs in response to demands; they generate new expectations, demands, and (perhaps) political "overloads." Such obvious considerations as these seem likely to become more consequential than they already are with the growing density and complexity of policy.

One classical democratic challenge lies in the technicality of much of modern policy. The problem of relating layman and expert in governance goes back to Plato; but science, technology, and economics have complicated it in ways still classically identified by Don K. Price.[16] Then there is the challenge of connection and comprehensiveness in large-scale government—how everything potentially relates to everything else—which administrative organization can only mitigate. The problem of clustering "policies" under "systemic" priorities and administrative rubrics is an organizational classic, if increasingly acute. In one formulation it is the problem of "planning," which has figured ambiguously in the language of economic policy since the Depression and the Employment Act of 1946, re-emerging now in the Humphrey-Javits bill and, with proposals for deregulation, challenging our capacities for more selective, less generally crescive policy-making.[17] One harbinger of "postindustrial society" may have been the advent of federal "planning" for professional manpower together with abundant subsidies of research and development in higher education after mid-century. Such policies create personal equities and fiscal entailments that tend to endure: they are hard to plan intelligently and hard to alter politically. In the same period the objectives of social policy have become more explicitly developmental and redevelopmental—by which I mean to suggest the promotion of individual and community improvement or rehabilitation through public services and subsidies. Such policies commonly depend on the motivation of individual subjects and the mobilization of particular communities for their results, so they are hard to implement effectively on a large scale. The range and penetration of public regulations have been extended impressively through national policy: civil rights and equal-opportunity legislation (and adjudication) are examples, as are the intensification of professional regulation and extension of measures for environmental protection and energy conservation already remarked.

A well-known analysis of public policies classifies them as distributive (e.g., most subsidies), redistributive, regulatory, and constituent (i.e., alterations of rules, structures, and opportunities for shaping policy).[18] One point of this analysis is that the characteristics of policies tend to determine the modes and loci of shaping policies. Conceding that these distinctions frequently apply more to perceptions than to effects (and that the classification seems incomplete), one may still suggest a general tendency to try not only to reach but to

Charles E. Gilbert

mitigate redistributive objectives through other types of policy. But it seems likely that redistributive perceptions in policy are becoming more general as policy is more extensive and as the quest for equality quickens. And regulatory measures, as they become more pervasive, may also appear more invidious and redistributive. So the emollient tendency toward "distributive" and "constituent" policies is understandable, though it may be running out of room and (as I'll suggest below) may not be unequivocally good for democratic institutions.

Finally, this may be the place to note the growing role of the federal trial judiciary in shaping public policy. Environmental and civil rights regulation are leading examples, wherein district courts function roughly as regulatory commissions pursuant to generous statutory delegations under relaxed rules of standing and of extended discovery, finding "legislative" facts and fashioning comprehensive remedies prospectively in analogs to equity for grievances based in "public-policy" claims. This extension of civil proceedings to public law has been paralleled by the expansion of statutory interests open to judicial review of administrative action at all levels through congressional objectives, including federal-grant standards, and perhaps through taxpayer standing to press certain constitutional interests against federal policy.[19] In short, more national policy is being made by courts (as much local policy long has been)—not through judicial review of legislation, but by judicial participation in administration, and increasingly by trial instead of appeal.

Some of the trends and prospects just suggested are undeniably real; others—their projections especially—are problematical. That goes for their institutional implications as well. One general implication only need be remarked now. In the terms of the Bicentennial Conference, tensions between governmental effectiveness, the popular role in the shaping of policy, and the evolution of Revolutionary values may continue to intensify. Some trends discussed above—e.g., the administrative state, the modern mixed economy, and the more pervasive regulatory role of the national government—are at odds with aspects of the doctrinal Revolutionary heritage. The "popular" and "righteous" aspects of that heritage are at odds not only with the large-scale "elite pluralism" of major American institutions, but with certain "republican" versions of the constitutional heritage that tend to reinforce the bargaining mode in policy-making. These tensions will be evident in the balance of this paper.

II. THE THEORY OF POPULAR SOVEREIGNTY

I take this section title with some reservations from the conference agenda.[20] Technically I take popular sovereignty to mean the grounding of government—both its constitution and its continuing rule— in the population at large as a legal or contractual understanding; or, practically speaking, "the people's ability to control their government."[21] It is an ancient notion, historically fundamental in democratic development, though fraught with ambiguities and hardly the whole of democratic thought. In modern usage it is apt to convey a populistic emphasis on absolute majority rule at the same time that, in modern political analysis, the formal conception of popular sovereignty is increasingly problematical.[22] In this form popular sovereignty conflicts potentially with conceptions of constitutionalism or limited government.[23] Still, the conception has figured prominently in American Revolutionary values, and in a limiting sense it is a useful rubric under which to consider democratic conditions for the shaping of public policy. Such conditions are considered most summarily here.

As to the dominant issues of 20th century constitutional criticism, I suppose the founding compromise was anti-populist but not anti-popular or anti-democratic. It provided a system of republican, or representative, government, but with emphasis on arrangements for balancing "responsiveness" by "responsibility." These arrangements —primarily the federal bargain and the separation of powers— reflected serious concerns for liberty, security, tranquility, and official effectiveness; and I believe they reflected also the framers' preponderant view of their society as one in which serious inequalities of condition (as distinct from sharp political competition or animosity) were unlikely to develop within the constitutional provisions for liberty and a national economy.[24]

According to some closely related lines of constitutional criticism the framework of federalism and imperfectly separated "powers" is at once redundant in distraint of tyranny and overabundant in restraint of majority rule. In the most general version of this view the "large republic" originally created through federalism is the sufficient condition of liberty through its natural pluralism, while the reinforcement of localism and fragmentation of majorities through formal constitutional arrangements are otiose or perverse or both with respect to liberty, equality, and public capacity. But I suspect that this view ignores the founding concern about how factional designs within government might encourage the mobilization of passionate or intolerant publics; and I suppose that this view identifies liberty with equality and responsibility with responsiveness in greater degree than did the preponderant republican opinion of the founders.[25]

These issues of assimilation or distinction of liberty and equality, and of responsibility and responsiveness, are a continuing heritage in American democratic theory, I think, though I have to neglect their various implications here.[26] Perhaps it will suffice to say that majority-rule and minority-rights conceptions of American politics, and pragmatic and formalistic conceptions of American politics, remain pertinent tensions in American democracy today in arrangements for the shaping of policy.[27]

Finally, I hope it will also suffice here merely to point to the pertinence of certain modern perspectives on American democracy. I'll identify these as elitist, pluralist, popular (or electoral), and participatory. The labels alone may suggest enough for present purposes to readers of contemporary American political science. In certain versions, as I observed in the original paper, each of these perspectives stands for critical attributes of American democratic politics. Within

Charles E. Gilbert

limits these pertinent versions include elite pluralism and elite electoral democracy, participatory pluralism and participatory electoral democracy; but I suppose the tension between pluralist and popular conceptions of American politics is central, even though such conceptions overlap in their attention to popular consultation and electoral competition. They also contend at least marginally with regard to conceptions of liberty and equality, majority rule and minority rights, responsiveness and responsibility. Thus summarily observed, these four perspectives may nevertheless provide some useful orientations in the following material.

III. THE PRACTICE OF POPULAR SOVEREIGNTY

The popular dimensions of the American Constitution are constitutional emanations historically in the basic organization of the party system deriving from federalism and the separation of powers and in the constitutional protections of political activity. But they are more largely conditioned today by factors of culture and technology outside the constitutional framework. While constitutional in an Aristotelian sense, and while deeply implicated in the shaping of policy, they are subject to shaping themselves more through the understandings of citizens and practitioners than by deliberate measures of policy—critical as the latter may be on the margins.

From the comments of the organizing committee for the Bicentennial Conference I take the practice of "popular sovereignty" to be the central concern of Committee III. And, in its extragovernmental dimensions, I'll consider the party system together with the institutional conditions of political pluralism and participation and the role of elections, omitting from the original paper material on the formation of public opinion (including mass communications) as well as elaboration on the functions and future of the party system.

1. The Party System

It is a commonplace of modern political analysis that parties are strictly critical in effectuating popular sovereignty—that institutional variations in party structure and functions tend centrally (but no doubt not ultimately) to determine theoretical issues discussed in the preceding section. They do this, presumably, by regularizing and legitimating opposition, organizing government (perhaps especially American government, with respect to the separation of powers), consolidating policy options for popular choice while structuring public opinion, providing labels and at least rudimentary organizational interests to the end of electoral accountability, contingently mitigating oligarchy and "mobilization of bias" through electoral competition, and (perhaps) by encouraging participation through electoral organization. There is less analytic emphasis on the centrality of party in democratic systems today than there used to be; it is hard to say how much this disposition reflects modern reality on the one hand or historical reanalysis on the other hand. In any case, there has always been a strong strain of anti-party thought in American politics and society, beginning with the founders' animadversions on "faction" and continuing with concern about partisanship and "the public interest."[28]

Naturally, some of this thinking has reflected official and factional dislike of opposition, but much of it appeals to views of liberty and justice discussed above. One result of this strain of thought has probably been the weakening of parties as agents of political equality; and, as I'll suggest presently, this strain of thought is strongly recrudescent today. Still, there are ample other reasons for the weakness of party in American politics.

One way to explore the role of party is through analysis of several putative party functions in the polity. Such analysis appears in the original paper anent the structuring of public opinion, social integration and the aggregation of policy interests, political "mobilization" and the encouragement of participation, the regularization of opposition and competition, nomination of candidates for office organization of government, and formulation of policy. It must suffice to say here that the American party system holds a monopoly position today in none of these putative functions, liberally but (I think) realistically understood, and approximates monopoly only in nominations—where the direct primary has much mitigated party's original role. As in nominations so in other functions also the organizational role of party has been diminished considerably in the 20th century; and this seems provisionally true of the ideological role of party in public and governmental alignments. Institutional reforms, educational and cultural change, and the progressive complexity of public policy all probably figure in this historical decline of party.

The contextual trends can be described as a progress from the conditions of a "traditional" to those of a "modern" party system, less traditionally organized and (perhaps) more rationally aligned. Arguably, such a "modern" party system will at last realize the designs of majoritarians for a more highly coherent, presumptively "responsible" two-party system; but my own argument in the original paper suggests, rather, that neither the organizational nor the ideological conditions of such a party system are cogent today.[29] Instead, the trend has been toward atrophy of party roles in communication, nomination, and organization of government across the separation of powers. Among many secular elements of this trend, recent developments in the presidential primary—abetted as I suppose by development of the electronic media—have perhaps been most influential, pulling presidency away from party in the large and apart from Congress in organization across the separation of powers.

So the condition of integral, organized leadership by Presidents in the "responsible-party" formula may be deteriorating. The conditions of party consolidation in Congress might improve a little with party realignment; but party reorganization in Congress has hardly enhanced this prospect. Presidential independence through personal coalitions and preoccupation with the media and bureaucracy may be no less a problem for party responsibility than congressional frag-

Charles E. Gilbert

mentation or intractability. The shaping of public policy follows coalitions of interests, including party. These may be increasingly discrete from one sector of policy to another. The more policy there is the more interests it engages. This might strengthen "party" against large interest groups; but it may also make it harder for party to hold together homogeneously.

The reality of coalitions suggests a similarity in all modern democratic systems, whether two-party or multi-party. Some people infer from this similarity that which kind of party system a nation has matters little for the prospects of governmental responsibility, re-responsiveness, and effectiveness. Some remark a convergence of party systems in much of Western Europe, the United States, and the British Dominions from either direction toward a highly qualified two-partyism, or hybrid arrangement, functioning in any case through executive/bureaucratic/interest group coalitions.[30] Some think the multi-party variant preferable for the United States—more responsive to the tendencies of "postindustrial society," and in any case a logical continuation of institutional developments in the present party system and of the role of minor parties in the past.

I won't conceal my own unreconstructed dislike of this idea. One needn't be an absolute majoritarian to conclude that responsibility in some balance of accountability, responsiveness and rationality is best served by a two-party system with sufficient discipline to play a considerable role in most of the functions just discussed. And "coalition" as an abstract noun too easily obscures, I think, the traditional distinction between coalitions formed prior to elections and those formed afterward, with its implications for governmental capacity and for obviating conflict. I mention this issue because of its bearing on issues for consideration in section V below.

I suppose that certain formal, effectively constitutional changes would much promote multi-partyism in modern America. Scholars disagree strongly on this point; but I believe the evidence compelling that the roots of the American two-party tendency are primarily institutional, having to do with the prevalence of single-member-district plurality elections, with the electoral college (which, with the exception of its aggregate majority requirements, is such an electoral system), and with the separation of powers. (I don't believe I should take space to argue this conclusion here.) Given the qualification "primarily institutional"—in recognition of the fact that institutions are not mechanical in effect but rather condition human aspirations and efforts—I think it problematical that any one of these institutions would suffice to preserve the two-party tendency in both branches under so-called postindustrial conditions. All of them together are not strictly sufficient for unalloyed two-partyism; and this, I think, has been a good thing in our history.

Another, related prospect for the American party system is much discussed today. That is its progressive "degeneration" or "decomposition."[31] This forecast starts with the growing independence of voters; the declining institutional and communicative role of party with the access of education and the changing popular impact and institutional position of mass media; and the culture of "postindustrial society" with respect to technology, authority, commitment, accommodation, and community. In one systemic version of this prognosis the progressive regional liquidation of party competition after 1876 and 1896, sustained by the Progressive reforms that followed, served the interests of industrial capitalism by suppressing relevant economic issues; and so eroded the party system organizationally and psychologically that its recovery in the Depression and New Deal realignment was incomplete. This version doesn't logically rule out party restoration through a further, fundamental realignment; but it suggests that the vestiges of party in American practice and opinion are unlikely to sustain such a realignment. In another view, many of the presumptive functions of party in the past are redundant or performed by other institutions today: modern party structures and functions reflect the perceptions and values of postindustrial culture. The substantial atrophy of party is less ineluctable in this perspective, but at any rate probable.

In none of these prognoses is the elimination of some kind (perhaps the present kind) of "party" labels in elections implied; but the label would cover a low-proof, if nonetheless volatile, blend: realignments would occur with high frequency, or electoral (especially presidential) conditions would be continuously labile and unstable. The present popular distrust of politics and low turnout in elections would presumably continue, possibly punctuated by populistic movements.[32] Government would likely lack effective composite majorities based on prescriptive popular alignments. More minor-party presidential (and perhaps congressional) campaigns would occur, abetted by recent campaign-finance legislation and imaginably by new election laws. Some minor-party continuities might develop, although many campaigns would be personal and episodic: absent effective institutionalization, the American demand for autonomous leadership would intensify. Conceivably some minor parties would in combination forestall electoral college majorities, forcing coalition politics to a new stage and enlarging the role of unpopular political bargaining. A likelier scenario, I suppose, relates the "modern" presidential primary process to the electoral college: in this prospect a popular candidate counted out in the convention pursues his campaign through the electoral college to Congress and the point of a "corrupt bargain."

None of the prognoses has, so far as I know, gone on to speculate in detail about which so-called functions or contributions of the sometime American two-party system would be most seriously diminished or missed in this scenario. The distributive implications of such a new populist mode in the educational and occupational "class" pattern of postindustrial society are, I think, disturbing. Competition for equalization of political influence would probably be destabilizing and perversely effective in the absence of secular "conservative majorities." The popular accountability of public bureaucracy and thus of much public policy would probably be diminished. So would the "integrative" effects of the two-party system if realignment were more substantially perpetual; politics would be much less emollient. Governmental capacity for decision, and the apparent "responsibility" of policy, would presumably be reduced. So, then, would authority and the prospects of liberal democracy.

I believe the foregoing prognoses should be taken seriously. But we are now in a period of some academic and popular skepticism about the contributions of party in the past (and especially in modern democracy), so not everyone will share this concern. Moreover, many scholars believe the prospect I have outlined uncertainly is likely to be avoided, indefinitely deferred, or even reversed by emergence of a "modern, responsible" party system. James Sundquist presents a strong case for the likelihood that the party alignment of circa 1960, appropriately modified, will be restored in the aftermath of issues of the 1960s orthogonal to the alignment.[33] Others think that alignment already much changed in its regional and class composition, if perhaps insufficiently so for party stability and capacity.[34] Still others think basic party realignment on regional, occupational, educational, religious, and maybe racial grounds possible or likely or perhaps necessary for restoration of the role of parties. Just now the imponderable claims of the young demographic bulge in the electorate are probably of critical significance for long-run consolidation of the party system. And there are others who perceive a trend toward more "rational," issue-oriented voting in recent presidential elections suggesting that, with appropriate realignment (and perhaps the reorganization of Congress), a more consolidated, "responsible" two-party system will result.[35] In this prospect party degeneration and voter alienation are far from inevitable; they are potentially signs of realignment and of demand for party reorganization.

If the future of party is in the balance, then we have a critical issue of how to provide for a system of institutionalized national leadership and opposition that is electorally responsible. That includes the issue whether a more consolidated, tightly aligned, and highly programmatic party system is either feasible or preferable to the party system of the recent past. In any case, no satisfactory substitute for party is in sight, or, I think, imaginable. We cannot count on necessity to reconstitute party. So we should consider the conditions of party restoration.

Foremost among those conditions today, I suggest, is some retreat from the current presidential-primary "system." One useful modification along this line might be Senator Walter Mondale's proposal for the regional scheduling of primaries. But I'll observe in the concluding section that a large role for the party convention and for congressional delegates in it seems to be desirable. And, lest the scenario mentioned above mislead, I'll also plead for continuation of the electoral college as a likely institutional support of two-partyism in the United States.

2. The Role of Interest Groups and Associations

The issues bearing on group and associational roles in shaping policy derive from issues of democratic theory mentioned in section II. They have to do with elite, pluralist, electoral, and participatory perspectives on national politics; with the articulation of liberty (or autonomy) with equality; and (ambiguously) with "responsible" versus "responsive" views of the public interest. In particular, two concerns mark current discussions of "pluralism" in the shaping of American public policy. One is whether the "group-competition" system is too considerably elitist and exclusive. The other concern is whether the shaping of policy is insufficiently "public"—i.e., whether the terms of group interaction with government, combined with conceivably excessive devolution of policy to participating or autonomous private organizations, impairs governmental responsibility.

There is no satisfactory way of settling these issues empirically. The participation of groups and private institutions in policy shaping is simply too diverse and profuse; and there is no agreed methodology for analyzing the interaction of group influence and governmental authority, or even its results in, say, the federal budget. I don't mean that patterns of group importunity in government, or specific decision-making procedures, can't be analyzed; and they have been analyzed extensively and intensively. I do mean that ultimately one consults one's general experience of American politics and one's normative conceptions of American democracy to evaluate the contribution of pluralist arrangements to the shaping of policy.

I think American intellectual perspectives on pluralism have been changing recently, and that the system of organized and corporate pluralism is increasingly seen as unduly elitist and exclusive. Popular and participatory concerns are more urgent today. So the perception of "undue" pluralism can create a kind of political malaise. At the same time, attempts to counter this in public policy through "distributive" and "constituent" policies (see section I. 10 above)—i.e., by extending the pluralist subsystem—may ultimately seem a hair-of-the-dog cure, warping and mortgaging the substance of policy through arrangements for the shaping of policy.[36] In any case, the problem of organized pluralism in popular and participatory perceptions is, I think, one of both appearance and reality; and, as I've suggested, the reality is hard to evaluate.

Pluralist interpretations of American politics usually have to do with cultural tendencies and "potential groups" and with circles or institutions of leadership, as well as with the direct access of organized interests to government. Pluralist interpretations make claims for the political "functions" of the pluralist system much like those made for political parties; indeed, a crucial issue in pluralism concerns the balance of pluralist with popular (electoral) elements, as well as with elite and participatory elements. For the group-competition system to serve its purported functions of informing policy, adjusting equal-

Charles E. Gilbert

ity with equity, modulating conflict through organization and over-lapping membership, and mediating "mass society" several conditions have been stipulated by both pluralists and their critics.[37] Group membership should be prevalent, overlapping, and voluntary; group interests should be largely homogeneous and group organization basically ubiquitous; group leadership should be responsive or accountable; opportunity for governmental access should be general, equitable, and applicable to all sectors of policy; and group competition or countervailing power should therefore be effective.

I think political scientists with no particular ideological axe to grind have increasingly challenged the foregoing assumptions empirically and in degree; and others contest them more categorically. For example, with respect to national politics, organizational membership is considerably less ubiquitous, more perfunctory, and less unprejudicially distributed than the assumptions require in any stringent sense. The extent to which overlapping group memberships tend to obviate or mitigate conflict is also uncertain, especially for the population at large, though the theory of "cross-cutting cleavages" with respect to more contingent cultural and economic alignments in relation to political-party identification, finds more empirical support. Such general consensus on liberal-democratic "rules of the game" as might prompt emergent organizational resistance to their violation by group arrangements with government is empirically problematical. So, on close inspection and consideration of potential issues and concerns, are the essential homogeneity of many group interests and the responsiveness or accountability of many group leaders. The voluntary nature of interest-group membership is frequently qualified by sanctions or incentives designed to "internalize" the benefits of membership—e.g., the union shop, or professional accreditation. So the organization and political negotiation of groups appear to reflect the entrepreneurialism of leaders more than the demands of members —from which follows a proclivity toward collusive or protective bargaining and the mutual recognition of spheres of influence.[38]

Such findings and inferences (some of them partial or primarily theoretical) tend to qualify the pluralist assumptions. But they are eclectic, as pluralism is disparate. Critics have tended to focus on economic policies—on subsidy, regulation (especially), or protection of certain large economic sectors and factors. Corporations, trade associations, labor unions, and farm organizations come prominently to mind. (Such issues as licensure, franchising, and contracting in state and local politics have seemed troublesome but less portentous.) There has been less concern about the trend of public devolution and subvention in the nonmarket sector that I have termed "private federalism" in section I.[39] No doubt whose ox is gored or whose axe is ground affects one's critical perspective.

Four major, intermingled concerns about the place of organized pluralism in the shaping of policy may be identified. One is the problem of vested, preemptive privilege in the reciprocal pervasion of governmental and private purposes.[40] A second is the problem of internal group organization—of bureaucratic management and entrepreneurial autonomy.[41] A third is the "mobilization of bias" that group strategic position and elite symbolic leadership may contribute to public opinion and electoral politics.[42] And a fourth is the implications of "interest-group liberalism" and group bargaining for administrative responsibility in discretion and administrative rationality in decision.[43] Scholars tend to argue now that congressional lobbying is more protective than aggressive—that constituent pressures and legislators' electoral independence together are, with the prompting of party loyalty and professional staff, effective counterweights.[44]

No doubt this depends on the nature of the legislative issue. But scholars tend to worry more today about administrative action—about regulatory "capture," agency "cooptation," bureaucratic decorum, and executive-branch coordination—where institutional public-interest norms are appropriately more stringent than in Congress, but also subject to more rigorous public expectations. Such tendencies and concerns suggest an establishmentarian style of policy shaping to populist critics.

In response to such concerns populist critics turn first to other topics of this section—to party organization for "responsible" leadership and popular influence through elections, and to distributed participation. The latter approach, as was observed in section II, has lately been a trend of national policy in numerous functional fields. As a subject of public policy it provides, I think, some evidence that pluralism flourishes "innovatively" as well as conservatively.

Another option, subject to constitutional limitations, is the promotion, protection, and regulation of opportunities for participation in associations \and functional constituencies as an object of public policy. Constitutional law has increasingly sustained legislative regulations of group organization and participation.[45] Here (determinations of socially harmful association aside) the problem is to balance organizational capacity with accountability, and collective purpose with individual rights. American public policy is less pervasive in this field than is the case in democratic nations with more Hobbesian or Rousseauian residues; and it is more normally a state than a national concern. Most commonly in national policy it accompanies group or constituent privilege, as in agricultural or labor organization, and more recently in the social services sector. Few policy issues entail more delicate calibrations of autonomy with equality. And the effective reach of statutory or judicial regulation has its limits, whatever the scope of affectation with a public interest or of formal participatory rights. But this recondite field of policy should not be ignored in contemplation of the shaping of policy.

Beside political organization and such regulation of interest-group organization as is politically and constitutionally feasible, two elements of the constitutional order should be considered seriously in concerns about imbalance or immobility in the pluralist demand-

Charles E. Gilbert

response system. These are the executive branch and the federal system. Anent the executive branch four perennial issues might be considered. One is closer congressional and/or judicial control of legislative delegation. Another is reconsideration of the independent-commission form of regulatory administration, together with selective "deregulation." A third is further "judicialization" of (primarily regulatory) administration through internal procedures, special appellate jurisdictions in the executive branch, or expansion of judicial review. And a fourth is personnel reform toward administrative consolidation and general management through something like the senior civil service proposal of twenty years ago.[46] These issues are more appropriately discussed in section V below. Here I'll merely observe that, together with proposals to reconstitute the party system toward enhancement of the "popular" demand-response system, they raise subtle issues of the meaning of "responsibility" in government and politics—issues adumbrated in section II above.

Finally, one should consider the larger role for public planning projected tentatively in section II, whatever "planning" may mean. Inter alia, I suppose it means at least an expansion of "regulation" of particular market practices under general legislative standards to the selective direction and control of investment and development pursuant to changing national objectives. Then the question is how national objectives are to be determined; that is, in what balance of governmental and industrial, legislative and executive determination.[47] If "the prerequisites of more rational collective choice begin with the prerequisites of improving hierarchy and polyarchy"—i.e., public bureaucracy and organized electoral responsibility—then more than marginal alteration of regulatory administration (and probably of legislative delegation as well) is implied.[48] The common criticism that regulation might gain in "planning" capacity through more integral location in the executive branch might become more cogent; and high-level civil service consolidation might become more pertinent in determining the balance of governmental and corporate or associational roles in planning. But ultimately, I suppose, this balance would depend on political organization toward legislative-executive "responsibility," including such patterns of political leadership and public opinion as would tend to preclude domination of the parties by economic organizations and radical instability of national objectives. And that, I think, means something less than the thoroughgoing "responsible-party-government" program, which seems infeasible anyway.

I'll return to these issues briefly in section IV. And I'll notice some issues of federalism in the following subsection.

3. Political and Civic Participation

The access of large-scale organization and the perceived practice of "elite pluralism" have produced an interesting doctrinal reaction. In this reaction the state-society distinction of "liberal" and classical "popular-control" democracy has been challenged both in substantive policy and popular sovereignty—largely on the ground that it no longer consists with political reality. Participatory and popular theorists urge that the scope of policy be extended more broadly into industrial and professional organization so as to broaden participation (and vice versa), both functionally and electorally.[49] In its functional thrust such theory is a partial reformulation of pluralism (with antecedents in early 20th century British and European thinking).

This approach may argue for functional supplementation of electoral participation, or it may go further toward displacement of majoritarian electoral control through proportional representation and functional participation. In the latter vein it tends to redefine traditional notions of political equality. In any case, it looks primarily to local government, functional quasi-governments, and regulated industrial self-government in some degree as the arenas of participation. While the first and third of these arenas have been the traditional foci of proposals for participation, the second has figured more prominently in federal public policy: here I have in mind such disparate instrumentalities as soil-conservation districts, community-action agencies, health-systems agencies. To these random examples one might add the recent consultative and advisory requirements in block-grant programs, or in child development and compensatory-education grants. One might also add the modern proposals for "community control," neighborhood government, and the territorial dismemberment of large cities.[50] Conceivably these are straws in a wind listing toward an extended conception of federalism as "distributed self-government."[51]

I mentioned above that issues of federalism figure in concerns about pluralism; and this seems an appropriate place at which to notice them. They have loosely to do with perspectives I have termed formalist and pragmatist. One issue concerns the erosion of general-purpose, broadly responsible local government under modern conditions. If there *is* a "classical" democratic theory, then one of its antipathies in early utilitarianism was toward separate functional jurisdictions, noncomparable and thus electorally unaccountable in politics.[52] Special-purpose public authorities and subsidized non-profit corporations as governmental surrogates for certain "public" functions, as well as "marble-cake" federalism with its functional bureaucratic articulation, are modern analogues of those concerns about oligarchies and electoral accountability. Such tendencies are ancient and basically irreversible in American politics.[53] Pure jurisdictional homogeneity isn't feasible; and federal-grant requirements are designed about as frequently to contain local "oligarchies" (including political organizations) as to sustain them.

Nevertheless, I shall suggest three considerations as critical for "distributed self-government" in the federal system. The first is the potentiality of general-purpose local government for political responsibility and participation; its functional dilution or gratuitous ter-

Charles E. Gilbert

ritorial enlargement is unlikely, I think, to serve "popular sovereignty." The second consideration is that strengthening of the states in our federal machinery can contribute to both local and national capacities respectively through constitutional responsibility for local action and prudent decentralization of national policy.[54] This is to suggest, finally, that federalism is functional for modern constitutional democracy as a system of public devolutions and appeals—for relieving national overload and controlling local improbity or prejudice.

It will not be appropriate to pursue these considerations further. I mention them because issues of centralization and decentralization in the shaping and implementation of policy are apt to concern us in discussion. In this connection it seems to me that, whatever the prospects for individual participation and vocational association, civic participation necessarily depends on definitions of locality and community or of functional responsibility. The problem is to organize local government to balance community and diversity, formality and responsiveness, functional generality and political scale, administrative capacity and accountability, fiscal responsibility and distributive equity—so as to encourage participation while protecting rights and promoting managerial capacities. These balances will seem banalities; but I think they support suggestions for attention to federalism in the preceding paragraph. That is, from the standpoint of participation, they imply local governments subject to responsible participation by ordinary residents, not simply by cosmopolitan professionals; and they imply state arrangements for protecting rights against local oligarchies or majoritarian aggrandizements.

While the foregoing conception of the federal system is no doubt utopian, accessible local government seems critical for civic participation. And civic participation seems prospectively—in the traditional, liberal view—more consequential than vocational forms of participation for individual development of political skills and for the shaping of public policy. But neither approach to participation is as relevant to *national* policy—or to the demands of management and challenges of large-scale pluralism—as participation relating to elections, especially voting by "ordinary" citizens.

This seems the more so in the light of recent research suggestions that, in the context of American political organization and ideology, participation tends to work perversely from the standpoint of equalization of influence, reinforcing socio-economic inequalities through its association with social status.[55] This inference, coupled with the well-documented effects of higher-level education in promoting civic competence and participation, and with the speculative tendencies toward a social-class system rather sharply demarcated by college education, and with the problems of large-scale organization in American pluralism, seems reason for concern about how to reduce disparities of influence in American politics and policy. Professional, "public-interest" participation hardly serves this concern, I suppose, by comparison with more general engagement of the population through partisan and electoral organization in ways to be considered now.

4. The Place of Elections in Shaping Policy

Accepting the centrality of elections for "popular sovereignty," and of party for electoral effectiveness, I'll raise summarily now some complicating issues.

Whatever the claims of incumbents, elections are rarely "mandates." While majoritarian convention might conceivably lend elections this character, the ambiguities of party alignment and of political communications (noticed below) leave large margins of official discretion in reality. Voting is probably more often retrospective than prospective. There is no doubt a certain rationality in this perspective: voters need not invest in comprehensive, high-level ideologies to evaluate policy in the light of their own condition; governmental incumbents nevertheless are circumscribed anticipatorily.

Still, there is persuasive evidence that the general, programmatic commitments of parties in presidential elections are intelligible and are characteristically honored by incumbents—at least in legislative effort, if not effectively.[56] Through secular alignments primarily, and in some respects more immediately, elections tend to settle basic issues—to remove them from controversy and to establish their resolutions as premises of policy. Subject to these premises, or a "moving consensus," many presidential elections are contested primarily over what have been termed "valence issues"—i.e., which candidate or party or program will better serve an emergent concern; not which party's conception of distributive justice should prevail.[57] There is also evidence of congruence between majority opinion in constituencies and the behavior of legislators, though it is reasonably clear that legislative discretion varies with the characteristics of issues and that there is commonly room for maneuver or for assertion of leadership.[58] Yet off-year congressional elections have been plausibly interpreted as referenda on the conduct of national administrations.[59]

In these degrees American national elections tend to be meaningful and effective, though our ability to characterize their influence (or their effects on the distribution of influence) more specifically is limited. For example, it appears that tight electoral competition frequently leverages organized groups—that, regarding equalization of influence, popular (electoral) democracy augments pluralist democracy, though it probably tends to redress political effects of large-scale organizations. But these permutations have yet to be worked through in democratic theory. Moreover, the logic of electoral coalitions suggests that even in less secular and consensual, more majoritarian systems than the American, there are limits to the electoral pursuit of distributive justice: the claims of small or (in particular) unpopular minorities are still likely to be discounted. Their electoral inclusion is likely to depend on legal protections or direct action within "a scheme of ordered liberty" and on popular allegiance to constitutional values.

Charles E. Gilbert

Within modern democratic ideologies, both totalitarian and liberal, popular elections are alleged to foster regime allegiance and stability through civic participation and responsibility.[60] However that may be, the evidence suggests that popular sovereignty in elections is more a matter of influence in government than of direct power over government—a matter of anticipatory circumscription: elections are contextual for the shaping of policy.[61] But this role seems more considerable today than it was in early constitutional expectation: the balance of electoral *demand* and electoral *protection* has altered with institutional and ideological evolution, especially in presidential elections. This is a way of saying that "traditional" party organization and alignments no longer control the electoral process so effectively by comparison with other institutions and determinants of opinion and also that electoral demand may tend to outrun electoral support.

Some observers believe a more "modern" and "responsible" American party system is now evolving to relieve these tendencies; but this claim raises serious issues of both prediction and evaluation.

5. A Reprise on Party

Insofar as partialities of large-scale pluralism, particularities of local participation, ambiguities of political communication, insufficiencies of voter information and sophistication, or limits of electoral accountability pose serious democratic problems, various incremental correctives are theoretically available with respect, e.g., to governmental organization, restraint of legislative delegation, public-personnel administration, reforms of federalism, educational improvement (dubiously), and (perhaps) public-service television. But reflection on such remedies suggests that, while they might be helpful, they also have practical and democratic shortcomings. They don't articulate the electorate with the shaping of policy, nor do they concert or constrain shapers of policy within the statutory and structural margins they provide. In uncertain degree they depend upon political organization, or party, for effective implementation. If the putative functions of party seem easily overstated in the light of other cultural and institutional conditions, this is partly, I suppose, because we tend to take party for granted.

But the decline of party, whether or not it turns out to be temporary, now finds ample documentation.[62] Like the phenomenon of party the decline is a matter of both electoral organization and popular alignments. These overlap, though they are distinguishable. In theory a stronger leadership structure (either tangible or ideological) might enable party to function effectively with weaker public identifications, or emergent popular ideologies and alignments on issues might help strengthen party organization; but in practice these factors are probably interdependent. So the question is whether some progressive restoration of party is in sight.

As to organization, voluntary and governmental policies have long been tending to weaken party control of nominations and campaigns —especially in recent years with respect to the presidency. The new

Democratic Party rules tend to render the Party more permeable than ever by other organized groups.[63] The campaign-finance legislation of 1974 tends to make presidential primary elections more party-destabilizing sweepstakes; and, in extending national regulation further into the central functions of party, it makes party a more public entity subject not only to congressional majorities and federal courts but also to the usual cumulative tendencies of regulation.[64] So public policy may tend to weaken party institutionally, appropriating party to the "public interest" and eroding the liberal state-society distinction that party has arguably both bridged and buttressed.

As to popular alignments, protagonists of a more "responsible" party system are discovering grounds for optimism in the recurrence of "issue voting" coupled with a rise of "issue consistency," or more nearly ideological voting behavior. Yet this behavior (if it is "behavior") seems also to be associated particularly with voter independence of party; and there are grounds for doubt that traditional party identifications will soon be restored.[65] Perhaps more consequentially, one may question whether any tight popular alignment, either in mass attitudes or interest-group positions, is now in sight or even conceivable that can reasonably comprehend the density, extensity, complexity, and technicality of public policy today. But the logic of future party alignments is too large a subject for consideration here.

Party alignments will presumably settle themselves without help from the Bicentennial Conference on the U.S. Constitution. But party organization can probably make a difference in the character of alignments and in their influence on the shaping of policy. So, without opting for the "responsible-party-government" program, there seems good reason to try to strengthen party organization for policy and elections. I'll comment briefly on policy in section V. As to elections, I'll suggest again that attention to presidential nominating procedures is in order, since they are at the heart of party organization, which is arguably impaired by the recent rules and legislation mentioned above. In this spring of 1976 we might well ask whether the role of presidential primary elections has grown beyond compatibility with adequate party organization.

IV. THE SHAPING OF POLICY BY PUBLIC OFFICIALS

Whatever the requirements of "popular sovereignty" for extragovernmental institutions and public behavior, I suppose these culminate constitutionally in the ultimate shaping of policy by elected officials. How definitive and pervasive one thinks this shaping should be will vary with one's position on issues indicated, but not explicated, in section II. How far one thinks such shaping may *feasibly* go is in part, though not entirely, another question—one of institutional capabilities and structure. Answers to that question are eternally problematical, but some aspects of it are considered in this section under four headings: the congressional role; the presidential role; problems of administrative responsibility; and prospects of constitutional reform.

Charles E. Gilbert

1. Congress

In this century "the decline of legislatures" has become a familiar lament. In the Western world party, lobby, executive authority, bureaucracy, and the complexity or exigency of policy have all been blamed for legislative "decline." And decline implies not only alteration of constitutional balance, but of both responsibility and responsiveness in the shaping of policy. Congress has not been thought exempt from these tendencies; yet Congress has remained—if in a dispersive rather than a collective or parliamentary sense—the strongest Western legislature. A critical issue for students of Congress is that of the extent to which its strength is constitutionally assured by the separation of powers or depends particularly today on the 20th century pattern of congressional decentralization of power and resistance to party discipline.

There is a beginning of wisdom in the perception that congressional performance isn't uniform. This is suggested by Theodore Lowi's distinction (see section I) between distributive, redistributive, regulatory, and constituent sectors of policy.[66] It appears in preliminary historical examination that Congress has probably been more effective (compared with other factors, governmental and nongovernmental) in some types of policy than in others; and moreover, that Congress tends to function collectively or parliamentarily in some types and fragmentarily in other types. Thus Congress probably cannot devise an energy policy, but it can exercise initiative in environmental regulation; it probably cannot function independently for global fiscal or monetary management, but it can draft tax legislation in copious detail. Congressional action takes different forms in different fields. In particular, Lowi argues, Congress tends to legislate most autonomously and parliamentarily with respect to regulation. Yet it is worth observing that this is the policy sector that gives rise to most concern about uncontrolled legislative delegation and administrative aggrandizement: it seems to be a sector where Congress is politically able to respond to popular concern essentially through identification of a "problem," adoption of either a categorical or vague (but in any case commodious) statutory standard, and establishment of an administrative agency or judicial jurisdiction to make the necessary adjustments. Where more particular or perspicuous legislation is required the congressional process tends to be more decentralized, or more dependent on presidential iniative.

A further complication is the multifunctionality of Congress as compared with most legislatures.[67] The functions of Congress have been endlessly and variously listed, but I shall identify four: legislation; control of administration; inquiry; and constituent service. In a strict sense, the confusion of the functions figures in the representative role of Congress as the "republican," nonplebiscitary element of the Constitution. This is so despite the efforts of institutional purists to discover constitutional distinctions among the functions.

Thus some critics argue that the job of Congress is to *legislate* generally, perspicuously, and parliamentarily; and that Congress should better organize itself to this end. In this view Congress is perceived as less representative of national interests than the President; Congress increasingly lacks legitimacy and legislative capacity. Yet the study of legislative etiology suggests that congressional initiative in policy is more common than appears to be the case in politics considered presidentially; the representative and technical roles of Congress in legislative revision are certainly considerable.[68] Arguably, some of our least successful public programs in recent years have resulted from exigent presidential leadership through large congressional majorities, when the representative role of Congress was attenuated or when Congress abdicated excessively in fields of conventional executive responsibility.

Critics who doubt the capacity of Congress to legislate in a sufficiently disciplined way suggest that Congress emphasize instead the *oversight of administration* in more nearly plenary style: in this residual manner Congress could contribute to policy and accountability through review of performance, statutory revision, and financial provision.[69] Such critics also tend to argue that congressional direction and control of administration are at present too pervasive, dispersive, particular, and irregular; and they have a point. Congress has increasingly relied on substantive understandings attaching to appropriations and "come-into-agreement" provisions to extend control of administration.[70] On the other hand, the decentralization and particularity of congressional oversight as well as its merger with legislative delegation and with statutory specification of administrative detail may in some degree be conditions of congressional effectiveness in this field. British and European parliamentary comparisons do not provide effective models of legislative control of administration; and the political incentives for congressmen and senators to concentrate on general oversight through plenary methods are not considerable. In this sphere congressional effectiveness almost certainly depends on specialization and decentralization—which is not to argue that congressional delegation of outright legislative determinations to committees is legitimate. Such methods of congressional direction and control of administration are constitutionally problematical (so is the legislative veto as a plenary method); but in any case this congressional function is increasingly critical for representative government and presumptively worth some price in rationality.

Controversy over the *investigative* role of Congress relates to oversight of administration where these are combined and to legislation when it appears not to serve that end directly. Its vindictive, privacy-violating, publicity-seeking abuses must be conceded with its uses for fact-finding, opinion sifting, issue definition, and public instruction. As grand inquest of the nation, Congress is sometimes best able to counter presidential prerogative and virtual representation. In oversight of administration congressional investigations are sometimes simply tools of *constituent service*; and in this sector some congressional reformers have urged a more impartial surrogate, such

Charles E. Gilbert

as an ombudsman.[71] In general the constituent-service function of Congress is subject to criticism for adulterating "policy," perverting bureaucracy, preserving incumbency, and abridging equity. But the potentialities of this function for mitigating bureaucratic inequities are also strong; and its contribution to ordinary citizens' sense of effective representation in the modern administrative state should not be ignored.[72]

These issues of congressional function are perdurable. So, in a general way, are issues of congressional structure, which are complicated now, however, by the fact of rapid change in Congress. Since World War II (to pursue a long tradition no further) Congress has been continuously criticized by reformers for structural obscurantism and particularism encouraging irrational compromise.[73] Recommending the consolidation of Congress through "responsible" parties, the critics have usually looked to the President for leadership. Conversely, congressional protagonists have commonly argued against the "party-government" doctrine on the ground that its realization would relegate Congress to a subordinate role. What critics and reformers often thought perversely unresponsive in Congress was accepted by some scholars as a system of institutionalized "responsibility" balancing independence of the presidency with insulation from importunate constituency pressures through a decentralized network of leadership resting on incentives and sanctions for congressional careers characterized by longevity in districts where electoral competition was more contingent than regular. If the machinery of Congress was apparently partisan in this system, policy alignments were more ambiguously so, leaving ample room for individual judgment and adjustment to constituency differences. However evaluated, in the House of Representatives this system was electorally conditioned by regional legacies dating from 1876, 1896, and the New Deal; over most of this period the advantages of incumbency increased and the electoral discretion of members on most issues seemed considerable.

By the 1970s, however, congressional reformers were having their day. From about 1958 electoral fortune several times favored liberal Democrats, who favored congressional reform and organized to bring it about. And the balance of legislative-executive relations after 1964 seems to have convinced members of both parties in Congress that they would benefit from some congressional reorganization. So, as a result of such measures in 1972, 1974, and 1975, we are witnessing a test of two common propositions about Congress. One is that party alignments and ideologies in Congress are not sufficiently defined or stable enough to sustain strong leadership based on the party caucus. The other is that, since the institutional strengths of Congress rest necessarily on decentralized and segmental procedures, congressional attempts to grapple integrally with national priorities or with policy in the large are likely to cripple Congress.

These are critical propositions, but there is no space for their analysis here. No one can know for certain whether they are sound in general, or just conditionally in degree, or even wrong in general. If they are right, then Congress may lose ground to the President again. Under the altered party balance and seniority distribution that now obtain in Congress, together with the current stress on legislative productivity, the evidence will accumulate; and in the meantime the standard academic literature on Congress will have become anachronistic.

There remains room for brief comment on three aspects of Congress; committee structure, staffing, and representation. It is perhaps the committee structure and the substantial autonomy of certain (primarily financial) committees that has exercised congressional critics most. This structure of specialization is arguably the source of congressional strength; but, coupled with the seniority rule and secure jurisdictions, it has also during this century been the basis of the dispersed congressional-leadership network.[74] The recent erosion of the seniority rule and redistribution of committee jurisdictions complement the current essay at caucus-based leadership in the House of Representatives. Altogether these developments tend to curb the independence and legislative influence of committees; yet committee performance is so central to congressional careers that strong pressure has developed for more subcommittees and jurisdictional rivalries among committees have increased. Congress has to specialize; morselization of policy seems essential to congressional effectiveness in shaping legislation. And there is probably no single optimal scheme of standing-committee jurisdictions, though Congress may be well advised to seek to cross-cut executive branch organization in this respect. And it can seek more comprehensive purviews through select and non-legislative committees, which, after the pattern of the Joint Economic Committee, might function effectively for several aspects of policy.

A striking departure in congressional committee structure has been the enlargement of staff; indeed, the doctrine of "salvation through staff" now applies to political direction and control of government in both branches. So do its practical problems in the theology of popular sovereignty and responsible government: *delegata postestas non potest delegari*; and too many cooks spoil the broth. The issue here is whether staff proliferation is reaching the point where the question arises seriously, with respect to legislative multifunctionality; is Congress attempting to do too much? Probably the question is less applicable so far to the shaping of policy in the large, where congressional responsibility functions necessarily through negotiation and voting by principals in the end, than it is to intervention with and investigation of administrative implementation of policy, where staffers can navigate independently.[75] In such congressional essays at comprehensiveness as the new budget committees or technology assessment ample professional staffing seems essential. But anyone comparing the Congress of today with that of a decade ago can see the signs of a growth industry and the danger that this form of "institutionalization" is accentuating dispersion and diluting repre-

Charles E. Gilbert

sentation. So greater emphasis on the pattern of institutionalization manifest in the General Accounting Office and the Congressional Research Service may be worth considering.

As to representation, the current emphases on comprehensive attention to priorities and on legislative accomplishment raise the prospect of alteration—marginally or perhaps more drastically—of the institutionalized congressional pattern that developed in this century, primarily in the House of Representatives. That pattern emphasized multifunctionality. In legislative and electoral organization it emphasized insulating properties (seniority, protection of incumbency, distributed leadership sanctions and incentives) to balance necessities of direct responsiveness.[76] This pattern gave Congress a dilatory and particularistic cast and probably favored the influence of "private interest" over "public-interest" groups. But it apparently fostered congressional response to aggregate national opinion as this emerged in congressional constituencies and permitted selective congressional initiatives; and it was consistent with the notion that there was no single (presumptively presidential) majority in the nation, but rather competing or complementary majorities attending to different interests and visions.[77] For most of the 20th century Congress has served a "conservative" function in this analysis; and it may be now that congressional and presidential roles will be reversed. Or the analysis may no longer be valid, in which case Congress may function less well in protecting particular interests and as a balance-wheel in our constitutional machinery.

2. The Presidency

I cannot avoid the standard observation that the presidential role, like that of Congress, is multifarious—though I shall neglect its specification here. The question arises whether the several presidential roles are also integral, mutually enhancing roles. If they are, then they are also apt to be reciprocally deleterious from time to time. There is strength in the combination of formal headship and political leadership; but there is also a danger to legitimacy since, save for generalized allegiance to constitutional values, so much combined responsibility rides on the President personally. Proposals for alteration of the separation of powers can hardly ignore the American problem of fusion of "dignified" and "efficient" functions.[78]

This problem becomes the more considerable as the presidency cuts loose from party organization progressively through the reciprocal effects of mass communications, popular nominating procedures, and deterioration of party structure. In any case, the presidential constituency tends to be "virtual" and vague; with respect to issues more nearly susceptible of direct accountability it is highly heterogeneous. Presidential representation thus has plebiscitarian elements and (depending on election-finance laws) plutocratic elements as well. Popular support of presidential performance can be mercurial—subject to precipitous decline and hard to recoup save through election campaigns or spectacular events. The dynamics of opinion formation figure in this vulnerability, but so do the functional problems of the presidency.

With respect to the executive branch the putative tools of the presidency for shaping and implementing policy have had increasingly to reckon with intractibility. Budgetary discretion and control, reorganizational authority, and personnel management are circumscribed by the economy, the Congress, and the conventions of civil service. The presidency is confined to selective initiatives in legislation and selective interventions in administration. The President as energetic general manager of the executive branch is not, I think, a workable conception.[79]

Within the ambiguity of presidential strength and weakness the question naturally arises whether the office can be "institutionalized" to the end of "responsibility" in its several significations. Short of constitutional amendment (to be considered below), the chief possibilities, I think, are three. One is progressive reorganization of the party system toward the "responsible" model in which presidential leadership would be more subject to partisan loyalties, collaboration, inhibition, and opposition. But party responsibility implies party organization—more than mere ideological agreement. In particular, the machinery of presidential nomination and campaigning would need reinstitutionalization, extending perhaps to congressional politics as well, and reversing current developments.

A second possibility, long advocated, looks to several objectives: stabilizing of executive-legislative relations, consolidation of legislative leadership, and collegial supplementation of the presidency. It takes the form of a legislative-executive council engaging the effective leadership of both branches in the shaping of policy.[80] The congressional membership might be bipartisan, or it might not; the council might de facto expand the Cabinet to congressional positions without portfolio, or legislative and managerial functions might (insofar as feasible) be distinguished. In one version or another this proposal emphasizes the stabilization, depersonalization, and containment of the presidency, or the integration and augmentation of general policy leadership in both branches.

A final possibility is movement toward a better balance of consolidation and devolution in the executive branch. This implies some retrenchment of presidential attempts to centralize direction and control in the White House. The managerial and collegial responsibilities of cabinet officers would be emphasized; the machinery of central administration (e.g., OMB) would be further institutionalized; perhaps a senior civil service would be established. The limits of presidential ability to manage the executive branch would be acknowledged; regularization of management would be emphasized within these limits; the old reorganization formula of executive branch consolidation in larger departments might be revised to emphasize smaller and more homogeneous departments even if this means that more secretaries must report to the President.

These three lines of development are logically compatible, I think.

Charles E. Gilbert

I also think the dispersive tendencies of American politics and administration are unlikely to favor the first and third developments alone or in combination; some governmental fulcrum or nexus is probably essential to either or both. Then the question is whether the second proposal would, in effect, supply enough institutional leadership and conventional leverage to serve the purpose. I suppose the best way to find out is to try it. The trouble is that presidential necessities seem to run the other way, and presidential incentives almost certainly do. The modern presidency seems mortgaged to personal ambitions, popular expectations, and functional contradictions beyond those operable in large-scale organizations generally, so its institutionalization is peculiarly difficult.

3. The Problems of Administrative Responsibility

These are, as already indicated, increasingly central considerations in popular sovereignty. Indeed, modern issues of bureaucratic rule, discretion, accountability, rationality, responsiveness, efficiency, and effectiveness are among the central issues of modern democratic theory in any practical sense.[81] Here the concerns of Committee III merge most integrally with those of Committee II.

I'll identify these issues in national administration under three heads: constitutional, internal, and external. The constitutional avenues of responsibility are those pertaining to President, Congress, and the courts distinctly and relatively in direction and control of administration.

As to the presidency, can the chief executive either lead or manage effectively the shaping and implementation of policy? Could he do so even if Congress were not so prominently in the picture? Has the trend toward White House centralization impaired departmental management? With the enlargement of the presidency, has staff "passion for anonymity" been coupled unduly with autonomy and authority? Are superdepartments or "czars" really superior to a larger number of more integrated departments? To raise these questions is to indicate concerns and at least a qualified perspective on the answer. If the presidential role in shaping policy is necessarily other than immediately and comprehensively managerial, then this implies more reliance on executive office, Cabinet, and departmental management assisted by restoration of presidential reorganization authority (subject to congressional veto), some consolidation of the higher civil service, and selective applications of managerial technique. As to the last of these "the triumph of technique over purpose" is a constant embarrassment of governmental management—one about as likely to emerge in modern policy analysis as in classical administrative methods, as can be seen in recent American experience.[82]

The role of Congress in direction and control of administration has been a staple problem in the American separation of powers. But its principal aspects—collective or "parliamentary" versus dispersive or fragmentary congressional oversight of administration, and the desire of presidential protagonists or bureaucratic rationalists that

Congress retreat from its pervasive administration intervention in many sectors—are basically intractable. Congress relates to administration as it does largely because Congress is organized and electorally conditioned as it is. Congressional priorities may change with imperatives of policy: the new budget procedures, general standard-setting legislation, and more use of the legislative veto (in despite of constitutional purists) are consolidating possibilities. But Congress will typically relate to administration through its committees, where its strength resides; and the more critical issue has to do with "institutionalization" of assistance in legislative oversight through, e.g., the General Accounting Office and Congressional Research Service.

While the judicial role in administrative responsibility is too technical for consideration here, it relates to a couple of large issues worth mentioning: the scope of legislative delegation, and the organization of regulatory administration. As to the latter, all three branches might make progress with the regulatory "fourth branch" together (short of its dismemberment and merger) through provision for presidential directives on general policy, investigation, or jurisdiction subject to judicial review and legislative veto.[83] And as to delegation, congressional provision for more extensive agency rulemaking and policy formulation might help tighten judicial review for consistency of decision, besides which the time may be ripe for more judicial pressure on legislative delegations independently through some sophisticated revival of the dormant non-delegation doctrine.[84]

The internal modes of administrative responsibility pose issues in civil service organization and regulation. The American public service is much less a guardian class or autonomous elite, much more a system of social and functional representation, than are most modern national bureaucracies.[85] These attributes are "in the wood"; they cannot be altered more than marginally with regard to the shaping of policy. Within these traditional limits two alternatives are worth considering anent the higher public service: one is its consolidation as a more corporate career service; the other is extension of presidential appointments to lower levels.[86] Of these I favor the former; but in either case the practical intractability arising from programmatic pluralism and the molecular tenacity of American bureaus, along with resistance from civil service unions, will be fundamentally troublesome.

Among the external dimensions of administrative responsibility I'll identify contracting, publicity, clientele participation, and intergovernmental relations for brief discussion. In contracting, especially for research, development, advice, and evaluation, the problem of administrative responsibility is to retain it unimpaired—that is, to maintain public capacities for definition, evaluation, and decision. This is no trivial problem today, but I need not review it here.[87]

Administrative publicity (and secrecy) pose similarly well-documented issues—publicity as a form of institutional or programmatic advertising and constituency cultivation, or as damaging persons or properties through adverse publicity attending regulation; secrecy in

Charles E. Gilbert

the competing requirements of "sunshine," journalism, public information, and equalization of interest-group access, or of national security, personal and corporate confidentiality, the encouragement of candor in administrative judgments, and of prudential autonomy in administrative decisions.[88] Such considerations figure ambiguously in the statutes on publicity and disclosure.[89] Insofar as publicity is influence and knowledge is power, the regulation of secrecy and publicity will always be critical in the shaping of policy.

By clientele participation, I mean arrangements more integral to policy shaping than ordinary negotiation with interest groups. These may range from advice to devolution; from formal to informal. They may be justified by the shortcomings of ultimate accountability and the need for something more immediate; by pragmatic or indigenous contributions to administrative information or to client motivation through participation; by the necessity of winning consent; as programmatic "targeting" and constituency building; as appropriately modulating bureaucratic uniformity; or as civil development through popular involvement. The problems of public purpose and governmental responsibility arise over the whole range from advice to devolution, and especially as arrangements depart from formality. In the shaping of policy and in democratic theory functional and electoral responsibility (or participation) are potentially at odds in distribution of the "new property" and regulation of the old. How shall we balance the claims of decentralization and participation with administrative responsibility?[90]

Finally, I'll recur to federalism as an external dimension of administrative responsibility, limiting its consideration to a couple of aspects of federal grants-in-aid. One has to do with their regulative effects (incidental or deliberate) on the structure and functions of "distributed self-government." I have in mind not so much the implicit conditioning of priorities through matching provisions as the more thoroughgoing "constituent" policies of restructuring state and local government through professionalization, regionalization, functional particularization, clientele targeting, and participative or consultative requirements. This is simply to suggest again that there is an issue of the future of general-purpose, electorally responsible jurisdictions in the federal system implicit in the programmatic and interest-group pluralism of national policy.

A second issue concerns the organization and balance of "fiscal federalism." The organizational possibilities range from narrow grant categories through functional or general block grants to true revenue sharing. We can probably expect this pattern to oscillate more or less as it has in the past. Programmatic categories have tended to reflect congressional concern for accountability as well as congressional response to group importunity. Project grants have favored federal administrative initiatives as well as "private federalism." They have also favored functional, territorial, and redistributive "targeting." Both categorical and project grants build constituencies. Functional block grants (with or without matching provisions or copious regulations) are a means of broadening national priorities and, especially, the federal position of the states. So-called general revenue sharing is likely, I think, to facilitate inflationary response to public-employee unions, though it is also a method of redressing fiscal disparities in the nation and its metropolitan areas while favoring general-purpose government.[91] The question is whether the "constituent" politics of federalism can be squared with a realignment of functions more rational financially and administratively. In the long run such a federal realignment might contribute marginally at least to resolution of problems of political alignment suggested in section III.

4. Constitutional Reform of the Separation of Powers and Federalism

More fundamental alteration of federalism—its constitutional abolition or reconstruction—figures briefly in the speculations of this section. But federalism has usually seemed to reformers more pragmatically malleable than has the separation of powers, and Article V is problematically intractable. Since the Civil War constitutional reformers have focused on the separation of powers, as I shall in the following synopsis of reform proposals. Among those who have believed that the distribution of checks and balances in the American branch-banking system tend toward governmental insolvency, four complex strands of revisionist thought can be distinguished.

One strand emphasizes *party* as organizer, normally subject to, and sustaining, more "responsible" presidential leadership. Constitutional reforms most commonly proposed to this end include four-year terms for members of the House of Representatives concurrent with the President's term, the addition of at-large members of the House elected by presidential slate on a winner-take-all basis to provide more national representation with workable executive majorities, and repeal of the "advice and consent" functions of the Senate—sometimes coupled with provision for override of Senate "vetoes" by the House. Along this line of reform the presidential veto power might or might not be retained; or it might become an "item veto."

Some reformers would abolish the electoral college, electing the President directly either by national plurality vote or through the weighted electoral college system without its present aggregate majority requirement. In the latter case a presumably critical issue arises regarding the consequences of election law for the two-party system: those who take such consequences seriously (as I do) are likely to favor retention of the present electoral college or, failing that, to fall back on a simple-plurality requirement in the national outcome; but proportional allocation of state electoral votes coupled with a minimum national plurality (usually 40 percent) have been proposed more frequently.[92]

In this line of thinking party organization would be consolidated basically through revival of the convention in presidential nominations, together with enlargement of the policy-shaping role of the party machinery. Conventions might comprise members of Congress and congressional candidates primarily or they might be based on

Charles E. Gilbert

grass-roots election of delegates by qualified "members" of more formal party organizations, or they might be structured more pluralistically through the allocation of seats to group interests. In any case, the party platform would assume larger importance in most such reform proposals: conventions might meet annually or biennially to shape the party program; presidential nominees would be expected to follow the party platform explicitly.[93] The place of presidential-primary elections in this scheme has been ambiguous: some "responsible-party" reformers have favored a role for primary elections, with or without the pledging of delegates, and perhaps in a consolidated national primary; but I think most members of the party-government school would minimize or eliminate presidential primaries in order to enlarge the role of party organization.[94]

A second strand of thought—not necessarily inconsistent with the first—emphasizes approximations to parliamentary or "presidential-parliamentary" government, in one version or the other. In the first version the President would be subject to formal votes of confidence in Congress; if he lost, a new election would be held.[95] In the other version, Presidents might dissolve Congress, failing a vote of confidence; then either Congress or both President and Congress would run for reelection.[96] The several forms of this general approach have in common a desire for closer legislative-executive liaison, more effective congressional leadership, and more stringent, contingent electoral discipline. But they differ sharply in their emphasis on Congress or President in the balance of powers. Critics of the former proposal think it would render presidential leadership too contingent and Congress too obdurate or domineering; proponents think it is a step toward more collective national management and prudent consultation. In the latter regard this proposal has affinities with the legislative-executive council or Cabinet discussed in section IV. 2, though the pure constitutional-reform proposal relies more heavily on the electoral sanction (which might, however, be combined with the joint-Cabinet proposal). Critics of the alternative version argue that presidential dissolution of Congress would risk the reelection of a similarly or more contumacious legislature, settling nothing or exacerbating matters—and that these problems might equally obtain if both branches stood for reelection, thus unsettling everything, including the direction of an already pluralistic bureaucracy. Supporters of dissolution have supposed elections would decide matters one way or the other; but they have also tended to favor reforms discussed above to foster party discipline and presidential leadership.

A third strand of thought would go further toward the fusion of powers. In the most tentative version President and Cabinet would sit in Congress, without vote, for the purpose of policy leadership.[97] The next step would be to repeal Article I(6)(2), thus permitting executive officers regular membership of Congress. And more thoroughgoing versions would move on toward parliamentary or cabinet government: the President's Cabinet would be chosen partly or entirely from Congress, perhaps with a congressional prime minister;

or the President would also derive from Congress, without independent election. The loose analogues here are present-day France and Britain; and one issue in the difference is provision for a stable chief of state. In all these versions, bicameralism is an obvious problem: short of unicameralism, the Senate might be diminished through constitutional amendments mentioned above, or the 17th Amendment might be repealed and a less popular mode of senatorial "election" contrived.

A number of concerns and intentions are combined in this strand of thinking: substitution of collective responsibility for the personalized and independent executive; stronger party organization and electoral accountability; more effective and programmatic support for political leadership; and, within a nationalized politics, a realignment of governmental "powers." As a contemporary analyst states the problem: the American system fragments "powers" and confuses "functions"; parliamentary systems consolidate "power" and provide a more sophisticated institutionalization of functions in which legislative intermeddling in management is minimized and administrative organization is more appropriately specialized—but in which policy-shaping power in legislation and administrative coordination is more effective governmentally and more responsible politically.[98] Indeed, one question about prospective abolition of the separation of powers today is whether it would adequately alter or consist with American administrative structure and tradition—whether executive direction and control of administration would be strong enough if the congressional role were altered, and whether the congressional role would indeed be altered. Among the other issues raised by parliamentary government in the United States are those of its majoritarian demands on a highly diverse polity, including its conceivable weakening of the two-party system and encouragement of coalition governments—an issue already suggested (section III) that seems to me of critical import. It is hard to imagine a less productive democratic polity than one combining coalition governments with the pluralism of American public administration. One's partiality to this approach is likely to depend as well on evidence that parliamentary governments have outperformed the American governmental system (*ceteris paribus*) in the past or are better suited to "postindustrial society."

The fourth major strand of thinking about constitutional revision begins with reanalysis of governmental "powers" and their appropriate relation to politics and popular sovereignty. One version of this approach figured in the thinking of Woodrow Wilson and, more particularly, Frank Goodnow, reflecting the reception of German doctrine in late 19th century American academic life.[99] It issued in the classical distinction between "politics" and "administration": the formulation and the execution of the people's will. Necessarily this approach tends to reprobate the separation of powers, given the modern role of the presidency. But it has always encountered practical problems in separating "administration" from "politics"—especially in the context of our Lockean and leveling tradition where the

Charles E. Gilbert

Rechtstaat is an alien legal notion and the deferential foundations of an administrative elite are lacking.[100] In Frank Goodnow's thinking, therefore, the distinction was pragmatically redefined in the Progressive tradition, toward the insulation from politics of more or less scientific, judicial, or business activities in government. And in this version (dating practically from, e.g., 19th century state regulatory commissions and local planning boards) the doctrine has been influential.

The reconsideration of "powers" was further developed in a more Hamiltonian direction by Rexford Tugwell—first in the conception of "planning" as a fourth branch of government; later by the addition of discrete appointed branches for regulation and for superintendence of political organization.[101] In Tugwell's thinking the separation of legislative and executive powers has been retained; but two Vice Presidents would be elected with the President: one as executive Vice President for general domestic affairs; the other for the "staff" and international departments—State, Defense, Justice, Treasury. (The next step in this line of thinking might be to elect a plural presidency, or Cabinet, as proposed by Herman Finer, to provide collective executive responsibility and relieve the personal burdens of the presidency.)[102]

The reanalysis of "powers" entails a tendency to inflate conceptions of governance without politics—of rational vision, technical discretion, virtual representation, and ambivalence regarding the liberal "state-society" distinction. American experience on this score has pretty clearly been that "out of (electoral) politics" implies susceptibility to more specialized and less explicit politics. And the American tendency has been to extend judicial controls over such sectors except as markets may provide discipline. But I suspect that "postindustrial" consideration of such problems as economic planning, wage-price adjudication, environmental regulation, energy development and conservation, or technology assessment will, in some dimensions of these topics, prompt further reanalysis of governmental functions or powers and of their institutional relation to politics and policy. One can imagine Congress creating its own agencies or ambiguously situated "branches" for advice or initiative on such subjects; and one can imagine their "rationalization" in an uncertain joinder of legislative and executive appointment, oversight, and reliance on their policy-shaping formulation. One can also imagine the progressive regionalization of some of these subjects, with implications for federalism, to be considered presently.

It is worth observing that the American separation of powers doctrine emerged two centuries ago from a tradition in which natural law and its more or less judicial application to policy bulked as large as popular sovereignty. Moreover, two centuries ago the "powers" we now identify conventionally were hardly conventional: they had been opaque in the *Second Treatise* and less than perspicuous in *The Spirit of the Laws*.[103] From this novelty there developed a remarkable uniformity among the "republican" structures of the states, varying mainly in application of the late Jeffersonian and Jacksonian principle extending election in all branches. (Within this basic federal frame-work local arrangements remained more heterogeneous.) One inter-esting approach to constitutional revision of the separation of powers (or development of new constitutional functions) today would be its essay in some state "experimental chambers," as civic reformers sometimes proposed in the early years of this century. If Pennsylvania could function with parliamentary government then, I suppose, so could any state. As for the nation, one issue worth considering is whether separated powers better serve its extent and diversity through multiple constituencies. This issue bears on the structure of federalism as well.

Both those who would abolish federalism and those who would reform it fundamentally tend to agree, I think, on the anachronism of existing governmental boundaries. It is harder, however, to agree on new ones. National "regions" (in the numerical range of a dozen), metropolitan areas, and local communities (urban and rural) figure in most reforming thought. Beyond this four major issues arise.

One issue is that of constitutional status: whether federalism in fundamental law should be dismantled; what in any case would be an appropriate allocation of functions; whether this allocation should strive for discreteness or encourage functional interpenetration; and what, if anything, should be done by way of provincial or local representation in the national government. (I'll pass over proposals for a functional, non-territorial federalism based on redefinition of "powers" and of relations between "polity" and "society.")

A second issue concerns the number of governmental levels in constitutional or pragmatical standing—that is, those with substan-tial autonomy or responsibility for supervision of constituent levels. Here conceptions of federalism or decentralization as systems of limited "sovereignties," of review and appeal, of fiscal redistribution and functional superintendence, and of political bargaining come into play. I think these considerations are critical in the mitigation of both central governmental burdens and local governmental pre-judice and impropriety as well as in political bargaining. In such considerations the argument for a strong intermediate governmental tier seems to me cogent.[104] Since I'm also persuaded of the contribu-tions of federalism to liberty or autonomy (as many of federalism's critics are not) and of its probable connections with the benefits of appropriate local and jurisdictional identifications, I'd preserve con-stitutional federalism for a variety of reasons there's no space or occasion to argue here.[105] And I would restrain regionalization of national administration out of deference to the states, whether or not the latter were consolidated in number and geographical logic. As for the last point, the logic of existence is certainly strong, even if not constitutionally ineluctable.

Thus a third issue concerns the permanence of territorial and jurisdictional delineations. Some reformers would accord constitu-tional standing to "states" but not to their boundaries and number.[106]

Charles E. Gilbert

Something like a national boundary commission would function (perhaps subject to legislative veto) in territorial and jurisdictional review, either at stipulated intervals or on occasion. A similar mechanism at the state level would function for adjustment of local boundaries. This proposal is easily caricatured as a floating governmental crap game; and it is easily classified as unrealistic in the light of American political traditions (or even of British experience). But, without reference to the national constitution, the state version of it—regarding local government, and probably subject to legislative veto—seems worth serious consideration as bearing on both territorial and functional jurisdiction.

Finally, there is the issue of general-purpose government, discussed in section III. 3 above, and related to the issue of the relative segmentation or commingling of functions. I say "relative" advisedly, since nothing more seems feasible or desirable. And beyond that I've already vented concerns on this subject and its implications for political organization and civic participation.

In all the constitutional proposals just hastily rehearsed I guess it goes without saying that tradition and the problem of articulation with existing institutions—perhaps especially the two-party system and the pattern of national administrative organization and responsibility—is an important consideration. I don't mean tradition for its own sake, but rather a concern for the prospective fit of reforms with consequential expectations and habits. There seems reason in this consideration for proceeding piecemeal through constitutional adjustments that may have strategic effects rather than through global reforms. But, given my own sense that the American system will probably work as tolerably with as without constitutional revision, this prudential advice may be merely prejudicial.

V. PUBLIC POLICIES FOR SHAPING THE SHAPING OF PUBLIC POLICY

It was suggested at the beginning of this paper that our ways of shaping policy are as subject to constructive change through public understandings as they are through legislative actions—though I should add that more explicit attention to the reflexive effects of substantive policies through their effects on public institutions is probably in order today. This paper concludes with a list of issues for committee consideration in the Bicentennial Conference—though not all of them have figured in the present version of the paper. The measures most worth considering can be classified as constitutional, pragmatic, and prudential for want of better terms—that is, as entailing constitutional reform or its functional equivalent, as subject to statutory action, or as depending on opinion leadership and civic endeavor. In my view the constitutional revisions are for the most part least important.

Among the difficulties, present and prospective, identified in section I, I tend to take most seriously the balance of competition and interpenetration between market, governmental, and subsidized "public-service" sectors in so-called postindustrial society along with that system's probable propensities toward inflation and cumulative educational "class" cleavages; the ambivalent trends toward centralization and private devolution in modern American government; the complexity of public organization and management resulting from the density and extensity of public policy and the trend toward public-sector trade unionism; the regulatory and allocative problems posed by endemic inflation, materials scarcity, and environmental stringency; the ideological assimilation of liberty to equality along with pressures toward public-service entitlements; and the likely challenges of "planning" in a society characterized by large-scale pluralism. Together with "garrison-state" tendencies, this constellation of difficulties seems likely to render the shaping of policy less subject to "popular sovereignty" as well as less susceptible to political leadership. This is the more so as it contributes—with the secular and reciprocal effects of congressional delegation, presidential aggrandizement, and electronic mass communications—to the erosion of party as a structure of leadership and participation as well as a buffer of responsibility.

Certain concerns will probably have been apparent in section II. These include the growing tension between government by institutionalized, electorally responsible elites and the populistic strain in American politics now fortified by highly educated aspirants to participation and respondents to electronic communication. I suppose a productive balance of responsibility and responsiveness in government implies some institutional insulation of decision and an ideological regard for liberty or autonomy consistent with, but not simply assimilated to, political equality. Still, the condition of political inclusion is critical. It implies, I think, not only continuing electoral organization and competition, but the improvement of local governing institutions subject to civic and electoral participation. Other avenues of participation surely contribute to the social conditions of popular sovereignty; but insofar as they tend to adulterate electoral organization and distributed self-government they may also be deleterious. In general, therefore, I suspect that liberal pragmatism and private federalism will tend to generate privilege, to dissipate legislative and administrative responsibility, and to frustrate political inclusion despite the recent reliance on delegation and devolution in national policy to redress imbalance in participation.

Several concerns dominate sections III and IV. For the shaping of policy through the concert and control of leadership and the diffusion of influence there seems no suitable substitute for the two-party structure. It is difficult today to take an oracular stand between the "responsible-party-government" optimists and the Cassandras on the score, or between the pluralist complacency of a decade ago and those who favor a corporate politics of programs without reference to party. I'm persuaded that the Cassandras have rightly identified some worrisome prospects for party organization and alignment; and I think the restoration of more than a modicum of party responsi-

Charles E. Gilbert

bility is a cause of high priority if public policy, leadership, and participation are to be institutionalized effectively. I guess it will be evident that my aspirations for the party system fall well short of high majoritarianism.

It may also be evident that I think the federal system needs attention. Indeed, I'm perverse enough to believe that the improvement of state governments as policy shapers and structures of sovereignty in relation to local government is conceivable and (for reasons adduced in sections III and IV) desirable. Inter alia, this implies some sorting out of functions and grant patterns at the national level, with early emphasis on public-welfare policy and long-run attention to its containment.

I suspect Congress will find it increasingly difficult to function adequately in its multiple roles, and especially in the deliberate shaping of policy. The technicality and schematic requirements of modern policy are less at issue here, I suppose, than decline of the conditions of legislative leadership and deterioration of the presidential connection. The materials of legislative leadership, like those of party restoration, are not apparent now, though the importance of preserving the several functions of Congress in its quintessential representative role is more apparent than ever.

Finally, whatever the inevitable dispersive effects of a strong Congress, together with those of liberal-pragmatic doctrines of administrative responsibility, I think we need to work toward more administrative consolidation. I don't mean by this larger departments or more immediate presidential supervision or even the bureaucratic merger of appropriately "independent" agencies. I do mean more managerial integration toward the top and through the line departments. I suppose the conditions of modest progress on this score lie in more collective consultative presidential leadership and liaison with Congress; in greater organizational integration of the "higher" civil service; and in managerial doctrine and practice that are both technically sophisticated and politically sensitive. These are also conditions of response to the challenge of "planning," not as desirably global and comprehensive, but as sufficiently purposive and articulate to render "planning" selective and politically responsible.

Even modest progress toward administrative consolidation in this sense is a tall order. Its proximate condition is probably the repair of checks and balances toward a system sustaining more collective leadership in both legislative and executive branches and more consultation between them. Some visible party organization and viable party alignments would help a lot in these connections. Here the problem is to reconnect presidency and party, and to that end some retrogression in presidential nominating arrangements might be helpful. That would mean party conventions without too many pledged delegates and with ample representation of congressional membership; and if such proceedings don't justify prime television time then perhaps they could be reported in the newspapers. Toward the connection of President and Congress I think the Cabinet expansion toward a legislative council discussed in section IV is worth trying. If that's insufficient then a constitutional amendment to provide for a vote of confidence might be considered.

Save possibly (with reservations) for adoption of four-year terms in the House of Representatives, concurrent with presidential terms, I don't look toward formal constitutional alteration for help.[107] That is partly because, with reference to issues suggested in section II, I suspect the separation of powers makes a practical, beneficial difference for liberal-democratic values in American society, on balance. (Among its institutional benefits a strong Congress and reinforcement of the two-party system merit mention.) In my reading, the founding compromise has served effectively and flexibly, for the most part, to balance responsibility and responsiveness in national leadership, and I doubt the interpretation that it induced civil war in the last century. In the course of this century, it seems to me, the balance of responsibility has gradually tilted too far on the presidential side, exceeding reasonable limits of executive capacity and accountability. Now the system's insulating and plebiscitarian properties there need more institutionalization and, especially, congressional participation in an age of massive administration and mass communication. Measured progress toward a "modern" party system seems paradoxically in order now, when the popular conditions of it seem problematical; but I'll suggest that we might best begin at the top, with presidential and congressional leadership, responding to a sense of necessity through more conciliar responsibility.

VI. ISSUES FOR CONSIDERATION

The effects of measures aimed at shaping the shaping of policy in the United States can be no more than conjectural. Necessity and uncertainty both suggest an incremental method. As suggested above, the measures worth considering can be classified as constitutional, pragmatic, and prudential. The following list of topics for discussion is simply a catalogue, with references to the foregoing discussion of issues, and concludes this long paper at last.

A. Should the separation of powers be attenuated or eliminated? Progressive steps in this direction include:

1. The conciliar approach, without constitutional reform: IV.2, IV.4.
2. The vote of confidence. IV.4.
3. Congressional dissolution, with or without presidential resignation. IV.4.
4. Presidential and Cabinet membership of Congress. IV.4.
5. Parliamentary or cabinet government. IV.4.

B. The redefinition of governmental "powers" and constitutional establishment of new "branches." IV.4.

C. Constitutional reconstruction of Congress:

Charles E. Gilbert

1. The four-year term in the House of Representatives. IV.4.
2. Retrenchment and/or reconstitution of the Senate. IV.4.
3. Unicameralism. IV.4.

D. The federal system.

1. Its constitutional abolition. IV.4.
2. Consolidation and reduction in the number of states. IV.4.
3. More thoroughgoing federal regionalization. IV.4.
4. The reconstruction of state government: experimentation with the separation of powers. IV.4.
5. The improvement of general-purpose local government. IV.4, III.3.

E. The electoral system.

1. Reform of the electoral college. IV.4, III.1.
2. Alternatives to single-member-district, plurality elections. IV.4, III.1.
3. The control of election expenditures. III.5.
4. Registration and minor-party ballot opportunities.
5. Electoral substitutes: the referendum.

F. Revision of the First Amendment.

1. With respect to regulation of the mass media.
2. With respect to regulation of parties and elections.
3. With respect to religious institutions as objects of public policy in a pluralistic society.

G. Reconstitution of the party system.

1. Reform of presidential nominating procedures. IV.4, III.5, III.1.
2. Through legislative-executive consolidation or liaison (above).

H. Executive branch reorganization short of constitutional reform.

1. Civil service consolidation. IV.3.
2. The improvement of managerial and analytic technique. IV.3.
3. Larger presidential reorganization authority. IV.3.
4. The enhancement of "planning" organization. IV. 3, III.2, I.2.
5. The merger of regulatory organization, or the further insulation of special functions. IV.3, IV.4.
6. The restriction of devolution to private parties. IV.3, III.2, I.8 and 9.
7. The control of policy shaping through governmental contracting. IV.3.
8. Judicialization, ethical and procedural standards, revision of conflict-of-interest statutes. IV.3.
9. Policy toward public-employee organization and collective bargaining. IV.3.
10. Can or should the presidency and executive-branch management be more fully "institutionalized"? IV.2 and 3.

Shaping of Public Policy

I. The reorganization of Congress short of constitutional reform.

   1. The committee structure. IV.1.
   2. The conditions of leadership. IV.1, III.1.
   3. The control of delegated legislation and the role of the legislative veto. IV.3, III.2.
   4. Congressional staffing and the institutionalization or professionalization of Congress. IV.1.
   5. More effective direction and control of administration. IV.3, IV.1.

J. The federal system short of constitutional reform.

   1. The enhancement of state government through reallocation of functions and alteration of federal-grant patterns. IV.4, IV.3, III.3, I.8.
   2. The balance and makeup of grants: categorical and block; program and project. Forms of revenue sharing. IV.3.
   3. The balance of special-purpose and general-purpose local government. IV.4, IV.3, III.2, I.8.
   4. The territorial jurisdiction of local government, primarily in urban areas. IV.4, III.3, I.7.

K. The regulation and encouragement of interest groups and associations.

   1. Regulation of group organization and participation opportunities. III.2 and 3.
   2. Governmental devolution and subsidy to private organizations. IV.3, III.2, I.2 and 8.
   3. Does the regulation of lobbying need revision in either Congress or executive branch or both? IV.3 and 1.

L. Participation as an object of policy.

   1. Devolution and "private federalism." IV.3, III.2 and 3, I.8.
   2. Group regulation, and industrial self-government. See K(1) above.
   3. Regulation of political-party organization. IV.4, III.1 and 3.
   4. The roles of general-purpose and special-purpose local government. See J(3) above.

M. Secrecy and publicity in government.

   1. The appropriate balance of "sunshine" and discretion. IV.3.
   2. The control of institutional advertising by governmental agencies. IV.3.
   3. The balance of responsibility between public officials and the fourth estate. IV.3, III.5, I.6.

N. The policy- and opinion-shaping role of the media.

   1. How, if at all, should the right to publication be limited? I.6.
   2. Is there a place for public broadcasting in public information; and, if so, how should it be organized? III.5 and I.6.

Charles E. Gilbert

3. What are the professional and cultural requirements of a "free and responsible press"? I.6.
4. Is economic concentration of the media a serious problem; and, if so, is it appropriately subject to regulation? I.6.
5. What can the media contribute to fundamental public understanding and realistic trust in politics? I.5 and 6.

O. Public education toward civic and political competence.

1. Can we enhance political understanding and competence through the public-school curriculum, and, if so, how?
2. How can public education (including post-secondary education) effectively counter the meritocratic class cleavages projected for "postindustrial society"? I.4.
3. Is the shaping of educational policy becoming too centralized for the welfare of a free society? I.8.
4. In particular, should we more freely subsidize sectarian schools in the interest of a pluralistic society? II.

P. How might public policy better serve such conditions of "civic culture," social diversity, and personal welfare as tend to favor liberal democracy?

1. What options of welfare, civil rights, and human-resources policy might be of strategic importance for autonomy, equality, and commonalty? II.
2. How can privileged and dependent relations on government best be minimized consistent with autonomy, equality, and commonalty? II.
3. How should group differentiation and decentralization be balanced with generality and centralization of policy consistent with autonomy, equality, and commonalty? II.
4. In the long run, are governmental arrangements for devolution to or close liaison with private organizations more or less likely than administrative consolidation to create perceptions of corruption and to impair public trust? IV.3, III.2, and 3.
5. Have the density and extensity of national policy carried us beyond our administrative capacity, with resultant loss of confidence in politics and government? IV.3, I.10.
6. Even if not, can we handle the Phillips curve, the problems of energy supply, and those of environmental preservation without degrees of regulation or expectations of planning capacity that overtax our governing and political capacities? IV.3, III.1 and 5, I.1, 2, 4, 9 and 10.

NOTES

1. Robert L. Heilbroner, *An Inquiry into the Human Prospect* (New York: W. W. Norton & Co., Inc., 1974).

2. Charles A. Reich, "The New Property," *Yale Law Journal* 73 (1964), p. 733; S. M. Miller and Frank Reissman, *Social Class and Social Policy* (New York: Basic Books, Inc., 1968).

3. Theodore J. Lowi, *The End of Liberalism* (New York: W. W. Norton & Co., Inc., 1969).

4. C. W. Mills, *The Power Elite* (New York: Oxford University Press, 1956); J. K. Galbraith, *The New Industrial State* (Boston: Houghton Mifflin Co., 1967).

5. Daniel Bell, *The Coming of Post-Industrial Society* (New York: Basic Books, 1973). See also Samuel P. Huntington, "Post-Industrial Politics: How Benign Will It Be?" *Comparative Politics* 6 (January 1974), pp. 163–91.

6. On the sectors, see Talcott Parsons, *Structure and Process in Modern Societies* (Glencoe: Free Press, 1960). On wage inflation in the service sector, see William J. Baumol, "The Macroeconomics of Unbalanced Growth," *American Economic Review* 57 (1967), p. 415.

7. An interesting statement on this point is that of Peter Drucker, "On the Economic Basis of American Politics," *The Public Interest* 10 (Winter 1968), p. 30.

8. The speculations I offer here derive primarily from Huntington, "Post-Industrial Politics"; Nicholas Rescher, *Welfare* (Pittsburgh: University of Pittsburgh Press, 1972), chap. 9; and M. Donald Hancock and Gideon Sjoberg, eds., *Politics in the Post-Welfare State* (New York: Columbia University Press, 1972), esp. pp. 1–113.

9. On overt and covert policies, see Robert A. Dahl, *Who Governs?* (New Haven: Yale University Press, 1961).

10. The bases of this allegation are discussed in Huntington, "Post-Industrial Politics," pp. 182–86. The allegation antedates Watergate, and is perhaps most persuasive with respect to the war in Vietnam.

11. This is a prominent theme of Scott Greer, *The Emerging City* (New York: Free Press, 1962).

12. Morton Grodzins, *The American System* (Chicago: Rand McNally & Co., 1966). For the minority view, see Harry N. Scheiber, *The Condition of American Federalism: An Historian's View* (Washington: U.S. Senate Committee on Government Operations, Committee Print, 1966).

13. Numbers in civilian public employment at the several governmental levels are not, I think, at issue here (cp. n. 15). Since World War II state and local public employment (excluding education) has risen much more rapidly than federal-government employment—at the state level most rapidly of all, and especially in the 1960s; and the state-local increase is still larger comparatively if educational employment is included.

14. The automobile figures in two random examples: EPA's mandated standards for state and local air-pollution control programs, currently under litigation (the Clean Air Act of 1970), and the grant condition that state laws permit right-hand turns at red lights (Energy Conservation Act of 1975).

15. Federal civilian employment increased by 70 percent, 1930–40; by 97 percent, 1940–50; by 17 percent, 1950–60; and by 20 percent, 1960–70. Per 1,000 population it increased by some two-thirds in the 1930s and by some three-fourths in the 1940s, levelling off thereafter in this ratio.

16. See, for example, Don K. Price, *The Scientific Estate* (Cambridge: Harvard University Press, 1965).

17. On this argument, see Galbraith, *The New Industrial State*; and Robert L. Heilbroner, "The American Plan," *New York Times Magazine*, 25 January 1976, p. 9. And consider the preference of business leadership for statutory and administrative regulation over effluent and emission charges as a form of environmental policy.

18. Theodore J. Lowi, "Four Systems of Public Policy, and Choice," *Public Administration Review* 32 (1972), p. 298.

19. See, for example, *Flast v. Cohen*, 392 U.S. 83 (1968); the discussions in *Barlow v. Collins*, 397 U.S. 159 (1970); and *U.S. v. Students Challenging Regulatory Agency Procedure* (SCRAP), 412 U.S. 669 (1973).

20. For purposes of discussion in the Bicentennial Conference it seemed important to review various perspectives on our founding, constitutional assumptions, and the conditions of democratic government today. But the limitations of space in publication preclude retention of that material here; and in this severely truncated section I mean simply to point allusively to issues that figure in subsequent sections of the paper.

21. Charles S. Hyneman, *Popular Government in America* (New York: Atherton Press, 1968), p. 8.

22. On the connection with majoritarianism, see Austin Ranney and Willmoore Kendall, *Democracy and the American Party System* (New York: Harcourt, Brace & Co., Inc., 1956). For some criticisms of the conception from different perspectives, see Robert A. Dahl, *A Preface to Democratic Theory* (Chicago: University of Chicago Press, 1957); and Giovanni Sartori, *Democratic Theory* (New York: Praeger Publishers, Inc., 1963).

23. S. M. Lipset, in *The First New Nation* (New York: Basic Books, Inc., 1963), argues that through the heritage of constitutionalism, American politics was able to maintain a distinction between the source of authority (or sovereignty) and the agents of authority, avoiding populistic excesses, or what Samuel P. Huntington terms "praetorian politics" in *Political Order in Changing Societies* (New Haven: Yale University Press, 1968).

24. A fine analysis of the framers' view on representation is contained in David G. Smith, *The Convention and the Constitution: The Political Ideas of the Founding Fathers* (New York: St. Martin's Press,

Charles E. Gilbert

Inc., 1965). More generally, from the compendious literature on the founding intentions one must mention Gordon S. Wood's magisterial *The Creation of the American Republic, 1776–1787* (Chapel Hill: University of North Carolina Press, 1969).

25. Dahl, *A Preface to Democratic Theory*; and cp. M. J. C. Vile, *Constitutionalism and the Separation of Powers* (Oxford: Clarendon Press, 1967). See also William H. Riker, *Democracy in the United States*, rev. ed. (New York: Macmillan Co., 1964); and *Federalism* (Boston: Little, Brown & Co., 1964).

26. J. Roland Pennock, "Responsiveness, Responsibility, and Majority Rule," *American Political Science Review* 56 (1952), p. 791. For an opposing view, advocating constructive accountability to electoral majorities, see Riker, *Democracy in the United States*.

27. David G. Smith, "Pragmatism and the Group Theory of Politics," *American Political Science Review* 58 (1964), p. 600; and Lowi, *The End of Liberalism*, pt. 1.

28. See, for example, Richard Hofstadter, *The Idea of a Party System* (Berkeley: University of California Press, 1969). See also Charles S. Hyneman and George W. Carey, *A Second Federalist* (New York: Appleton-Century-Crofts, Inc., 1967), pt. IV, for selections from early congressional debates on the role of faction or party.

29. On the "responsible-party-government" doctrine, see Ranney and Kendall, *Democracy and the American Party System*, esp. chaps. 6, 17, 20–22. On the argument for a larger party role in congressional organization, see Samuel P. Huntington, "Congressional Responses to the Twentieth Century," in David B. Truman, ed., *The Congress and America's Future* (Englewood Cliffs: Prentice-Hall, Inc., 1965).

30. See, e.g., Gordon Smith, *Politics in Western Europe* (New York: Holmes & Meier Publishers, Inc., 1973).

31. For divergent views on this prospect see, for example, David S. Broder, *The Party's Over* (New York: Harper & Row Publishers, 1972); W. Dean Burnham, *Critical Elections and the Mainsprings of American Politics* (New York: W. W. Norton & Co., Inc., 1970); Everett Carll Ladd, Jr., *Transformations of the American Party System* (New York: W. W. Norton & Co., Inc., 1975); Samuel Lubell, *The Hidden Crisis in American Politics* (New York: W. W. Norton & Co., Inc., 1971); Kevin Phillips, *Mediacracy* (Garden City: Doubleday & Co., Inc., 1975); Gerald Pomper, *Voters' Choice* (New York: Dodd, Mead & Co., 1975); James L. Sundquist, *Dynamics of the Party System* (Washington: Brookings Institution, 1973).

32. Such current tendencies in the electorate are discussed in Arthur H. Miller, Warren E. Miller, Alden S. Raine, and Thad A. Brown, "A Majority Party in Disarray: Policy Polarization in the 1972 Election" (The Center for Political Studies of the University of Michigan, Mimeo).

33. Sundquist, *Dynamics of the Party System*.

34. Phillips, *Mediacracy*.

35. Pomper, *Voters' Choice*.

36. A couple of such participatory arrangements may be provocative illustrations: the community action program and comprehensive health planning (based on legislation of 1964 and 1966). There were cogent reasons for both in the "targeting" of policy—in one case largely on neighborhoods; in the other on regions. And there were persuasive "constituent" reasons in the countering of state and municipal bureaucracies or of hospitals and medical societies. But in each case there was also much diffusion of policy instead of more focused redistribution of income in the Poverty Program or effective regulation of medical facilities to reach a major source of escalating health care costs.

37. For example, David B. Truman, *The Governmental Process* (New York: Alfred A. Knopf Inc., 1951).

38. The vast literature on this subject is reviewed in J. David Greenstone, "Group Theories," in Fred I. Greenstein and Nelson W. Polsby, eds., *Handbook of Political Science*, vol. 2 (Reading, Mass.: Addison-Wesley Publishing Co., Inc., 1975); and Robert Salisbury, "Interest Groups," vol. 4, ibid. Two remarkable recent analytic treatments are: Mancur Olson, *The Logic of Collective Action* (Cambridge: Harvard University Press, 1965), and James Q. Wilson, *Political Organizations* (Cambridge: Harvard University Press, 1973).

39. Not that officials of the federal government have been unconcerned about problems of accountability in this trend. See, for example, the looseleaf *Grants Administration Handbook* of DHEW.

40. Grant McConnell, *Private Power and American Democracy* (New York: Alfred A. Knopf Inc., 1966); Lowi, *The End of Liberalism*.

41. McConnell, *Private Power*; Galbraith, *The New Industrial State*.

42. E. E. Schnattschneider, *The Semisovereign People* (New York: Holt, Rinehart & Winston, 1960); Peter Bachrach, *The Theory of Democratic Elitism* (Boston: Little, Brown & Co., 1967); Murray Edelman, *The Symbolic Uses of Politics* (Urbana: University of Illinois Press, 1964).

43. Lowi, *The End of Liberalism*; Robert A. Dahl and Charles E. Lindblom, *Politics, Economics, and Welfare* (New York: Harper & Bros., 1953), chap. 12. See also Smith, "Pragmatism and the Group Theory of Politics."

44. See, for example, Heinz Eulau, "Lobbyists: The Wasted Profession," *Public Opinion Quarterly* 28 (1964), p. 27; Raymond Bauer, et al., *American Business and Public Policy* (New York: Atherton Press, 1964). Compare E. P. Herring, *Group Representation before Congress* (Baltimore: Johns Hopkins University Press, 1929).

45. There is some discussion of these issues in Hans. A. Linde and George Bunn, *Legislation and Administrative Processes* (Mineola: Foundation Press, Inc., 1976).

46. Readers may recognize in these suggestions—the first and fourth especially—the program of Lowi, *The End of Liberalism*.

47. For some tendentious but provocative views of the former balance today and tomorrow, see Gal-

braith, *The New Industrial State*; and Robert L. Heilbroner, *Business Civilization in Decline* (New York: W. W. Norton & Co., Inc., 1976).

48. Dahl and Lindblom, *Politics, Economics, and Welfare*, p. 436.

49. For example, Bachrach, *The Theory of Democratic Elitism*.

50. Alan Altschuler, *Community Control* (New York: Bobbs, Merrill Co., Inc., 1970); Milton Kotler, *Neighborhood Government* (Indianapolis: Bobbs-Merrill Co., Inc., 1969); Robert A. Dahl, "The City in the Future of Democracy," *American Political Science Review* 61 (1967), p. 953.

51. On distributed self-government, see Charles S. Hyneman, *Popular Government in America* (New York: Atherton Press, 1968).

52. See, for example, Elie Halevy, *The Growth of Philosophic Radicalism* (London: Faber & Faber, Ltd., 1928) pt. 2, chap. 1; pt. 3, chap. 2.

53. Grodzins, *The American System*.

54. For an interesting discussion of this point, see Daniel J. Elazar, "The New Federalism: Can the States be Trusted?," *The Public Interest* 35 (Spring 1974), p. 89.

55. Sidney Verba and Norman H. Nie, *Participation in America* (New York: Harper & Row Publishers, 1972).

56. Gerald M. Pomper, *Elections in America* (New York: Dodd, Mead & Co., 1968).

57. Angus Campbell, Philip Converse, Warren E. Miller and Donald E. Stokes, *Elections and the Political Order* (New York: John Wiley & Sons, 1968), chap. 9; V. O. Key, *Politics, Parties and Pressure Groups*, 5th ed. (New York: Thomas Y. Crowell & Co., Inc., 1964), chap. 8.

58. Warren E. Miller and Donald E. Stokes, "Constituency Influence in Congress," *American Political Science Review* 57 (1963), p. 45. As to the expressed policy positions of candidates interviewed, this survey found generally greater congruence with majority constituent opinion among winning candidates than among the losers.

59. Edward R. Tufte, "Determinants of the Outcomes of Midterm Congressional Elections," *American Political Science Review* 69 (1975), p. 812.

60. Richard Rose and Harve Mossawir, "Voting and Elections: A Functional Analysis," *Political Studies* 15 (1967), p. 173.

61. Pomper, *Elections in America*, p. 253.

62. On the decline of party in the electorate, see, especially, Norman H. Nie, Sidney Verba, and John R. Petrocik, *The Changing American Voter* (Cambridge: Harvard University Press, 1976).

63. See, for example, Richard L. Rubin, *Party Dynamics: The Democratic Coalition and the Politics of Change* (New York: Oxford University Press, 1976); and for some suggestive speculations, Richard M. Merelman, "Electoral Instability and the American Party System," *Journal of Politics* 32 (1970), p. 115.

64. On this score the comments of Burger, C. J.,

dissenting in part in *Buckley* v. *Valeo*, 424 U.S. 1 (1976), are suggestive.

65. Nie, Verba, and Petrocik, *The Changing American Voter*, and Paul R. Abramson, "Generational Change and the Decline of Party Identification in America," *American Political Science Review* 70 (1976), p. 469.

66. Lowi, "Four Systems of Public Policy, and Choice." The nature of redistributive and regulatory policies will seem clear enough (despite their frequent indistinguishability in practice). "Distributive" policies confer benefits without apparent costs to other parties; "constituent" policies alter institutional opportunities for access and influence.

67. On this point, see Nelson W. Polsby, "Legislatures," in Greenstein and Polsby, *Handbook of Political Science*, vol. 5.

68. See, for example, J. R. Johannes, "Congress and the Initiation of Legislation," *Public Policy* 20 (1972), p. 281; and Ronald D. Moe and Steven Teel, "Congress as Policy Maker: A Necessary Reappraisal," *Political Science Quarterly* 85 (1970), p. 443.

69. For example, Samuel P. Huntington, "Congressional Responses to the Twentieth Century," in Truman, ed., *The Congress and America's Future*.

70. See, e.g., Michael W. Kirst, *Government Without Passing Laws* (Chapel Hill: University of North Carolina Press, 1969); Robert W. Dixon, "Congress, Shared Administration, and Executive Privilege," in Harvey C. Mansfield, ed., *Congress Against the President* (New York: Praeger Publishers, Inc., 1975); John E. Schwartz and L. Earl Shaw, *The United States Congress in Comparative Perspective* (Hinsdale: Dryden Press, 1976), chap. 7.

71. On proposals for such regularization, see e.g., Walter Gellhorn, *When Americans Complain* (Cambridge: Harvard University Press, 1966).

72. There is impressive testimony to this contribution in, for example, Robert E. Lane, *Political Ideology* (New York: Free Press, 1962).

73. Representative treatments include Stephen K. Bailey, *Congress Makes a Law* (New York: Columbia University Press, 1950); and *The New Congress* (New York: St. Martin's Press, Inc., 1966); James M. Burns, *Congress on Trial* (New York: Harper & Bros., 1949); and *The Deadlock of Democracy* (Englewood Cliffs: Prentice-Hall & Co., 1963); Richard Bolling, *House out of Order*, (New York: E. P. Dutton & Co., 1966); and Joseph S. Clark, *Congress: The Sapless Branch* (New York: Harper & Row, Publishers, 1964).

74. The discussions in Truman, ed., *The Congress and America's Future* are pertinent to this point.

75. As to the shaping of policy, the rise of some senatorial staff empires, reflecting the financial means of individual Senators as well as more liberal staffing provisions, may well be an unbalancing influence. As to investigative activities, a current case in point as this paper is revised is the House Select Committee on Assassinations, whose chief counsel is recommending a staff of 170. *New York Times*, 14 November 1976, p. 30.

Charles E. Gilbert

76. See, for example, Nelson W. Polsby, "The Institutionalization of the U.S. House of Representatives," *American Political Science Review* 62 (1968), p. 144; H. Douglas Price, "The Congressional Career: Risks and Rewards," in Nelson W. Polsby, ed., *Congressional Behavior* (New York: Random House Inc., 1971); and Lewis Mayhew, *Congress: The Electoral Connection* (New Haven: Yale University Press, 1974).

77. A forceful but useful statement of this perspective is Willmoore Kendall, "The Two Majorities," *Midwest Journal of Political Science* 4 (1960), p. 317.

78. Walter Bagehot, *The English Constitution* (1867; London: Oxford University Press, 1928).

79. I thing a useful recent treatment of these matters is Erwin C. Hargrove, *The Power of the Modern Presidency* (Philadelphia: Temple University Press, 1974). See also George E. Reedy, *The Twilight of the Presidency* (New York: World Publishing Co., 1970).

80. For different versions of this proposal, see Edward S. Corwin, *The President: Office and Powers*, 3rd ed. (New York: New York University Press, 1948); and Charles S. Hyneman, *Bureaucracy in a Democracy* (New York: Harper & Bros., 1950).

81. A general discussion of some of these issues may be found in Mark V. Nadel and Francis E. Rourke, "Bureaucracies," in Greenstein and Polsby, *Handbook of Political Science*, vol. 5, esp. pp. 411–29, with references to the large literature of the subject. I sought to identify some of the issues in the meanings and modes of responsibility in "The Framework of Administrative Responsibility," *Journal of Politics* 21 (1959), p. 373.

82. The quoted phrase is that of the late Wallace S. Sayre, who applied it to personnel administration in "The Triumph of Technique over Purpose," *Public Administration Review* 8 (1948), p. 134.

83. See Lloyd N. Cutler and David R. Johnson, "Regulation and the Political Process," *Yale Law Journal* 84 (1975), p. 1395, and James O. Freedman, "Crisis and Legitimacy in the Administrative Process," *Stanford Law Review* 27 (1975), p. 1041.

84. Compare Kenneth Culp Davis, *Discretionary Justice* (Baton Rouge: Louisiana State University Press, 1969), chap. 2; and James O. Freedman, "Delegation of Power and Institutional Competence," *University of Chicago Law Review* 43 (1976), p. 307.

85. Kenneth J. Meier, "Representative Bureaucracy: An Empirical Analysis," *American Political Science Review* 69 (1975), p. 526; V. Subramaniam, "Representative Bureaucracy: A Reassessment," *American Political Science Review* 61 (1967), p. 1010; Frederick C. Mosher, *Democracy and the Public Service* (New York: Oxford University Press, 1968); John Armstrong, *The European Administrative Elite* (Princeton: Princeton University Press, 1973).

86. See esp. Mosher, *Democracy and the Public Service*; and Paul Van Riper, *History of the United States Civil Service* (Evanston: Row, Peterson & Co., 1958).

87. See, for example, *Report of the Commission on Government Procurement* (Washington: GPO, 1972), 4 vols.; Clarence Danhoff, *Government Contracting and Technological Change* (Washington: Brookings Institution, 1968).

88. Useful discussions include Francis E. Rourke, *Secrecy and Publicity* (Baltimore: Johns Hopkins University Press, 1961); Francis E. Rourke, ed., "A Symposium, Administrative Secrecy: A Comparative Perspective," *Public Administrative Review* 35 (1975), p. 1; Joseph W. Bishop, Jr., "The Executive's Right of Privacy: An Unresolved Constitutional Question," *Yale Law Journal* 66 (1957), p. 477; Douglass Cater, *The Fourth Branch of Government* (Boston: Houghton Mifflin Co., 1959); Norman Dorsen and Stephen Gillers, *None of Your Business* (Baltimore: Penguin Books, 1975); James O. Freedman, "Summary Action by Administrative Agencies," *University of Chicago Law Review* 40 (1972), p. 1; Ernest Gellhorn, "Adverse Publicity by Administrative Agencies, *Harvard Law Review* 86 (1973), p. 1380; Edward Newman, "Government and Ignorance," *Harvard Law Review* 63 (1950), p. 929; Archibald Cox, "Executive Privilege," *University of Pennsylvania Law Review* 122 (1974), p. 1383.

89. On the Freedom of Information Act, see, for example, Note, "The Freedom of Information Act and the exemption for Intra-Agency Memoranda," *Harvard Law Review* 86 (1973), p. 1047; U.S. Senate Judiciary Committee, *Freedom of Information Act Source Book* (1974).

90. For conflicting views on just two such participative programs, see John D. Lewis, "Democratic Planning in Agriculture," *American Political Science Review* 35 (1951), p. 232, and R. Frieschknecht, "The Democratization of Administration: The Farmer Committee System," *American Political Science Review* 47 (1963), p. 705 on the farm committee system; and Peter Bachrach and Morton Baratz, *Power and Poverty* (New York: Oxford University Press, 1970); and Daniel P. Moynihan, *Maximum Feasible Misunderstanding* (New York: Free Press, 1969), on the Community Action Program of the War on Poverty.

91. See, for example, Wallace Oates, *Fiscal Federalism* (New York: Harcourt Brace Jovanovich, 1972); Charles E. McLure, Jr., "Revenue Sharing: Alternatives to Rational Fiscal Federalism?," *Public Policy* 19 (1971), p. 457; and Richard A. Musgrave and A. Mitchell Polinsky, "Revenue Sharing: A Critical View," *Harvard Journal on Legislation* 8 (1971), p. 196. For a politically sophisticated discussion, see Daniel J. Elazar, "Fiscal Questions and Political Answers in Intergovernmental Finance," *Public Administration Review* 32 (1972), p. 471.

92. Recent contributions to several perspectives on the electoral college include: Alexander Bickel, *Reform and Continuity* (New York: Harper & Row Publishers, 1971), chaps. 1–2; Lawrence D. Longley and Alan G. Braun, *The Politics of Electoral College Reform* (New Haven: Yale University Press, 1972); Donald R. Matthews, ed., *Perspectives on Presidential Selection* (Washington: Brookings Institution, 1973), chaps. 7–8; Neal R. Peirce, *The People's President* (New York: Simon & Schuster Inc., 1968); and Wallace S. Sayre and Judith Parris, *Voting for President* (Washington: Brookings Institution, 1970).

93. Recent discussions of presidential primaries

and conventions include: Bickel, *Reform and Continuity*; Paul T. David, et al., *The Politics of National Party Conventions* (Washington: Brookings Institution, 1960); James W. Davis, *Presidential Primaries: The Road to the White House* (New York: Thomas Y. Crowell Co., Inc., 1967); Matthews, ed., *Perspectives on Presidential Selection*; Judith Parris, *The Convention Problem* (Washington: Brookings Institution, 1972); Nelson W. Polsby and Aaron Wildavsky, *Presidential Elections* (New York: Charles Scribners Sons, 1973); Gerald Pomper, *Nominating the President* (Evanston: Northwestern University Press, 1966); and Austin Ranney, "Turnout and Representation in Presidential Primary Elections," *American Political Science Review* 66 (1972), p. 21.

94. A convenient recent source for the constitutional-reform proposals is Charles M. Hardin, *Presidential Power and Accountability: Toward a New Constitution* (Chicago: University of Chicago Press, 1974). The party-government position is discussed in Austin Ranney, *The Doctrine of Responsible Party Government* (Urbana: University of Illinois Press, 1954). For statements of this position, see, for example, Henry Jones Ford, *The Rise and Growth of American Politics* (New York: Macmillan Co., 1898); American Political Science Association, *Toward a More Responsible Two-Party System* (New York: Rinehart & Co., 1950); E. E. Schnattschneider, *The Struggle for Party Government* (College Park: University of Maryland Press, 1948); James M. Burns, *The Deadlock of Democracy* (Englewood Cliffs: Prentice-Hall, Inc., 1963).

95. See, for example, James L. Sundquist, "Needed: A Workable Check on the Presidency," *Brookings Bulletin* (Fall 1973) (Washington: Brookings Institution), p. 7.

96. Perhaps the best statement of this position is in Thomas K. Finletter, *Can Representative Government do the Job?* (New York: Harcourt, Brace & Co., 1945). As in most versions of this proposal, Finletter favored concurrent terms for the President and both houses of Congress, failing dissolution—in his case, six years. Discussion of this position and of other, more sweeping, constitutional reforms may be found in, for example, William Y. Elliott, *The Need for Constitutional Reform* (New York: McGraw-Hill Book Co., Inc., 1935); and C. Perry Patterson, *Presidential Government in the United States* (Chapel Hill: University of North Carolina Press, 1947).

97. Among Progressives in the early years of this century, this approach may be found in the thinking of Herbert Croly, *The Promise of American Life* (New York: Macmillan Co., 1909), and *Progressive Democracy* (New York: Macmillan Co., 1914, who advocated it in state government; and in the practice of Woodrow Wilson as President. The proposal to admit Cabinet members and other presidential officers to Congress to submit to "parliamentary" questioning is a variant barely worth consideration, I think. See Estes Kefauver, "The Need for Better Executive-Legislative Teamwork in the National Government," *American Political Science Review* 38 (1944), p. 317; and, on practical deficiencies of the British question period, Bernard Crick, *The Reform of Parliament* (New York: Doubleday & Co., Inc., 1965).

98. Huntington, *Political Order in Changing Societies*, chap. 2. So far as I know, Huntington is *not* a proponent of abolition of the American separation of powers.

99. Frank J. Goodnow, *Politics and Administration* (New York: Macmillan Co., 1900); Woodrow Wilson, *Constitutional Government in the United States* (New York: Columbia University Press, 1908); and "The Study of Administration," *Political Science Quarterly* 2 (1887), p. 204.

100. On this point, see Norton Long, "Power and Administration," *Public Administration Review* 9 (1949), p. 257; "Bureaucracy and Constitutionalism," *American Political Science Review* 46 (1952), p. 808; and "Public Policy and Administration: The Goals of Rationality and Responsibility," *Public Administration Review* 14 (1954), p. 61.

101. Rexford G. Tugwell, "Implementing the Public Interest," *Public Administration Review* 1 (1940), p. 32; and *The Emerging Constitution* (New York: Harper's Magazine Press, 1974).

102. Herman Finer, *The Presidency: Crisis and Regeneration* (Chicago: University of Chicago Press, 1960).

103. See, for example, the discussion in M. J. C. Vile, *Constitutionalism and the Separation of Powers*, p. 24. Legislation was then, by derivation from positive necessity and popular sovereignty, a reasonably definite function; but its appropriate scope and contemplation in the shaping of national policy were ill-defined in relation to magistracy, prerogative, and adjudication as well as to such local institutions as commissioners, justices and juries.

104. See, for example, Paul Ylvisaker, "Criteria for a 'Proper' Areal Division of Powers," in Arthur Maass, ed., *Area and Power: A Theory of Local Government* (New York: Free Press, 1959); Leonard D. White, *The States and the Nation* (Baton Rouge: Louisiana State University Press, 1953); and Charles E. Gilbert and David G. Smith, "The Modernization of American Federalism," in Murray S. Stedman, Jr., ed., *Modernizing American Government* (Englewood Cliffs: Prentice-Hall, Inc., 1968).

105. For the contrary view, see William H. Riker, *Federalism: Origin, Operation, Significance* (Boston: Little, Brown & Co., 1964); and "Federalism," in Greenstein and Polsby, eds. *Handbook of Political Science*, vol. 5. See also the following exchange of views on federal institutions as better reflecting public preferences than unitary institutions: William H. Riker and Ronald Schaps, "Disharmony in Federal Government," *Behavioral Science* 2 (1957), p. 276; and J. Roland Pennock, "Federal and Unitary Government—Disharmony and Frustration," *Behavioral Science* 4 (1959), p. 147.

106. For example, Tugwell, *The Emerging Constitution.*

107. On practical difficulties in the four-year term, see Charles O. Jones, *Every Second Year* (Washington: Brookings Institution, 1967).

The Pennſylvania Packet, *and Daily Advertiſer.*

[Price Four-Pence.]   WEDNESDAY, SEPTEMBER 19, 1787.   [No. 2690.]

WE, the People of the United States, in order to form a more perfect Union, eſtabliſh Juſtice, inſure domeſtic Tranquility, provide for the common Defence, promote the General Welfare, and ſecure the Bleſſings of Liberty to Ourſelves and our Poſterity, do ordain and eſtabliſh this Conſtitution for the United States of America.

REPORT on the DELIBERATIONS of COMMITTEE III
by Gerald Frug and John Honnold

PRESIDENTIAL PRIMARIES AND THE DECLINE OF THE POLITICAL PARTY SYSTEM

Committee III turned its attention first to the role of political parties in the United States. Although the party system has been the traditional method by which the widely divergent groups in our society have shaped their goals into proposals for government action, the strength of the party system has declined in recent years, as evidenced by the rise in split-ticket voting and the increase in the number of people calling themselves independents. Since a major ingredient of this decline has been the rise in prominence of the direct primary as a method for selecting nominees for President, the presidential primaries became the principal focus of the first session's discussion. Our focus on the presidential primary, the committee felt, could help us determine whether the disadvantages of the diminished role of political parties in one of their central functions, choosing a presidential nominee, were offset by other values. Such a focus also served to delimit what we meant by "political parties." The committee's concern was the quadrennial coalition of groups that form the presidential Democratic or Republican party, and not the different entities that constitute the congressional or state parties.

In discussing the presidential primary, the committee first turned to the reasons for its existence, reasons articulated by the Progressive movement where the idea of presidential primaries originated. These justifications for direct primary elections were not cited merely as historical references, however, since a number of committee members asserted their continuing validity. Two basic justifications of the presidential primary system were advanced. First, some stated that the basis of the long-standing anti-party feeling in America—a feeling demonstrated by the pride people take in the saying that they vote for the man and not the party—is the belief that nominees will be better if selected without party domination of the process. Party organizations, it is said, not only fail to add to the process of selection but cause unnecessary and undesirable factors to enter into the selection process. Secondly, even if it could not be shown that the results of the primary system are better than those achieved by a party-dominated selection process, there is value in itself in democratizing the presidential selection process. By eliminating the party organization separating the people and the nominating process, government becomes more accountable directly to the people.

Those who were concerned about the effect of the emergence of presidential primaries on political parties contended that the logical result of the arguments advanced for the presidential primaries would be the creation of one national primary to select the presidential candidates. Such a device, they asserted, would eliminate an important function that the parties have traditionally served: uniting disparate elements of society behind two competing presidential candidates. The party system, by requiring potential candidates to negotiate with the divergent elements that make up modern political parties, has helped to reduce the nation's ideological differences. A national primary, on the other hand, would increase those differences, since primaries normally have low voter turnouts, with those voting having strong ideological views. Reliance on a national primary would therefore threaten to produce candidates not truly representative of a broad range of American opinion.

A second argument advanced by those who criticized the direct primary system was that there is a danger that primary results can be determined by style, particularly style on television, without adequate reference to substantive programs. The committee was referred to the then ongoing process of choosing a new British prime minister. There, the candidates were being screened by fellow members of the parliamentary party, people familiar with their capabilities and views. Thus, it is likely that a candidate would be selected on his record, without reference to matters of style. The primary system, on the other hand, offered such rewards of publicity that people were likely to run simply for public exposure. Indeed, the amount of this exposure itself may determine the outcome. Such a process is not likely to eliminate undesirable candidates or to attract to the race candidates capable of the job but wary of the primary process.

A final argument against the diminished party role in the nominating process was that a meaningful and effective choice by voters was diminished as well. Presenting the electorate with policy choices was less likely to be achieved in the state-by-state media campaign engendered by the primary system than it would be by the formation of coalitions within a party to gain nomination. Such a lack of content in the electoral choice engenders apathy, weakening the democratic process itself. It at the same time complicates the ability of a President once elected to work with Congress, since the absence of a strong party tie might further fracture the government process, leading to divisions which would undermine the ability to govern.

Gerald Frug and John Honnold

Those who argued in favor of the presidential primary system responded to the arguments in favor of a party role in the nominating process in a number of ways. First, they argued that cohesiveness between the President and Congress based on party ties rarely existed and, when it did, often was undesirable. Secondly, they found the attack on the primary system fundamentally anti-democratic in tone, based on a reluctance to let the people decide themselves on the candidates. Finally, they questioned the proposition that a primary system prevented the adequate formulation of issues. To the extent that the party was a method of articulating a set of governmental objectives, they argued, the party system was not in a decline. Rather, the decline was in the party as an organization. Party philosophy still affected the voters, and the building of a governing consensus within a party can best be made by allowing a candidate to form coalitions by attracting voters. This process not only increases interest in politics, but also encourages the type of entrepreneurial candidate—the outsider—whom we ought to encourage. The choosing of an insider, as in Britain, may not always be desirable.

Though the debate was by no means resolved, there seemed to be a good deal of support from people supporting both points of view for what might be considered a compromise position, a system of regional presidential primaries. Such a plan envisions a series of state primaries on a given day in one region of the country, with other regions holding similar primaries over a period of several weeks. Such a system would allow a second look at the candidates after a first vote, so that new coalitions could form and new candidates could emerge. It also would cut down on campaign costs. Most importantly to some, it would permit the continued existence of a type of uncommitted delegate—either elected on a no preference or favorite son slate—who could help stabilize and direct the selection process at a convention. Some saw this kind of regional primary as a way to create a balance between the role of the primary system and of the party system in candidate selection.

THE SEPARATION OF POWERS: EXCESSIVE DELEGATION OF CONGRESSIONAL POWER TO THE PRESIDENT

A number of committee members were concerned that effective operation of government required an improved working relationship between Congress and the President. Some argued that the method of achieving this result should be greater congressional control over presidential decisions; others saw instead the need for greater presidential power to gain congressional support for his program. These inconsistent approaches to a more unified government program both rested on a common assumption: that intergovernmental conflict could threaten the ability of the government to function effectively. Although no committee member argued for a strengthened party system as the principal device for easing this conflict, some felt that greater weakening of the party system would dangerously exacerbate the system's current difficulties.

The aspect of this problem most extensively discussed by the committee was the excessive extent of legislative delegation of power in recent times to the executive branch. Although some saw hopeful signs of reversing this increase in delegated authority because of the recent formation of congressional budget committees[1] and the rising influence of party caucuses in developing policies independently of presidential initiative, others argued that the tendency remained for Congress to leave major decisions to the executive. While this tendency derives at times from a congressional determination that details of policy must of necessity be filled in by executive implementation, it stems at other times from the inability of Congress to decide what its policy or program ought to be. The result too often is that Congress merely says to the President: here is a problem—do something about it.

Some committee members felt than an extensive amount of delegation to the executive was inevitable, since details could never be adequately decided in advance. In addition, as long as the basic constitutional structure of prohibiting legislators from serving as administrators of public policy remains,[2] there can be no effective congressional role in formulating specific policy through participating in implementation. The issue then became whether there can be a congressional role in policy formulation after policy implementation by the executive has begun.

A number of committee members argued that Congress can adequately reassert its authority through legislative oversight of executive action. Given the recently strengthened congressional committee system caused by the decline of its baronial structure, Congress can review how the executive is administering its policies and, through an informal but important give and take, can cause the modification of these policies. Congressional oversight, therefore, allows sufficient latitude for executive discretion, but provides Congress with the ability continuously to monitor and check the exercise of that discretion.

Other committee members felt that congressional oversight was an insufficiently powerful tool to control executive action. First, they argued, oversight could be effective only in those cases of delegation in which Congress had agreed on a policy and had delegated only the details of implementation. In those cases in which delegation simply reflected the fact that Congress had never formulated a policy, congressional oversight could not enforce a nonexisting congressional mandate. If a policy dispute between a committee of Congress and the executive agency arose in such a case, there would be no method for resolving it. Only a new act of Congress could effectively cause the executive to change the policy Congress authorize him to adopt. Another troubling result of these types of policy disputes is that recently they have often ended in litigation, thus transferring to the courts the task of determining the policy Congress failed to define. Although some saw this attempt to shift important political issues to the nonpolitical branch of government as an

Gerald Frug and John Honnold

inevitable feature of democratic systems, many felt it to be an inadequate and undesirable method of checking on administrative abuse. The Employment Act of 1946[3] was cited as an example of a delegation of congressional power without adequate definition of policy, leaving Congress unable to check executive policy by oversight. Surely, it was argued, the courts cannot specify congressional policy in such a case.

A second problem with reliance on congressional oversight raised by committee members is that even when it can be effective—where Congress has formulated a policy—oversight may come too late, since many executive actions taken are irreversible. Although Congress could correct future abuses in those cases in which policy development is slow and time consuming, in other situations, particularly those involving foreign affairs, executive action may be taken so quickly and be so final that no congressional role is possible. The result is executive domination of government policy.

Finally, since oversight is not widely seen as a glamorous part of the congressional function, some feared that oversight would simply be left to congressional staff. The result would be the undesirable situation of one nonelected group of individuals, working for Congress, negotiating with another nonelected group of individuals, working for the President, with their agreement resulting in government policy. This was not seen as an acceptable method of public policy decision-making.

Those unsatisfied with reliance on congressional oversight sought ways to force Congress to formulate policy adequately prior to its enactment of legislation. One approach suggested was the resurrection of the dormant judicial doctrine of unconstitutional delegation of legislative power.[4] In some cases, Congress should not be allowed to evade its constitutional responsibility to set government policy, and if it tries to do so, the courts should invalidate its delegation of power to the executive. Congress then would be forced to formulate its policy more specifically when it reconsidered the legislation. Another suggestion was the addition of a provision in some legislation for the automatic termination of the legislation at a given date. This device would force Congress to periodically take a look at its programs. In this way, after the executive has had a chance to implement the legislation for a number of years, Congress would be able to specify more clearly its own objectives, thus narrowing executive discretion. The committee also noted the increasingly common provision for a one-house veto of executive action, or even a congressional committee veto of such an action. The constitutional difficulties in relying on these schemes were considered too serious to see them as a solution to the need to check executive discretion.[5]

One committee member felt that none of the proposals for recapture of congressional power over policy formulation dealt adequately with the magnitude of the problem. In light of the recent experience during Watergate, he argued, there is a need for congressional ability to force a President from office if he is incapable of governing. If the President was handling an economic crisis badly or ineptly managing a war, the Constitution now permits no effective change until the years remaining to the end of the presidential term have passed. Incompetence is not an impeachable offense, and there may be no physical or mental breakdown of the incumbent to bring the 25th Amendment into effect.[6] Such an inability to alter disastrous presidential policies, he argued, was intolerable. One method for preventing such an eventuality was a constitutional amendment giving Congress the power to vote no-confidence in the President, thus forcing him to seek reelection. To ensure that such a vote would not lightly be used, the entire Congress, Senate and House, would be required to seek reelection at the same time. Although use of such a power may be rare, recent events demonstrate that a crisis can arise which may lead Congress to be confident enough of the seriousness of the crisis and of its own position to force a new election.

ALLOCATION OF GOVERNMENTAL POWER BETWEEN THE NATION AND THE STATES

The committee recognized that at the Constitutional Convention of 1787 it was possible to secure agreement on a stronger national government only by dividing power between the nation and the states—i.e., a "federal" structure. The committee devoted a session to structural problems that have developed as governmental programs have multiplied for the nation and for the states and, most especially, for cities and metropolitan regions.

Erosion of General-Purpose Government and of Local Controls

The keynoter referred to the progressive erosion of general-purpose government. Part of this erosion has resulted from the creation of special-purpose institutions such as urban-renewal authorities and regional health-planning councils. It was suggested that this development tends to undermine the capacity of the people affected by these programs to participate in the shaping of policy. There were strong pressures toward special-purpose institutions but, in the view of the keynoter, these pressures should be resisted. Attention should be given to ways to enhance popular participation in the shaping of policy at the local level. This would also lighten the load of decision-making at the national level. The national government has become overburdened; wherever feasible, decision-making should be redistributed to local units.

The keynoter added that in the last fifteen years there has been a striking change in intergovernmental relations.[7] Federal grant policy has produced quasi-governments—private organizations with governmental functions.

Attention was drawn to the following dilemma: we need planning at the regional level for health care and other local problems. But we do not have a structure of government at the regional level to control these programs.[8]

Gerald Frug and John Honnold

The keynoter observed that a second significant aspect of the federal system of grants is a pattern whereby grants are made directly to local governments without reference to the states.[9]

One member observed that it was important to distinguish between two kinds of governmental functions: regulatory functions and those that are predominately the supplying of services. It was suggested that the states are needed to check discriminatory or corrupt behavior of local governments.

The supplying of services has become increasingly important. The crucial problem, when localities must supply the services, is that the sources of tax revenues are not located at the places of greatest social need. To coordinate tax resources with the need for services, the taxing function must be heavily concentrated on the basis of national uniformity. When the funds are allocated to local communities on the basis of need, one faces inevitably a separation of the responsibilities to impose taxes and to spend the money. Congress could be expected to establish general standards for the use of funds but, as one member observed, experience in the health-care field indicated that general oversight over expenditures was adequate. The problem of oversight would be more acute if a private group were given regulatory power.

National or Local Government: A Dilemma?

Some committee members supported the view that, wherever possible, functions should be allocated to smaller, local groups. It was suggested that important values are inherent in the nature of the political process itself, and that these values may be as precious as any concrete results that could be produced by the governmental process. One of these values is the creation of a wide variety of decision-making centers—units that can try projects on a subnational scale. It was noted that in many instances, the states and localities had served as laboratories for testing ideas; this testing sorted out projects that were useful from those that had theoretical appeal but presented unforeseen problems of implementation.

Other members of the committee responded to the suggestion that one should rely more heavily on the states and localities. This suggestion overlooks the fact that the federal government has taken on problems, such as relief, only because the states weren't doing the job.[10] There is no expectation that many of the states will ever be able to deal adequately with problems such as education and health. In these states, without national assistance, adequate education and health would be denied to entire generations. In addition, it would be an over-simplification to consider merely which governmental unit should do the job; the choice between governmental units determines whether the job would be done. Analytically, one might conclude that education is a local problem.[11] But this decision would mean that the strongest resources cannot be tapped for education, with the result that there would be less education. This is borne out by the fact that upper-income taxpayers, who are hit hard by national taxes, have generally opposed national programs, while people need-ing services are in favor of national programs since the national government has the money for financing.

This exchange of views recalled the distinction, mentioned earlier in the discussion, between (1) gathering and distributing revenue and (2) shaping and administering programs for the supplying of services. It seemed that the concerns of many members of the com-mittee would be met if the federal government would provide the funds while the states and localities shaped and administered the programs supplying public services.

A member of the committee suggested that at both national and local levels, planning in respect to governmental programs often proceeded in the dark for lack of basic information. It was suggested that there was need for independent or institutional fact-finding and for analysis of the facts on a systematic basis; reference was made to the work done by the congressional budget group and the Brook-ings Institution. Without such advance study, programs are launched without any solid basis for predicting the results of the new pro-grams; this leads to disappointment and waste of resources.

Governmental Units Shaped for the Size of the Problem

A member of the committee noted that in allocating authority to different governmental units, one might conclude that a separate governmental unit should be constructed for each problem. Thus, for water planning one would create a water basin authority; for air pollution, a different area; and for sewage disposal still another area. But this approach, in spite of its theoretical appeal, is impractical since too many governmental units are created for effective political control. The only practical approach is to use geographical units with boundaries which are rough compromises so that a govern-mental unit will do reasonably well for a wide range of functions. In support of this approach, it was noted that a large metropolitan area needs to develop a unified approach to a wide variety of problems such as the following: health-care delivery; water pollution; water basin administration; air pollution; education; transportation from home to place of employment and to public services; access to housing.

Another member of the committee pointed out that in allocating functions between state, regional and local bodies, it was important to define precisely the function to be performed and that it was inadequate to speak in general terms of transportation or pollution or health. For example, the state of Pennsylvania can handle the pollution problem in the Schuylkill River but not in the Delaware River.

The committee then turned to problems of government presented by urban areas which cut across state lines; examples mentioned were the metropolitan areas surrounding Kansas City, Chicago and New York City. It was noted that municipal governments depend for powers upon the state,[12] and that there is no governmental unit

Gerald Frug and John Honnold

with power to deal with metropolitan problems on a unified basis. It also was noted that some of the most critical social and governmental problems of today are concentrated in such metropolitan areas. The problems are aggravated when one of these states offers low tax rates to encourage affluent persons to move to or stay in that state. This leads to further cleavage between the people who have money and the people who need services. Unsolved social problems in one area (such as the center city) lead to ever-increasing flight to the suburbs, so that the fiscal and social problems in the city become unmanageable. In this setting, cities have been appealing urgently for federal help. However, national legislatures have been reluctant to pour adequate funds into the cities.

A member of the committee pointed out that, within a metropolitan region, many problems are interrelated. For example, effective health-care delivery may depend on the establishment of a transportation system that allows the disadvantaged to reach available clinical facilities. In addition, within a water basin it is important to deal on a unified basis with recreation, potability of the water supply and the use of the drainage system for the removal of wastes. It was suggested that such interrelated problems needed to be dealt with by a water basin authority.[13]

Population Density: A Subject for Control?

Concentrating the population in urban centers, one member observed, had proved to be a social disaster. It was suggested that it would be poor national policy to encourage the continuation of such concentrations of the population. If such concentrations were not subsidized, the population would tend to disperse and more viable social units would emerge. It was suggested that the migration of peoples to seek better living conditions—Europe to America; from the East to the West; from the farms to the cities—had played a vital part in the nation's development. In fact, migrations now seem to be taking place which are reversing the earlier movement from the rural South to the northern and eastern industrial centers.

One view laid before the committee was that since migrations of economic units and of individuals were the source of serious social problems, direct control over relocations of businesses and individuals might be considered. The committee was generally of the view that direct control over the movement of individuals created unacceptable problems of administration and of human rights. Constitutional protection is now given to freedom of movement,[14] and it would be unwise to remove such constitutional protections. And direct controls were considered unnecessary, since zoning could prevent excessive congestion of business and residential units. It was also noted that tax subsidies could be given to industries which located in areas of unemployment or economic underdevelopment. It was noted that these latter indirect measures avoided the problems of administration and of human rights that would be presented by attempt to control directly the movement of peoples or businesses.

Deliberations of Committee III

Interstate Compacts for Regional Problems:
Can Control be Given to the Region?

In connection with the problems of regional governmental units, it was noted that several regional problems have been approached by way of interstate compacts. It was recognized that the Constitution (Art. I, Sec. 10, Cl. 3) permits such interstate compacts with the approval of Congress. It was noted, however, that no way had yet been found to establish a regional constituency to control such programs. The following question was posed for the committee's consideration: under the Constitution, would it be possible to give voting power to the people of a metropolitan, interstate region and thereby establish regional control over the program? Examples were given of regional bodies that had run into serious difficulties for lack of a political unit or constituency to exercise oversight and control.

Several members of the committee were of the view that strengthening the governmental powers of regional units would be useful, and that there seemed to be no obvious barrier in the Constitution. On the other hand, it was noted that there were serious political barriers resulting from the reluctance of states to enter into such a compact. In addition, implications from the basic structure of the constitutions of the states might bar such reallocation of political powers.

These difficulties lead to a further question: in the absence of state approval, would the federal government have the power to establish such regional limited-purpose governmental units? The experience of the Tennessee Valley Authority was considered, but it appeared that the TVA had not been provided with a regional constituency with voting power to control its programs.

It was noted that various national programs had included provisions for approval of specific programs by local groups. It was suggested that if the program could be controlled from Washington there should be no legal barrier to relinquishing some of that control to a locality. It was suggested, however, that an attempt by the national government to confer special taxing power on a locality would present difficulties under the Constitution in view of the limitation on the national taxing power (Art. I, Sec. 8) that "all Duties, Imposts and Excises shall be uniform throughout the United States."[15] On the other hand, it was suggested that this difficulty might not be fatal. Some regional authorities can raise revenues by charging for services (e.g., bridge or tunnel tolls); where such revenues are insufficient, funds could be provided through grants from the national government.

THE EFFECT OF GOVERNMENT ORGANIZATION ON ITS ABILITY TO FORMULATE POLICY

In its fourth session, the committee turned to another problem caused by our system of separation of powers. The fear was expressed that our current governmental system fails to provide a way to decide

Gerald Frug and John Honnold

major government policies or to plan for an increasingly complex future.

In discussing this aspect of the shaping of public policy, the committee turned first to the problems of policy formulation at the state level. Although many people feel that most government policy ought to be made at the state and local level, the governmental system itself frustrates this objective. State legislators, generally without staff and inadequately paid, cannot effectively exercise their responsibility to decide local policy issues. Moreover, most state and local executives also cannot function effectively. If they seek aggressively to solve local problems, the regressive local tax system and the danger of forcing taxpayers and industry to move to other jurisdictions undercut their ability to do so. Too often the result of aggressive policy is that those who adopt it find themselves unable to win reelection. Inadequacies at the local government level thus help explain why vast amounts of responsibility have been transferred to the federal executive, not only by Congress but by the states as well. The states have tended to abandon their roles of policy formulation and implementation to become special pleaders for federal funds.

When these responsibilities end up at the federal executive level, however, they are handled by an executive branch divided between politically responsive administrators and career civil servants. Reference was made to the political administrators such as the assistant secretary of a cabinet department; usually his term of office is too short to enable him to learn about, let alone deal with, the problems he faces. An additional problem is that to the extent one appoints officials who already have expertise in the field in question, one brings into the government, along with the expertise, a built-in conflict-of-interest. The individual, having come from the private sector being regulated, will likely return to the same industry. This problem is particularly severe for the independent regulating agencies, where the likelihood of careful appointment is diminished and the chance is increased of the agency becoming a captive of the regulated industry. The result is that policies contemplated in the creation of the agencies are thwarted by the nature of the personnel hired to implement them. Some felt that the problems of conflict-of-interest in administrative agencies are so severe that a return of many functions now handled by the independent agencies to cabinet officials responsible to the President would be desirable. The basic problem, however, would remain—our political leadership constantly changes. No sooner has an official learned his job, than the turnover caused by a presidential election puts another person in it.

Beneath the layer of political leadership is the career civil service. Although many committee members expressed concern that the unresponsive nature of government was enhanced by the civil service system, the committee did not have a chance to explore the issue adequately. Simply stated, the problem is that while sometimes people are pleased when the civil service continues to function while the country's political leaders are disabled by crisis, as in 1974, at other times this fact gives us reason to wonder whether either the President or the Congress actually controls the operation of government.

As an example of the problems of conflict between the goals of political leadership and established government interests, the committee discussed an issue taken from the local level, the desire to strengthen metropolitan governments. The movement toward regional government in this country has been undermined by the strength of provincial interests seeking self-preservation, interests epitomized to one committee member by volunteer fire departments. Of course, the deeply felt need to control government locally is often constructive, but the fact that no political leadership has been able to curb the entrenched power of local interests, even when metropolitan solution is preferable, underscores the staying power of the current system of governmental organization.[16]

Given the inadequacies of state and local government, the divided structure of the federal executive branch, and the conflict between the legislative and executive branches discussed earlier, the critical issue of governmental effectiveness today is whether this governmental system can deal with today's complex problems, such as economic and energy policy. The issue, in short, is whether government as presently constituted can plan. The need for such planning was widely accepted by the committee, with the recognition that the extent of government planning and the extent of governmental intervention into the private sector are two separate matters. Indeed, unexplained and unarticulated governmental intervention was often seen as more dangerous than intervention based on an articulation by the government of its goals and objectives. Planning, then, was supported generally not as a form of gazing into a crystal ball, but as a way of forcing the government to articulate objectives and alternative means of reaching those objectives. Such a plan would serve as a way to educate the public and the Congress, enabling them to formulate policy. Of course, the ability to plan assumes the existence of data—a healthy assumption as some observed—but many felt that such data would never be acquired until the decision to plan is made. If one accepts the need to plan, the question remains: can our government plan? And if it can, can that plan be implemented?

On the capacity of the government to plan, some saw signs of encouragement. The Humphrey-Hawkins Full Employment and Balanced Growth Act[17] was seen as an example of a congressional attempt to define broad objectives of government policy and to require the executive to submit plans to meet those objectives. Congress would retain the power to evaluate the plan once formulated. In the bill, planning is thus properly recognized as an executive function, but an important congressional function remains—the power to force revisions in the plan.

Some saw greater difficulty in the prospect of a plan being implemented, because Congress has not generally organized itself to con-

Gerald Frug and John Honnold

sider a complex piece of legislation as a whole. Rather, numerous individual committees normally review individual proposals, fracturing the process and the hope of an overall attack on a problem. The new congressional budget process,[18] however, was noted as an example to the contrary, a process encouraging congressional self-discipline and allowing an overall congressional proposal to emerge.

The ability to implement a plan is, of course, always complicated by the fact that our democratic process allows constantly changing values, so that any plan once formulated is subject to modification or abandonment as our values change. While some saw this a reason for pessimism, others reminded the committee that ours is the oldest functioning democratic government in the world, with democracy today being rare at any age. The vitality of the system over 200 years gave some reason to hope that these future challenges can be met as well.

CITIZEN PARTICIPATION IN AND CONTROL OVER GOVERNMENT

The final session of the committee was devoted to ways in which citizens can influence government—in other words, the implementing of the democratic ideal. Two aspects were considered: first, ways to enhance direct participation in the processes of government; second, ways to strengthen control through the ballot.

Direct Participation

Citizen participation, apart from the ballot, has been encouraged in recent years by legislative provisions for public hearings before programs are finalized. An early development was the community action program under the Office of Economic Opportunity;[19] more recent instances have been provisions for hearings with respect to environmental problems, and the use of federal funds allocated under revenue sharing programs.[20]

Members of the committee reported that citizen involvement and influence under these programs had been disappointing. Some noted that the public had not been given adequate notice of the opportunity to participate in public hearings; in addition to providing a formal notice buried in a newspaper, invitations should be extended to the public by announcements on radio and television. Others suggested that public involvement was limited because of the difficulty of becoming informed about the complex issues involved in public programs.

It was also reported that when citizens did present informed views and suggestions they were disappointed and frustrated since there was little indication that officials took account of the citizens' views. One suggestion was that officials be required to accompany their decisions with responses to the views that citizens had presented; on the other hand, it was noted that this would merely add to the present overwhelming mass of paperwork, and might contribute to further delays and add to the opportunities for obstructive legal attacks. The courts, it was observed, had limited capacity to solve governmental problems; excessive demands were being made on the courts to deal with issues that should be resolved through the political processes.

The committee turned to the role of public interest organizations such as the League of Women Voters, Common Cause, the National Women's Political Caucus, environmental groups and similar citizens' organizations. It was noted that organized pressure by interest groups had long played a significant part in American political life. A significant development in recent years was the attention given issues affecting larger numbers of people, such as the quality of the environment and protection for consumers; even more basic was the attention given issues involving the structure of political processes, such as public financing of elections, and conflicts-of-interest by congressmen.

It was noted that public interest groups have little direct impact on votes in the legislature; their major influence was exerted indirectly, by informing voters of current issues so voters could write to congressmen and express an informed choice at elections. It was also noted that conscientious legislators who wanted to make principled decisions on public issues were grateful for the studies and recommendations of groups who were devoted to the public interest.

Do public interest groups really reflect the views of their members? In response to this question one committee member reported that he had noted instances where the position of the group had been decided by the leaders with little advance consultation with the members. Representatives of public interest groups acknowledged that advance consultation was not always feasible. The general objectives of the organization are known at the time that individuals join; on current issues that arise thereafter the procedures for consultation with members were being improved, but could not always be used with respect to specific steps to further the general objectives of the group.

Did the public interest groups divert citizens from participation in party politics? Contrary to this suggestion it was observed that the public interest groups mobilized citizens who were not active in politics. On the other hand, it was noted that television and public financing of elections had made it easier for new groups to take the lead in political campaigns.

Were there dangers in democratic pressures? One member reported that insistent demands for added services and benefits had, at least in New York, led to fiscal disaster. Was it possible to mobilize groups that were interested in long-range issues such as solvency? It was noted that the state and federal government, in helping the city, had imposed controls; the committee also recalled its earlier discussion of the need for larger governmental units for metropolitan regions.

Structures for Voting and for Representation

The committee also considered proposals for legislative or constitutional changes: universal registration of voters; modification of congressional terms; disclosure by candidates and legislators of financial interests; the method of selecting the Vice President.

Could wider participation in elections be aided by changes in the process of voter registration? It was noted that many voters were unaware of the deadlines for registration, or did not have the initiative to register in advance of elections. Proposals have been made for simpler registration (e.g., by postcard) or by compulsory universal registration by a door-to-door canvassing comparable to the census.

In the past, objections to such proposals had come from varying quarters: from a party that anticipated that the new voters would tend to vote for the opposing party; and from political leaders who were secure in their position with the registered voters and who feared that adding a new group of voters might have an unsettling effect.

Most members of the committee favored measures to widen voter registration, and thereby facilitate a larger turnout in elections, although it was recognized that these measures could not be expected to improve the quality of participation in the political process.

The committee considered proposals to modify the terms in office of members of Congress. One suggestion, which would require a constitutional amendment, would place an outside limit on the number of consecutive terms: e.g., a limit of six or seven terms for representatives and two or three terms for senators.[21] It was suggested that this would dislodge entrenched members and would make legislators more responsive to the voters.

It was observed that some of these objectives had been met by recent inroads on seniority as a basis for committee chairmanships. In addition, a limit on the number of terms curtailed the use of accumulated experience, and would override the wishes of the electorate who would prefer to reelect their representative. Most members of the committee did not favor this proposal.

Another proposal, also requiring constitutional change,[22] would extend the terms of members of the House to four years. It was noted that under such a proposal, a significant issue was whether the representatives would be elected at the same time as the President or in the middle of the President's term of office. The first alternative would encourage unity between the President and Congress; the second would encourage independence of Congress. It was noted that most congressmen favored the second alternative.

The basic proposal for a four-year term was supported on the ground that congressmen now must spend too much of their time campaigning for reelection; in addition, the present two-year term renders congressmen vulnerable to pressures and makes it difficult for them to support measures (like energy conservation) which sacrifice instant gratification for long-range goals. On the other hand, most members of the committee opposed the proposal on the ground that it would make Congress less responsive to the electorate. The Senate, by its six-year term, provided adequate independence; the House of Representatives in contrast, should be closely responsive to the people.

Deliberations of Committee III

The committee turned to proposals that would require congressmen (as candidates and while in office), as well as administrative officials, to make public disclosure of their income and its sources, and possibly of their assets.

It was noted that disclosure requirements could be implemented more readily with respect to persons appointed to public office since legislation could disable them from acting in situations where there was a conflict of interest. A congressman, elected after full disclosure, could not be barred from voting without disenfranchising the voters who elected him. It was suggested that for elected officials, disclosure played its most significant part during a campaign.

There was considerable support for some disclosure requirements for legislators, as well as for administrators, but no decision was reached as to the most appropriate scope of disclosure.

Should the officials' federal income tax returns be made public? It was noted that requiring disclosure of the complete tax return presented problems, since the return may include confidential and irrelevant material such as medical deductions and charitable contributions. In addition to current income, should total assets (such as ownership of land or corporate securities) be disclosed? One view was that disclosure of income should be sufficient. On the other hand, it was noted that assets that did not generate current income might give rise to conflicts-of-interest. It was agreed that measures for public disclosure were important, and deserved further attention.

Finally, the committee considered procedures for selection of the Vice President. It was noted that current procedures can result in hasty and unrepresentative action, with serious consequences when the Vice President must assume the office of President. Attention was given to a proposal that only a President be elected; the President would then nominate a Vice President who would be subject to confirmation by both houses of Congress, as under the 25th Amendment.[23]

In view of the limited time for consideration, no final position was taken. The committee, however, concluded that it was important that further attention be given to the procedures for selection of the Vice President, and that the need to improve the present procedures might well justify amendment of the Constitution. It was also agreed that, under these proposals, the Vice President should become an active member of the administration, so that he would be informed and experienced in the event he must assume the presidency.

Gerald Frug and John Honnold

NOTES

1. The Congressional Budget and Impoundment Control Act of 1974, P.L. 93–344; 88 Stat. 297, 31 U.S.C.; sec. 1301 *et seq.*

2. United States Constitution, Art. I, sec. 6, cl. 2.

3. 15 U.S.C., sec. 1021, *et seq.*

4. *Panama Refining Company* v. *Ryan,* 293 U.S. 388 (1935); *Schechter Poultry Corporation* v. *U.S.,* 295 U.S. 495 (1935); see generally, James O. Freedman, "Delegation of Power and Institutional Competence," *University of Chicago Law Review* 43 (1976), p. 307; J. Skelly Wright, "Beyond Discretionary Justice," *Yale Law Journal* 81 (1972), p. 575.

5. Such a procedure can take the form of enabling one house of Congress or one congressional committee to veto proposed regulations or even wording of such regulations without affirmative congressional action. See generally, H. Lee Watson, "Congress Steps Out: A Look at Congressional Control of the Executive," *California Law Review* 63 (1975), p. 983.

6. U.S. Constitution, 25th Amendment (Ratified Feb. 10, 1967).

7. Steinberg, *State Involvement in Federal-Local Grant Programs* (Advisory Commission on Intergovernmental Relations), pp. 1–2, 10–11 (1969).

8. For materials dealing with some of the problems and suggested solutions, see Frank I. Michelman and Terrance Sandalow, *Government in Urban Areas,* (St. Paul: West Publishing Co., 1970), pp. 815–34.

9. According to one study, there was an acceleration of grant-in-aid programs beginning in 1961. These direct federal-local programs included community health services for chronically ill and aged, air pollution, neighborhood youth corps, equal employment opportunity, law enforcement, urban beautification, and model cities. See Steinberg, *State Involvement in Federal-Local Grant Programs.*

10. See Steinberg, *State Involvement in Federal-Local Grant Programs,* at pp. 10–15.

11. For discussion from the point of view of constitutional law, see, for example, *Milliken* v. *Bradley,* 418 U.S. 717, 741–42 (1974); *San Antonio Independent School District* v. *Rodriguez,* 411 U.S. 1, 40, 44 (1973); *Epperson* v. *Arkansas,* 393, U.S. 97, 104 (1968).

12. This principle is commonly known as Dillon's Rule. See Michelman and Sandalow, *Government in Urban Areas* at pp. 252–55.

13. For an example of an interstate water basin authority, see the Delaware River Basin Compact, Act of September 27, 1961. P.L. 87–328; 75 Stat. 688; N.J. Stat. Ann., sec. 32; 110–1 (1963); 32 P.S., sec. 815.101 (1961); Del. Code Ann. 7; sec. 6501, 6511; ECL, sec. 21-0701 to 21-0723 (McKinney's 1961). For a general discussion of the Compact, see Bruce Ackerman and James Sawyer, "The Uncertain Search for Environmental Policy: Scientific Factfinding and Rational Decisionmaking Along the Delaware River," *University of Pennsylvania Law Review* 120 (1972), p. 419.

14. The right of interstate travel or freedom of movement has repeatedly been recognized as a basic constitutional freedom. See, for example, *Memorial Hospital* v. *Maricopa County,* 415 U.S. 250, 254 (1974); *Dunn* v. *Blummstein,* 405 U.S. 330, 338 (1972); *United States* v. *Gurst,* 383 U.S. 745, 758 (1966); and *Edwards* v. *California,* 314 U.S. 160, 163 (1941).

15. The uniformity exacted by the Constitution is geographical uniformity. It has long been settled that within the meaning of the uniformity clause a tax is uniform when it operates on the subject matter with the same force and effect in every state in which the subject of the tax is found. See *Fernandez* v. *Wiener,* 236 U.S. 340, 359 (1945); *In re Estate of Bonash,* 432 F.2d 308 (9th Cir. 1970).

16. See generally, Note, "The Urban County: A Study of New Approaches to Local Government in Urban Areas," *Harvard Law Review* 73 (1960), p. 526. Part of the problem involves the effect of legislative and constitutional home rule provisions, as well as the existence of adverse local political conditions.

17. P.L. 95–523, 92 Stat. 1887, 27 October 1978.

18. The Congressional Budget and Impoundment Act of 1974, P.L. 93–344, 88 Stat. 297, 31 U.S.C., sec. 1301 *et seq.*

19. Economic Opportunity Act, 42 U.S.C., sec. 2796 (1970).

20. Revenue Sharing Act, 31 U.S.C., sec. 1241(b) (Supp. 4. 1976) (amending U.S.C., sec. 1241 (1970).

21. Art. I, Sec. 2, Para. 1 and 2, describe the terms and qualifications for the members of the House of Representatives. No limit is placed on the number of terms a person may serve in the House. Art. I, Sec. 3 and the 17th Amendment prescribe the election and qualification requirements for Senators. As with members of the House, there is no limit on the number of terms which may be served. Of course, the President is limited to two terms by the 22nd Amendment.

22. See n. 21, *supra.*

23. Sec. 2 of the 25th Amendment provides that "whenever there is a vacancy in the office of the Vice President, the President shall nominate a Vice President who shall take office upon confirmation by a majority vote of both Houses of Congress." U.S. Constitution, 25th Amendment (Ratified 10 February 1967).

COMMITTEE IV

THE UNITED STATES AND THE WORLD
by Covey T. Oliver

It would be interesting to know whether the American people believe there is a crisis today in the management of American foreign relations under the Constitution of 1789. Most expert American observers of, or participants in, the conduct of the nation's official dealings with the rest of the world would agree that we have a unique, complicated, energy-depleting system of public law for the allocation of authority for the governance of our official conduct offshore. And they would find the present situation of this system at least somewhat controversial, both at home and abroad.

But these same American experts would divide as to whether anything can or should be done structurally. A considerable majority, probably, agree with the general thrust of Appendix L[1] to the Report of the Commission for the Study of the Organization of the Government for Foreign Affairs,[2] that by mutuality, patience, and other attitudinal acts of moderation, the qualified players of the "Foreign Relations Game" for the American side can improve the "game plan" result for the United States. So far as the evidence from writings goes, it seems that the preponderant opinion of experts, with some exceptions (as always among experts), is that it is unnecessary, unthinkable, or illusory to contemplate changing significantly the structure of American government for any reason linked to "The United States and the World." Nonetheless, some believe that it might be useful now to go through the exercise of reviewing the basic law controlling America's relationships with the rest of the planet.

Basic issues of governmental structure for foreign relations should not always be examined, as they usually are, only from the standpoint of our internal concerns and expectations about the Constitution and our associations with the rest of the world. The rest of the world is also vitally concerned with, is affected by, and hence reacts to, how America does things internationally.

Let us begin by seeing ourselves as others see us. We are a country that in its first 200 years has been phenomenally successful in every way in which the achievements of nations are measured; but usually the world does not credit our institutions and our way of life for this, as we tend to do, but rather believes that the good fortune of natural riches explains our success. Major resources, however, are seriously depleted now; and substitutes have not yet been assured. Some foreigners, following Adam Smith's view as to the fundamental wealth of nations, are willing to credit the American people also for the nation's success. But even this limited perception of us, the people, as the true wealth of the nation, is in decline now.

The United States is a federal, participatory democracy, whose state and federal constitutions all incorporate some version of separation of powers with checks and balances—thus requiring the interrelated independence of three branches of government. This makes us unique—*truly solitary*—in the world community. As Ambassador Moynihan did not tire of saying, democracy itself is no longer the form of government that a majority of states provide for or practice. Within participatory democracies, only a very few (not more than a dozen) states are federal in form, and of these options federalism is a serious legal factor in the foreign relations of only five![3] Finally, no other federalistic democracy has an operational separation of powers/checks and balances constitutional system. Nor, for that matter, do unitary (non-federal) states often practice separation of powers. In Iberic-America, for example, where the American Constitution was the model, of the few remaining democracies, only in Colombia and Costa Rica have separation of powers problems occasionally arisen in regard to relations with other states.

Although in the world community the American system of governance for foreign relations is thus exotic, our national tendency, exhibited even in the evaluation of our Constitution, is to disregard this basic fact and to treat the problem of foreign affairs and the Constitution largely as a matter of internal values and preferences. We ascribe an almost incontestable value to the constitutional status quo and expect the rest of the world to adjust to it; or, at most, we assume that the domestic gains outweigh the possible foreign affairs losses, now and possibly for all time to come.

But there is a rising tide of evidence that the rest of the world—especially the shrinking world of our friends—is finding our blandness in this particular increasingly irritating and destabilizing. We should not accept such evidence as conclusive, but we should not disregard it either. Thus, consider two recent illustrations:

> 1. Alfonso Lopez Michelsen, elected President of Colombia, observed, in regard to an unannounced shift in United States policy (from supporting a Colombian cut-flower export industry as relevant to Colombia's development to a Congress-pressured Treasury investigation of Colombian cut-flower imports as being subject to extraordinary [dumping] duties) that the episode brought sharply to attention questions of the reliability and

Covey T. Oliver

authoritativeness of United States foreign policy declarations and assurances.

2. The Prime Minister of Singapore at a White House dinner in his honor remarked in his toast that the friends of the United States are becoming increasingly uncertain and concerned as to who effectively speaks for the United States.[4]

Hence, as we proceed in accordance with the wishes and interests of the participants to examine issues of (or close to) constitutional dimensions arising from America's contemporary and projected roles in the world community, let us consider the perspectives of that community, as well as our attachment to our present system. "Interdependence" requires no less.

As we go forward, I remind you that the official report cited previously, and whose Appendix L was sent to the conference participants for prior study, is the eighty-third[5] officially commissioned study of United States foreign relations arrangements since World War II![6] These studies are not famed for focus on the types of questions that the conference should focus on here.[7] It has been 200 years, after all, since our government under the Articles began, and the soon-perceived inadequacy of this original system for the conduct of the nation's foreign relations was one of the major inducements to the Constitutional Convention of 1787. That conclave did result in a new system. It seems fitting now to move ahead with reevaluation, freed from the limitations of realism, practicality, and ethnocentricity that seemingly always bind official commissions. Perhaps if the framers had been practical—or realistic—they would merely have adjusted the Articles of Confederation a bit. We know to our advantage that they let their minds be bold.[8] Let us be bold enough to inquire.

FOREIGN POLICY AND THE SEPARATION OF POWERS

The Internal Situation Today

The American system of separation of powers with checks and balances is a system that, at the constitutional level, allocates action and commitment authority related to foreign affairs functions between the two political branches of government. The nonpolitical (judicial) branch, generally speaking, has shown almost "unjudicial" awareness of the practical needs of untroubled foreign relations where issues have arisen as between people and the executive,[9] but so far the courts have not ventured far into Constitution-level resolution of conflicts of jurisdiction between the executive and the legislative branches.

Those who have read Appendix L, who have studied Professor Louis Henkin's elegant small treatise,[10] or have otherwise absorbed our constitutional fundamentals know that the Constitution of 1789 creates an executive who (although this is not said in so many words) internationally is the American chief of state (not merely head of government). The powers of this executive are not elaborately enumerated, as are those of the Congress. The Constitution says the President has the executive power. It is clear that under the Constitution the President personally or through his delegates is the sole organ of official communication with other states. Broadly speaking, the Constitution as written does not give to Congress a general power to legislate as to foreign affairs,[11] although some of the specified powers, such as over foreign commerce, have high degrees of foreign affairs relevancy.

The Constitution gives one-third plus one of the senators present and voting both a veto and a delaying power over "treaties." And in America even the traditional "envoys extraordinary and ministers plenipotentiary" of age-old ambassadorial communications patterns between chiefs of state cannot be appointed by the American chief of state alone, although after Senate approval (by simple majority), office is held at the pleasure of the President. The Constitution makes the President the commander-in-chief of the armed forces of the United States, without specific distinction as to where he may command these forces to be. But only Congress may declare war.

This brief recitation of constitutional fundamentals, amply buttressed and elaborated elsewhere, suffices to support these descriptive observations:

1. The constitutional architecture of separation of powers with checks and balances requires executive and legislative cooperation and compromise as to most major or enduring aspects of American foreign relations. A President cannot for very long do very much that is highly significant in foreign relations on his own; and Congress on its own is not legally authorized to deal with other states and international organizations. The result is a dualism. Viewed from abroad, it has happened with some frequency in our history that deficiencies in American reliability that really result from the inherent nature of the system are seen elsewhere as excuses for American manipulation, evasion, and breach of commitment.

2. At best, the Constitution and its gestation are enigmatic as to a question that, had it ever been answered clearly and definitely, would have mitigated the problems sketched in 1, above. The question: between Congress and the President, who is to be master in the realm of international affairs?

The Constitution is generally silent—some say secretive—as to the foreign affairs roles of the three branches. There is also reason to doubt the conflicts-resolution utility—if not the authoritativeness—of some rather fanciful Supreme Court "doctrines of obiter" about the direct descent of the foreign affairs executive power from the British Crown to the "executive in Congress" of the Articles and on to the President under the Constitution of 1789.[12]

In providing a scheme of government "for ages to come," did the

Covey T. Oliver

founding fathers consciously decide to avoid coming to grips with the issue of who is ultimately to be master? If so, why? Or did they assume that Congress remained paramount, as it had perforce been under the Articles? Contrariwise, did they choose to leave it to the two political branches to grapple and contend and eventually to adjust as circumstances would make necessary, from epoch to epoch and from one President and Congress to another?

Perhaps, though, the silences of the Constitution simply reflect a now-obsolete perception of the foreign relations process. In this regard, it bears noting that one thread running through several of the viewpoints expressed in Appendix L of the Murphy Commission Report is that things really have not changed as to the process, because in our formative years under this Constitution our foreparents in office had to contend with the infinite complexities of America's relations with the convoluted "European System" of the 18th century.[13] Do the writers really mean this? Do *you* agree that picking America's way between revolutionary France and the pre-Concert of Europe presents the policy choices and the operations difficulties that face this country today, on a planet of 150 states, rich-poor, socialist-nonsocialist, old-new, with nuclear proliferation, run-away arms races, a population explosion, and environmental exhaustion blended in? I personally differ, and furthermore I suspect that the framers did not, in 1787, see foreign relations for what it has become, particularly the rather threatening reality that, in terms of survival—of values as well as of the nation—there is no longer any sharp line between internal and external affairs.

Nor should we lose sight of the political fact that the separation of powers system has been bridged almost from the beginning of our history under the present Constitution by party politics, a term and concept as to which the Constitution is entirely silent. A fundamental question cutting through all of the topics of this conference is whether the American people may not have come, after nearly 200 years, to have to try to live for the first time with unrelieved separation of powers.

In orthodox American governmental theory, the Congress and the executive were once thought to be coordinated through the President's political leadership of the dominant party in Congress. Woodrow Wilson, early in this century, shifted coordination theory to the concept of the President (if to be "strong," that is, "effective") as the articulate voice, vis-à-vis Congress, of the ideals, values, and wishes of the American people in his time. From time to time, particularly in the aftermath of World War II, foreign policy has been characterized as outside political contention—as "bipartisan."

Now, however, looking back we note that since World War II, Truman, Eisenhower, Nixon, and Ford have been part- or full-time "minority" Presidents and that Kennedy never had, and ultimately Johnson lost, the support of majorities of their own parties in Congress.

The Wilsonian version of the strong President putting the fear of

God into the Congress in the name of the people did not, tragically, work for him, or for any President after him except for Roosevelt—and even he failed in efforts to purge senatorial recalcitrants.

Bipartisanship in foreign affairs began to die when Eisenhower campaigned on "I will go to Korea," despite occasional efforts since to revive it.

Strangely—eerily almost—today there may even be a kind of reverse bipartisanship at work, in that the foreign affairs issues that divide the President and the Congress are not so much based upon political differences as on different senses of mission between the two sets of institutions involved. Certainly today the issue "Who shall be master?" is not a party issue but an issue of congressional power versus presidential power, as the Democratic Majority Leader in the Senate never hides.[14]

Major Issues of Foreign Policy and the Separation of Powers

The basic, externally-oriented issues of constitutional limitation are herewith stated and explained. The panel may wish to disregard, debate, restate, or accept them as a backdrop to the evaluation of other issues. As already indicated, I consider these factors to be neglected or undervalued in conventional American appraisals of the Constitution and foreign policy. The issues are mainly ones of separation of powers and of checks and balances, although possible constitutional restrictions upon the types of official actions that representatives of the United States may take are also involved.

Issue: What is the capacity of the United States to act in ways and along lines that other states in the world community use?

Discussion of Issue: Customary international law and international relations modalities still reflect their origins in Western state systems between 1300 and 1500, when the people and their representatives had no legal power or authorized role in any aspect of foreign statecraft. Even in Great Britain, where Parliament developed to the level of virtual omnipotence in domestic affairs behind elaborate fictions as to the continuation of monarchial prerogatives, the Crown has kept control of foreign relations, including the making of international agreements. Thus, in Britain to this day Parliament is not called upon to approve a treaty as a condition of its coming into existence.[15] Her Majesty's principal secretary of state for foreign affairs, although a member of the cabinet and sitting in Parliament, is usually not effectively questioned[16]—or his party turned out—where issues of controverted foreign choice are present in the political atmosphere. Recently, even, the Court of Appeal has held that, despite the doctrine that no Parliament may bind another, the national legislation required to enable Britain to perform its obligations under the European Community treaties is impervious to fundamental variance by another Parliament thereafter.[17]

The American President, acting personally or through the Department of State or other executive agencies, is treated on the world scene as being authorized to act for the United States as if an absolute monarch. He and his subordinates may commit the country, notwithstanding the Constitution, internationally. Lack of capacity domestically is no legal defense internationally to an undertaking made by a chief of state.[18] When presidents, secretaries of state, ambassadors, and other authorized Americans meet with their peers from other countries, the inheritance from what for modern democracies is an outmoded but still living system tends to influence the way things go, especially where the issues involved relate to the intensity with which policy objectives of the chiefs of state are pursued.

Despite all this, however, the American chief of state increasingly finds himself cut down well below his peers in the world system as to powers related to foreign affairs operations that even in other modern democratic societies are exclusive to the foreign affairs executive there.

And, of course, absolute power-wielding chiefs of state have increased in numbers in modern times as participatory democracy has been displaced or is not practiced in fact. I know of no other government in the world in which the legislative branch claims, as Congress seems to be claiming today, that the executive departments are not privileged to keep internal operations communications to themselves (executive privilege) and that state secrets must be revealed to legislative assemblies. In most other democratic states, the foreign affairs executive is able to maintain executive privacy and state security, because the constitution places the control of parliament in a group of officials who occupy dual roles, those of executives and legislators.

Anyone who, knowing of congressional inquisitions in Washington, has observed question time at Westminster and has seen the foreign affairs executive blandly answer, "No, sir" (which means "No comment"), to a pointed parliamentary question related to foreign affairs operations understands the difference between the systems. Which is not to say, of course, that one of them is, in the nature of things, preferable to the other. It is only to say that the American executive, charged with giving course and direction to American foreign affairs, is not, in law, as invulnerable to destabilizing internal counterpressures as are his opposite numbers in other countries, including democratic allies as well as dictatorships.

In this analytical summary, it is also worthy of brief reference that in the United States, unlike most other states, there are constitutional limitations upon the subject matter of international agreements. The pointed dicta of Holmes in *Missouri* v. *Holland*[19] and of Black in *Reid* v. *Covert*[20] establish that it is beyond the capacity of the United States to comply with an international agreement obligation to give internal legal effect to an exercise of authority that the Constitution prohibits, such as a treaty, for example, under which the gist of the agreement is that the contracting states each agree to suppress defamatory utterances about the government, leaders, or people of the other.

The Supreme Court, moreover, in *Youngstown Sheet and Tube Co.*

v. *Sawyer*,[21] and in other decisions, has shrunk to negligibility notions that the President has "inherent executive power," linked to foreign policy considerations, under which he may ensure to other states the internal legal effectiveness of mutually agreed foreign policy lines of action that depend upon parallel internal application.

Finally, as to constitutional limitations upon the legal capacity or the immunity of American officials from liability when they act abroad, instead of at home, there may be emerging an extension of the old "When does the Constitution follow the flag?" problem. Mr. Dooley, with the Insular Cases[22] of our Spanish-American War period of imperialism in mind, used to say that the Constitution followed the flag on certain days of the week only. But the basic issue in those cases was whether United States governmental action on American-conquered and -acquired territory offshore was controlled by the Constitution as to process, other fundamental rights, and the like.

Today, problems in this regard seem to be much more complicated. Consider the situation in *United States* v. *Jordan*,[23] recently before the United States Court of Military Appeals: is evidence obtained by search and seizure to be excluded at a court-martial of an American airman charged with off-base burglary in the United Kingdom, because American airbase police accompanied but did not participate in an on-base search of the accused's quarters by the British police?

The military appeals court held that the Supreme Court decision in *Mapp* v. *Ohio*, a domestic case,[24] had shifted the invalid search rule from an evidentiary base to a "positive command of the Constitution," thus compelling the abandonment of all precedents in prior military justice that made inadmissibility of search and seizure evidence in foreign base cases turn upon the participation, *vel non*, of the American military police in the search. The court concluded:

> In sum, then, we hold that evidence obtained by search and seizure in a foreign country must meet Fourth Amendment standards in order to be admitted in evidence in a trial by court-martial, *regardless of whether it is obtained by foreign police acting on their own or in conjunction with American authorities.* (Emphasis added)

Readers who know something about the workings of our *Status of Forces Agreements* are in a good position to conjecture as to what the consequences of such a decision are apt to be when, in the next case of an off-base, off-duty offense by an American soldier, the United States base authorities wish the host state to yield primary jurisdiction to try the defendant in the American military courts. Yet, could such a reader agree as a matter of constitutional analysis with the dissenting judge? He began:

> To say that our armed forces carry with them the Constitution as well as the flag is one thing. To say that the Constitution operates against a foreign government in its own country is quite another.

Covey T. Oliver

And who among us could give with complete assurance a categorical negative answer to this question: could an American official be held liable, assuming statutory specification, for the violation in another country of the "constitutional rights" of an alien under the Bill of Rights?

Another type of restriction on United States power to act in the foreign affairs field exists de facto only, but it exists nonetheless. It is the actual reluctance of the executive to negotiate arrangements with other states, especially self-executing ones, that under the Constitution lie within the range of the treaty power but are believed to be apt to cause objections within the states of the Union—or among congressional groups. This reluctance is not entirely new, but it has certainly become a negative factor of wider ambit since the Bricker Amendment controversy of the 1950s.

One embarrassing aspect of this reluctance is that from time to time the United States seeks special exceptions to its obligations under a treaty, to which other states are unconditionally bound, on the ground that "considering its constitutional structure" the United States is obligated only to use its good offices to persuade the states of the Union to perform.[25] The hypocrisy—and known as such in international circles—is that the constitutional structure of the United States does not impose limitations upon the power of the federal government to override "states' rights" by a treaty.

As bearing on this Issue very specially (although relevant to some others also), consideration should be given to contemporary courses of conduct of the Congress (mainly through key committees and subcommittees thereof) that trench directly upon the traditional powers of chiefs of state as to the conduct of international relations:

1. Secrets of state: Until contemporary times the general assumption, certainly so within the foreign affairs component of the American executive branch, has been that Congress and its committee staffs have no legal right to share in the knowledge of, and certainly not to publicize without the consent of, the executive "secrets of state," leaving open for the moment the content of this phrase. Until recently, indeed, it was the assumption of perhaps most interested legislators that the classified information collected by the foreign affairs apparatus of the American chief of state could not be demanded under claim of right, but could only be used by the legislative branch at the discretion of the executive. Now, as the activities of the House Select Committee on Intelligence and various proposals for legislation to provide for prior clearance by the Congress of clandestine intelligence operations inform us, different winds are blowing from the Hill. Compare, further, the discussion below of a proposal that, building upon legislation now existent (requiring that *all* international agreements made by the executive, even those under inherent executive authority, be reported to the Congress) would further provide for legislative rescission of some types of such executive agreements without presidential veto. The trend noted cannot but have inhibiting effects (even before final determinations of validity, if such are possible) over a very wide field of normal conduct for the chief of state of any state, including, for example, political, intelligence cooperation, international organizations voting plans, and other informal operating understandings.

2. What remains of executive privilege? Also very much under attack from congressional quarters today is the claim of executive privilege (or bureaucratic right of privacy) as to the internal workings of the executive branch with regard to foreign operations. Foreign affairs operations decisions are often "made" by the human affairs equivalent of resultants of forces in traditional physics. And it has been the contention recently of both the President and Secretary Kissinger that required revelation to the Congress (which they imply means virtually always revelation to the media as well) consigns the process just described to unworkability. The issue joined goes out beyond where the legal trail ended in *United States* v. *Nixon*,[26] for it is to be recalled that the Supreme Court was careful, when balancing public interests in that case, to note that sensitive issues of foreign affairs operations would not be exposed by denying executive privilege under the facts before the Court.

3. Legislative trends toward denying the President the veto: In "Hoover Commission" days, few difficulties were seen with arrangements under which the Congress delegated to the President authority to reorganize the government in accordance with congressional guidelines and subject to congressional invalidation of any particular executive plan by *concurrent resolution* voted within stated (fairly short) time periods. In modern times, however, Congress has drawn upon the concept that a concurrent resolution, unlike a *joint resolution*, is not legislation (and hence is not subject to the veto over laws given to the President by the Constitution) to claim for itself a capacity to rescind, as to internal legal effect, international undertakings made by the chief of state.

Useful illustrations of the process and of some problems it creates can be found in the Trade Reform Act of 1974.[27] Until renewal of legislative authorizations that ended at midnight, June 30, 1967 (the expiration date of the Trade Expansion Act of 1962), it was not worthwhile for there to be further tariff and non-tariff barrier reduction negotiations (through the General Agreement on Tariffs and Trade or otherwise) in the world community, because the American executive had no authority to put negotiated reductions into effect in the tariff laws of the United States.

The executive departments, naturally, bore the brunt of concern about the situation, seeing as imperative the enactment of new trade legislation. Eventually it came, in 1975, burdened with a number of nontrade preconditions required by Congress. (Some of these, such as the Jackson-Vanik Amendment on emigration, were foreign affairs innovations, for hitherto it had not been international practice to attach nontrade conditions to trade concessions.) An important economic need in the new trade legislation was for more effective reduc-

Covey T. Oliver

tion of non-tariff barriers to international trade, such as quantitative restrictions (quotas), the valuation of certain imports at "American Selling Price," and the like.

For trade reasons, it was necessary for the present executive to accept an extension of the concept of congressional post hoc review and possible invalidation by concurrent resolution of presidential negotiations under the powers delegated to him. (A rather exquisite question here is whether the President's nonveto of the trade bill—he could not afford to—has barred him and his successors, by some sort of constitutional-level estoppel, from attacking the circumvention of his normal power through the veto to require Congress to muster two-third votes in both houses to override his rejection of congressional action that has legal effects.)

Internationally, the apparent power of the Congress to undo a trade negotiation to which the United States is a party is already seen as both inhibiting the chief of state and creating an unsettling degree of uncertainty in regard to the next or "Tokyo" round of multilateral trade negotiations.

The augmentation of earlier usage of the concurrent resolution seems still to be of some interest to groups in Congress. There is now before Congress what may possibly be a high-water mark among legislative efforts to insulate from the veto the will of Congress that certain executive agreements not come into effect if disapproved by concurrent resolution. This proposal is not here discussed in detail, because it is still pending.[28]

4. Selective use of traditional powers by Congress: The Issue above directs attention to the actual capacities of the United States as a state among states and of the American chief of state among chiefs of state. The view is from the pit of the world arena. It is submitted that the situation of the United States, unique from the beginning, seems to be moving toward even more unusualness.

In this subanalysis, the obvious powers of Congress as to appropriations and investigative post-audit have not been discussed, because as to the first of these powers, history shows that even absolute monarchs have been vulnerable to it and, as to the second, even dictators are reviewed by those who overthrow them.

It does not follow, however, that the use of certain entirely classic and traditional powers of Congress is always directed truly toward the powers used. Subcommittees of regular committees, such as of Government Operations, Armed Services, and, of course, Appropriations, can be and are used by the legislators who dominate them to seek to force the executive to move along foreign policy lines that reflect the foreign policy preferences, not of the Congress as an entity, but of particular legislators and sometimes those of committee staffers, who, no more than the executive bureaucracy, were ever elected by anybody.

A newly created discrimination against the Department of State that is linked to particularized interests in explicit influence on foreign affairs operations should now be noted: it has come to pass that the first ministry to be established under the Constitution of 1789 is now, alone among the established departments of government, required to be reauthorized as an agency periodically by Congress.

Watchers of the United States government, here and abroad, have over time become familiar with the fact that a major difference between the permanent executive agencies (the ministries) and temporary agencies, such as, say, the United States Agency for International Development and its many-titled predecessors since the Economic Cooperation Administration of Marshall Plan days, is that the latter die if not periodically reauthorized by Congress.

But now, as a result of the "advise and consent" drive of the Senate Foreign Relations Committee from roughly 1964 on, the Department of State carries on under a second-class agency requirement of having to answer on money matters, not only to the appropriations committees, but to the Senate and House committees for foreign affairs at an "authorization" stage. In contrast, the Treasury Department—the second oldest of the established ministries and one of immense consequence in international relations—need not answer in Congress other than as to its actual appropriations. Of course, if Treasury were to support a particular piece of legislation, such as the replenishment of the American share of the soft-loan capital of international development banks, it would have to go on the merits to the relevant committees, one of which is not charged in Congress with general responsibilities for foreign affairs matters.[29]

Issue: How will the reaction of other entities in the world community affect United States interests if present constitutional structure and practice thereunder are continued into the next century?

Discussion of Issue: To ensure discussion of issues not very often examined in appraisals of the United States Constitution in relationship to international relations, we referred earlier to the evidence of rising foreign impatience with what, in world terms, is a peculiar American system for the conduct of foreign relations. The legal and structural aspects of our present situation in foreign affairs policy-making and performance have also been sketched. Additionally, as to the Issue, there are these questions:

1. Is there buried in a national attitude toward our way of life, including the inertia of normalcy, an assumption that for reasons of virtue, power, or democratic institutional values the United States is entitled to expect to continue to enjoy special toleration for its foreign affairs system?

2. If the answer to (1) is "yes," does world response to rapidly changing world environment (as to international law, forms of government, ideology, resource allocations, population, ecology, neonationalism, irrationality in the conduct of foreign relations, and the like) justify a continued expectation of no-cost toleration?

Covey T. Oliver

These questions are intended simply to call attention to the undesirability of letting events take us by surprise, as they have the former colonial powers in one particular and the United States in another. The former did not see early enough the end of a cycle and we did not anticipate the present chaos in the national state system that the end of colonialism has brought.

It may be offensive to some even to suggest considering that our highly valued constitutional system may be a product of times that, for the world as a whole, have passed or are passing.[30]

Realistically, nonetheless, for the near future at least, America is not getting the general deference it once could take for granted. No matter how we may paper it over to ourselves at home, the world knows that America has been defeated—in a professional, Von Clausewitzian sense—in a war; that, although our institutions worked to turn a power-abusing President out of office, they did not earlier reveal his defects to the electorate that voted him into office; and that for the first time in the country's history the chief of state cannot match the authority that members of Congress derive from having been elected.

As we turn again, in the next section, to the more familiar home ground viewpoint, let us ask ourselves whether the sense of mission as to integrity and effectiveness in foreign relations operations that comes to characterize virtually all who are involved in the process as acting parties in the executive branch can really be shared by the Congress as a whole or the people as a whole.

In all democracies—usually in nondemocracies too—there is a suspicion of those fellow citizens, the "foreign office chaps," who deal with foreigners and become sensitive to their expectations of rights, comity, reciprocity, respect, and even justice. If this reserve becomes rejection, how will the United States ever be able to attempt to explain itself abroad?

PROBLEM CASES THAT TODAY INFLUENCE
THE SHAPING OF EXTERNAL RELATIONS

Linkages

We are aware that constitutional issues were not considered in a vacuum at Philadelphia in 1787.[31] As to foreign affairs, real problems of national concern about international relations and of the national interest under the Articles existed. Today, many pressing questions of value-choice, rather than of structure, also link to our governance for foreign affairs.

I shall attempt to raise the appraisal of these in a governmental context, but without foreclosing others that members of the panel may propose to the chairman and their colleagues. One problem, "Disarmament and Arms Control," I have added to the outline, out of an affectionate respect for the person and profound admiration for the conscience, wisdom, and vision of a Philadelphian so great as to have assuredly been among the founding fathers had he lived in 1787, Senator Joseph S. Clark.

Military Policy

Korea, Vietnam, unbelievable budgets, and a general sense that President Eisenhower was saying something of great importance in his farewell warning as to a military-industrial complex have brought about a situation in which many representatives of the people—we do not know as much about the people themselves—feel that Congress must "do something," because the executive will not or cannot control a runaway military state within the state.

In contrast, military affairs professionals, not all of whom are in the armed services by any means, look dubiously at détente, appraise what they consider to be an unchanged (and probably unchangeable) threat situation, and align themselves with certain seniority-entrenched elements in the Congress to resist legal and financial restraints upon American military power-in-being.

So far, the results of this contention have been rather erratic. To illustrate: a few years ago, there arose within the anti-armaments group in Congress a strong determination to force United States development assistance recipients in Latin America to eschew even a modicum of modernization in their military equipment, such as replacing thirty-five-year-old piston-engined military aircraft with the only kind now manufactured, jets.

What then Assistant Secretary of State Lincoln Gordon called an "arms crawl" in Latin America, dominant congressmen called, in support of riders to the Foreign Assistance Act, "a run-away arms race." Actually, Latin America then, as now, spent less of its gross national product on arms and the military than any other sector of the planet.[32] And at that time of amendments to the annual Foreign Assistance Authorization Act enforcing the above views, Southeast Asia, the Middle East—even Ethiopia—were freed by waivers from these congressional controls.[33] Result: more and more, the military took over governments in Latin America and the countries turned elsewhere for modern materiel. Also, the Latin countries saw the United States action as not only interventionist, but what is worse, ridiculous or hypocritical.

Structurally viewed, the most significant result of the pulls and hauls partially illustrated here is the War Powers (Joint) Resolution, passed in 1973 over presidential veto.[34] In constitutional terms, the issue presented is between the President's power as commander-in-chief to deploy forces and the power of Congress to protect its power to declare war from situational preemption by such deployment. Although at the time of its consideration, enactment, veto, and passage over the veto, issues of constitutionality figured in debate, President Ford has so far bowed to its mandate.

While it may be that (standing to sue aside) the decision of the Supreme Court as to the Federal Election Commission,[35] January 30, 1976,

Covey T. Oliver

will spark a revival of separation of powers adjudications and that the federal courts will not reject the present issue as a political question, the basic issue for us here seems to be whether there should be resolution by constitutional respecification of congressional power to curb the President's volition on deployment of forces.

On a somewhat broader front, the landmark decision referred to above may presage a judicial endeavor to set limits beyond which Congress may not go in acting authoritatively under the Constitution with intent to administer, rather than to legislate or investigate.

Expenditure Levels

There are two possible questions for us here:

1. The control of Congress over expenditure levels and disposition of government property being plenary under the Constitution, should there be some mechanism, other than waiting until the next election, to correct asserted-to-be serious congressional damage to foreign policy goals of the United States stemming from reductions or cutoffs of programs, such as military cooperation, foreign intelligence operations, and support for bilateral and multipartite development assistance?

As to expenditures, I join those who say, "We just have to live with what we have." I do so, because even major constitutional change, such as going to ministerial responsibility, would surely leave the money power squarely with the legislative body. Perhaps there could be experimentation with bicamerally-approved foreign assistance international agreements under which the House of Representatives would be committed, along with the Senate, to fund, for periods of years, certain types of foreign assistance programs.

Or, perhaps, the House might initiate a "foreign development tax" to provide for our general welfare through reducing the turbulence of a world otherwise irreversibly divided between rich and poor nations.

It is important to ponder, in passing, why it has been that Congress has been so very reluctant to use its most unquestioned and most powerful control over external operations, the money power. American foreign policy is today—and for some time has been—based upon large expenditures of money. Ergo, even foreign policy is controllable under the money power. Answers seem to lie along one or the other of these lines: (1) internal factors that congressmen cannot ignore are also in play; (2) Congress does not want to wreck, but only influence, major aspects of foreign policy, as to the substance of which it does not disagree with the executive; (3) using the money power to enable Congress to shape foreign policy throws the control within Congress to inappropriate committees; (4) Congress is aware that it should not use the money power to distort the Constitution.

2. The question of the constitutionality of executive impoundment of foreign affairs appropriations has not moved in practice beyond President Truman's rejection of a congressional directive to spend on Spain funds that he did not wish to spend on Spain, even though

executive domestic impoundment seems controllable by congressional specification in law.[36] The separation of powers issue as to executive impoundment related to international operations is an issue seemingly left unresolved by the present Constitution. Perhaps it will appeal to some of our participants for further—or divergent—analysis or as a topic for revisionary attention. Again, perhaps, the election law case speaks to the separation of powers issue here, although I doubt that it does.

Arms Control and Disarmament

The first of Professor Louis Henkin's useful books on the Constitution and America's public affairs projected an international agreement on arms control and disarmament and proceeded to analyze, solidly and imaginatively, the constitutional issues that might be raised.[37]

Unhappily for us and for the world, Professor Henkin's projections have never had an opportunity to guide events. Today, arms control and disarmament seem far from presenting us with constitutional problems.

As with regard to military policy and levels of military expenditure, the heart of the difficulty seems to be that polarizations of viewpoints cut across separation of powers and involve pro and anti alignments in both the executive and legislative branches. The state of readiness/threat situation professionals in the executive departments find counterparts in the legislative branch, especially among the authoritative chairmen of some key committees. It is very difficult for any responsible person to be detached about the situation, because deeply held moral feelings are so strongly involved, the risks so awful, and the unknowns so enigmatic. Some say the area is one in which nothing much will be accomplished until the world has a severe but survivable nuclear experience or, short of that and in the case of the United States, until the country shall have—if ever it does—an executive chief who is both a fully effective national leader and a person assuredly knowledgeable on nuclear arms and threat matters.

It is almost impossible, in my opinion, for steadfast leadership of the required level of effectiveness to develop in Congress, even though substantial numbers of individual legislators be committed to sound principles as to the fundamentals of arms control and disarmament.

This observation on the probable exclusive effectiveness of executive leadership on arms control and disarmament derives from personal experience with leadership as to levels and continuity of American contributions to development—to the international war on poverty. Congress has never taken leadership initiatives on foreign aid, and the spiraling-down of our development assistance effort largely reflects presidential disinclinations or perceived inabilities to lead affirmatively in this field. And these two deficiences in leadership may become tragically linked—in a rich-poor world of nuclear proliferation.

Covey T. Oliver

THE CONSTITUTION AND UNITED STATES PARTICIPATION IN TRANSNATIONAL GOVERNMENTAL PROCESSES

Evolution Beyond the National State System—Something to Consider?

Nine democratic, free, developed countries, all allies of the United States, have found it necessary to create by treaty regional institutions that have authority to act directly upon persons, including governmental agencies, within the member states, much as the federal government acts directly within the federal sphere in this country. These countries, too, have a community Court of Justice, which is the final legal authority over national courts on matters of interpretation of the organic treaties creating the European Economic Communities. Several of the European Community countries had to alter their constitutions to permit this result.

No one is suggesting that the United States—at this time, at least —seek to join the European Communities or to become a member of a Western hemisphere common market with our Latin American neighbors. The latter would be impossible for the neighbors to live with economically, considering the overwhelming cost-effectiveness of American industrial production in comparison to theirs.

But there is Canada, with which we already have a free trade area in motor vehicles and parts, and which could probably hold its own if all tariff walls should come down between us. More importantly, there is the century ahead to think about. The logical result of the "interdependency" that present leaders in the executive and in the Congress support is evolution beyond the present national state system and the present types of international organizations that are not directly organs of human governance.

Would Supranationality Be Constitutional?

Could the United States under its present Constitution enter into a regionalistic or planetary federalism of limited powers? I fear that, without standing the Constitution, written and unwritten, on its head, we could not.

Item: to provide by treaty for an external agency to make and enforce law in the United States would involve the use of the treaty power to do what the Constitution prohibits as to due process, delegation of legislative power, and the exercise of executive and judicial powers; and the Court has said, twice at least, that the treaty power cannot be used to do by treaty that which the Constitution prohibits.

Item: American legal opinion, including that of secretaries of state and attorneys-general, has consistently held that the Constitution does not permit appellate review by international tribunals of process in domestic tribunals.

Item: beyond the issue of federalism settled by *Missouri v. Holland* lies the question of whether the treaty power may validly be used to displace states' rights in favor of some rulemaking and authority-wielding entity other than the federal government.

Item: a national plebiscite of the sort that eventually settled—for now, at least— the troubled question of British entry into the European Communities is difficult indeed to fit into our present constitutional system.

Are not these matters that are worth thinking about as we peer ahead as best we can into a murky future, from a present in which we are constantly being told that multinational enterprise has already seen the future of society on this small planet better than governments have?

THE STATES OF THE UNION AND FOREIGN AFFAIRS

Other than the problem of "federal reluctance" to use the treaty power, where doing so invades legal domains that fall to the states in the absence of treaties, and legalistic odds and ends of federalism, such as the recently restored power of the states to impose nondiscriminatory property taxes on imports not yet in the stream of commerce, formal federalistic issues are not of present or of foreseeable future difficulty as to the conduct of foreign relations under the present Constitution. To overstate a bit, whatever remained of "states' rights" in foreign affairs after *Missouri* v. *Holland* probably was swept away by the Supreme Court's self-made version of a "non-treaty supremacy clause" in *Zschernig* v. *Miller*.[38]

Even the theoretical question of secession in a new guise, self-determination of peoples, seems quite remote in a nation increasingly homogenized as to values, tastes, outlooks, and life-styles. The main question about the states of the Union and foreign affairs under the Constitution is whether states "as we know them" (that is, in present numbers and distributions of population) are any longer utile. This is a matter that has been addressed in a stimulating and provocative study by Dr. Rexford Tugwell and others.

This is not to say, of course, that the states do not have certain bearings on foreign affairs, as when the state police insist on escorting speeding but immune Soviet diplomats off the New Jersey Turnpike, which the Department of State tells the Russians they must not deviate from in motoring between New York and Washington.

And it not to say, either, that the very existence of a federal structure does not impose some restraints upon national foreign policy. It is a reality that the states—and the cities—tend not to become affirmatively involved in foreign relations matters and hence do not give much weight to what is desirable in foreign policy, especially when a transnational perspective threatens an expectation that federal financial assistance to them might be affected.

THE PEOPLE AND FOREIGN AFFAIRS

The discourse just concluded leads to a very significant matter, one that justifies being stated as a third Issue:

Covey T. Oliver

Issue: Do present constitutional arrangements adequately provide for the participation of the citizenry in value choices related to foreign policy?

Discussion of Issue: Statistical realism requires us to admit that a very large proportion of our population does not even understand basic aspects of our Constitution, such as the Bill of Rights, to say nothing of its convoluted arrangements as to foreign relations and its even more complicated unwritten growth in this sector. Nonetheless, modern mass media, TV especially, have brought the world and America's stance therein very close to a concerned minority of the citizenry; and, if an international relations issue is a very big (and therefore a starkly simple) one, even the populace as a whole may involve itself.

Assuming a significant degree of popular involvement, particularly in election years, in foreign policy, let us consider constitutional theory and practice in regard to the people's role. In constitutional theory, the President is not chosen by the people; but in practice, and making allowance for the "winner-take-all" effect of our state-linked electoral voting pattern, the people now select the President by popular majority. In doing so, the people elect a chief of state who is not legally or politically explicitly committed for his four-year term to follow any course of action, but only to use his best judgment in giving course and direction to American foreign policy.

The House membership is also elected on a theory that the people of a congressional district choose, not "mouthpieces," but wise and good people to go to Washington and make wise and good decisions. Originally the Senate may have had a different function,[39] but since the 17th Amendment, providing for the statewide popular election of senators, there has been a shift from the senator as delegate of his state to the Washington government to the senator as a "super-congressman" (having a bigger district and a longer term, but no higher pay).

In practice, over the whole range of political values, the picture is much less clear. The prevailing popular belief is probably that all members of Congress jerk into motion when predominant interests of the left or right, capital-labor-farmer, ethnic) in their electoral constituencies pull the strings. Yet, it is observable fact that some senators and some representatives usually vote as to international issues in accordance with their own judgments, although there are usually also some distortions, for which some otherwise independent solons become well known. Discounting personality factors, what is the line of cleavage? It is the safety of the member's seat; and even with longer Senate terms, there is notable correlation between a senator's independence of mind and his confidence in being reelected.

It seems reasonable to conclude that, generally speaking, members of the House and Senate are in practice more independent-minded in foreign relations than in domestic matters, mainly because their constituencies do not have definite views on foreign relations issues, unless the issue be as basic as staying in or getting out of Vietnam or of electoral district concern. A plausible hypothesis is that the theory of delegation of popular sovereignty to elected representatives works in foreign relations most of the time as the founders assumed and that it does so because the people of the constituencies are not massively attracted to personal involvement in foreign affairs activism.

If this analysis is correct, then the people have delegated their popular sovereignty as to foreign affairs to both the President (on a national basis) and their representatives and senators on voting district bases. The result is that the people do not, in practice, decide who wins when there are controversies between the President and the Congress, but only watch the fray.

It may well be that our panel should speculate about what the people ought to be doing in foreign relations, how they could be induced to do it, and how they should be prepared informationally to discharge their responsibilities if they should become active. This is to ask: for the future on a rapidly changing planet, should the American people more closely couple themselves to the making of basic choices, such as the shaping of external relations, peace or war, negotiated arms reductions or unilateral disarmament, military policy, contributions to development, doing or not doing "dirty tricks" abroad, and many others? Or should the present system continue, with the people leaving these questions to those they select by vote to make choices? Is our present system too reflective of a bygone age at a time when "Yea-Nay" buttons on the family cable television set could give a national viewpoint on an issue within milliseconds? Or is it still wise and desirable for the people to let others decide values for them, subject to post hoc correction at the polls? If so, why? avoidance of having to decide? specialization of knowledge? an assumption that the representatives chosen are superior to the people in ability to make these decisions?

At this point, it is appropriate to make a cross-reference to a later discussion of the question of whether there is utility in considering on the merits a shift in our form of government to a system of "legislative domination with cabinet responsibility." The linkage relevant here was well expressed by a British laborer who, when asked why it was useful to have a general election at a particular time, responded: "So's we can throw the buggers out!" This is another way—an older and pre-TV button way—of bringing the people closer to the actual processes of decision-making. But, as noted earlier, it is not often in the political practices of "ministerial-responsibility" democracies that the "buggers" get turned out on foreign affairs issues.

Finally, in regard to this Issue, we should evaluate the roles and the power of modern mass media in foreign affairs choice-making. The American people are not fully informed by their government. (No people anywhere are.) We are just beginning, under the Freedom of Information Act, to use a statutory people's right to know (with security limitations) what has been done in the past. So far, there is no recognition of a citizen's constitutional right to be kept informed as to

Covey T. Oliver

ongoing operations. The question might be asked, in the light of a present separation-of-powers controversy between the President and two congressional committees, "If the Congress has a right to know, what about the people?" Note that if only Congress but not the people shall have the right to know, the people—to the extent interested at all—remain ineluctably relegated by informational disadvantage to the secondary and passive role ascribed to them by the 18th century theory of representative government, unless, of course, they decide to intervene on the basis of what the "TV tube masters" and other media "authorities" tell them they should know—and do.

THE INTERNATIONAL AGREEMENTS POWERS AND GOOD FAITH PERFORMANCE OF THE INTERNATIONAL OBLIGATIONS OF THE UNITED STATES

Congressional Disregard of International Agreements

By judicial decisions and in governmental practice, Congress is recognized as having the capacity to rescind the legal effect of a treaty as internal law, even though to do so puts the United States into breach of the treaty internationally.[40]

Today, as we have seen, Congress practices veto-proof invalidation of executive agreements based upon congressional authorization, and it may claim the power to review and similarly invalidate executive agreements made under the inherent powers of the President as chief of state and commander-in-chief.

In his commentary upon Professor Henkin's presentation in Appendix L to the Murphy Commission Report, Professor Falk calls for greater respect in practice for international law by the United States. This appeal includes a preference for constitutional stipulations under which an international agreement, having internal effect as law, cannot be undone by a later inconsistent act of the legislature.

The question of whether the Constitution should be amended to conform in this fashion to the constitutions of some other countries is a matter for consideration. This concern is voiced, of course, against the background that, increasingly, an objective of treaties and other international agreements is to provide for parallel internal legal treatment of matters that touch and concern the interests of all the parties —and often of the planet as a whole.

Additionally, Americans should consider seriously whether their assumption that the United States almost always performs its international obligations is correct. There is reason to believe that, largely for structural reasons, there is sometimes ineffectual government agency policing of the requirements of international agreements. Private parties may assert treaty rights affirmatively or defensively in legal proceedings brought in federal and state courts; but, unless a treaty setting performance standards has been implemented by domestic criminal or regulatory law, there is no governmental agency but the Department of State, motivated by diplomatic considerations, to push for observance. And some other former officers of the Department of

State might recall, as I do, a tendency within the department to leave worries about seeing to it that an international agreement is "lived up to" to the persons and/or office that negotiated it. This tends to make *uberrima fides* respect for treaties vulnerable to the passage of time and shifts in the attention and interest spans of the higher echelons.

Consider in this regard this question: assume that the Third United Nations Law of the Sea Conference does produce a full-range law of the sea convention, one that, as to nine or ten major areas of normation, involves the spheres and interests of almost every one of our executive departments and a number of independent agencies and commissions as well. What agency will be responsible for the overall coordination of United States application of the convention? If there is no localization of sense of mission as to United States official performance, United States compliance cannot but be disjointed and episodic. The problem is highly important for the future, as it is foreseeable that more and more matters of planet-wide concern will come to be regulated by treaty in the same way for all nations.

Should "Treaties" Be Approved Only by Simple Majorities in Both Houses?

One of the conference participants, Professor Myres McDougal, with a co-author, demonstrated some years ago to the satisfaction of most students of the subject that "executive-legislative" agreements that come into effect by bills voted in both houses are entirely interchangeable with treaties ratified and promulgated by the President after he has received the advice and consent of two-thirds of the senators present and voting.[41]

The fine question whether international agreements coming into effect in this bicameral way are "treaties" within the supremacy clause may be debated here, but the issue approaches mootness as judicial restrictions on the legislative powers of Congress have been relaxed.[42]

The more important question now is whether the time has come to "democratize" the treaty process by deleting from the Constitution the old bias in favor of the Senate (the two-thirds principle), which has both made the Senate "the graveyard of treaties" and fed senatorial pretensions that they, but not members of the House of Representatives, are entitled by the Constitution to advise and give consent to presidential foreign policy lines of action that are not sent to the Senate for approval as treaties.

In this connection, it is perhaps useful to keep in mind both the well-known account of President Washington's formal consultation with the Senate,[43] never repeated by him or by any other President since, and the uniqueness of the unicameral, weighted majority, upper chamber treaty-approval provision of our Constitution among the constitutions of other modern, developed, democratic states. In most other democratic states, indeed, the upper house is vestigial and can

Covey T. Oliver

only delay, but not eventually prevail over, the legislative will of the more populous branch.

Self-Executing Treaties

On most matters, the President and two-thirds of the senators may legislate (give internal effect as positive law) by treaty. Self-executing treaties are possible in a few other democratic systems, but not in most. They are impossible in Great Britain, where there is complete disjunction between the Crown's sole power to bind the realm internationally and Parliament's essential role in making the law of the land. In the constitution of the German Federal Republic, international agreements may only be ratified by legislation that first comes into effect as national law.

In the United States, self-executing treaties have given some problems. These are problems of (1) determining which treaties are self-executing and which are not, usually a matter for judicial determination; (2) whether the President and the Senate may, by treaty, preempt the rights of the House to initiate (and a fortiori to vote on) revenue measures and to participate in laws for the disposition of the property of the United States. The last-stated problem may become crucial in the proposed new treaty with Panama as to the Canal and Zone.[44]

Should self-executing treaties continue to be permitted? There is a link between this question and the one posed in the previous section. However, it should be noted that in executive practice—apparently acquiesced in by the Senate—treaties intended to have internal effect as law are no longer put into effect by use of the self-execution principle, because the Department of State no longer forwards treaties to the Senate for advice and consent until any needed implementing legislation is certain of approval by regular majorities in both houses. This practice, of course, tends to slow materially the completion of the treaty-approval process itself; and such delays are inherently contrary to the normal expectations of other nations that ratifications be speedily sought by any party signing a treaty *ad referendum* to such action.

CONSTITUTIONAL REVISION FOR FOREIGN AFFAIRS REASONS: STRUCTURAL ISSUES AND THE RANGE OF CHOICE

We have now reviewed, mainly from the standpoint of substantive policy preferences, the making and management of foreign policy under the Constitution of 1789. Attention should now shift to some very significant Issues of structure and function and to a sketch of possible constitutional revision, in a range from major change to no change. The Issues set out and discussed immediately following are seen as preliminary or conditioning factors in regard to revision, *vel non*, the last Issue posed herein.

Four Conditioning Issues

Issue: Under the present Constitution, is there a reliable and definitive process for deciding the respective foreign affairs authorities of the two political branches of the government?

Discussion of Issue: Attention here very rapidly comes to adjudication and impeachment-and-removal-from-office. However, the latter is almost as impracticable an alternative as two others that are only mentioned for analytical completeness, due to their entire inappropriateness to situations of international crisis, where speed as well as sharpness of resolution are of the essence. The two possibilities rejected out-of-hand are: (1) the President or his congressional opposition goes to the country, à la Woodrow Wilson; (2) waiting for a series of "eyeball-to-eyeball" confrontations to cause one side or the other to blink—but not necessarily with all blinks in the series coming from a single side.[45]

The only additional comment that occurs as to impeachment-removal-from-office is that it settles nothing in a normative, authoritative manner, being always a highly political process as well as one that causes discontinuity in government, as distinguished from shifts in the law by which governors are to be governed. The question of whether the judicial process should expand to deal with areas clearly within the power of Congress to indict and remove from office, but not yet clearly declared by the Supreme Court also to be within judicial jurisdiction and willingness to adjudicate, is not, analytically, essential to this evaluation.

Turning, then, to the fundamentals given to us so far by the Supreme Court, we find one line of judicial utterances ("holdings" is too strong a word here)—the *Curtiss-Wright Export Corporation*[46] line—that tends to discourage resort to litigation to resolve separation-of-powers issues in the foreign relations field, precisely because the Court appears to give constitutional carte blanche to the claimants of power. If, as Justice Sutherland's pre-appointment viewpoint that he later wrote into his *Curtiss-Wright* opinion asserts, the foreign affairs sovereignty of the nation is not limited by the Constitution, there seems very little more that the courts can do to resolve power struggles between the President and the Congress. However, the famous dictum probably lives today mainly in *U.S. v. California*[47] and its progeny, denying to the states of the Union the benefits of any independent juristic existence in the international legal order; and this is a matter of federalism that is off the mark for us here.

A relevant speculation as to the predictable limits of judicial resolution of the respective foreign affairs authorities of the President and the Congress must project from *Baker v. Carr*[48] through *Powell v. McCormack*[49] to the Federal Election Act decision[50] of this past January. In the first of these cases, known to our political history for "one man-one vote," the Supreme Court (in dealing with the argument that the application of the guarantee of a republican form of

Covey T. Oliver

government to the states had been held a nonjusticiable "political question" in *Luther* v. *Borden*[51]) reviewed the concept of "political question" as a limitation on justiciability. In a discourse designed to show the relativism of "political question," the majority said:

> *Foreign relations*: There are sweeping statements to the effect that all questions touching foreign relations are political questions. Not only does resolution of such issues frequently turn on standards that defy judicial applications, or involve the exercise of a discretion demonstrably committed to the executive or legislature; but many such questions uniquely demand single-voiced statement of the Government's views. Yet it is error to suppose that every case or controversy which touches foreign relations lies beyond judicial cognizance. Our cases in this field seem invariably to show a discriminating analysis of the particular question posed, in terms of the history of its management by the political branches, of its susceptibility to judicial handling in the light of its nature and posture in the specific case, and of the possible consequences of judicial action. For example, though a court will not ordinarily inquire whether a treaty has been terminated, since on that question "governmental action . . . must be regarded as of controlling importance," if there has been no conclusive "governmental action" then a court can construe a treaty and may find it provides the answer.

Consider whether there is, in the above, any promise of a workable rule for resolution of the problem of this Issue, or in this, from the opinion in Representative Powell's successful suit against not having been allowed by the House to take his seat:

> Respondent's alternate contention is that the case presents a political question because judicial resolution of petitioner's claim would produce a "potentially embarrassing confrontation between coordinate branches" of the Federal government. But [our interpretation of Art. I, Section 5] falls within the traditional role accorded courts to interpret the law, and does not involve a "lack of respect due (*a*) coordinate branch of government," nor does it involve an "initial policy determination of a kind clearly for nonjudicial discretion." *Baker* v. *Carr*. Our system of government requires that federal courts on occasion interpret the Constitution in a manner at variance with the construction given the document by another branch. . . .

> Nor are any of the other formulations of a political question "inextricable from the case at bar." *Baker*. Petitioners seek a determination . . . for which clearly there are "*judicially manageable standards*" (emphasis added)

U.S. v. *Nixon*,[52] of course, distinguishes, from what the Court decided in that contention was within its power to say "what the law is," an executive-legislative jurisdictional dispute about foreign affairs powers. And Holtzman's effort against Secretary of Defense Schlesinger to have the judiciary rule on the constitutionality of American combat presence in Southeast Asia attracted only two justices.[53] As Cox has put it: "The task of formulating a workable principle for delimiting the President's power to engage in military activities overseas is far from easy."[54] True enough for courts, but seemingly not for Congress under the War Powers Resolution, unless the courts should be willing (and a movant have standing) to review the Congress!

The Federal Election Act case[55] seems to track the "*Marbury* v. *Madison* revived" line of cases just outlined, that is, while it is indeed the courts' business to say what the law is, they do so largely on the Supreme Court's terms. And these terms seem not sharp enough or predictable enough for reliable resolution of power contention between the two political branches as to their respective foreign affairs authorizations.

Hence, the answer to this Issue, it would seem, is "no." So the question becomes, should the Constitution be changed so as to fix authority to resolve these contentions speedily, effectively, and normatively? This can be a question of the evolutionary structural adequacy of what we have. Consideration of this question need not necessarily lead to a proposal for amendment. Institutional determination by the judiciary might suffice, assuming there are not too many doubts about a "Book of Judges" approach to America's future governance.

Issue: Under present constitutional arrangements and congressional traditions, can Congress act effectively to discharge the new foreign affairs authorities that are being claimed in its name?

Discussion of Issue: This conditioning Issue as to future structure is well known to any person who has had acquaintance with Congress at work. There are two basic problems: (1) *the conditions under which the executive branch must attempt to cooperate with the Congress*; (2) *the committee structure and traditional practices of the Congress.*

Even in the best of times there are conditions of endemic civil war between the two political branches. On the Hill, executive spokesmen are suspect because, at the least, they are wary. Often they are deceivers. Sometimes they are perjurers. Congress tends to conceive of itself as "un-engaged," as not being a part of the government in the sense of sharing responsibility, even for the continuation of foreign affairs lines of action that would not have been possible without its concurrence at an earlier time, as Dean Rostow's contribution to Appendix L of the Murphy Commission Report demonstrates.

The committee structure of Congress is notorious for its multifariousness and for the undemocratic seniority system. As bearing upon operations across the separation-of-powers chasm, it is well known that the multiplicity of congressional committees and empire-building chairmen and subchairmen depresses the quality of govern-

Covey T. Oliver

ment in a range from undue demands upon the time of ministers and subministers of the executive to legislation-distorting conflicts of jurisdiction between committees and even subcommittees.

Also, the committee staffs are growing phenomenally, rapidly tending toward becoming a second bureaucracy. And this second bureaucracy, unlike the bedeviled first (of the executive branch), is not compelled by congressional intervention to be alert to or answerable to public interest. Doubters may resort to a simple test: as a citizen, try to get an answer from (a) the executive bureaucracy and (b) the Hill bureaucracy. You will not get it from (b) unless you are important to an important legislator on that committee or subcommittee. You can almost always command it from (a), if other means fail, by getting your legislator to write to the agency where the executive bureaucrat works.

Perhaps the situation just described is merely transitory. In the beginnings of executive bureaucracy under the Constitution of 1789, it may have been that Mr. Jefferson's several clerks at the "Department of Foreign Relations" were as remote from the demands of the citizenry as congressional staffers tend to be now—the mores of primitive bureaucracies being that the clerks answer to their masters, not to the public.

And so, an old question repeats itself: *Quis custodiet ipsos custodes* —not at the next election, but during the first three or four years, say, of a "safe" Senate term?

There are, here, other questions pertinent to the governance of foreign affairs. I limit myself to posing only those of particular relevance, assuming the continuation without substantial modification of the present separation-of-powers system:

1. Why continue the special foreign affairs powers of the Senate? For that matter, why a Senate any longer—at least beyond an upper house that, representing establishmentarian interests, may delay but not prevent legislation? Perhaps our senatorial tradition, amply buttressed by the attitudes of certain members of that "club," is a bit more Roman than is safe if we are to ensure a non-Roman future.

2. If we were to consider essential unicameralism for the future, is the House too large? Are the terms of representatives too short?

3. What of congressional committee structures, functional non-parallelism with the executive departments, overlapping jurisdiction, seniority?

The main problem the American people have to face, though, as to the future role of Congress in relationship to foreign affairs, is this Issue:

Issue: Does Congress accurately represent the outlooks and attitudes of the American people from time to time as to America's relationship to the rest of the world? Or does it distort both the people's outlooks and their attitudes?

Discussion of Issue: Serious appraisers should at least think about the above Issue. Does Congress—always, usually, sometimes, or at this point in time—reflect better the foreign affairs goals of the American people than does the President? If the answer is "always" or "usually," and if what have been normal congressional attitudes continue, we may have to resign ourselves to a maverick and isolated role in the world community, unless we are willing—and if willing, know where and how—to change our constitutional structure. Alternatively, what of the possibility that Congress might develop a continuous sense of responsibility to the country's relationships with the rest of the planet? As Justice Brandeis used to argue in another context, perhaps it is also true here that only from having real responsibility will true congressional effectiveness evolve.

Issue: How much do contemporary problems being experienced by the United States in foreign policy formulation and execution arise from temporary conditions of American politics? and how much from the early stages of structural defects that will eventually require correction?

Discussion of Issue: The pattern of increasing discontinuity between the political alignments of Presidents and of congressional majorities has been referred to previously, and the singularity of the Ford presidency is too well known to require comment.

The question seems to come to be whether the present situation is too unusual to last, but to others it seems to be whether the present situation is or is not a mere variation of a fairly stable new pattern.

It is hard for us to imagine unorthodox change under stress in this country. But ten years ago, unilateral, unannounced internationally unauthorized devaluation of the dollar was also unthinkable, and America's shift toward what other nations do in financial trouble was at first indirect and inadequate. But, before long we engaged in a straight-out write-down, as if we had been France, Germany, Great Britain, or numbers of other countries "less of the law" than these or we. And a President has been driven from office by his vulnerability to legislative trial. Unorthodoxies do happen!

It is a simple fact of international life, amply recognized in customary international law, that states are more enduring than their forms of government. Stresses incompatible with governmental structure will change it to preserve the state itself. It is only our good fortune that so far has immunized us from this reality. Or is our Constitution less vulnerable than others have been? If so, why?

The Range of Structural Change in the Constitution

Issue: Shall there be constitutional revision for foreign affairs reasons, and, if so, what should be its dimensions?

Discussion of Issue: It is beyond the function of this issues paper to propose an answer to this Issue or, if it should be answered "yes," to submit a plan for change. The function of this writer ends with the following sketch of attitudinal alternatives and of schematic variables that are to be taken as merely suggestive, not as exclusionary or definitive.

A Synopsis of Constitutional Revision for Foreign Affairs Reasons

I. "Practicality" aside, is constitutional change worth considering? Why or why not?

II. Alternatives to revision—the range of: (a) institutional and individual self-restraint as between the "political branches" and the actors therein; (b) institutional rearrangments not requiring legislation or constitutional change: the institutionalization of executive-legislative cooperation; limits of, under the Federal Election Act case, if any; (c) legislative changes not involving constitutional revision—as against the backdrop of the proceeding Issue and the Federal Election Act decision.

III. Changing the Constitution—the range of possibilities: (a) major change: abandon separation of powers and put the executive for foreign affairs in the legislature (a cabinet form of government for foreign affairs); (b) constitutional adjustments not negating separation of powers (some possibly by "judicial amendment").[56]

1. State the territorial reach of the Constitution, function-by-function, if need be.

2. Eliminate the exclusive role of the Senate in approving treaties and provide that international agreements (all but very minor or technical ones) come into internal legal effect only by simple majority approval in both houses.

3. Create a treaty-performance agency to ensure that in day-to-day operations the international treaty obligations of the United States are, in fact, lived up to throughout the federal government and by the states. (This could probably be done without amendment of the Constitution.)

4. Permit certain types of regional or international entities which the United States may enter to act directly (*erga omnes*) upon persons and interests in the United States.

5. Fix the limits of validity, if any, of executive privilege and of official secrecy in a foreign affairs context.

6. Clarify the authority of the judiciary in contentions between the Congress and the executive as to their respective authorities ("political questions").

7. Make structural changes in the Congress (not that Congress could not make these without amendment, but because it does not do so).

8. State clearly whether the President's power as commander-in-chief includes sole or controlled authority (other than the congressional money power) to deploy military force outside the United States.

9. Modernize the concept of declaration of war.

10. Settle by positive constitutional determination the question whether Congress may participate in foreign affairs operations especially in regard to: *(i)* negation free of presidential veto of executive agreements made under previously delegated authority and under the President's chief of state (inherent) powers; *(ii)* mandatory executive application or not of appropriations to fund congressionally chosen foreign affairs goals; (iii) Senate "advise and consent" beyond its treaty-approval function; *(iv)* constitutional principles of separation of powers unsettled (if unsettlement there was) by the Supreme Court's decision in the Federal Election Act case as to the inability of congressional appointees to engage in other than legislative and investigative functions.

11. Weigh the desirability of giving the people plebiscite, initiative, and referendum powers, possibly by electronic voting.

12. Abolish or curtail the foreign relations powers of the Senate now denied to the House.

13. Provide longer terms and fewer numbers for members of the House of Representatives.

14. Expand congressmen's standing to sue and to object administratively to governmental foreign policy lines of action.

15. Provide that subsequent inconsistent legislation may not contradict the internal legal effect of a treaty until it is legally no longer in effect.

16. State clearly whether the power to end international agreements, including those with internal legal effects, is solely executive; or, alternatively, provide for legislative participation in the treaty-termination power.

17. Decide whether the executive shall have (as presently the judiciary claims to have, not in decisions but in approaches to Congress) a right to funds adequate to maintain basic effectiveness as to its foreign affairs responsibilities.

18. Clarify the inquiry power of Congress as to the President's nondepartmental assistants and advisers.

19. Readjust federal-state relationships in the foreign affairs area if any such readjustment seems necessary in the overall interests of the nation.

20. Evaluate a plural presidency or some redistribution at the constitutional level of the present vast range of presidential responsibility.

21. Reexamine the amendment process under the Constitution of 1789 to determine whether it is too rigid and too difficult to achieve.

22. Reappraise, if relevant, the extent to which the Supreme Court has expanded the concept of judicial review and the use of contingent and conditional mandates and decide whether the powers of the courts in these particulars should be moderated or denied.

23. Shall the President be authorized to veto items in appropriations bills relating to the conduct of foreign affairs?

Covey T. Oliver

NOTES

1. This report, "Organizing the Government to Conduct Foreign Policy: The Constitutional Questions," was distributed along with this issues paper to participants in the work of Committee IV through the courtesy of the *University of Virginia Law Review* 61 (1975), p. 747.

2. Widely referred to as the "Murphy Commission" in honor of its chairman, the Honorable Robert D. Murphy. a distinguished senior American diplomatist, this commission was required by Sec. 603(a) of the Foreign Relations Authorization Act of 1972, P. L. 92-352, 86 Stat. 489. The singularity of the requirement for reauthorization, as distinguished from fiscal appropriation, of the Department of State among the established departments of the executive branch is discussed herein. A livelier account of the origins of the commission than that of its general counsel in his *Introduction* to the law review printing cited above is to be found in B. Welles, "The Genesis of the Murphy Commission—Congress, Commissions, and Cookie-Pushing," *Foreign Service Journal* 53 (January 1976), p. 11.

3. Covey T. Oliver, "The Enforcement of Treaties by a Federal State," chap. 3, I-1974, *Recueil des Cours*, pp. 346, 348, Hague Academy of International Law.

4. Remarks of the Prime Minister of Singapore at the White House, *Weekly Compilation of Presidential Documents* 11 (12 May 1975), p. 501, at p. 502.

5. The tally is that of B. Welles, "The Genesis of the Murphy Commission."

6. Even by 1949 in the writer's recollection, "reorganizing the Department of State" had become rather repetitive in Washington.

7. The reasons for modest scope in official reports on the reorganization of the government, especially as to its basic structure, are quite understandable. They are, perhaps, the same reasons the Congress of the United States, under the Articles of Confederation, did not undertake directly the revisory tasks that came to be performed by the Federal Convention of 1787. See, generally, Max Farrand, *The Framing of the Constitution* (New Haven: Yale University Press, 1913), chap. 1.

8. J. Brandeis, dissenting in *New State Ice Co.* v. *Liebmann*, 285 U.S. 262 (1932), from the then-reigning notion that substantive due process required invalidation of state legislation limiting entry into a business denominated in that legislation as one affected with the public interest.

9. In the matter of the determination of the immunity of defendants from suit under the claim of "sovereign" immunity, settlement of nationalization claims, and so on. See generally, *Restatement of the Law Second: The Foreign Relations Law of the United States* (St. Paul: American Law Institute Publishers, 1965), sec. 69, R.N. 1; 71; 212; 213; 214.

10. Louis Henkin, *Foreign Affairs and the Constitution* (Mineola: Foundation Press, 1972).

11. Why it did not is often said to be one of the several enigmas of silence in the Constitution as to arrangements for foreign relations operations. However, Farrand, *The Framing of the Constitution*, by his time-sequence rearrangement of what went on at Philadelphia, tends to show that no mysteries were involved but, rather, that the framers had far more delicate and difficult internal issues of union than foreign affairs ones to face and settle and, having done so, engrossed their document and adjourned, leaving us with ". . . the 'bundle of compromises' known as the constitution of the United States . . . a practical piece of work for very practical purposes" (p. 201). "[The framers] were dependent upon their experience under the state constitutions and the articles of confederation. John Dickinson expressed this very succinctly in the course of the debates when he said: 'Experience must be our only guide. Reason may mislead us' " (p. 204).

Nowadays, thanks to the Supreme Court's accretive creation of an unwritten constitution, the "foreign affairs legislative power of Congress" has become a commonplace. Compare Henkin, *Foreign Affairs and the Constitution*, chap. 3, pp. 74–76.

12. The reference is to an interpretation of the wide-ranging obiter dictum of Justice Sutherland as the opinion-writer in *United States* v. *Curtiss-Wright Export Corp.*, 299 U.S. 304, 315–20 (1936).

13. Note, particularly, the comments of Professor Gerhard Casper, "Organizing the Government," p. 777.

14. Consult the dissent of Senator Mike Mansfield to the Report of the Murphy Commission. Welles, "The Genesis of the Murphy Commission," selects these phrases from this nonconcurrence of a commissioner: ". . . even a cursory reading of the Commission's report reveals a . . . timidity and paucity of substance . . . obvious lack of any consensus among the Commissioners . . . *almost total absence of any consideration of the role of Congress.*" (Emphasis added.) The same source quotes Senator Mansfield on interview as characterizing the Murphy Commission Report as ". . . thin gruel . . . served in a very thick bowl."

15. See Oliver, *The Enforcement of Treaties*, chap. 4, pp. 363–65, for a short explanation of the classic British discontinuity between treaty-making and internal treaty performance needing legislation and of the "Ponsonby Rule," whereby HMG usually provides Parliament with informational scrutiny of treaties by laying them on the table for a time.

16. This generalization is based upon personal observations and the reality that if the foreign minister's party has the votes, the opposition cannot make much of a not untypical "No, sir" refusal to respond at question time.

17. *Blackburn* v. *Attorney-General* [1971] Common Market L. Reps. 784 [1971] 1 W.L.R. 1037 (Ct. of App.).

18. Compare Arts. 27 and 46 of the United Nations (Vienna) Convention on the Law of Treaties; *Restatement Second: Foreign Relations Law of the United States* (1965), sec. 123, 132, 163; Oliver, *The Enforcement of Treaties*, pp. 354–60.

19. 252 U.S. 416 (1920).

20. 354 U.S. 1, 16–17 (1957).

21. 343 U.S. 579 (1952).

22. Contrast *Downes* v. *Bidwell*, 182 U.S. 244 (1901) with *Hawaii* v. *Mankichi*, 190 U.S. 197 (1903); *Dorr* v. *U.S.*, 195 U.S. 138 (1904); *Balzac* v. *Puerto Rico*, 258 U.S. 298 (1922). See, generally, Henkin, *Foreign Affairs and the Constitution*, chap. 10.

23. No. 29, 592, ACM 21707, 22 August 1975. Modified on reconsideration, 44 LW 2466 (1976).

24. 367 U.S. 643 (1961).

25. Loper, " 'Federal State' Clauses in Multilateral Instruments," 1960, *University of Illinois Law Forum* 1960 (Fall), p. 375 (a reprinting in monographic compendium); Oliver, *The Enforcement of Treaties*, chap. 6, pp. 404–7.

26. 418 U.S. 683 (1974).

27. P.L. 93-618, 3 January 1975, sec. 102(e), 125, 151, 152, 161.

28. Readers may wish to consider H.R. 4438, 94th Cong., 1st Sess. A high-water mark among legislative efforts to insulate the will of Congress as to the effectiveness of foreign affairs undertakings of the United States from presidential veto is a proposed "Executive Agreements Review Act of 1975," which deserves wider, scientific attention than so far it appears to have received.

29. The key committee in the Congress as to this vital aspect of foreign affairs policy is the House Banking and Currency Committee, not the House Committee on International Relations. In the Senate, consideration is by the Committee on Foreign Relations.

30. This is intended as a serious reflection on what may be the typical political organization of most of the world in a time of resource depletion and population increase, assuming for this purpose that mankind's seeming problems are not dissipated by benign development not now foreseeable.

31. Farrand, *The Framing of the Constitution*, repeatedly brings his readers back to the fundamental fact that the opposite was true in the beginning and in his time. He summarizes pertinently in his conclusion:

> Neither a work of divine origin, nor "the greatest work that ever was struck off at a given time by the brain and purpose of man," but a practical, workable document is this Constitution of the United States. Planned to meet certain immediate needs and modified to suit the exigencies of the situation, . . . it has been adapted by an ingenious political people to meet the changing requirements of a century and a quarter.

(The year was 1913).

But compare Henkin, *Foreign Affairs and the Constitution*, who ends his book with an approving requotation of what some others have considered "the sneer implicit" in Gladstone's peroration on the American Constitution, quoted and rejected above by Farrand, and the Liberal Prime Minister's contrasting reference to the British constitution as ". . . the most subtile [sic] organism which has proceeded from the womb and the long gestation of progressive history."

32. William Giandoni, "Latin Americans Spend Little On The Military," Copley News Service, *Dallas Morning News*, 10 March 1976, p. 70.

33. The President, who had been given the power to waive these but not all conditions precedent to American development assistance if, in his determination, the foreign affairs interests of the United States should so warrant (but with a burden of reporting and explaining), knew that the congressional groups involved would tolerate waivers as to countries in other areas for a variety of reasons but not as to the recipients of development assistance in the Western hemisphere.

34. P.L., 93-148 (1973).

35. *Buckley* v. *Valeo*, 424 U.S. 1, 109 (1976). In holding that the Federal Election Commission created by the Federal Election Campaign Act of 1971 could not continue to function in a rulemaking and executive management way for more than thirty days after mandate, the Court relied upon the separation-of-powers system of the Constitution and, following *Springer* v. *Philippine Islands*, 277 U.S. 189 (1922), held that legislative appointees to governmental bodies cannot perform executive functions. Compare H. Lee Watson, "Congress Steps Out: A Look at Congressional Control of the Executive," *California Law Review* 63 (1975), p. 983, at pp. 1029–48. The holding in part 4 of the lengthy opinion was unanimous in the per curiam decision.

36. I am indebted to William Bailey Lockhart, Yale Kamisar, and Jesse H. Choper, *Constitutional Law—Cases, Comments, Questions* (St. Paul: West Publishing Co., 1975), pp. 277–88 for very useful notes on impoundment and for reassurances as to the position taken in the text as to impoundment and foreign affairs. A disclaimer provision (Sec. 1001 (1)) declares that nothing in the Congressional Budget and Impoundment Control Act of 1974 ". . . shall be construed as asserting or conceding the constitutional powers or limitations of either the Congress or the President."

37. Louis Henkin, *Arms Control and Inspection in American Law* (New York: Columbia University Press, 1958).

38. 389 U.S. 429 (1968). Henkin, *Foreign Affairs and the Constitution*, chap. 9, is more moderate and restrained in his evaluation of this case. In it the Supreme Court, even with a disavowal of foreign affairs concern filed by the federal executive, held invalid an Oregon escheat statute denying inheritances to persons behind the Iron Curtain, unless the Oregon probate courts should be satisfied that these persons would actually be able to receive and enjoy the inheritances. Professor Henkin notes that the Court declared this to be an unconstitutional ". . . intrusion by the State into the field of foreign affairs which the Constitution entrusts to the President and the Congress." He adds:

> This is new constitutional doctrine. No doubt, an act of Congress or a treaty, probably an executive agreement, perhaps an official executive declaration, possibly even a rule made by the federal courts, could have forbidden what Oregon purported to do. Here there was no relevant exercise of federal

Covey T. Oliver

power and no basis for deriving any prohibition by 'interpretation' of the silence of Congress and the President. . . . [The case] then, imposes additional limitations on the States but what they are and how far they reach remains to be determined.

39. The widely-accepted notion that the framers assumed from the beginning that the Senate should represent the states (almost as if official delegations from the states to the seat of the federal government) may be another of the numerous post hoc myths about the creation; see Farrand, *The Framing of the Constitution*, chap. 7. The Virginia Plan provided for the lower house to elect the Senate from nominees made by each state. The small states resisted a system of representation proportional to population in both houses; the "Great Compromise" was to give them an assured two seats in the Senate, not necessarily to provide for the selection of these two by state legislatures.

40. *Restatement of the Law Second*, sec. 145.

41. Myres S. McDougal and Asher Lans, "Treaties and Congressional-Executive or Presidential Agreements: Interchangeable Instruments of National Policy," *Yale Law Journal* 54 (1945), pp. 181, 534. Consult, generally, Henkin, *Foreign Affairs and the Constitution*, chap. 6.

42. The point is often made that at any time since roughly 1938—at the latest—it would not have required a treaty with Canada to provide internal legal effect for preemptive federal legislation on migratory game birds because of judicial relaxation of old judicial limitations upon the subject-matter reach of ordinary legislation under the Article I enumerated powers—or even the evolved legislative powers, such as the "foreign affairs legislative power." Compare *Missouri* v. *Holland*, 252 U.S. 416 (1920).

43. Bernard Schwartz, *A Commentary on the Constitution of the United States: The Powers of Government* (New York: Macmillan Co., 1963), pp. 101, 150.

44. In some congressional and public opinion quarters, opposition to modification in Panama's favor of the 1903 treaty has taken to a "high ground" defense that, regardless of the constitutional power of the President and two-thirds of the Senate to alter our "as if sovereign" status in the Canal Zone, the land area is owned (in fee simple) by the United States by purchase and hence cannot be disposed of without the consent of both houses. (Compare Art. IV, Sec. 3 and Art. I, Sec. 8). However, at the present time, the degree of opposition in the Senate itself suggests that even a new treaty arrangement would not receive the requisite extraordinary vote in the upper chamber.

45. Sometimes, as January 1976 news items remind us, the Congress blinks, as when the House refused to uphold the sweeping claims of its Select Committee on Intelligence.

46. *United States* v. *Curtiss-Wright Export Corp.* See *supra* n. 12.

47. 332 U.S. 19 (1947).

48. 369 U.S. 186 (1962).

49. 395 U.S. 486 (1969).

50. *Supra* n. 35.

51. 7 How. 1 (U.S. 1849)—guarantee of a republican form of government; not a foreign relations "political question" case.

52. 418 U.S. 683 (1974).

53. 484 F.2d 1307 (2d Cir. 1973), cert. den. with opinions by Marshall and Douglas, JJ, 414 U.S. 1304 (1973).

54. The citation is available thanks to the richness of the notes in Lockhart, Kamisar and Choper, *Constitutional Law Cases*; Archibald Cox, "The Role of Congress in Constitutional Determinations," *University of Cincinnati Law Review* 40 (1971), p. 199, at p. 204.

55. *Buckley* v. *Valeo*. See *supra* n. 35.

56. There are very few proposals for general change on a major scale. See generally, Rexford G. Tugwell, *The Emerging Constitution* (New York: Harper's Magazine Press, 1974), issued under the imprimatur of the Fund for the Republic and based upon studies prepared for the Center for the Study of Democratic Institutions. This plan for major revision is not, on the whole, oriented particularly toward the crisis of separation of powers in foreign relations; but there is a perspective in the introduction (p. xv) that is highly pertinent to the perspective of this issues paper:

A serious difficulty with any agreement embodied in a document and widely accepted, as the Constitution of 1787 eventually came to be, is that its provisions eventually tend to become scriptural. . . . Because this charter is thus massively founded it may easily . . . become obsolete as economic and social changes occur.

The American instance of obsolescence is a serious one, strangely ignored in constitutional commentaries even by students of public law.

Adam Yarmolinsky, "Organizing for Interdependence: The Role of Government," *Interdependence Series* No. 5/Aspen Institute for Humanistic Studies, Program in International Affairs (1976), proposes elaborate reorganization of the executive branch and slight changes in congressional structure as necessary for the United States in a future of planetary "interdependence." The study also notes the existence now of a congressional bureaucracy, adding that as of the beginning of fiscal year 1976 there were 11,500 members of congressional staffs. The major thrust of the reorganization plan is that there be recognition in law of a diminished role for the Department of State, provision for the redistribution of powers in the executive branch to reflect the senses of mission and of capabilities for coping of a number of other executive units, and congressional-legislative cooperation based upon the concept that no valid line exists any longer between "domestic" and "foreign" lines of action. The current crisis at the constitutional level and the *erga omnes* problem are not featured in this study of "interdependence," which is, of course, not necessarily an idealized ingredient of the future, but a likely necessity.

REPORT on the DELIBERATIONS of COMMITTEE IV
by Noyes Leech and Stephen J. Schulhofer

Part 1 by Stephen J. Schulhofer

INTRODUCTION

The mission of Committee IV was to assess the present constitutional framework for the conduct of relations between the United States and the rest of the world. The committee's deliberations focused upon the strengths and weaknesses of the present system and upon the desirability of changing particular features of our legal framework either by legislation or by constitutional amendment. In the second part of this paper my colleague Professor Leech analyzes those facets of the committee's discussions that focused upon the overall distribution of authority between the President and Congress, and upon the specific legal principles that govern the making and breaking of international agreements. This part of the paper considers the issues that arise, outside the scope of formal agreements between or among nations, in connection with the conduct of military and diplomatic affairs.

The problems to be examined accordingly are large ones. They include the formation of American policy toward foreign countries, the day-to-day conduct of our relationships with the rest of the world, control of the military establishment, spending for defense and foreign aid, decisions regarding the use of military force and finally, decisions with particular regard to the use of nuclear force. But the committee did not, for the most part, consider it appropriate to discuss the specific policies that should or should not be formulated with respect to the substance of any of these matters. Rather, the committee addressed only the much narrower question whether we have organized ourselves in such a way as to make sound decision-making on these problems even possible in our third century. The present paper likewise concerns itself only with this relatively limited, structural question.

It is well to stress at the outset that the committee approached its task with a keen sense of the significance of the issues on its agenda. Senator Joseph Clark reminded the panel at the outset of its deliberations that the first question underlying its discussions would, in effect, be "[I]s America going to *have* a third century?" Indeed, at the opening of the Bicentennial Conference, Dean Louis Pollak pointedly drew the attention of all conference participants to the fact that as America closes its second century, it does so under the cloud of the tragedy of Vietnam.[1] The committee therefore undertook, with a strong sense of purpose, the responsibility of examining in some detail the arrangements that condition whether catastrophes of that magnitude, or of even greater, will be among the events that we should anticipate or must anticipate during the one hundred years to come.

The committee did not find the kind of tendency observed by Committee III, a tendency on the part of Congress to delegate more and more authority to the executive branch of the government. On the contrary, the committee found in the field of foreign affairs a growing congressional will to participate actively in the conduct of the government's business. The view taken in the committee was that this will should be encouraged, but not encouraged by giving Congress new powers or new weapons to use against the executive. Rather it was the general view that we should seek ways to build bridges that will permit more effective cooperation between the two branches of government.

Now, how can this aspiration be fulfilled? The committee considered first the possibility of changes at the constitutional level and then considered a variety of subconstitutional changes.

CONSTITUTIONAL CHANGES

Among the constitutional changes, one that was discussed in some detail concerned the procedures for declaring war. The Constitution presently provides only the terse statement that "The Congress shall have Power . . . To declare War, . . ."[2] The realities of military deployment under contemporary conditions were, of course, scarcely contemplated when this language was drafted, and the committee therefore examined the desirability of modernizing this provision by including specific constitutional requirements for congressional and/or presidential authorization prior to military undertakings of particular kinds.

Other possibilities for constitutional change were also considered. The committee discussed the usefulness of granting explicitly to Congress the executive power to manage certain types of foreign relations activities, such as trade negotiations. The committee also examined the desirability of including in the Constitution a provision spelling out the authority of the executive branch to withhold information from Congress on grounds of official secrecy or executive privilege.

With respect to each of these proposals, the general view in the

Stephen J. Schulhofer and Noyes Leech

committee was that constitutional change was not necessary or even desirable at the present time. One reason for this reluctance to press amendments to the Constitution was very forcefully expressed by Bayless Manning:

> What we see or perceive right now in the short-term focus of our political glasses as structural difficulties in the Constitution are profoundly reflective of what are essentially underlying political bubblings and splits.

> Not only do we have the interjection of a different design for the doing of international business, the Senate, and not only do we have underlying nonconsensus of a political character, . . . and have all of these things simultaneously in the most heated political environment the society has seen since the Civil War. . . . It would seem to me that is hardly the most appropriate time to inquire and to have a clear vision as to whether the structural arrangements which have served with rather remarkable aggregate success for 200 years will continue to serve us.

While a number of committee members expressed disagreement with this analysis, they likewise concluded that constitutional change was inappropriate. These committee members found evidence of significant structural weakness in our constitutional system, but took the view that the present constitutional language provides an appropriately flexible framework within which creative solutions for these structural problems may over time evolve. These committee members therefore turned their attention to the kinds of subconstitutional changes that would lay the foundation for this sort of structural improvement.

SUBCONSTITUTIONAL CHANGES

In the course of the committee's examination of proposals for subconstitutional change in our governmental structure, four problems received particularly detailed attention. These were the use of military force, Congress's ability to obtain and use information bearing on foreign relations issues, congressional oversight, and the role of the courts.

The Use of Military Force

The War Powers Resolution, enacted over President Nixon's veto in 1973,[3] marks the beginnings of congressional control over the deployment of American forces. Under the resolution, whenever American armed forces are introduced "into hostilities or into situations where imminent involvement in hostilities is clearly indicated by the circumstances," the President must within forty-eight hours provide Congress with a written report explaining the circumstances necessitating the involvement and the estimated scope and duration of the involvement.[4] The resolution also provides that the forces must be withdrawn within sixty days unless Congress has declared war, enacted a specific authorization for the continued use of American forces, or enacted legislation extending the sixty-day period.[5] Finally, the resolution requires that without regard for the sixty-day time limit:

> [A]t any time that United States Armed Forces are engaged in hostilities outside the territory of the United States, its possessions and territories without a declaration of war or specific statutory authorization, such forces shall be removed by the President if the Congress so directs by concurrent resolution [a form of congressional action not subject to presidential veto].[6]

There has been considerable public discussion concerning the constitutionality of this historic legislation. In his veto message, President Nixon asserted flatly that the resolution was "clearly unconstitutional."[7] Although this view is not wholly without scholarly support,[8] there was strong support within the committee for the position that the measure represents a legitimate exercise of powers granted to Congress under the Constitution and does not constitute an improper interference with the President's authority as commander-in-chief.[9]

On the contrary, the concern that was expressed, and very forcefully expressed by some members of the committee, was that the War Powers Resolution does not go far enough. In the War Powers Resolution and in congressional action generally, there has been great insensitivity to evolving restrictions under international law upon the use of force. The committee spent some time discussing the nature and effectiveness of these restrictions. The Kellogg-Briand Pact of 1928,[10] to which the United States and nearly all other major powers are signatories,[11] provides that the signatory nations "renounce [war] as an instrument of national policy in their relations with one another." Similarly, Article 2(4) of the United Nations Charter provides that "All Members shall refrain in their international relations from the threat or use of force against the territorial integrity or political independence of any state."[12]

In spite of these apparently clear and unequivocal restrictions, the precise scope of the prohibition against the use of force as an instrument of national policy remains uncertain. In part, this uncertainty is attributable to the fact that the U.N. Charter itself authorizes the use of force in "individual or collective self-defence,"[13] an exception that continues to defy workable definition. Beyond this, the commentators and publicists continue to debate the validity of other, unwritten exceptions permitting the use of force in anticolonial or humanitarian interventions, and the like. And in the absence of a functioning mechanism for *enforcing* international law, it seems undeniable that state-supported violence not falling within any conceivable exception continues on a large scale throughout the world.[14] Under these circumstances not all members of the committee were prepared to recognize that meaningful restrictions upon the use of force do exist under international law. But Professor Louis Henkin probably reflected a prevalent view among panel members when he concluded that "the principle [against the use of force] is firm and generally accepted, [although] the opening up of exceptions has made that, unhappily, less clear than it could be." And as Ambassador Philip Jessup put it:

> [I]nternational law is not like a teacup which, when once broken, is irretrievably ruined; and the fact that you have these breaches of international law is no evidence that the rule does not exist.

Against this background, Professor Richard Falk stated a view shared by many on the panel when he expressed his shock that "the War Powers Act itself is completely drafted as if the United Nations Charter . . . never existed, and it assumes presidential discretion to use force in a kind of legal vacuum." A number of participants therefore stressed the need for much greater attention to the evolving restrictions upon the use of force, not only in day-to-day practice, but also in the applicable domestic legislation.

Beyond this, the committee saw a need for special attention to the use of nuclear force. Discussed in some detail were the procedures that could permit congressional consultation prior to the use of nuclear weapons. These procedures are not nearly so impractical as they might at first blush appear, because in some situations several days or even weeks may elapse before a decision to make tactical or defensive use of nuclear weapons will be acted upon. Committee members did not generally express support for requiring approval by the full Congress in such cases, but it was considered desirable to explore the possibilities of constituting a standing committee of five or six members of Congress, whose concurrence in this very momentous type of decision would be required.

The committee also considered the possibility of imposing substantive limits on the use of nuclear force, as a matter of domestic law. An example of such a limit would be a rule prohibiting first use by the United States. Many members of the committee favored exploring the feasibility of a restriction of this type.

The committee's view, it is fair to summarize, was that expansion of congressional control over the use of force, in the various ways described above, would be constitutional. The attitude was somewhat less widespread that all the proposals mentioned would be desirable, but the committee nevertheless endorsed, as a general matter, the notion of exploring these possibilities very seriously.

Congressional Ability to Obtain and Use Information

Despite the support expressed in the committee for the proposals thus far described, the committee was clearly unanimous in feeling that changes of this kind, whether desirable or not, cannot by themselves accomplish very much.

Regardless of the statutory principles in force, the effectiveness of congressional control in the final analysis depends upon Congress's ability to evaluate particular fact situations, usually at a time of crisis. In this Congress has not been particularly successful. Prior to the War Powers Resolution, the experience with Tonkin Gulf makes it quite clear that, even if that resolution had been in effect, Congress would have issued the necessary authorizations based on the information initially available to it.[15] Subsequent to the War Powers Resolution, the initial congressional response to the *Mayaguez* incident pointed in exactly the same direction.[16] So the committee concluded that there was need for changes of a very different type.

This second group of changes concerns getting information to Congress and improving its ability to use that information. Here, the first area of difficulty involves the problems of state secrets and executive privilege. The present procedures for classifying and declassifying national security information are set forth in an executive order promulgated in 1972.[17] Even when disclosure of foreign affairs information could not endanger national security, however, Congress and the public may, under some circumstances, be denied access to that information by operation of the doctrine of executive privilege.[18]

Many committee members very strongly expressed the view that these privileges of secrecy and confidentiality are invoked far too often by the executive branch of the government. On the other hand, there was a recognition that some confidentiality and indeed a good deal of confidentiality is necessary not only to protect American security but also to insure full debate at the lower levels of government.

In this area, the committee saw a need for much greater restraint by the executive in invoking privileges of confidentiality. In addition, a total overhaul of our classification system for official secrets was considered desirable.[19]

The other facet of the information problem is the need to strengthen congressional capacity to use effectively the information that, hopefully, it will be able to obtain. In this area, Congress already has three very important arms for research and analysis. These are the Office of Technology Assessment,[20] the Library of Congress[21] and the General Accounting Office.[22] To date, however, these tools have not been used as frequently in the foreign relations area as they could be. The committee found a definite need to strengthen these three arms of Congress and, in particular, to involve them actively in the problems of defense and foreign relations. A notable example of the kind of involvement the committee had in mind was provided some months after the close of our deliberations, with the publication of the General Accounting Office investigation of the *Mayaguez* incident.[23]

The budget process is another area in which Congress has not been well organized for effective action. Until recently, congressional authority over expenditures was dispersed throughout a number of independent committees. Coordinated review of spending priorities and of the overall impact of the budget on the national economy was therefore impossible. In addition, Congress had no staff comparable to the President's Office of Management and Budget, and presidential

272   *Stephen J. Schulhofer and Noyes Leech*

budget proposals were normally submitted only a few months before congressional action on them was required.[24]

In an effort to cope with these problems Congress has recently enacted legislation establishing a budget committee in each house of Congress, and creating a Congressional Budget Office with responsibility for analyzing the impact of budget proposals and reporting on them to the budget committees.[25] The legislation also establishes new timetables that will permit better long-term planning and more thorough analysis of requests for expenditure authorizations. Committee members viewed these reforms as most promising and urged that they be put to active use in evaluating military and foreign relations questions.

Congressional Oversight

Even if all the recommendations in the two areas thus far considered should be fully implemented, the committee unfortunately was not particularly optimistic about the prospects for a vast change in the quality and nature of decision-making. Congressional participation in advance of decisions on major issues is seldom likely to be effective in influencing the result. Therefore, the need that was perceived by many was for a much more active use of the technique of legislative oversight after the event.

The committee did not share the reservations that were expressed with regard to this technique by Committee III. The predominant view taken in Committee IV was that Congress should be the Monday morning quarterback and should play that role not rarely and reluctantly but willingly and often, not only when executive actions are unpopular or would appear to be unsuccessful from the military standpoint, but whenever foreign policy or military initiatives of major significance are instituted.

The proposals for improvement in the three areas thus far considered represent very basic changes, but they do not appear to be barred by constitutional concepts of separation of powers. In the issues paper, Professor Oliver did raise the question whether, in light of the recent Federal Election Commission decision,[26] the Supreme Court may be taking a stricter view of the required division of functions among the branches of government.[27] The committee did not view this decision as posing an impediment to the particular kinds of cooperation between the branches that I have outlined. If, however, judicial decisions should evolve in such a way as to cast doubt upon the validity of such measures, then many committee members would endorse constitutional amendment to permit the kind a sharing of authority in the foreign relations field that they considered appropriate.

The Role of the Courts

The committee considered a variety of issues relating to the role of the judicial branch within the constitutional framework for the conduct of foreign relations. In the companion paper Professor Leech discusses the possibility of using the courts to help resolve questions concerning statutes in derogation of treaty obligations. The same possibility arises in connection with questions regarding claims of executive privilege, the validity of deployments of troops under the War Powers Resolution, and other issues of law that might arise under the type of legislation that I have described.

The scope of judicial involvement in questions of this kind presently depends upon the various doctrines of "justiciability." In order to be considered justiciable, a dispute must involve a genuine "case or controversy" between the parties, rather than a mere request for an advisory opinion.[28] The dispute also must be "ripe" for decision, in the sense that judicial involvement is not deemed premature,[29] but the dispute must not be "moot," in the sense that judicial involvement is deemed to come too late.[30] The party bringing the case must have "standing," that is "such a personal stake in the outcome of the controversy as to assure that concrete adverseness which sharpens the presentation of issues upon which the court so largely depends for illumination of difficult constitutional questions."[31] And the issue presented to the courts must not be regarded as a "political question,"[32] a requirement that is easy to state but virtually impossible to define.[33]

The importance of these doctrines became all too obvious during the course of efforts to challenge the constitutionality of the war in Vietnam. Although the decisions were not uniform, most courts found an absence of "standing" in suits brought by taxpayers[34] or by members of Congress.[35] And where the "standing" requirement was met, as in cases brought by servicemen facing duty in Vietnam, most courts held the suit to involve a nonjusticiable "political question."[36]

The view has been expressed, perhaps most notably and most forcefully by Dean Louis Pollak in his President's Lectures last year at the University of Pennsylvania, that these doctrines should be modified by statute so that the courts may play a larger role in determining the validity under our own Constitution of military operations undertaken by the President.[37] Dean Pollak proposed that Congress be given standing to use, in its own name, to obtain a judicial declaration of what the law is, if the executive and legislative branches should be in disagreement concerning the legality of action involving the use of American forces.

Some committee members expressed reluctance to take that step. Their concern seemed to center primarily on two factors. First was a hope that restraint will prevail. Several members of the committee argued that in the field of foreign relations, separation of powers will work best if each branch of government refrains from pushing its power to the limit.

Second, if a clash between the executive and legislative branches should occur, these committee members argued that the existing doctrines of justiciability provide more flexible and more appropriate tools, with which judges may determine for themselves whether they ought to become involved in questions of this delicate nature. The concern expressed by these members was that a more active judicial

Stephen J. Schulhofer and Noyes Leech

role in matters of this kind might put a strain upon the courts and, in particular, upon their ability to contribute to the resolution of the many controversial domestic problems with which they undoubtedly will be faced. Other members of the committee, however, appeared to view a relaxation of the prevailing notions of justiciability as well worth its costs. All agreed, however, that the very sensitive questions concerning the role of the courts should remain in the forefront of those under examination.

It is well to stress that there was no unanimity with respect to the various issues that have been discussed. There was, however, a very pervasive attitude in the committee that a more active role by Congress is desirable and that a number of institutional changes, some of as yet uncertain shape, need to be pursued to make this role possible. These changes, all of them subconstitutional, many of them even substatutory, will nevertheless yield what has to be regarded as a quantum change in the level of congressional involvement in the foreign relations field and hopefully a quantum change in the quality of that involvement.

Part 2 by Noyes Leech

This part of the paper reports the varying responses of a diverse group of individuals to Professor Oliver's paper. It does not report my own point of view and my own reaction to his paper. The committee did not consider the issues paper as an adversary document, but rather as, in fact, what it purported to be: a statement of issues that ought to be considered by the committee.

A CONSTITUTIONAL CRISIS?

There was a thematic point of view that ran through Professor Oliver's paper, to which the committee members responded. In his statement of several of the issues, Professor Oliver observed that Congress is currently expressing a strong will to participate in the making of foreign policy. He also noted that we are presently operating in a state of unrelieved separation of powers. In his judgment, these two conditions impose serious impediments on the ability of the executive branch, and therefore of the United States, to enter into immediate and reliable commitments with foreign states.[1] Committee members appeared ready to recognize that the phenomenon described by Professor Oliver, namely, the crisis in the exercise of our foreign relations power, did exist in some measure and that this was created by the congressional will to participate, complicated in part by the system of separation of powers. Possibly the clearest expression of this point of view within the committee came from Professor Gardner, who reported:

> The United States is now behind by quite a few years in its commitments to the replenishment of the International Development Association and various regional development banks. Can we think of any other major country in which a commitment by the president to put money up for international development purposes is two, three, four, five years later not implemented because of the refusal of the legislature? As a second example, we are embarked on a series of multilateral trade negotiations in Geneva in which everyone concedes the heart of the matter to be non-tariff barriers. The agreement of the President's representative in Geneva is a very dubious thing. It has to be implemented under the provisions of the trade bill by Congress, and no one can say with assurance whether the Congress will carry out those commitments. Is there any other major country in the world whose executive branch cannot deliver with respect to commitments on those matters? I think pragmatically, whatever the formalities may be, we are really unique among major countries.

However, many members of the committee did not share the view that, in international affairs generally, the United States was in such a peculiar position that it was unduly hampered in its power to carry

276   Stephen J. Schulhofer and Noyes Leech

on foreign relations effectively. Although it was recognized that the requirement either of Senate advice and consent to treaties or of congressional approval of international agreements did impede the making of commitments that could be immediately and confidently relied upon by foreign states, it was observed by committee members that other countries are frequently impeded by parliamentary rules with like effect, although of a different structure. A number of members of the committee voiced the view that the difficulties of the United States in this regard are not necessarily structural but depend upon differing political points of view held by the President and the Congress.[2]

In any event, the committee was almost completely of the view that no need presently exists for amendments to the foreign affairs provisions of the Constitution. Although the committee was reminded that its charge enjoined it to look off into the distance of the United States' third century, no one was able confidently to predict that there would be developments that would inevitably require constitutional amendment. However, as I will discuss later, there was recognition of some remote contingencies that might signal the need for some specific amendment.

EXECUTIVE AND CONGRESS

In the main, the disposition of the committee was to deal with the relationship between the executive and the Congress as one of continuing political balance that could be comfortably (and by that term I do not mean "serenely") accommodated within the confines of the present constitutional structure. The tension that exists between the two branches was recognized as a more or less permanent feature of governmental structure in the United States, with the ultimate balance of power the product of a process variously described as a "tug of war," "push come to shove," and "ebb and flow." It was emphasized that many of the evils that are seen flowing from the so-called imperial presidency resulted not from Congress's lack of constitutional authority but from its non-use of its admitted powers. The cure for these evils was perceived as attainable through what came to be called in the committee "subconstitutional means": new practices, new institutions, new legislation—in short, through ordinary political and legislative processes.

One particular point of view about Congress's alleged inability to act with efficiency should be mentioned. This point of view was not shared wholly by all members of the committee, but it does represent a distinct and different attitude that should be described. As Professor Falk posed the issue, it is "the question as to whether, in the absence of a popular consensus, one wants an efficient foreign policy." The argument proceeds somewhat as follows. There is not a popular consensus favoring national action in many matters, for example, United States involvement in Angola. The executive branch should not act without a widespread consensus. Congress is now a better institution than the executive branch to record the existence of such consensus as may develop. The executive should not act until Congress supports national action on the basis of whatever consensus it observes, reports, or represents. If, as a consequence of congressional participation in the process, the executive cannot take immediate action of its own choosing, that is simply an inevitable consequence of a process that promotes desirable political values. Again quoting Professor Falk:

> So I think a lot of the concern with structure, in a way, is a displaced concern with policy, and I think that is important to keep in mind because it leads one toward looking to constitutional remedies for what are largely political frustrations. . . . I think that one of the characteristics of the present period is that there is a failure of consensus in a number of fundamental dimensions. The most obvious dimension is the dimension of policy. I think the Vietnam experience has created a fundamental policy split between an interventionary activist diplomacy in the world and essentially a predisposition for a kind of neo-isolationist withdrawal. That is part of what is reflected in the congressional-executive tension. If you look at the key issues, Angola being the most recent one, it is a congressional predisposition toward withdrawal and nonintervention and an executive predisposition toward activist interventionary diplomacy. In my view, it is better for society as a whole not to be drawn into activist pastures in the absence of a very powerful consensual mandate, because the absence of a powerful consensual mandate is what I think places the domestic system under tremendous strain, as one saw in the latter part of the Vietnam period, where there wasn't a genuine consensus underlying the policy. That led to tremendous encroachments upon a lot of other aspects of congressional patterns of government, just to mobilize enough support to carry on the policy that didn't possess the wide popular basis of support.

Professor Falk concluded this analysis with the observation that the "ineffectuality" that has resulted from the present congressional-executive tension is taking place in a period of transition toward a new kind of consensus. He saw this as "essentially a healthy by-product of the constitutional arrangement rather than something one should seek to overcome."

Although other members of the committee did not expressly endorse this analysis of the present political position, some of them appeared to agree that the current satisfactions or dissatisfactions with the operation of the separation of powers principle do not arise from constitutional structure itself but rather from what was referred to by one member as "essentially underlying political bubblings and splits." For the most part, the members of the committee were in agreement that it was in order to hold a conference to study the constitutional problems of foreign affairs, as distinguished from the

Stephen J. Schulhofer and Noyes Leech

political ramifications of the subject. However, one member, Senator Clark, expressed concern over a narrow reading of the committee's charge which would exclude consideration of a number of issues other than constitutional interpretation, issues he considered essential to "a sound consideration of America's third century." These issues are set forth in the note in the Senator's own words.[3] The committee recognized the imposing and impending nature of these problems. Members of the committee nevertheless asserted that it was highly appropriate for the committee to focus its own study on the question of the ways in which the United States could organize itself to deal rationally with those problems. Therefore, it identified the constitutional and subconstitutional issues to which it was addressing itself at this conference as useful questions to be considered in order to create the necessary organization of the resources of the United States government and of its people for the solution of those vital substantive problems.

INTERNATIONAL AGREEMENTS

The challenges posed by Congress's assertion of its will to participate in the making of foreign policy raised a number of discrete constitutional problems. The committee considered how certain problems of congressional-executive branch organization relating to international agreements might be approached. These problems are: the making of international agreements, the termination of the effect of international agreements as internal United States law, and joining and participating in the work of international organizations. My colleague, Mr. Schulhofer, addressed a number of other questions that have arisen in the area of separation of powers; I will deal with these three matters relating to international agreements.

Making International Agreements

International agreements are made by the United States in three principal forms: (1) the treaty, requiring a two-thirds vote of "advice and consent" by the Senate; (2) the executive agreement made pursuant to authority given by treaty or by Congress; and (3) the executive agreement made pursuant to the President's constitutional authority.[4]

A number of members of the committee expressed a preference for entering into international agreements through the device of the agreement made by the executive branch under authorization by both houses of Congress, including in some cases broad policy authorization. Authorization might be given prior to the making of the agreement or by ratification after the agreement has been made. In any event, authorization would be given through the normal legislative process: a simple majority vote by the House and the Senate, followed by the signing of the authorizing bill by the President. Of course, this mode should be contrasted with the treaty-making process, requiring a two-thirds vote by the Senate.[5] The committee gave consideration to proposing an amendment to remove from the Constitution the requirement of two-thirds Senate advice and consent. With such an amendment, the main agreement-making device would then consist of presidential action authorized or ratified by the two houses in the normal legislative process. In the committee there was a widespread feeling that, in principle, the two-thirds vote was not desirable or, indeed, rationally supportable under today's conditions, and that the ability of one-third of the Senate plus one senator to block international agreements should not be imbedded in the Constitution.[6] But most members of the committee were reluctant, and at least one member was unwilling, to assume the serious political costs they thought would be needed to procure that amendment at this time. One other member, however, was of the opinion that these costs might well have to be paid at some time not too far in the future. There was inconclusive discussion of the question of the constitutional problems that might arise in connection with the making of a new agreement relating to the Panama Canal. The need for such an agreement was perceived as so great that, if a treaty were to be blocked by a minority of senators, it was thought possible that the two houses of Congress might try to approve such an agreement by simple majority vote.[7] It was suggested that this would be a critical test of the survival of the right of a Senate minority to insist upon an exclusive Senate role in the making of international agreements.

The committee addressed the further question of Congress's regulation of the executive agreement by devices other than normal legislative authorization or ratification. The committee considered a procedure that could operate as a congressional veto but that would itself be free of the presidential veto. Under this procedure, all executive agreements would be reported to Congress, but Congress could veto the agreement if, within a period of time, it should vote by concurrent resolution of both houses not to allow the agreement to stand.[8] Since the concurrent resolution does not require presidential signature, this procedure would operate to give Congress a veto over agreements entered into by the President.[9] It was asserted in the committee that, in view of the fact that in congressional practice the concurrent resolution had not been subject to the President's veto and had not been used for basic legislation,[10] it was inappropriate to use it to control such basic matters as international agreements. In general, members of the committee accepted this argument, although there was recognition of the fact that one reason there was a movement to give Congress such a strong role in the area of executive agreements was the fact that the Case Act, requiring the reporting of executive agreements to the Congress, had been evaded in the past.[11]

Peculiar problems were recognized with respect to one type of executive agreement: the agreement entered into by the President on the basis of his own constitutional authority, e.g., as commander-in-chief.[12] It was agreed that a congressional veto by way of the concurrent resolution would be unconstitutional if applied to a presidential agreement based on his individual powers. One member was con-

Stephen J. Schulhofer and Noyes Leech

cerned whether the President's constitutional authority, as presently understood, would cover such commitments as an agreement to use nuclear weapons in defense of South Korea. Asserting that an agreement of that scope ought not be made by the executive alone, he suggested that a constitutional amendment was needed to limit the President's power. While not going so far as to support amendment of the Constitution, one other member supported Congress's emerging effort to be involved in the making of international agreements. Professor Henkin sought to sharpen the issue as follows:

> [T]he question is: involvement in what way? The Case Act is involvement, and if you broaden it, strengthen it, etc., you have congressional involvement. [One of our members] suggested involvement by broad policy outlines in advance, and in areas like trade, which are areas clearly in the congressional domain, no one would quarrel with that. . . . But if you are talking about involvement in all executive agreements, and if you are talking about this particular device of concurrent resolution, then I have serious problems about certain kinds of agreements, and it seems to me that it is there that we might have some lines to be drawn.[13]

The committee did not essay to draw those lines, perhaps reflecting Professor McDougal's "individual statement" that "the gentlemen who sat here two hundred years ago thought it most unwise to try to define in detail the powers of the President; they preferred to leave this to future exigence."

Termination of Internal Effect of International Agreements

It is currently understood to be the law that, although a treaty made under the authority of the United States is the supreme law of the land,[14] if Congress enacts a statute inconsistent with a prior treaty the statute (which is also the supreme law of the land) supplants the treaty as internal law.[15] The committee deplored the casual use of such a practice by the Congress, since it leaves the country in violation of its international duties under the treaty. There was a strong disposition to devise procedures to make Congress aware of the seriousness of breaching international obligations in this fashion. Suggestions were made—and appeared well received by members of the committee—that treaties be drafted to include sanctions to be suffered by the United States in the event of treaty breach (which would include breach resulting from congressional enactment of inconsistent legislation). It was pointed out that the General Agreement on Tariffs and Trade provides a procedure for making a form of compensation to a party whose interests have been prejudiced by a violation of that agreement.[16] Some thought there ought to be a constitutional amendment that would place the international agreement in a position superior to legislation, even legislation enacted later than the agreement. One operative effect of such an amendment could be to allow the Supreme Court to declare an act of Congress ineffective as internal law if it should conflict with an obligation under an international agreement.[17] Most who spoke in favor of such an amendment thought it was not presently likely to be adopted. Judge Jessup suggested:

> Suppose short of . . . constitutional amendment, which I would favor but hold to be away in the future, you set up by statute, which of course could be repealed, . . . that if the President based a veto of a statute on the ground that passage of that statute would be a violation of our international obligations, Congress could then . . . be authorized to take the issue to court and let the court determine whether this was violation of our international obligations and, if so, Congress would not be able to override the veto.[18]

There was inconclusive discussion in the committee about this suggestion and questions raised about whether a constitutional amendment would be required to accomplish the result. Professor McDougal made a strong plea for preserving largely intact the present system for terminating treaties, which he saw as allowing the Congress to take the lead in some cases, the President to take the lead in others.

> I don't think there should be any one branch of government that predominates over the others. I like this very fluid system in which they can all get in a say, and it's really priority in time that prevails. When you are dealing with conflicting treaties, conflicting statutes, conflicting presidential agreements, and so forth, if they are within their competence, the Court has always held that the latest in time prevails. . . . [I]t seems to me that in its broad framework this is a pretty good system, and we have a way of ultimately getting answers [that are] compatible with our long-term common interest.

The committee reached no consensus on a single way to deal with the question of the enactment of legislation violative of the international obligations of the United States. Political difficulties appeared to stand in the way of some of the suggestions, not the least of which would be the difficulty of procuring the constitutional amendments that would be required in some cases. Professor Lipson thought that repeal of the Connally Reservation[19] "may be politically difficult . . . but politically a good deal easier" than a number of other suggestions. He asserted:

> [A] measure that would as a matter of statute declare the willingness of the United States to accept the jurisdiction of an international tribunal, seized with [the] question whether a measure is inconsistent with the international obligations of the United States, would have some difficulty, but repeal of the Connally Reservation would be a step on the way.

Stephen J. Schulhofer and Noyes Leech

INTERNATIONAL ORGANIZATIONS

The question of joining and participating in international organizations resulted from the committee's looking down the years into the next century. The committee projected that there would be a desire on the part of the United States to join international organizations of an increasingly sophisticated type. Such highly developed organizations, possibly regional in character and dealing with technical concerns such as economic integration, might follow the pattern of some European organizations that provide for dealing directly with persons and entities within the territory of the member states.[20] Organizations of this type do not act simply on the state alone. Professor Oliver posed to the committee the question whether under our constitutional structure (on such matters as the judicial power of the United States[21] and the guarantees of the Bill of Rights) the United States could lawfully join such organizations without violating constitutional provisions. It was the view of some of the committee members that the cases that appeared to nullify international agreements that conflicted with the Constitution[22] may not in fact do so in this instance. No one argued that the courts should cease to measure the provisions of charters of international organizations by constitutional standards; such charters are a form of treaty in themselves. However it was urged by some that judicial development might well accommodate the United States' joining such organizations without the necessity of constitutional amendment.

This is not to suggest that the courts would not be alert to protect United States citizens against deprivation of liberties. Presumably the courts will insist upon the employment of fair procedures by any international organization of which the United States becomes a member, even though the procedures do not follow the same patterns as those established in this country. Some members of the committee expressed the view that the constitutional problems arising upon joining some kinds of international organizations could be quite complex, if the matter were approached without amendment of the Constitution.[23] The committee members appeared to agree with one member who asserted that this was an area in which the necessity of constitutional amendment ought to be reserved on what he called a contingency basis. If, at some time in the possibly distant future, the courts are not sufficiently sensitive to national needs, and do not interpret the Constitution so as to permit United States membership in highly developed international organizations essential to its interests (and possibly to its survival), he asserted that it would then be necessary to make membership possible in those organizations through whatever amendments of the Constitution were required.

NOTES
Part 1

1. Louis Pollak, "Keynote Address," *The Annals of the American Academy of Political and Social Science* 426 (July 1976), p. 9 at p. 18.

2. U.S. Constitution, see Art. I, Sec. 8, Cl. 11.

3. P.L. 93-148, 87 Stat. 555, 50 U.S.C. Sec. 1541 *et seq.* (Supp. III, 1973).

4. Ibid., Sec. 1543(a)(1).

5. Ibid., Sec. 1544(b). The President can unilaterally extend the sixty-day period by not more than an additional thirty days, if he certifies that military necessity requires the continued use of American forces to effectuate the prompt and safe removal of these forces.

6. Ibid., Sec. 1544(c).

7. "Veto of War Powers Resolution," *Weekly Compilation of Presidential Documents* 9 (27 October 1973), p. 1285, at p. 1286.

8. For example, Eugene Rostow, "Great Cases Make Bad Law: The War Powers Act," *Texas Law Review* 50 (May 1972), p. 833.

9. For a full development of this view, see, for example, Raoul Berger, "War-Making by the President," *University of Pennsylvania Law Review* 121 (1972), p. 29.

10. 46 Stat. 2343, 94 U.N.T.S. 59 (1929).

11. See Noyes Leech, Covey T. Oliver and Joseph Sweeney, *The International Legal System* (Mineola: Foundation Press, 1973), p. 1210.

12. *1970 Yearbook of the United Nations*, p. 1001.

13. See Art. 51, ibid., p. 1007.

14. For a useful collection of materials dealing with these matters, see Leech, Oliver & Sweeney, *The International Legal System*, at pp. 1202–68.

15. See Gulf of Tonkin Resolution, P.L. 88–408, 78 Stat. 384 (1964), repealed, P.L. 91–672, sec. 12, 84 Stat. 2053 (1971). Information that subsequently became available put the matter in quite a different light. See *Hearings on the Gulf of Tonkin, the 1964 Incidents, Before the Senate Committee on Foreign Relations,* 90th Cong., 2d Sess. (1968).

16. See generally, Jordan Paust, "The Seizure and Recovery of the *Mayaguez*," Yale Law Journal 85 (May 1976), p. 774. Eighteen months after the incident, the General Accounting Office issued a report taking a far more critical view of the way the incident had been handled. See GAO report, "The Seizure of the *Mayaguez*: A Case Study of Crisis Management," ID-76-45, 11 May 1976.

17. Executive Order No. 11, 652, 6 March 1972, *Federal Register* 37, 33 C.F.R. sec. 339 (1974), p. 5209.

18. See Archibald Cox, "Executive Privilege," *University of Pennsylvania Law Review* 122 (1974), p. 1383.

19. For a discussion of some of the principal shortcomings of the present system and suggestions for reform, see Charles R. Nesson, "Aspects of the Executive's Power over National Security Matters: Secrecy Classifications and Foreign Intelligence Wire-taps," *Indiana Law Journal* 49 (Spring 1974), p. 399; Note, "National Security and the Amended Freedom of Information Act," *Yale Law Journal* 85 (1976), p. 401.

20. See Technology Assessment Act of 1972, 2 U.S.C. secs. 471–81 (1973).

21. The Library of Congress was established on 24 April 1800. See 2 Stat. 56. Its responsibilities which have expanded substantially over time, are set out in 2 U.S.C. secs. 131–69 (Supp. 1975). See also Office of Federal Reporter, *U.S. Government Manual* (Washington: Government Printing Office, 1975), pp. 53–58.

22. The General Accounting Office was created by the Budget and Accounting Act of 1921, 31 U.S.C. sec. 41 (1976). For an analysis of its present responsibilities, see *U.S. Government Manual*, at pp. 44–49.

23. See GAO, "The Seizure of the *Mayaguez*: A Case Study of Crisis Management."

24. For discussion of these matters, see the Report of the House Rules Committee on the Congressional Budget and Impoundment Control Act, H.R. Rep. 93–658, 93rd Cong., 1st Sess. (1973).

25. Congressional Budget Act of 1974, P.L. 93-344, 88 Stat. 297 (1974).

26. *Buckley* v. *Valeo*, 424 U.S. 1 (1976).

27. Covey T. Oliver, "The United States and the World," *The Annals of the American Academy of Political and Social Science* 426 (July 1976), p. 166.

28. *United States* v. *Freuhauf*, 365 U.S. 146 (1961); *Muskrat* v. *United States*, 219 U.S. 346 (1911).

29. *Postum Cereal Co.* v. *California Fig Nut Co.*, 272 U.S. 693 (1927).

30. *California* v. *San Pablo & T.R. Co.*, 149 U.S. 308 (1893).

31. *Baker* v. *Carr*, 369 U.S. 186, 204 (1962). See also *Flast* v. *Cohen*, 392 U.S. 83 (1968).

32. *Luther* v. *Borden*, 48 U.S. (7 How.) 1 (1849); see *Baker* v. *Carr*, n. 31, *supra*.

33. See Louis Henkin, *Foreign Affairs and the Constitution* (Mineola: Foundation Press, 1972), pp. 210–16; Louis Henkin, "Is There a 'Political Question' Doctrine," *Yale Law Journal* 84 (1976), p. 597.

34. See, for example, *Pietsch* v. *President of the United States*, 434 F.2d 861 (2d Cir. 1970), cert. den., 403 U.S. 920 (1971); *Velvel* v. *Nixon*, 415 F.2d 236 (10th Cir. 1969), cert. den., 396 U.S. 1042 (1970).

35. See, for example, *Holtzman* v. *Schlesinger*, 484 F.2d 1307 (2d Cir. 1973), cert. den., 416 U.S. 936 (1974); *Gravel* v. *Laird*, 347 F. Supp. 7 (D. D.C. 1972). Contra, *Mitchell* v. *Laird*, 488 F.2d 611, 614 (D.C. Cir. 1973).

36. See, for example, *Da Cosna* v. *Laird*, 471 F.2d 1146 (2d Cir. 1973); *Luftig* v. *McNamara*, 373 F.2d 664 (D.C. Cir. 1967), cert. den., 387 U.S. 945 (1967); *Atlee* v. *Laird*, 347 F. Supp. 689 (E.D. Pa. 1972), aff'd., 411 U.S. 911 (1973). In one contrary

Stephen J. Schulhofer and Noyes Leech

decision, the Court held the question not to be "political" and reached the merits, but then rejected the challenge to the constitutionality of the war on the ground that Congress had in fact authorized or ratified the relevant military operations. *Orlando* v. *Laird,* 443 F.2d 1039 (2d Cir. 1971), cert. den., 404 U.S. 869 (1971).

37. Louis H. Pollak, "The Constitution as an Experiment," *University of Pennsylvania Law Review* 123 (1975), p. 1318, at pp. 1337–38.

NOTES
Part 2

1. Indeed, Professor Oliver spoke to the committee of the "concern, irritation and loss of confidence abroad in the predictable performance of the United States along this or that foreign affairs line of action" and asserted "that our potential capacity is somewhat limited and that our actual capacity for operations in the world arena as other states operate is significantly limited now."

2. As pointed out in the committee, the basic difficulty in the foreign affairs field arises from the fact that the executive and the legislative branches may represent different political parties. Structural (i.e., constitutional) changes would be required to change that fact, as for example to institute a British parliamentary style of government.

3. "One, is there a need for a new world order?

"Two, are global resources so finite that we must plan better on a global basis for their just use?

"Three, what limits, if any, should be imposed on national sovereignty?

"Four, what are Americans going to do about poverty, hunger, and disease, if anything?

"Five, is there a need for improved population control, and, if so, what does America do about it?

"Six, how can we build effective machinery to keep the peace?

"Seven, what should American policy be with respect to the oceans?

"Eight, air and water pollution. How should America deal with them in a global setting?

"Nine, what should our policy be with respect to international trade and monetary reform?

"Ten, what should our attitude be towards expanding the scope of international law?"

4. The constitutional bases for the making of international agreements are detailed in secs. 117–21 of *Restatement of The Law Second: Foreign Relations Law of the United States* (St. Paul: American Law Institute Publishers, 1965). See also, Daniel Patrick O'Connell, *International Law,* 2d ed. (Dobbs Ferry: Oceana Publications, Inc., 1970). The author sets forth a select list of executive agreements entered into by the United States in recent years (categorized by reference to prior and subsequent congressional approval and by inherent presidential power). The list is reprinted in Leech, Oliver and Sweeney, *The International Legal System,* p. 1013. See *supra* n. 11.

5. United States Constitution, Art. II, Sec. 2.

6. One member asserted that even at the time of the framing of the Constitution there was no rational basis for the two-thirds rule and that the rule was a compromise that had led, over the years, to the development of the congressional-executive agreement device to by-pass the strict treaty-making process. See generally, Myres S. McDougal and Asher Lans, "Treaties and Congressional-Executive or Presidential Agreements: Interchangeable Instruments of National Policy," *Yale Law Journal* 54 (1945), pp. 181, 534. In committee discussion it was asserted:

Nobody has been able to give a rational reason in contemporary times. If the one-third is needed to protect some special interest, it is a special interest. If you ask yourself what special interest is to be protected, if you don't relate it to long-term common interests, it's just naked power, and there is no place for that in our constitutional structure.

7. See the account in William W. Bishop, Jr., *International Law,* 2nd ed. (Boston: Little, Brown & Co., 1962) at p. 103 of the admission of Texas to the Union by joint resolution after Senate rejection of an annexation treaty.

8. The Executive Agreements Review Act of 1975, H.R. 4438, 94th Cong., 1st Sess., provides for transmittal to Congress of each executive agreement regarding a "national commitment" (defined to cover agreements on deploying armed forces abroad or the provision of military or nuclear technology or other resources to a foreign country). The bill provides for the coming into effect of the executive agreement sixty days after such transmittal unless both houses by concurrent resolution state they do not approve the agreement.

9. U.S. Constitution, Art. I, Sec. 7 provides: "Every Order, Resolution or Vote to which the Concurrence of the Senate and House of Representatives may be necessary . . . shall be presented to the President of the United States" (and be subject to his veto). Under long-standing congressional practice, concurrent resolutions have not been submitted to the President, under an interpretation of the foregoing provision.

10. "It has been employed as a means of claiming for the houses the power to control or recover powers delegated by Congress to the President." Edward S. Corwin's *The Constitution and What It Means Today* (Princeton: Princeton University Press, 1973), p. 31, (citing the Reorganization Act of 1939, the Lend-Lease Act of 1941, the First War Powers Act of 1941, the Emergency Price Control Act of 1942, the Stabilization Act of 1942 and the War Labor Disputes Act of 1943).

11. 1 U.S.C., Sec. 112b (Supp. V 1975):
The Secretary of State shall transmit to the Congress the text of any international agreement, other than a treaty, to which the United States is

a party as soon as practicable after such agreement has entered into force with respect to the United States but in no event later than sixty days thereafter. However, any such agreement the immediate public disclosure of which would, in the opinion of the President, be prejudicial to the national security of the United States shall not be so transmitted to the Congress but shall be transmitted to the Committee on Foreign Relations of the Senate and the Committee on Foreign Affairs of the House of Representatives under an appropriate injunction of secrecy to be removed only upon due notice from the President.

12. For example, armistice agreements are entered into under that authority. The famous Litvinoff Assignment arose under the President's constitutional power to recognize foreign governments. (U.S. Constitution, Art. II, Sec. 3: ". . . receive Ambassadors and other public Ministers"). See *United States* v. *Belmont*, 301 U.S. 324 (1937).

13. The Trade Agreements Act of 1934 inaugurated Congress's delegation of power to the President to make agreements in this field. The current legislation is to be found at 19 U.S.C. sec. 1351.

14. U.S. Constitution, Art. VI, Cl. 2.

15. "This Court has also repeatedly taken the position that an Act of Congress . . . is on a full parity with a treaty, and that when a statute which is subsequent in time is inconsistent with a treaty, the statute to the extent of the conflict renders the treaty null. *Reid* v. *Covert*, 354 U.S. 1, 18 (1957).

16. The General Agreement on Tariffs and Trade of 30 October 1947, 61 Stat. Part 5, A 12, 55 U.N.T.S. 187, provides in Art. XXVIII for a reciprocal withdrawal of tariff concessions by a party confronted by another state's modification or withdrawal of a prior concession.

17. There is an analogy to the Supreme Court's declaring a statute ineffective because it conflicts with a provision of the Constitution (i.e., it declares the statute "unconstitutional").

18. With respect to the standing of Congress to maintain such a suit, the committee member recalled an analogous suggestion by Dean Louis Pollak that, under certain circumstances, Congress by concurrent resolution should be authorized to bring suit in its own name in federal court in connection with certain issues under the War Powers Resolution. Pollak, "The Constitution as an Experiment," at p. 1338. See *supra* n. 37.

19. 61 Stat. 1218. As is well known, the so-called Connally Reservation to the submission of the United States to the compulsory jurisdiction of the International Court of Justice contains a provision whereby the United States itself determines whether or not a matter falls essentially within its domestic jurisdiction. This "self-judging" reservation is thought to give the United States the power to decide in a particular case whether or not it will submit to the court's jurisdiction, the antithesis of a genuine compulsory submission to that jurisdiction.

20. In the European Community, individuals and corporations, though nationals of member states of the community, can be found by the community's commission to have violated its antitrust laws and other regulations.

21. "The judicial power of the United States, shall be vested in one supreme court, and in such inferior courts as the Congress may from time to time ordain and establish." U.S. Constitution, Art. III, Sec. 1.

22. For example, *Reid* v. *Covert*; see *supra* n. 15.

23. See, for example, Nathaniel L. Nathanson, "The Constitution and World Government," *Northwestern University Law Review* 57 (1962), p. 355.

The
Constitution
OF THE
UNITED STATES
OF AMERICA

We the People of the United States, in Order to form a more perfect Union, establish Justice, insure domestic Tranquility, provide for the common defence, promote the general Welfare, and secure the Blessings of Liberty to ourselves and our Posterity, do ordain and establish this Constitution for the United States of America.

SECTION 1. All legislative Powers herein granted shall be vested in a Congress of the United States, which shall consist of a Senate and House of Representatives.

SECTION 2. The House of Representatives shall be composed of Members chosen every second Year by the People of the several States, and the Electors in each State shall have the Qualifications requisite for Electors of the most numerous Branch of the State Legislature.

No Person shall be a Representative who shall not have attained to the Age of twenty-five Years, and been seven Years a Citizen of the United States, and who shall not, when elected, be an Inhabitant of that State in which he shall be chosen.

[Representatives and direct Taxes shall be apportioned among the several States which may be included within this Union, according to their respective Numbers, which shall be determined by adding to the whole Number of free Persons, including those bound to Service for a Term of Years, and excluding Indians not taxed, three-fifths of all other Persons.]* The actual Enumeration shall be made within three Years after the first Meeting of the Congress of the United States, and within every subsequent Term of ten Years, in such Manner as they

*Changed by section 2 of the fourteenth amendment.

287

shall by Law direct. The Number of Representatives shall not exceed one for every thirty Thousand,* but each State shall have at Least one Representative; and until such enumeration shall be made, the State of New Hampshire shall be entitled to chuse three, Massachusetts eight, Rhode-Island and Providence Plantations one, Connecticut five, New-York six, New Jersey four, Pennsylvania eight, Delaware one, Maryland six, Virginia ten, North Carolina five, South Carolina five, and Georgia three.

When vacancies happen in the Representation from any State, the Executive Authority thereof shall issue Writs of Election to fill such Vacancies.

The House of Representatives shall chuse their Speaker and other Officers; and shall have the sole Power of Impeachment.

SECTION 3. The Senate of the United States shall be composed of two Senators from each State, [chosen by the Legislature thereof,]** for six Years; and each Senator shall have one Vote.

Immediately after they shall be assembled in Consequence of the first Election, they shall be divided as equally as may be into three Classes. The Seats of the Senators of the first Class shall be vacated at the Expiration of the second Year, of the second Class at the Expiration of the fourth Year, and of the third Class at the Expiration of the sixth Year, so that one-third may be chosen every second Year; [and if Vacancies happen by Resignation, or otherwise, during the Recess of the Legislature of any State, the Executive thereof may make temporary Appointments until the next Meeting of the Legislature, which shall then fill such Vacancies.]***

No Person shall be a Senator who shall not have attained to the Age of thirty Years, and been nine Years a Citizen of the United States, and who shall not, when elected, be an Inhabitant of that State for which he shall be chosen.

The Vice President of the United States shall be President of the Senate, but shall have no Vote, unless they be equally divided.

The Senate shall chuse their other Officers, and also a President pro tempore, in the absence of the Vice President, or when he shall exercise the Office of President of the United States.

The Senate shall have the sole Power to try all Impeachments. When sitting for that Purpose, they shall be on Oath or Affirmation. When the President of the United States is tried, the Chief Justice shall preside: And no Person shall be convicted without the Concurrence of two thirds of the Members present.

Judgment in Cases of Impeachment shall not extend further than to removal from Office, and disqualification to hold and enjoy any Office of honor, Trust or Profit under the United States: but the Party convicted shall nevertheless be liable and subject to Indictment, Trial, Judgment and Punishment, according to Law.

SECTION 4. The Times, Places and Manner of holding Elections for

*Ratio in 1965 was one to over 410,000.
**Changed by section 1 of the seventeenth amendment.
***Changed by clause 2 of the seventeenth amendment.

The Constitution of the United States of America

Senators and Representatives, shall be prescribed in each State by the Legislature thereof; but the Congress may at any time by Law make or alter such Regulations, except as to the Place of Chusing Senators.

The Congress shall assemble at least once in every Year, and such Meeting shall [be on the first Monday in December,]* unless they shall by Law appoint a different Day.

SECTION 5. Each House shall be the Judge of the Elections, Returns and Qualifications of its own Members, and a Majority of each shall constitute a Quorum to do Business; but a smaller number may adjourn from day to day, and may be authorized to compel the Attendance of absent Members, in such Manner, and under such Penalties as each House may provide.

Each House may determine the Rules of its Proceedings, punish its Members for disorderly Behavior, and, with the Concurrence of two thirds, expel a Member.

Each House shall keep a Journal of its Proceedings, and from time to time publish the same, excepting such Parts as may in their Judgment require Secrecy; and the Yeas and Nays of the Members of either House on any question shall, at the Desire of one fifth of those Present, be entered on the Journal.

Neither House, during the Session of Congress, shall, without the Consent of the other, adjourn for more than three days, nor to any other Place than that in which the two Houses shall be sitting.

SECTION 6. The Senators and Representatives shall receive a Compensation for their Services, to be ascertained by Law, and paid out of the Treasury of the United States. They shall in all Cases, except Treason, Felony and Breach of the Peace, be privileged from Arrest during their Attendance at the Session of their respective Houses, and in going to and returning from the same; and for any Speech or Debate in either House, they shall not be questioned in any other Place.

No Senator or Representative shall, during the Time for which he was elected, be appointed to any civil Office under the Authority of the United States, which shall have been created, or the Emoluments whereof shall have been encreased during such time; and no Person holding any Office under the United States, shall be a Member of either House during his Continuance in Office.

SECTION 7. All Bills for raising Revenue shall originate in the House of Representatives; but the Senate may propose or concur with Amendments as on other Bills.

Every Bill which shall have passed the House of Representatives and the Senate, shall, before it become a Law, be presented to the President of the United States; If he approve he shall sign it, but if not he shall return it, with his Objections to that House in which it shall have originated, who shall enter the Objections at large on their Journal, and proceed to reconsider it. If after such Reconsideration

*Changed by section 2 of the twentieth amendment.

two thirds of that House shall agree to pass the Bill, it shall be sent, together with the Objections, to the other House, by which it shall likewise be reconsidered, and if approved by two-thirds of that House, it shall become a Law. But in all such Cases the Votes of both Houses shall be determined by Yeas and Nays, and the Names of the Persons voting for and against the Bill shall be entered on the Journal of each House respectively. If any Bill shall not be returned by the President within ten Days (Sundays excepted) after it shall have been presented to him, the Same shall be a Law, in like Manner as if he had signed it, unless the Congress by their Adjournment prevent its Return, in which Case it shall not be a Law.

Every Order, Resolution, or Vote to which the Concurrence of the Senate and House of Representatives may be necessary (except on a question of Adjournment) shall be presented to the President of the United States; and before the Same shall take Effect, shall be approved by him, or being disapproved by him, shall be repassed by two-thirds of the Senate and House of Representatives, according to the Rules and Limitations prescribed in the Case of a Bill.

SECTION 8. The Congress shall have Power To lay and collect Taxes, Duties, Imposts and Excises, to pay the Debts and provide for the common Defence and general Welfare of the United States; but all Duties, Imposts and Excises shall be uniform throughout the United States;

To borrow money on the credit of the United States;

To regulate Commerce with foreign Nations, and among the several States, and with the Indian Tribes;

To establish an uniform Rule of Naturalization, and uniform Laws on the subject of Bankruptcies throughout the United States;

To coin Money, regulate the Value thereof, and of foreign Coin, and fix the Standard of Weights and Measures;

To provide for the Punishment of counterfeiting the Securities and current Coin of the United States;

To establish Post Offices and post Roads;

To promote the Progress of Science and useful Arts, by securing for limited Times to Authors and Inventors the exclusive Right to their respective Writings and Discoveries;

To constitute Tribunals inferior to the supreme Court;

To define and punish Piracies and Felonies committed on the high Seas, and Offenses against the Law of Nations;

To declare War, grant Letters of Marque and Reprisal, and make Rules concerning Captures on Land and Water;

To raise and support Armies, but no Appropriation of Money to that Use shall be for a longer Term than two Years;

To provide and maintain a Navy;

To make Rules for the Government and Regulation of the land and naval Forces;

To provide for calling forth the Militia to execute the Laws of the Union, suppress Insurrections and repel Invasions;

To provide for organizing, arming, and disciplining the Militia, and for governing such Part of them as may be employed in the Service of the United States, reserving to the States respectively, the Appointment of the Officers, and the Authority of training the Militia according to the discipline prescribed by Congress;

To exercise exclusive Legislation in all Cases whatsoever, over such District (not exceeding ten Miles square) as may, by Cession of particular States, and the acceptance of Congress, become the Seat of the Government of the United States, and to exercise like Authority over all Places purchased by the Consent of the Legislature of the State in which the Same shall be, for the Erection of Forts, Magazines, Arsenals, dock-Yards, and other needful Buildings;—And

To make all Laws which shall be necessary and proper for carrying into Execution the foregoing Powers, and all other Powers vested by this Constitution in the Government of the United States, or in any Department or Officer thereof.

Section 9. The Migration or Importation of such Persons as any of the States now existing shall think proper to admit, shall not be prohibited by the Congress prior to the Year one thousand eight hundred and eight, but a tax or duty may be imposed on such Importation, not exceeding ten dollars for each Person.

The privilege of the Writ of Habeas Corpus shall not be suspended, unless when in Cases of Rebellion or Invasion the public Safety may require it.

No Bill of Attainder or ex post facto Law shall be passed.

No capitation, or other direct, Tax shall be laid, unless in Proportion to the Census or Enumeration herein before directed to be taken.*

No Tax or Duty shall be laid on Articles exported from any State.

No Preference shall be given by any Regulation of Commerce or Revenue to the Ports of one State over those of another: nor shall Vessels bound to, or from, one State, be obliged to enter, clear, or pay Duties in another.

No Money shall be drawn from the Treasury, but in Consequence of Appropriations made by Law; and a regular Statement and Account of the Receipts and Expenditures of all public Money shall be published from time to time.

No Title of Nobility shall be granted by the United States: And no Person holding any Office of Profit or Trust under them, shall, without the Consent of the Congress, accept of any present, Emolument, Office, or Title, of any kind whatever, from any King, Prince, or foreign State.

Section 10. No State shall enter into any Treaty, Alliance, or Confederation; grant Letters of Marque and Reprisal; coin Money; emit Bills of Credit; make any Thing but gold and silver Coin a Tender in Payment of Debts; pass any Bill of Attainder, ex post facto Law, or Law impairing the Obligation of Contracts, or grant any Title of Nobility.

No State shall, without the Consent of the Congress, lay any

*But see the sixteenth amendment.

Imposts or Duties on Imports or Exports, except what may be absolutely necessary for executing its inspection Laws: and the net Produce of all Duties and Imposts, laid by any State on Imports or Exports, shall be for the Use of the Treasury of the United States; and all such Laws shall be subject to the Revision and Controul of the Congress.

No State shall, without the Consent of Congress, lay any duty of Tonnage, keep Troops, or Ships of War in time of Peace, enter into any Agreement or Compact with another State, or with a foreign Power, or engage in War, unless actually invaded, or in such imminent Danger as will not admit of delay.

ARTICLE II.

SECTION 1. The executive Power shall be vested in a President of the United States of America. He shall hold his Office during the Term of four Years, and, together with the Vice President, chosen for the same Term, be elected, as follows.

Each State shall appoint, in such Manner as the Legislature thereof may direct, a Number of Electors, equal to the whole Number of Senators and Representatives to which the State may be entitled in the Congress: but no Senator or Representative, or Person holding an Office of Trust or Profit under the United States, shall be appointed an Elector.

[The Electors shall meet in their respective States, and vote by Ballot for two persons, of whom one at least shall not be an Inhabitant of the same State with themselves. And they shall make a List of all the Persons voted for, and of the Number of Votes for each; which List they shall sign and certify, and transmit sealed to the Seat of the Government of the United States, directed to the President of the Senate. The President of the Senate shall, in the Presence of the Senate and House of Representatives, open all the Certificates, and the Votes shall then be counted. The Person having the greatest Number of Votes shall be the President, if such Number be a Majority of the whole Number of Electors appointed; and if there be more than one who have such Majority, and have an equal Number of Votes, then the House of Representatives shall immediately chuse by Ballot one of them for President; and if no Person have a Majority, then from the five highest on the List the said House shall in like Manner chuse the President. But in chusing the President, the Votes shall be taken by States, the Representation from each State having one Vote; a quorum for this Purpose shall consist of a Member or Members from two-thirds of the States, and a Majority of all the States shall be necessary to a Choice. In every Case, after the Choice of the President, the Person having the greatest Number of Votes of the Electors shall be the Vice President. But if there should remain two or more who have equal Votes, the Senate shall chuse from them by Ballot the Vice President.]*

*Superseded by the twelfth amendment.

The Congress may determine the Time of chusing the Electors, and the Day on which they shall give their Votes; which Day shall be the same throughout the United States.

No person except a natural born Citizen, or a Citizen of the United States, at the time of the Adoption of this Constitution, shall be eligible to the Office of President; neither shall any Person be eligible to that Office who shall not have attained to the Age of thirty-five Years, and been fourteen Years a Resident within the United States.

*[In Case of the Removal of the President from Office, or of his Death, Resignation, or Inability to discharge the Powers and Duties of the said Office, the same shall devolve on the Vice President, and the Congress may by Law, provide for the Case of Removal, Death, Resignation or Inability, both of the President and Vice President, declaring what Officer shall then act as President, and such Officer shall act accordingly, until the Disability be removed, or a President shall be elected.]

The President shall, at stated Times, receive for his Services, a Compensation, which shall neither be encreased nor diminished during the Period for which he shall have been elected, and he shall not receive within that Period any other Emolument from the United States, or any of them.

Before he enter on the Execution of his Office, he shall take the following Oath or Affirmation:—"I do solemnly swear (or affirm) that I will faithfully execute the Office of President of the United States, and will to the best of my Ability, preserve, protect and defend the Constitution of the United States."

SECTION 2. The President shall be Commander in Chief of the Army and Navy of the United States, and of the Militia of the several States, when called into the actual Service of the United States; he may require the Opinion in writing, of the principal Officer in each of the executive Departments, upon any subject relating to the Duties of their respective Offices, and he shall have Power to Grant Reprieves and Pardons for Offenses against the United States, except in Cases of Impeachment.

He shall have Power, by and with the Advice and Consent of the Senate, to make Treaties, provided two-thirds of the Senators present concur; and he shall nominate, and by and with the Advice and Consent of the Senate, shall appoint Ambassadors, other public Ministers and Consuls, Judges of the supreme Court, and all other Officers of the United States, whose Appointments are not herein otherwise provided for, and which shall be established by Law: but the Congress may by Law vest the Appointment of such inferior Officers, as they think proper, in the President alone, in the Courts of Law, or in the Heads of Departments.

The President shall have Power to fill up all Vacancies that may happen during the Recess of the Senate, by granting Commissions which shall expire at the End of their next Session.

*This clause has been affected by the twenty-fifth amendment.

Section 3. He shall from time to time give to the Congress Information of the State of the Union, and recommend to their Consideration such Measures as he shall judge necessary and expedient; he may, on extraordinary Occasions, convene both Houses, or either of them, and in Case of Disagreement between them, with Respect to the Time of Adjournment, he may adjourn them to such Time as he shall think proper; he shall receive Ambassadors and other public Ministers; he shall take Care that the Laws be faithfully executed, and shall Commission all the Officers of the United States.

Section 4. The President, Vice President and all civil Officers of the United States, shall be removed from Office on Impeachment for, and Conviction of, Treason, Bribery, or other high Crimes and Misdemeanors.

ARTICLE III.

Section 1. The judicial Power of the United States, shall be vested in one supreme Court, and in such inferior Courts as the Congress may from time to time ordain and establish. The Judges, both of the supreme and inferior Courts, shall hold their Offices during good Behaviour, and shall, at stated Times, receive for their Services, a Compensation, which shall not be diminished during their Continuance in Office.

Section 2. The judicial Power shall extend to all Cases, in Law and Equity, arising under this Constitution, the Laws of the United States, and Treaties made, or which shall be made, under their Authority;— to all Cases affecting Ambassadors, other public Ministers and Consuls;—to all Cases of admiralty and maritime Jurisdiction;—to Controversies to which the United States shall be a Party;—to Controversies between two or more States;—between a State and Citizens of another State;—between Citizens of different States;—between Citizens of the same State claiming Lands under Grants of different States, and between a State, or the Citizens thereof, and foreign States, Citizens or Subjects.

In all Cases affecting Ambassadors, other public Ministers and Consuls, and those in which a State shall be a Party, the supreme Court shall have original Jurisdiction. In all the other Cases before mentioned, the supreme Court shall have appellate Jurisdiction, both as to Law and Fact, with such Exceptions, and under such Regulations as the Congress shall make.

The trial of all Crimes, except in Cases of Impeachment, shall be by Jury; and such Trial shall be held in the State where the said Crimes shall have been committed; but when not committed within any State, the Trial shall be at such Place or Places as the Congress may by Law have directed.

Section 3. Treason against the United States, shall consist only in levying War against them, or in adhering to their Enemies, giving them Aid and Comfort. No Person shall be convicted of Treason unless on the Testimony of two Witnesses to the same overt Act, or on Confession in open Court.

The Congress shall have Power to declare the Punishment of Treason, but no Attainder of Treason shall work Corruption of Blood, or Forfeiture except during the Life of the Person attainted.

ARTICLE IV.

SECTION 1. Full Faith and Credit shall be given in each State to the public Acts, Records, and judicial Proceedings of every other State. And the Congress may by general Laws prescribe the Manner in which such Acts, Records and Proceedings shall be proved, and the Effect thereof.

SECTION 2. The Citizens of each State shall be entitled to all Privileges and Immunities of Citizens in the several States.

A Person charged in any State with Treason, Felony, or other Crime, who shall flee from Justice, and be found in another State, shall on demand of the executive Authority of the State from which he fled, be delivered up, to be removed to the State having Jurisdiction of the Crime.

[No Person held to Service or Labour in one State, under the Laws thereof, escaping into another, shall, in Consequence of any Law or Regulation therein, be discharged from such Service or Labour, but shall be delivered up on Claim of the Party to whom such Service or Labour may be due.]*

SECTION 3. New States may be admitted by the Congress into this Union; but no new State shall be formed or erected within the Jurisdiction of any other State; nor any State be formed by the Junction of two or more States, or parts of States, without the Consent of the Legislatures of the States concerned as well as of the Congress.

The Congress shall have Power to dispose of and make all needful Rules and Regulations respecting the Territory or other Property belonging to the United States; and nothing in this Constitution shall be so construed as to Prejudice any Claims of the United States, or of any particular State.

SECTION 4. The United States shall guarantee to every State in this Union a Republican Form of Government, and shall protect each of them against Invasion; and on Application of the Legislature, or of the Executive (when the Legislature cannot be convened) against domestic Violence.

ARTICLE V.

The Congress, whenever two-thirds of both Houses shall deem it necessary, shall propose Amendments to this Constitution, or, on the Application of the Legislatures of two-thirds of the several States, shall call a Convention for proposing Amendments, which, in either Case, shall be valid to all Intents and Purposes, as part of this Constitution, when ratified by the Legislatures of three-fourths of the several States, or by Conventions in three-fourths thereof, as the one or

*Superseded by the thirteenth amendment.

the other Mode of Ratification may be proposed by the Congress: Provided that no Amendment which may be made prior to the Year One thousand eight hundred and eight shall in any Manner affect the first and fourth Clauses in the Ninth Section of the first Article; and that no State, without its Consent, shall be deprived of its equal Suffrage in the Senate.

ARTICLE VI.

All Debts contracted and Engagements entered into, before the Adoption of this Constitution, shall be as valid against the United States under this Constitution, as under the Confederation.

This Constitution, and the Laws of the United States which shall be made in Pursuance thereof; and all Treaties made, or which shall be made, under the Authority of the United States, shall be the supreme Law of the Land; and the Judges in every State shall be bound thereby, any Thing in the Constitution or Laws of any State to the Contrary notwithstanding.

The Senators and Representatives before mentioned, and the Members of the several State Legislatures, and all executive and judicial Officers, both of the United States and of the several States, shall be bound by Oath or Affirmation, to support this Constitution; but no religious Test shall ever be required as a Qualification to any Office or public Trust under the United States.

ARTICLE VII.

The Ratification of the Conventions of nine States shall be sufficient for the Establishment of this Constitution between the States so ratifying the Same.

DONE in Convention by the Unanimous Consent of the States present the Seventeenth Day of September in the Year of our Lord one thousand seven hundred and Eighty seven and of the Independence of the United States of America the Twelfth.

In Witness whereof We have hereunto subscribed our Names.

Go *WASHINGTON*
Presidt and deputy from Virginia

New Hampshire.

John Langdon
Nicholas Gilman

Massachusetts.

Nathaniel Gorham
Rufus King

New Jersey.

Wil: Livingston
David Brearley.

Wm Paterson.
Jona: Dayton

Pennsylvania.

B Franklin
Robt. Morris
Thos. FitzSimons
James Wilson
Thomas Mifflin
Geo. Clymer
Jared Ingersoll
Gouv Morris

Delaware.

Geo: Read
John Dickinson
Jaco: Broom
Gunning Bedford jun
Richard Bassett

Connecticut.

Wm Saml Johnson
Roger Sherman

New York.

Alexander Hamilton

Maryland.

James McHenry
Danl Carrol
Dan: of St Thos Jenifer

Virginia.

John Blair
James Madison Jr.

North Carolina.

Wm Blount
Hu Williamson
Richd Dobbs Spaight.

South Carolina.

J. Rutledge
Charles Pinckney
Charles Cotesworth
Pinckney
Pierce Butler

Georgia.

William Few
Abr Baldwin

Attest:

WILLIAM JACKSON, *Secretary.*

Articles in Addition To, and Amendment Of, the Constitution of the United States of America, Proposed by Congress, and Ratified by the Legislatures of the Several States, Pursuant to the Fifth Article of the Original Constitution.*

(The first 10 Amendments were ratified December 15, 1791, and form what is known as the "Bill of Rights")

AMENDMENT I

Congress shall make no law respecting an establishment of religion, or prohibiting the free exercise thereof; or abridging the freedom of speech, or of the press; or the right of the people peaceably to assemble, and to petition the Government for a redress of grievances.

AMENDMENT II

A well regulated Militia, being necessary to the security of a free State, the right of the people to keep and bear Arms, shall not be infringed.

*Amendment XXI was not ratified by state legislatures, but by state conventions summoned by Congress.

AMENDMENT III

No Soldier shall, in time of peace be quartered in any house, without the consent of the Owner, nor in time of war, but in a manner to be prescribed by law.

AMENDMENT IV

The right of the people to be secure in their persons, houses, papers, and effects, against unreasonable searches and seizures, shall not be violated, and no Warrants shall issue, but upon probable cause, supported by Oath or affirmation, and particularly describing the place to be searched, and the persons or things to be seized.

AMENDMENT V

No person shall be held to answer for a capital, or otherwise infamous crime, unless on a presentment or indictment of a Grand Jury, except in cases arising in the land or naval forces, or in the Militia, when in actual service in time of War or public danger; nor shall any person be subject for the same offence to be twice put in jeopardy of life or limb; nor shall be compelled in any criminal case to be a witness against himself, nor be deprived of life, liberty, or property, without due process of law; nor shall private property be taken for public use, without just compensation.

AMENDMENT VI

In all criminal prosecutions, the accused shall enjoy the right to a speedy and public trial, by an impartial jury of the State and district wherein the crime shall have been committed, which district shall have been previously ascertained by law, and to be informed of the nature and cause of the accusation; to be confronted with the witnesses against him; to have compulsory process for obtaining witnesses in his favor, and to have the Assistance of Counsel for his defence.

AMENDMENT VII

In suits at common law, where the value in controversy shall exceed twenty dollars, the right of trial by jury shall be preserved, and no fact tried by a jury, shall be otherwise reexamined in any Court of the United States, than according to the rules of the common law.

AMENDMENT VIII

Excessive bail shall not be required, nor excessive fines imposed, nor cruel and unusual punishments inflicted.

AMENDMENT IX

The enumeration in the Constitution, of certain rights, shall not be construed to deny or disparage others retained by the people.

AMENDMENT X

The powers not delegated to the United States by the Constitution, nor prohibited by it to the States, are reserved to the States respectively, or to the people.

AMENDMENT XI
(Ratified February 7, 1795)

The Judicial power of the United States shall not be construed to extend to any suit in law or equity, commenced or prosecuted against one of the United States by Citizens of another State, or by Citizens or Subjects of any Foreign State.

AMENDMENT XII
(Ratified July 27, 1804)

The Electors shall meet in their respective states and vote by ballot for President and Vice President, one of whom, at least, shall not be an inhabitant of the same state with themselves; they shall name in their ballots the person voted for as President, and in distinct ballots the person voted for as Vice President, and they shall make distinct lists of all persons voted for as President, and of all persons voted for as Vice President, and of the number of votes for each, which lists they shall sign and certify, and transmit sealed to the seat of the government of the United States, directed to the President of the Senate;—The President of the Senate shall, in presence of the Senate and House of Representatives, open all the certificates and the votes shall then be counted;—The person having the greatest number of votes for President, shall be the President, if such number be a majority of the whole number of Electors appointed; and if no person have such majority, then from the persons having the highest numbers not exceeding three on the list of those voted for as President, the House of Representatives shall choose immediately, by ballot, the President. But in choosing the President, the votes shall be taken by states, the representation from each state having one vote; a quorum for this purpose shall consist of a member or members from two-thirds of the states, and a majority of all the states shall be necessary to a choice. [And if the House of Representatives shall not choose a President whenever the right of choice shall devolve upon them, before the fourth day of March next following, then the Vice President shall act as President, as in the case of the death or other constitutional disability of the President.—]* The person having the greatest number of votes as Vice President, shall be the Vice President, if such number be a majority of the whole number of Electors appointed, and if no person have a majority, then from the two highest numbers on the list, the Senate shall choose the Vice President; a quorum for the purpose shall consist of two-thirds of the whole number of Senators, and a majority of the whole number shall be neces-

*Superseded by section 3 of the twentieth amendment.

sary to a choice. But no person constitutionally ineligible to the office of President shall be eligible to that of Vice President of the United States.

AMENDMENT XIII
(Ratified December 6, 1865)

SECTION 1. Neither slavery nor involuntary servitude, except as a punishment for crime whereof the party shall have been duly convicted, shall exist within the United States, or any place subject to their jurisdiction.

SECTION 2. Congress shall have power to enforce this article by appropriate legislation.

AMENDMENT XIV
(Ratified July 9, 1868)

SECTION 1. All persons born or naturalized in the United States, and subject to the jurisdiction thereof, are citizens of the United States and of the State wherein they reside. No State shall make or enforce any law which shall abridge the privileges or immunities of citizens of the United States; nor shall any State deprive any person of life, liberty, or property, without due process of law; nor deny to any person within its jurisdiction the equal protection of the laws.

SECTION 2. Representatives shall be apportioned among the several States according to their respective numbers, counting the whole number of persons in each State, excluding Indians not taxed. But when the right to vote at any election for the choice of electors for President and Vice President of the United States, Representatives in Congress, the Executive and Judicial officers of a State, or the members of the Legislature thereof, is denied to any of the male inhabitants of such State, being twenty-one years of age,* and citizens of the United States, or in any way abridged, except for participation in rebellion, or other crime, the basis of representation therein shall be reduced in the proportion which the number of such male citizens shall bear to the whole number of male citizens twenty-one years of age in such State.

SECTION 3. No person shall be a Senator or Representative in Congress, or elector of President and Vice President, or hold any office, civil or military, under the United States, or under any State, who, having previously taken an oath, as a member of Congress, or as an officer of the United States, or as a member of any State legislature, or as an executive or judicial officer of any State, to support the Constitution of the United States, shall have engaged in insurrection or rebellion against the same, or given aid or comfort to the enemies thereof. But Congress may by a vote of two-thirds of each House, remove such disability.

SECTION 4. The validity of the public debt of the United States, authorized by law, including debts incurred for payment of pensions

*Changed by section 1 of the twenty-sixth amendment.

and bounties for services in suppressing insurrection or rebellion, shall not be questioned. But neither the United States nor any State shall assume or pay any debt or obligation incurred in aid of insurrection or rebellion against the United States, or any claim for the loss or emancipation of any slave; but all such debts, obligations and claims shall be held illegal and void.

SECTION 5. The Congress shall have power to enforce, by appropriate legislation, the provisions of this article.

AMENDMENT XV
(Ratified February 3, 1870)

SECTION 1. The right of citizens of the United States to vote shall not be denied or abridged by the United States or by any State on account of race, color, or previous condition of servitude—

SECTION 2. The Congress shall have power to enforce this article by appropriate legislation.

AMENDMENT XVI
(Ratified February 3, 1913)

The Congress shall have power to lay and collect taxes on incomes, from whatever source derived, without apportionment among the several States, and without regard to any census or enumeration.

AMENDMENT XVII
(Ratified April 8, 1913)

The Senate of the United States shall be composed of two Senators from each State, elected by the people thereof, for six years; and each Senator shall have one vote. The electors in each State shall have the qualifications requisite for electors of the most numerous branch of the State legislatures.

When vacancies happen in the representation of any State in the Senate, the executive authority of such State shall issue writs of election to fill such vacancies: *Provided*, That the legislature of any State may empower the executive thereof to make temporary appointments until the people fill the vacancies by election as the legislature may direct.

This amendment shall not be so construed as to affect the election or term of any Senator chosen before it becomes valid as part of the Constitution.

AMENDMENT XVIII
(Ratified January 16, 1919)

[SECTION 1. After one year from the ratification of this article the manufacture, sale, or transportation of intoxicating liquors within, the importation thereof into, or the exportation thereof from the United States and all territory subject to the jurisdiction thereof for beverage purposes is hereby prohibited.

[SECTION 2. The Congress and the several States shall have concurrent power to enforce this article by appropriate legislation.

The Constitution of the United States of America   301

[SECTION 3. This article shall be inoperative unless it shall have been ratified as an amendment to the Constitution by the legislatures of the several States as provided in the Constitution, within seven years from the date of the submission hereof to the States by the Congress.]*

AMENDMENT XIX
(Ratified August 18, 1920)

The right of citizens of the United States to vote shall not be denied or abridged by the United States or by any State on account of sex.

Congress shall have power to enforce this article by appropriate legislation.

AMENDMENT XX
(Ratified January 23, 1933)

SECTION 1. The terms of the President and Vice President shall end at noon on the 20th day of January, and the terms of Senators and Representatives at noon on the 3d day of January, of the years in which such terms would have ended if this article had not been ratified; and the terms of their successors shall then begin.

SECTION 2. The Congress shall assemble at least once in every year, and such meeting shall begin at noon on the 3d day of January, unless they shall by law appoint a different day.

SECTION 3. If, at the time fixed for the beginning of the term of the President, the President elect shall have died, the Vice President elect shall become President. If a President shall not have been chosen before the time fixed for the beginning of his term, or if the President elect shall have failed to qualify, then the Vice President elect shall act as President until a President shall have qualified; and the Congress may by law provide for the case wherein neither a President elect nor a Vice President elect shall have qualified, declaring who shall then act as President, or the manner in which one who is to act shall be selected, and such person shall act accordingly until a President or Vice President shall have qualified.

SECTION 4. The Congress may by law provide for the case of the death of any of the persons from whom the House of Representatives may choose a President whenever the right of choice shall have devolved upon them, and for the case of the death of any of the persons from whom the Senate may choose a Vice President whenever the right of choice shall have devolved upon them.

SECTION 5. Sections 1 and 2 shall take effect on the 15th day of October following the ratification of this article.

SECTION 6. This article shall be inoperative unless it shall have been ratified as an amendment to the Constitution by the legislatures of three-fourths of the several States within seven years from the date of its submission.

*Repealed by section 1 of the twenty-first amendment.

AMENDMENT XXI
(*Ratified December 5, 1933*)

SECTION 1. The eighteenth article of amendment to the Constitution of the United States is hereby repealed.

SECTION 2. The transportation or importation into any State, Territory, or possession of the United States for delivery or use therein of intoxicating liquors, in violation of the laws thereof, is hereby prohibited.

SECTION 3. This article shall be inoperative unless it shall have been ratified as an amendment to the Constitution by conventions in the several States, as provided in the Constitution, within seven years from the date of the submission hereof to the States by the Congress.

AMENDMENT XXII
(*Ratified February 27, 1951*)

SECTION 1. No person shall be elected to the office of the President more than twice, and no person who has held the office of President, or acted as President, for more than two years of a term to which some other person was elected President shall be elected to the office of the President more than once. But this Article shall not apply to any person holding the office of President when this Article was proposed by the Congress, and shall not prevent any person who may be holding the office of President, or acting as President, during the term within which this Article becomes operative from holding the office of President or acting as President during the remainder of such term.

SECTION 2. This article shall be inoperative unless it shall have been ratified as an amendment to the Constitution by the legislatures of three-fourths of the several States within seven years from the date of its submission to the States by the Congress.

AMENDMENT XXIII
(*Ratified March 29, 1961*)

SECTION 1. The District constituting the seat of Government of the United States shall appoint in such manner as the Congress may direct:

A number of electors of President and Vice President equal to the whole number of Senators and Representatives in Congress to which the District would be entitled if it were a State, but in no event more than the least populous State; they shall be in addition to those appointed by the States, but they shall be considered, for the purposes of the election of President and Vice President, to be electors appointed by a State; and they shall meet in the District and perform such duties as provided by the twelfth article of amendment.

SECTION 2. The Congress shall have power to enforce this article by appropriate legislation.

AMENDMENT XXIV
(*Ratified January 23, 1964*)

SECTION 1. The right of citizens of the United States to vote in any

The Constitution of the United States of America   303 primary or other election for President or Vice President, for electors for President or Vice President, or for Senator or Representative in Congress, shall not be denied or abridged by the United States or any State by reason of failure to pay any poll tax or other tax.

Section 2. The Congress shall have power to enforce this article by appropriate legislation.

AMENDMENT XXV
(*Ratified February 10, 1967*)

Section 1. In case of the removal of the President from office or of his death or resignation, the Vice President shall become President.

Section 2. Whenever there is a vacancy in the office of the Vice President, the President shall nominate a Vice President who shall take office upon confirmation by a majority vote of both Houses of Congress.

Section 3. Whenever the President transmits to the President pro tempore of the Senate and the Speaker of the House of Representatives his written declaration that he is unable to discharge the powers and duties of his office, and until he transmits to them a written declaration to the contrary, such powers and duties shall be discharged by the Vice President as Acting President.

Section 4. Whenever the Vice President and a majority of either the principal officers of the executive departments or of such other body as Congress may by law provide, transmit to the President pro tempore of the Senate and the Speaker of the House of Representatives their written declaration that the President is unable to discharge the powers and duties of his office, the Vice President shall immediately assume the powers and duties of the office as Acting President.

Thereafter, when the President transmits to the President pro tempore of the Senate and the Speaker of the House of Representatives his written declaration that no inability exists, he shall resume the powers and duties of his office unless the Vice President and a majority of either the principal officers of the executive department or of such other body as Congress may by law provide, transmit within four days to the President pro tempore of the Senate and the Speaker of the House of Representatives their written declaration that the President is unable to discharge the powers and duties of his office. Thereupon Congress shall decide the issue, assembling within forty-eight hours for that purpose if not in session. If the Congress, within twenty-one days after receipt of the latter written declaration, or, if Congress is not in session, within twenty-one days after Congress is required to assemble, determines by two-thirds vote of both Houses that the President is unable to discharge the powers and duties of his office, the Vice President shall continue to discharge the same as Acting President; otherwise, the President shall resume the powers and duties of his office.

SECTION 1. The right of citizens of the United States, who are eighteen years of age or older, to vote shall not be denied or abridged by the United States or by any State on account of age.

SECTION 2. The Congress shall have power to enforce this article by appropriate legislation.

INDEX

SUBJECT INDEX

and enlargement of congressional
districts, 136
representative function of, 251–52
lengthening terms of, 136–37, 196,
262. *See also* Congress
Hughes, Charles Evans, 145, on
Supreme Court and public opinion,
122
Hume, David
on human rights and liberty, 72
on politics as a science, 45

impeachment
House Judiciary Committee draft
article of, 35
of Samuel Chase, 29–30
of Andrew Johnson, 31. *See also*
President
individual rights. *See* constitutional
rights; natural rights
interest groups
regulation of, 206
role of, in shaping public policy,
178–81, 206, 228
international agreements. *See* Foreign
affairs

Jackson, Robert H., 145
on judicial review, 150
on Supreme Court and public
opinion, 122
Jefferson, Thomas
on Constitution and change, 19
on equality, 52, 75
on partisanship, 29
Revolutionary values of, 52, 66
Jessup, Philip
on internal effect of international
agreements, 282
on international law, 271
Johnson, Andrew
administration of, 32
impeachment of, 31
Johnson, Lyndon, Vietnam War
policies of, 34–35
judicial activism
as compared to judicial restraint,
112, 119, 149–50
and judicial "legislation," 112, 118–
21
in nationalizing constitutional
liberty, 86. *See also* judicial branch
judicial branch (federal and state)
and adequacy of federal tribunals,
114–22
and adversary process, 112–14, 148
and appellate courts, 39
as conceived of in Constitutional
Convention, 69

and diversity jurisdiction, 114–15,
148
and effect of federal trial courts on
public policy, 171
and interpretation of constitutional
values, 97–101
and judicial review, 29
public view of, 111, 143–44
and reform and reorganization of
federal courts, 112–18, 148–49
role of, in conduct of foreign
relations, 273–76, 283
and selection of judges
federal, 116–18, 144–47
state, 149
staffing of, 115
subconstitutional changes in, 261
and three-judge district courts, 114,
148–149. *See also* Supreme Court
judicial restraint. *See* judicial activism
judicial review. *See* judicial branch

Kellogg-Briand Pact of 1928, 270
Kenyon, Cecelia M., 45
on equality and happiness as
Revolutionary goals, 51–52

Laski, Harold, 13–14
legislative-executive relationship. *See*
Congress; Executive-legislative
relationship; President
Levy, Leonard
on 1st Amendment, 69–70, 79
on Warren Court, 87
Lewis, Anthony, on judicial branch,
111, 119
Lincoln, Abraham, 30
Lipson, Leon, on Connally Reservation,
282
Locke, John
on definition of natural rights, 64–65
Second Treatise of Government, 51,
64, 199
Lowi, Theodore, 139, 187

McDougal, Myres S., on international
agreements, 254, 281–82
Madison, James
on factions, 49
on federal-state relationship, 48
on political parties, 29
on Supreme Court, 121
Mandeville, Bernard, 48
Manning, Bayless, on constitutional
amendment, 269
Marshall, John, 145
on Constitution, 26
on federal supremacy, 30, 124
on "political questions," 29, 37

Martineau, Harriet, 75
Meiklejohn, Alexander, on 1st
  Amendment, 69–70
military subordination to civil power,
  70–71, 79
Miller, Samuel F., 31, 145
Morris, Gouverneur, on new Consti-
  tution, 1787, 13
Moynihan, Patrick, on democratic
  governments, 234

natural law. *See* natural rights
natural rights
  American view of, as departure from
    British tradition, 46–47
  and Bill of Rights, 69–71
  as contrasted to magisterial tradition
    in American society, 67–69
  in Declaration of Independence,
    66–67
  as defined by Locke, 51–52, 64–65
  and egalitarianism, 67, 72, 75, 81
  as emerging in Revolutionary era,
    63
  evolutionary changes in theories of,
    71–74
  and fundamental rights of English-
    men, 65–66, 74
  Jefferson's concepts of, 66
  philosophers of, 52, 63–65, 72
Nelson, Samuel, on federal-state
  relationship, 31–32
New York City's fiscal crisis, 123, 152–
  53, 155–56. *See also* federalism
Nixon, Richard M.
  article of impeachment re, 35
  U.S. v. *Nixon*, 37, 89, 121, 144, 242,
    257–58

Otis, James, 71

Paine, Thomas
  on equality, 51–52
  on formation of government, 45–46
  on liberty, 51
  Rights of Man, 51
  on role of government, 47, 56
  on union of the states, 53
Paterson, William, 86–87
Paul, Jerry, on Joan Little trial, 113
Pinckney, Charles, on purpose of
  government, 51–52
Plato, on nature of law and the state
  in *Republic*, 63–64
Pocock, J. G. A., 45
Pole, J. R., 45
political parties
  decline of, 173–77, 185–86, 215–17
  effect of
    on popular sovereignty, 173–77

  on presidential primaries, 177,
    185–86, 197, 215–17
  on separation of powers, 237–38
  erosion of, as leadership factor,
    202–3
  function of, 215–17
  and influence of two-party system
    on public policy shaping, 174–77,
    202–3
  and issue voting, 186
  and President, 175, 203–4
  realignment of, 174–77, 186, 189
  and reorganization of party system,
    192, 196–97, 205–6
  as representative of diverse interests,
    29, 49
Pollak, Louis, on congressional standing to sue, 274
popular sovereignty, 171–86
  delegation of, to elected representa-
    tives, 251–52
  and elections, 184–85
  practice of, in policy shaping, 173–
    86
  as a Revolutionary value, 47–48
  theory of, in policy shaping, 171–73
Pound, Roscoe, 72
Powell, Thomas Reed, 122
President
  ability of, to shape policy, 191–93
  and arms control and disarmament,
    248
  and Cabinet, 197
  and commander-in-chief role, 35,
    236, 246, 261, 269–70, 280–81
  commitments of, to foreign powers,
    276
  congressional delegation of power
    to, 181, 194, 217–20
  and control of bureaucracy, 142, 180,
    192, 225–26
  effect of White House staff on,
    140–42
  and executive agreements, 253, 279–
    81
  and executive branch reorganiza-
    tion, 193–96, 205
  and executive-legislative relation-
    ship, 31, 188, 192–93, 203, 217–20,
    268, 271, 277–79
  and executive privilege, 141, 239,
    242, 261, 268–69, 272
  foreign affairs powers of, 35, 235–
    36, 241, 276–78
  and impoundment of funds, 247–48
  and presidential primaries, 185–86,
    197, 215–17
  removal of, from office, (impeach-
    ment), 142–43, 219–20, 256

separation of powers—*continued*
  effect of, on conduct of foreign
    relations, 235–45, 276–77
  and legislative oversight of executive
    action, 218–19, 273
  and major issues in foreign policy,
    238–45
  subconstitutional changes in, 269–75
  as a Revolutionary value, 47. *See
    also* executive-legislative relation-
    ship
Seward, William H., and the slavery
  extension crisis of 1850, 72
slavery
  attitudes toward, in Revolutionary
    era, 52–53, 67
  ban against, in Northwest
    Ordinance, 67
  in Declaration of Independence, 94
Society for Political Inquiries, 45
Spirit of the Laws, 199
state action doctrine, 101
state constitutions, 19
Sundquist, James, on party alignments,
  177
Supreme Court
  and resolution of constitutional
    issues, 121–22, 143–44
  and executive privilege, 89, 121, 144,
    242
  and free expression, 82–84
  and individual rights, 72–73, 74–77
  and nationalization of constitutional
    liberty, 86–90
  on religion and education, 84–85
  role of, 149–50
  on seditious activity, 79–81
  selection of justices of, 144–47
  on separation of powers, 273
  subconstitutional changes in, 261
  treatment of "political questions"
    by, 36, 256–57, 261, 274
    See also judicial branch

Taney, Roger, 30, 145
Thomson, Charles, on private versus
  public interests, 56
Tocqueville, Alexis de, on equality in
  America, 55, 66, 75
Tonkin Gulf Resolution. *See* Vietnam
  War
treaty power. *See* Congress; foreign
  affairs; President
Tugwell, Rexford G.
  on federal system, 115, 122, 152
  on separation of powers, 199
  on states in the Union, 250
two-party system. *See* political parties

United Nations Charter, 270–71. *See
  also* foreign affairs

Vandenberg, Arthur, on conduct of
  foreign policy, 35
Vice President, procedures for selec-
  tion of, 230
Vietnam War
  and Cambodian bombing, 35–36
  Johnson administration policies
    during, 34–35
  legality legislation, 40, 258
  Nixon administration policies dur-
    ing, 34–36
  and Tonkin Gulf Resolution, 34–35
Virginia Declaration of Rights, 50
Virginia Plan (Resolutions), 18
Virginia Statute of Religious Liberty,
  74

War on Poverty, 156–58. *See also*
  citizen participation in government
War Powers Resolution. *See* Congress;
  executive-legislative relationship
Warren Court, 145
  on concept of equality, 74
  on constitutional rights, 100
  on 14th Amendment, 87–88
  on nature of right and justice, 73–74
  on "open society," 80–81
  on reconciling 1st Amendment
    rights, 83–84
  on Smith and McCarran Acts, 80–81.
    See also Supreme Court
Washington, George
  on formation of government, 46
  on new Constitution, 1787, 13
  on public interest, 53
Wechsler, Herbert, on neutral principles of constitutional law, 39, 118
Wildavsky, Aaron, on presidential
  popularity, 131–32
Williams, Samuel
  on early American spirit, 54
  on equality, 52
  on reason in government, 45
  on role of government, 47, 55–56
  on societal values, 54
Wilson, James, on Bill of Rights, 69,
  71
Wilson, Woodrow
  on Constitution, 18
  on government and politics, 198
  on presidency, 237–38
Wolfgang, Myra, on Equal Rights
  Amendment, 78–79
Wood, Gordon S., 45

CASE INDEX

RECOGNIZED BY
AMERICAN REVOLUTION
BICENTENNIAL
ADMINISTRATION

Historical prints courtesy of the Historical Society of Pennsylvania

Photography by Harvey Michael Newman

Designed by Robert M. Luebbers